MOVING
LIFE COURSE THEORY
INTO ACTION

MAKING
CHANGE
HAPPEN

MOVING
LIFE COURSE THEORY
INTO ACTION

MAKING
CHANGE
HAPPEN

APHA PRESS
AN IMPRINT OF AMERICAN PUBLIC HEALTH ASSOCIATION

EDITED BY
SARAH VERBIEST
DrPH, MSW, MPH

American Public Health Association
800 I Street, NW
Washington, DC 20001-3710
www.apha.org

Georges C. Benjamin, MD, FACP, FACEP (Emeritus), Executive Director

Printed and bound in the United States of America
Book Production Editor: Maya Ribault
Typesetting: The Charlesworth Group
Cover Design: Alan Giarcanella
Printing and Binding: Sheridan Books

Library of Congress Cataloging-in-Publication Data

Names: Verbiest, Sarah, editor. | American Public Health Association, issuing
    body.
Title: Moving life course theory into action : making change happen / edited
    by Sarah Verbiest.
Description: Washington, DC : American Public Health Association, [2018] |
    Includes bibliographical references.
Identifiers: LCCN 2018009833 (print) | LCCN 2018010643 (ebook) | ISBN
    9780875532967 (e-book) | ISBN 9780875532950 (pbk.)
Subjects: | MESH: Public Health | Human Development | Life Change Events |
    Models, Psychological | Social Support | Maternal-Child Health Services |
    United States
Classification: LCC RA425 (ebook) | LCC RA425 (print) | NLM WA 100 | DDC
    362.1--dc23
LC record available at https://lccn.loc.gov/2018009833

Contents

Preface

Each decade and generation of leaders face challenges in advancing programs, policies and strategies to support the nation's promise of life, liberty, and the pursuit of happiness for all. While progress has been made, the United States faces major systems of inequity, poorer health outcomes than other industrialized countries, significant wealth/health gaps, and emerging crises such as the opiate epidemic sweeping the country. Disparities in outcomes and indicators across the maternal and child health spectrum illuminate the need for adaptive and courageous leadership coupled with new approaches to address the complexity of these challenges and their multifaceted solutions. Life Course Theory offers a framework to prompt strategic thinking and action that is aligned with the difficult and rewarding work that needs to be done.

Over the past decade, practitioners in the field of maternal and child health have gained a general understanding of Life Course Theory and its potential application to practice, particularly through the work of the Health Resources and Services Administration's Maternal and Child Health Bureau (HRSA MCHB) and the introduction of crosscutting life course national performance measures for the Title V program. Partners at the federal, state, and local levels have called for renewed attention to the social determinants of health and their influence on the health of women, men, children, adolescents, and families. Similarly, the American Public Health Association aims to create the healthiest nation in one generation with priorities including building public health infrastructure and capacity, as well as ensuring the right to health and health care and creating health equity (see https://www.apha.org). Achieving this vision requires new ways of thinking and working.

At the same time, social workers have grounded their work in the life course perspective since the beginning of the profession, although in the past several decades the focus has trended toward individual approaches instead of a more macro system application. As the field from the academy to the community considers new approaches, Life Course Theory has become a springboard for not only getting "out of the box" but also stepping into new spaces. For example, in 2012 the American Academy of Social Work and Social Welfare launched the Grand Challenges of Social Work Initiative to improve individual and family well-being, strengthen the social fabric, create a more just society, energize the field, and focus on larger, societal issues. The Grand Challenges include the following: ensuring healthy development of all youth, stopping family violence, eradicating social isolation, ending homelessness, promoting smart decarceration,* reducing extreme economic inequality, harnessing technology for social good, achieving equal opportunity and justice, and advancing long and productive lives (for a complete list, see http://aaswsw.org).

The concept for a book focusing on moving Life Course Theory into practice emerged from an expressed need from practitioners across a variety of fields for more information and strategies for application of this approach. Many of these practitioners are working overtime, addressing competing priorities in complex environments with limited resources for continuing education. Therefore, the resulting book was designed to fit into the busy lives of practitioners with new ideas and strategies delivered in a focused, handbook-style format. Each chapter includes key points, which offer a quick summary of the main lessons the authors are advancing. Some chapters also have a list of resources for ongoing learning.

The first three chapters of the book lay the foundation, with a comprehensive discussion of the life course perspective. Chapter 1 by Lu and colleagues provides a solid grounding in Life Course Theory, including its definition, framework, core concepts, critiques, and implications for practice. Paired with this chapter are three appendices that identify unique perspectives of the Life Course Approach to practice for the American Indian community by Locklear Hertel and for men and fathers by Lanier. Chapter 2 elevates the opportunity that Life Course Theory offers for understanding and disrupting disparities in health and well-being. Authors Abresch and Wyche-Etheridge offer a set of strategies and call upon practitioners to build equity by creating conditions where all children, adolescents, young adults, seniors, and families can thrive. In Chapter 3, Kotelchuck offers a unique retrospective view of the work of early public health and social work and the foundations laid for today's renewed call for action centered on a Life Course Approach. The chapter provides a rich history lesson along with guidance for practitioners in moving forward.

Life Course Theory prompts practitioners at all levels to consider the impact of systems such as education, health care, and child welfare on individuals and families at sensitive time periods of development. The second group of chapters describes opportunities for broadening traditional maternal and child health work to better serve populations that are caught in systems of oppression, by addressing social determinants of health, expanding current models of care to fit a Life Course Approach, and trying new strategies for improving outcomes for all. In Chapter 4, McLemore and colleagues describe challenges in the criminal justice that have intergenerational effects on health and life trajectories. The authors provide a series of strategies and questions for practitioners to consider, spotlighting the need for more attention to this often forgotten population of people caught in the criminal justice system. In Chapter 5, Braughton and colleagues highlight

---

*Decarceration is a government policy of reducing either the number of persons imprisoned or the rate of imprisonment in a given jurisdiction. It may also be described as the process of removing people from institutions such as prisons or mental hospitals. It is the opposite of incarceration.

the advantages that place-based initiatives offer for influencing local social determinants of health, with implementation strategies and examples of this work in practice. Infusing maternal and child health perspectives into place-based initiatives provides a platform for new and unique ways to reduce risks and augment protective factors.

In Chapter 6, Brady and Johnson illustrate the potential for expanding an existing maternal and child health program-home visiting-to align more closely with a Life Course Approach. They describe the influence of home visiting history on the evidence-based practices being utilized today across the country. The authors present new designs for deepening the potential positive impact of home visiting on communities. The social determinants of health (SDOH) are key actors throughout this book. In Chapter 7, Allen and Wolin provide insights into one very important SDOH-housing. The housing industry is not particularly well understood by maternal and child health practitioners, even though it has a significant influence on families' ability to achieve health, employment, and educational goals. This chapter offers an overview of the reasons why all practitioners should be concerned about safe and affordable housing in their communities and provides information about key influencers in the industry, as well as some food for thought on addressing housing needs for young families.

The third section of the book suggests strategies for managers and leaders who are convinced that applying life course to practice makes sense but are not quite sure how to move forward and make it happen. In Chapter 8, Cilenti and Harris lead the section with their chapter on partnerships and collaboration. Building relationships and working with new people and organizations/industries are central to addressing existing risk and protective factors for communities. In Chapter 9, Berkowitz and colleagues challenge the field to think differently when developing projects and interventions with their introduction of Human-Centered Design. Taking a page from science and engineering, Human-Centered Design holds the potential to increase the success of programs by putting the needs, wishes, and interests of the target population front and center. In Chapter 10, Malin and colleagues illustrate the application of Life Course Theory to planning—an important first step in realigning focus and action steps at the program, agency and state level. The authors provide examples from three states that have intentionally focused on working from a life course perspective, along with reality-based advice for practitioners who may wish to take a fresh approach to their work.

Caplan and Gase discuss the importance of the concept of Health in all Policies in Chapter 11. The authors describe the five key elements of Health in All Policies along with eight activities for practitioners who wish to capitalize on the influence that policy can have on health and well-being. Whether at the organizational/local small "p" level or at the state/federal capital "P" level, the capacity to effect more wide scale innovation and progress requires policy skills. In Chapter 12, Farfalla and Shea focus on communicating about Life Course Theory—an essential component of engaging partners and communities and advancing policy and programs. The authors discuss framing techniques for talking about Life Course Theory along with conversation starters and a warning about potential messaging missteps. In Chapter 13, Stampfel and Shiman take on one of the bigger challenges of integrating Life Course Theory into action-evaluation and assessment. Generating proof that new approaches can create change and have impact over the life course is essential for securing resources and advancing the field. While it can be difficult to measure and weigh the complexity of intergenerational effects, this is an essential component of this work offering a rich area for study. The authors include many suggestions and resources for taking on this important task. In Chapter 14, Bachman picks up on themes from Chapter 13 in her work, which focuses on financing for programs that have a life course perspective. She provides background on traditional funding sources for maternal and child health services and offers insight into future directions and strategies for sourcing this work. Innovation, complexity and confronting oppression are inherent components within the Life Course Approach that require thoughtful, boundary-spanning, adaptive leadership skills. In Chapter 15, I conclude the book with a discussion about leading for change, proposing that all practitioners regardless of their formal position or role within an agency have a critical part to play in advocating for change and improving life course trajectories for vulnerable and historically oppressed populations.

As the chapters were completed, several themes emerged naturally from this work. First, equity is a lifeline principle—a main artery—that runs across all of the chapters. Without a laser focus on ameliorating the risk factors and augmenting the protective factors that keep different populations from reaching their full potential, practitioners run the risk of continuing to perpetuate inequities. Recognizing that maternal and child health populations are influenced by numerous systems that are designed to advantage some groups over others, practitioners must wake up to their role in changing these patterns, programs, and policies. While this is not a small task, especially for professionals who are members of advantaged groups and therefore not always able to see these patterns well, avoiding adaptive challenges is not an option for life course practitioners.

The necessity of building new partnerships and collaborations is a second theme that aligns well with an equity approach. Regardless of the type of work at hand (e.g., planning, policy, evaluation, fundraising) or the problem being tackled, developing new relationships with colleagues from different sectors and industries is essential. This partnership extends to clients and the community, without whom it is impossible to influence lasting change. The application of Human-Centered Design is one of several strategies that can be employed to allow practitioners to work around their own culture and privilege and identify workable programs and interventions in partnership with the people they wish to serve.

Without question, life course–aligned strategies will force paradigm shifts and move practitioners into some less familiar territory. For example, preconception health—focusing on the health and wellness of adults prior to pregnancy—is widely understood to be a critical strategy for improving intergenerational health outcomes. Yet, there has been limited funding, programming, and political capital aimed at this population and stage of development. Applying Life Course Theory to practice means that maternal and child health program focus needs to expand to areas such as reproductive health and justice and the well-being of young adults who do not have and may never have children. Likewise, Life Course Theory requires programs aimed at sexually transmitted infections, chronic disease, interpersonal violence, behavioral health, early childhood education, aging, and contraceptives to expand their partnerships and consider new alignments that link them into a more comprehensive, multigenerational direction.

Shifting from an individual focus to a more expansive intergenerational approach to health and wellness will certainly stretch practitioners. A value of the Life Course Approach is that it encourages a program aimed at one age-specific population to assess the interconnected protective factors and influences on that person's life over time. Whether for programs or services designed for pregnant women, new mothers, young children, adolescents, young adults, or the elderly, these "populations" need communities and are influenced by them in many ways. The commonly understood American frame of individualism and "pulling oneself up by the bootstraps" is continually accentuated in services and programs. Practitioners should review the programs they offer and find mechanisms to stop reinforcing the "go it alone" American ideal. This approach has not worked well for many public health goals. Perhaps there will be healthier people and families if the focus shifted to engage and reinforce social support. What would programs look like if they provided an opportunity for a family (by birth or choice), including men, aunties, uncles, and others, as well as informal/formal community leaders, to fully participate in conversations around infant safe sleep, breastfeeding, postpartum recovery, and perinatal depression? Behaviors that are difficult to change and maintain—weight loss, tobacco cessation, and healthy, safe relationships—are clearly influenced by a person's social circles, support systems, and local resources. While this is certainly not new knowledge, systems have not yet responded—potentially because this more communal approach is a departure from the way institutions are designed and practitioners are trained. The reward for this change and broadened efforts has the potential to be significant for communities, particularly those that have been historically excluded.

Life Course Theory introduces a layered approach to programming, evaluation, and resource utilization, as well as a new level of complexity to traditional maternal and child health interventions. As maternal and child health continues to operate in changing environments, practitioners need to understand how systems connect with one another to shape and deliver clinical, social, and public health services to families. Life Course Theory encourages the engagement of new and different systems outside of traditional health and public health, including schools, child welfare, employment, transportation, housing, criminal justice, and more. Systems thinking is required to tease apart the many levers that need to be adjusted to allow for innovation and change. Understanding how systems work allows for a more proactive approach to achieve desired outcomes and identify behaviors, relationships, policies, and perspectives that lead to disparities.

Finally, bridging ideas and strategies across two fields that claim common ancestry—social work and public health—is an excellent way to begin to broaden the work in both schools of thought. Practitioners in both fields contribute unique perspectives, research, and skill sets and may capitalize on the synergy that can be achieved with a fusion of their work. These professions along with a growing number of kindred spirits in fields such as community development, city planning, and medicine can join together to develop more community-engaged, consumer-focused prevention strategies using Life Course Theory as a common language.

Just as a Life Course Approach requires the convening of many hearts and minds, the development of this book called upon the gifts and talents of many. Special thanks are due to the professionals who reviewed the chapters and provided excellent feedback to authors—Aileen Aylworth, MPH, MSW; Erin Bonzon, MSPH, MSW; Sarah Buisson, MSW, MSPH; Megan Canady, MSW, MPH; Piia Hanson, MSPH, MBA; Morgan Jeter, BA; Jamie Lea, MPH; Carla Salvo Lewis, MSPH, MPH; Erin K. McClain, MA, MPH; Jasmine Getrouw-Moore, MPA; Monica Murphy, MPH; Rebecca Sink Smith, MSW, MPH; Laura Snebold, MPH; and Amanda Zabala, MPH. These women are creating change in public health and social work spaces across the country and will be leading the way in the decades to come.

This book contains the work of 38 authors representing many different perspectives, areas of expertise, and career points—from seasoned leaders to new, emerging voices. Hopefully, the wisdom, practice suggestions, and strategies proposed will support professionals across fields in advancing the application of Life Course Theory in maternal and child health practice and beyond. Weaving the Life Course Approach into practice opens the door for creative thought and programming, real community engagement, and the chance for practitioners to lean into the most pressing problems of the time to effectuate lasting change for generations to come.

This book is written in honor of the generations in my life course—my grandparents John, Pearl, Eddie, and Ethel; my parents David and Patricia; my siblings Tim and Amy; my life partner Dirk; his parents Edmond and Rosa; and our children Kylie and Tai.

Many thanks to the chapter authors who made space in their busy calendars to offer such significant contributions to this work. They truly model a Life Course Approach in all that they do, and it is a blessing to have them as colleagues and cocreators on this journey toward change.

I offer deep gratitude for my team at the University of North Carolina Center for Maternal and Infant Health as well as my running tribe for their patience and encouragement throughout the writing and editing process. This book would not have been written without Cheri Pies who is a matchmaker, cheerleader, mentor, and a true legacy leader.

Sarah Verbiest, DrPH, MSW, MPH

Life Course Theory: An Overview

Michael C. Lu, MD, MPH, Sarah Verbiest, DrPH, MSW, MPH, and Tyan Parker Dominguez, PhD, MPH, MSW

A thriving and productive society requires a healthy population, in which the talents, skills, and contributions of every member are valued and cultivated.[1,2] When this is not the case, the well-being of society as a whole is compromised.[3] Many different professions and organizations are dedicated to making the world a better place for everyone. Whether the focus is on physical, mental, or spiritual health; housing; employment; the environment; education; safety; or another domain, thousands of people spend their days working to advance equitable opportunities for life, liberty, and the pursuit of happiness. A Life Course Approach holds great promise for elevating this work and deepening its impact.

Life Course Theory (LCT) offers an innovative, broad-based model for integrating the complex array of factors—from the biological to the environmental, the individual to the communal, the historical to the contemporary—that shape health and well-being patterns in individuals and populations. The science across multiple disciplines indicates that a Life Course Approach is essential for improving understanding of how health develops and how disparities are created and perpetuated over time.[4] As such, LCT is especially well suited to efforts to promote health equity and social justice.[5] This opening chapter provides an overview of LCT, with a focus on the context of maternal and child health (MCH). The core constructs, major critiques, and implications of LCT for MCH practice, research, and policy are presented. To highlight the wider utility of LCT, this chapter also includes several illustrations of how LCT can be applied in practice as well as how this perspective affects different communities.

LIFE COURSE THEORY: THE FOUNDATION

Life course thinking is an integration of advances in multiple disciplines over the past century in understanding the interconnections, interdependence, and dynamic interactions across time and space of persons and their environments.[4] Simply put, LCT is a way of understanding human development and adaptation across the life span. An example of the scientific work that has informed LCT is biological research into the epigenetic mechanisms by which the environment can shape gene expression and affect the development and function of biological systems. Other influences include epidemiological research into developmental origins of chronic disease, the social patterning of health and illness, and the "weathering" effect of cumulative disadvantage. Sociological research into changing pathways of different generational cohorts and psychological research on stress, adaptation, and life span development have also contributed to life course thinking.[4]

LCT offers a multidimensional lens for understanding how life experiences have an impact on health and well-being. This theory emphasizes the biological–psychosocial–cultural–environmental–historical context within which life begins and unfolds over time and across generations. Life course draws from systems and socioecological theory to explain the interconnected and interdependent relationship between the person and the environment. Systems theory originated with Ludwig von Bertalanffy's General Systems Theory (1968), which explained biological life as the constant interaction among interlocking systems. Systems are both part and whole. They are distinct entities comprised of smaller (sub) systems, as well as component parts of larger (supra) systems. Each system affects function in other systems. Systems theory has wide application across a variety of disciplines; social scientists and health researchers have used this concept to create biopsychosocial models of human behavior.[4]

Developmental psychologist Urie Bronfenbrenner[6,7] recognized that human development was inextricably linked to the social environment. His ecological theory includes five levels of social influence on development, beginning with the immediate social environment and the interrelationships among its various components (e.g., families and communities), then extending outward in concentric layers to include the indirect influence of wider social forces, such as public policy, culture, and values, and changes in these contexts over time. Bronfenbrenner viewed people as engaged in a dynamic process of adaptation, both shaping and being shaped by the environments in which they were embedded. Practitioners in fields such as public health and social work have adopted ecological theory to guide practitioners, program planners, and advocates to consider interventions, programs, and policies that move beyond individual risks, protections, behaviors, and services to consider wider social influences on health and disease. Figure 1-1 provides an illustrated depiction of this model.

LIFE COURSE THEORY: THE CORE CONSTRUCTS

Fine and Kotelchuck[9] described LCT by using four domains: timeline, timing, environment, and equity. Lu and Halfon[10] synthesized two core constructs—early programming and cumulative pathways—into a longitudinal model of disparities. The concepts are not entirely distinct from each other. LCT offers a framework to explore the "intergenerational transmission" of health, expressed biologically (epigenetically) or by nature of shared family/community exposures. Risk and protective factors influence the trajectory

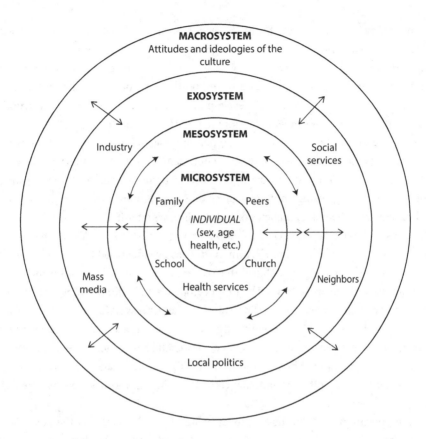

Source: Hchokr.[8] Reprinted from Wikimedia Commons.

Figure 1-1. Bronfenbrenner's Ecological Theory of Development

of an individual, family, and community's well-being. This section will describe these constructs in greater detail to weave a more complete picture of LCT.

Early Programming

The concept of early programming has roots in developmental biology and emphasizes the importance of sensitive developmental periods in utero or early life during which future health and function become programmed.[4] This model builds on the work of David Barker and his colleagues at the University of Southhampton, who found an unexpected association between low birth weight and increased risk for coronary artery disease, diabetes mellitus, and hypertension.[11] The Barker hypothesis was met with a great deal of skepticism and even some ridicule initially.[11] But over the past two decades, a whole field of scientific research has emerged, collectively known as developmental origins of health and disease. Although the biological mechanisms by which in utero exposures may influence adult health have not been fully understood, one possible mechanism for early programming is the regulation of gene expression.

Epigenetics can be described as the volume control for genes. Gene expression can get turned up or down, or switched on or off, on the basis of environmental exposure, especially during critical periods of development. Barker and his colleagues hypothesized that there are periods in fetal development during which the functions of an organ or system are being "programmed."[11] If something goes wrong during early programming, that organ or system may not function optimally over the life course. For example, a fetus that is undernourished during the second trimester when the pancreas and kidneys are rapidly growing could end up with a smaller pancreas or smaller kidneys, which might raise the risk of diabetes or kidney diseases later in life.

One area of biological research has found that maternal stress can "cross" the placenta in a way that activates fetal stress.[12,13] Animal studies have identified two areas of the fetal brain that are particularly vulnerable to the toxic effects of cortisol (stress hormone): the hippocampus and the amygdala.[12] The hippocampus is a site for learning and memory formation; rat pups exposed to a great deal of prenatal stress have a hard time forming memories and learning new tasks. Similarly, the amygdala is a site that mediates anxiety and fear, and rat pups exposed to a great deal of prenatal stress show a lot of anxiety and fear in aversive situations. More importantly, the hippocampus and the amygdala regulate the hypothalamic–pituitary–adrenal (HPA) axis, which in turn mediates the fight-or-flight response.

The hippocampus can be described as a brake pedal that slows the activities of the HPA axis. The amygdala can be described an accelerator pedal that accentuates the activities of the HPA axis. When a mother is stressed out during pregnancy, her fetus is exposed to stress hormones, which during critical periods of fetal development could decrease the number of stress receptors in the hippocampus, making the brake pedal less sensitive. At the same time, excess stress hormones can increase the number of receptors in the amygdala, making the accelerator pedal more sensitive. By making the brake pedal less sensitive and the accelerator pedal more sensitive, maternal stress could program a fetal brain in a way that influences the way the infant's system regulates stress over the life course. As such, maternal stress during pregnancy may elevate risks for attention-deficit/hyperactivity disorder,[14,15] future chronic health conditions,[16] infectious diseases,[17] and even preterm birth[18] in that infant's future offspring.

Sensitive Periods

In a similar line of thought to timeline, the timing of exposures and experiences during critical periods of development can influence life trajectories. As Halfon et al. have described, "addressing the health risks that occur early in life is important not just in terms of improving later adult health, but in setting a strong foundation for the entire nation's well-being."[4] There are unique periods in human growth where interventions may be particularly sensitive to timing. Infant feeding offers a good example. The positive impacts of breastfeeding extend throughout an infant's early development, reducing risks for infection and sudden infant death syndrome[19] in the short term and reducing risks for obesity[20] over time. Likewise, breastfeeding can assist mothers in losing pregnancy weight and serves as a protective factor against breast cancer in the future. However, there is a limited window of time when an infant and mother establish their breastfeeding relationship. If this opportunity is missed because of lack of resources and support, then the long-term benefits of breastfeeding for both mother and baby are lost. As such, LCT elevates the importance in investing in lactation specialists and focusing on populations at risk to improve outcomes and close health disparities over time.

Although there is little doubt that the early years of a person's life are very important, there are sensitive periods at many places across the life course during which interventions are particularly salient. Developmental screenings[21,22] as well as vision[23,24] and hearing[25] tests during early childhood can support successful transition to school. Reading level at third grade likewise affects longer learning trajectories.[26] Providing quality medical care and health education to adolescents as they go through puberty is critical, as is attending to the social–emotional needs of teenagers. Offering comprehensive support and resources to lesbian, gay, bisexual, transgender, and queer adolescents can have an impact on health issues for them, such as weight and unintended pregnancy. Life course models tend to stress physical development, but there are also important life experience transitions that may be as important to mark, such as commitment to a long-term relationship, graduation from high school, and retirement from the paid workforce. LCT opens the door for new conversations and research among practitioners and agencies to consider the timing of service delivery and investment of resources accordingly.

Risks and Protective Factors

Across the life span, all individuals face challenges to their well-being and health as well as advantages that help them cope and thrive. In LCT lexicon, challenges translate to risk factors. Some of these factors might be genetic or physical such as being born with spina bifida, cystic fibrosis, or autism and/or to carry a genetic code that predisposes one to breast and ovarian cancer. Others result from family and environmental contexts such as being born to teenaged parents, experiencing housing issues, surviving sexual assault, or residing in a community with a poor school system. Bad events happen to people—car crashes that take the lives of family breadwinners, cancer, natural disasters, and so forth.

Likewise, everyone has some advantages or protective factors as a sort of counterbalance. These advantages could include having a resilient spirit, a special talent, and the capacity to communicate well. Examples of environmental protective factors include having access to high-quality health care, being part of a vibrant faith community, growing up surrounded by loving and supportive family members, access to high-speed internet services, and having access to safe places outdoors to run and play. These positive opportunities can buffer risk factors and support an upward life course trajectory. For example, children born with special health care needs who have access to clinicians, therapists, teachers, and playgrounds that support their development have the chance to grow to their fullest potential.

LCT provides a platform for communities and practitioners alike to focus on reducing risks and increasing protective factors to improve health, wealth, and happiness for individuals, families, and populations. Practitioners need to consider factors that support and hinder health and wellness at all levels for the people they wish to serve in order to design and implement interventions that are effective. This concept requires discussion and consideration of the social determinants of health—the conditions in which people are born, grow, live, age, work, and play. The distribution of resources, influence, money, and power has an impact on these determinants in deeply significant ways. For example, when natural disasters such as hurricanes strike, entire communities are affected. However, people with insurance, clear documentation of home ownership, homes located in areas with vocal policymakers, and who have other financial assets will recover more quickly and completely than people without these protections. As leaders consider new programs and policies, they must consider how these protections will affect everyone in the community. Providing sidewalks and walking trails, for example, offers benefits for weight control, stress reduction, community connection, and enjoyment. However, if the sidewalks are only laid in affluent sections of town or new parks are not accessible by public transportation or if the sidewalks in low-income neighborhoods do not have the needed lighting, call boxes, and police bike patrols to support safety, the resources deployed provide support for some, but not everyone, in the community.

Equity

Although everyone has risks and protections, some populations and communities have far more protections than others. Differential risks and protections over the life course contribute to differential pathways or trajectories, thereby producing disparities. In the hurricane example discussed previously, communities of color and individuals who are low-income are the least likely to have the assets they need to recover quickly from a disaster. Furthermore, the location of their neighborhoods, build of their homes, and even drainage systems may be subpar, increasing their risk of harm during weather events. Racism is a persistent factor that leads to inequitable distribution of public goods and services in the United States. Classism usually follows a few steps behind. Chapter 2 elevates the opportunity that LCT offers for understanding and disrupting these inequities. With all the advantages that LCT provides to practitioners, the opportunity and necessity of addressing inequities is the most central.

Cumulative Impact

The cumulative pathways model suggests that chronic stress (both biological and psychological) can cause wear and tear on the body's regulatory systems, which over time can lead to decline in health and function. LCT posits that the impact of biological, behavioral, and social risk factors builds up over time, resulting in "weathering" or the gradual degradation of health. This perspective helps explain the social patterning of health and disease, as those with fewer resources will experience greater risks. Essentially, this is how inequality can "get under the skin."[4]

The human body is self-regulating; it knows to shut itself off once a stressor has been removed. Allostasis describes the body's adaptations to predictable or unpredictable changes in the environment (e.g., sighting a bear). Allostasis works like a thermostat. When the room temperature falls below a preset point, the thermostat turns on the heat. But as soon as the preset point is reached, the thermostat shuts off the heat to prevent the room from becoming overheated. However, in the face of repeated or chronic stress, the body loses the ability for self-regulation. This loss of self-regulation as a result of chronic accommodation to stress results in a high allostatic load and elevated levels of stress hormone known as cortisol.[27,28]

Studies have found elevated stress hormones and exaggerated responses to natural or experimental stressors in animals and humans subjected to chronic stress.[28,29] As a result, repeated stress accumulated over the life course may lead to increased risk for cardiovascular diseases, cancers, autoimmune disorders, and a host of chronic adult diseases that contribute to health disparities. Research by Geronimus et al.[30] supports this cumulative pathway or weathering hypothesis. Her work found a four-fold increase in the risk of low birth weight and very low birth weight births with increasing age among African American women, but not among White women.[31] Moreover, among African American women, the elevated risk with increasing age was seen only in women of low and average socioeconomic status (SES), not in those of high SES.[31]

Geronimus also noted a more rapid decline in the health status of African American women, particularly those who are low-income, than that of White women with increasing age.[31] Geronimus attributed this disparity to the chronic stress and strain that African American women have to weather day in and day out throughout their life.[31] The cumulative effect of the allostatic stress load on reproductive health and the next generation is evident in the increasing rates of poor birth outcomes with increasing age.[31] In a different study of a large cohort of homeless women in Los Angeles, California, the percentage of life a woman had spent homeless had a stronger association with low birth weight and preterm delivery than whether or not she was homeless during the pregnancy.[32] This spotlights the importance of preconception health and wellness, as the stress a woman has endured before pregnancy may have equal if not greater impact on the outcome of the pregnancy than what happens during it.

A SYNTHESIS

Together, the core constructs and models described previously comprise the LCT. Figure 1-2 provides a visual depiction of the theory, emphasizing the developmental trajectory over time. For simplicity, the figure only depicts one individual life course. Scientists who are part of the Life Course Research Network led by Halfon and colleagues have developed complex models that demonstrate multiple generations and relationships.

The horizontal axis represents development over time, showing some of the different sensitive periods during growth in which interventions may be particularly salient. The dotted lines create a link between generations as it depicts the health and wellness of parents before conception. The point in time depicting fetal development (epigenetics/early programming) is a second time, when two life trajectories—mother and fetus—intersect at the most intimate biological level possible. The longitudinal nature of the horizontal access also suggests the presence of cumulative pathways over time. The vertical axis represents a person's health and well-being potential, with the line higher up on the axis indicating fuller potential. This elevates the core goal for public health, social work, and related fields that seek to support people in achieving health, productivity, and even happiness.

The trajectory is drawn as curves rather than straight lines to underscore the concept of sensitive periods, such as early childhood and puberty, during which development is

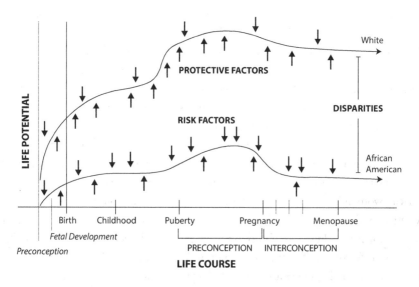

Source: Lu and Halfon.[10] Adapted with permission from Springer.

Figure 1-2. Life Course Model of Health Disparities

particularly vulnerable. The influence of risk factors such as poverty and limited access to quality childcare or kindergarten is depicted as downward arrows. Protective factors such as a nurturing home environment, access to nutritious food, and employment security are depicted as upward arrows. Clearly, very few individuals do not have some risk factors and some protective factors. However, when the factors become imbalanced, their weight can shift the life course of an individual, family, and community.

Although this is a stagnant model, in real time, at any point in a person's life course, an increase in protective factors theoretically can narrow that gap by improving health and well-being. The gap between the two lines represents health inequities. In the United States, the upper line may be labeled as depicting the trajectory for someone who is socially advantaged (e.g., non-Hispanic Whites, the wealthy) and the lower line as the trajectory for someone who is socially disadvantaged (e.g., African Americans, American Indians, the poor). By focusing on the risk and protective factors that influence the life trajectory, this model creates a space for innovation and calls for a focus on the social determinants of health to close the gaps. Lu and Halfon originally used this visual to describe a woman's reproductive potential as influenced by her developmental trajectory set forth by early life experiences (early programming) and altered by chronic adaptation to stressors (cumulative pathways) over the life course (Figure 1-2).[10]

LIFE COURSE THEORY AND MATERNAL AND CHILD HEALTH

Infant mortality is a sensitive and long-standing gauge of societal well-being.[33,34] In the United States, socioeconomic and racial disparities in infant mortality, as well as other key MCH indicators, have persisted over a century and, in some cases, are widening.[35,36] These seemingly intractable population health differentials are a major reason that the United States ranks behind much of the industrialized world in MCH.[37] The typical response to these disparities involves "age and stage" medical model approaches focused on individual-level risks, protections, and interventions, which, while unquestionably important, have not been sufficient to eliminate the problem.[5] Health is more than health care, and disparities are more than health differentials. National and international calls for health equity are aligned in their message: closing the gap requires courageous, coordinated, and far-reaching efforts to address the multiple determinants of health, especially those factors that fundamentally shape the context of social life and the distribution of social resources.[1,38,39]

In 2003, Lu and Halfon[10] proposed a life course perspective as a new approach to an old problem. Then, as today, African American infants experienced two to three times the incidence of adverse birth outcomes (e.g., preterm and very preterm delivery) and infant death as non-Hispanic Whites.[9,40] These disparities were not explained by conventional medical, behavioral, sociodemographic, or psychosocial risks or protections.[41-44] National data even revealed paradoxical trends in several risk parameters, wherein infant mortality was higher among low-risk African Americans than high-risk non-Hispanic Whites.[45,46] And there was little scientific evidence that genes were to blame.[47-50]

For decades, MCH research, practice, and policy efforts to support healthy pregnancies and address racial disparities focused on individual-level risks and protections during pregnancy. Lu and Halfon argued that a pregnancy outcome was the culmination of a woman's total life experience up to that point in her development, not simply her experiences during the pregnancy itself.[10] Life unfolded, not as disconnected stages of development but as an integrated continuum of experiences. Each stage of life was predicated on all the stages that preceded it. The prenatal period, therefore, is late to start intervening to optimize pregnancy outcomes and reduce disparities. Disparities could be better understood longitudinally as the result of a complex array of differential risks and protections across multiple domains (biological, psychological, social, behavioral, environmental) and levels of experience (individual, family, community, society, culture, generation) that affected health and development trajectories across the life span.

One important note—this perspective, although new in public health, has been understood by social workers since Jane Addams began her work in the late 1800s. Although the context may be different, over time, social workers also drifted, perhaps not from seeing individuals in the context of their family, community, and larger environment but in their more "micro" focused efforts on individuals and less "macro" on the community development and policy issues that greatly influence the people they serve. Chapter 3 provides a historical context for these shifts in perspective and focus.

Lu and Halfon's promotion of life course within MCH has helped practitioners take a complex view of MCH and explore new strategies and partnerships to effect change.[10] In Appendix 1A, McClain discusses how tobacco use is a risk factor that has intergenerational impact. Furthermore, this perspective has elevated the importance of working upstream in the life course, so to speak, in fields such as chronic disease prevention, mental health, tobacco cessation, economic development, violence prevention, and environmental justice. The Life Course Approach also offers a language to use when one is considering the way different cultures and populations may understand LCT and its application. Locklear Hertel applies a life course perspective to the history of American Indians as well as their intergenerational perspective in Appendix 1B at the close of this chapter.

CRITIQUES

Although the Life Course Approach offers many opportunities for advancing the field, there are pitfalls that may prove problematic if not addressed with care. One critique of this theory is the emphasis placed on early life—the beginning of an individual's life cycle. Programmatically, it makes sense to invest resources and focus research at the critical juncture in time when two generations connect at the cellular level during pregnancy. Research has demonstrated that early infant and childhood exposures—fetal development, nutrition, safety, and care—set the stage for future well-being. The call for investment in this sensitive period of time is necessary and, if done correctly, can have long-term payoffs. This is particularly true for chronic disease prevention—proper nutrition and healthy behaviors for youths and young adults is a wise investment for their own well-being but also influences fetal exposures and infant/child feeding practices in the future—an excellent example of primary prevention. However, a genuine focus on life course requires an intergenerational approach that necessitates considering the health and economic success of young adults before they become parents, the wellness of new parents who care for children, and the social, financial, and physical well-being of older adults in a family circle—whether they serve a primary caregiving role as grandparents, provide monetary support to their children, or themselves require considerable care and financial resources. LCT calls practitioners to consider and address the many factors that intertwine with different developmental stages and to practice creativity and depth when seeking innovative solutions to long-standing challenges.

If not approached thoughtfully, elements of LCT such as sensitive period of time and cumulative impact can appear to be deterministic in nature. This is dangerous both in potentially reduced funding for public health programs and services beyond early childhood and in creating a sense of hopelessness among communities and populations who may see themselves as destined for lifelong health inequities. The reality is that there are sensitive points in development across the life course—adolescence, early adulthood, pregnancy, menopause—when supports and services can reduce risks and improve well-being. Furthermore, other elements of this theory highlight the impact that positive changes in a person's environment—the social determinants of health—can have on health trajectories. For example, although a baby who was exposed to tobacco in utero may have greater risks of having attention-deficit disorder or developing a chronic disease, access to educational supports, quality clinical care, healthy food, and safe places to exercise can counter that risk and close gaps in outcomes. Practitioners must be mindful of language when communicating about LCT, walking a careful line between making a case for intervention at a certain period of time and creating a sense that any investment after that time is less valuable.

Another common concern with this theory, particularly in the MCH arena, is the emphasis that is placed on the woman in her role as a mother. This is reinforced by the current system of care for reproductive health, which focuses with great intensity on women while pregnant, yet ignores needs for care before, in between, and beyond prenatal care. Preconception care, the health of young adults, is a critical period of time that has been shown to improve outcomes for individuals regardless of childbearing and families.[51] Yet it has been difficult to advance this work, particularly for programs focused on pregnancy prevention. Policymakers are more inclined to support programs for children than women, which has led to framing care for women in the context of pregnancy. This neglects the fullness of a woman's health and well-being at the same time that it may alienate individuals who chose not to have children, have experienced a fetal or infant death, and/or are unable to become pregnant.

Furthermore, this focus removes men and their role as fathers from the equation. Men exert significant influence on the women and children in their lives by their presence or absence, support or neglect. Their access to services and supports matters for their own life course trajectory as well as how their trajectory is inextricably linked with that of their partners, families, and children. Emerging research on sperm demonstrates that men's early exposures, stress, and behaviors alter DNA, which in turn affects their future offspring.[52] LCT presents a unique opportunity for practitioners, teams, and the community to discuss shared perceptions on motherhood, fatherhood, reproductive justice, and feminism. Lanier provides a perspective of LCT and fatherhood in an Appendix 1C at the close of this chapter.

Victim blaming is a fourth pitfall that LCT may present. Discussions about pregnancy and life course quickly turn toward maternal behaviors such as tobacco use, nutritional supplements, oral care, and stress. Rarely do these discussions expand further to discuss the woman in context in terms of resources, access to care, and racism. For example, a woman may not breastfeed her child because she does not have the support, information, and community, family, or employment environment needed for lactation success. Instead of implicitly or explicitly judging her infant feeding choices, the Life Course Approach insists that we consider all of the factors that contribute to this decision. While often inadvertent, language and phrasing used by practitioners in this context may cause harm—particularly by professionals who have more power and privilege than those they serve. Paying attention to language is essential, as the last thing that professionals aim to do is to inadvertently blame someone for the stress that they carry because of racism, gender discrimination, and intergenerational poverty!

Finally, the focus on evidence-based practice is critical at the same time that it may pose a roadblock. Given the innovation that LCT requires, the field is challenged to weigh and balance a singular application of evidence-based practice compared with a broadening of perspective toward evidence-informed practice. Rigor and expectation for success are necessary for funders and practitioners alike. However, LCT at its core offers complexity and the need to adapt interventions for communities according to their input and guidance. Implementation science offers strategies and concepts that may address this need for balance within practice. There is a rich array of models and methods that can build evidence and accountability while allowing space for adaptation.

IMPLICATIONS

Practice

The life course perspective calls for clinical, social, and public health interventions that are longitudinally and contextually integrated into practice. For example, improving health requires access to quality health care not only during the reproductive years but also across the life span. Integrated care and medical homes reduce the risk that people "fall through the cracks" of a fragmented health system and, instead, ensure they receive the education, screening, and treatment they need at each developmental stage of life. Although the Life Course Approach suggests that prenatal care may be limited in its effectiveness to reverse the cumulative impact of early life influences and chronic allostatic load on the mother, it recognizes the potential contributions of prenatal care to early programming of the baby's organs and systems, including the reproductive system, for optimal lifelong functioning. The benefits of prenatal care for improving birth outcomes may be more intergenerational than immediate. However, using prenatal care as an entry point to cohesive, comprehensive, coordinated, woman-centered care for the mother is an opportunity not to be missed. Improving women's health outcomes is equally (if not more) critical.

Women's health is not only the product of clinical health care; it is also the result of many factors operating at multiple levels and interacting with each other over the life course. Thus, eliminating disparities in birth outcomes will take a more integrative approach that simultaneously addresses these multiple (biological, psychological, behavioral, and social) determinants of women's health.[53] Health care providers, licensed clinical social workers, and public health professionals are not exempt from addressing causes outside the clinical domain.[54] It is imperative that they understand how multiple factors interact to influence health across generations.

As an example, it has been shown that the typical cost of food is approximately 15% to 20% higher in poor neighborhoods, while the quality of food available is lower.[55] In many disadvantaged communities, there are more liquor stores than grocery stores, and more fast food restaurants than healthy restaurants.[55] For individuals growing up and living in those communities, the relative unavailability of nutritious food may pattern a lifelong habit of making unhealthy food choices that becomes difficult to change. Similarly, in many disadvantaged communities, parks and recreation areas are scarce and often unsafe. The relative lack of opportunities (e.g., lack of space, childcare needs, transportation, working long hours) for physical activities may pattern an inactive lifestyle that often continues from youth to adulthood. This may also explain why even the most intensive smoking cessation interventions during pregnancy appear to be only modestly effective.[56] Most programs do not adequately address the social stressors that underlie the addictive behavior.[55] Integrated biopsychosocial–environmental health promotion and intervention strategies can better support complete care and ability to change. Interventions to eliminate racial disparities in birth outcomes are unlikely to be widely effective if they do not address the social contexts of health behaviors.

The 12-Point Plan to Close the Black–White Gap in Birth Outcomes, developed by Lu et al. (Box 1-1), is an example of the creativity and breadth that a Life Course Approach engenders.[57] The 12-Point Plan moves beyond a current focus on prenatal care to addressing the health care needs of girls and women across their life course—beyond the current focus on changing individual behaviors to strengthening family and community systems.

Box 1-1. A 12-Point Plan to Close the Black–White Gap in Birth Outcomes: A Life Course Approach

1. Provide interconception care to women with prior adverse pregnancy outcomes.
2. Increase access to preconception care to African American women.
3. Improve the quality of prenatal care.
4. Expand health care access over the life course.
5. Strengthen father involvement in African American families.
6. Enhance coordination and integration of family support services.
7. Create reproductive social capital in African American communities.
8. Invest in community building and urban renewal.
9. Close the education gap.
10. Reduce poverty among African American families.
11. Support working mothers and families.
12. Undo racism.

Source: Lu et al.[57] Adapted with permission of ISHIB, publisher of Ethnicity & Disease.

And the plan shifts the direction from biomedical models to begin to address the social and economic inequities that underlie much of the disparities in MCH. States as described in Chapter 10 have become serious about applying a life course perspective to their work, whether through this framework or approaches described throughout this book.

Research

LCT calls for research that considers cumulative experiences over a person's life. As a first step, it calls for better data integration. Databases need to be linked across different stages of life. Maternal and paternal data need to be linked not only to birth outcomes data but also to data on long-term child health and developmental outcomes. Data also need to be collected and linked at multiple points in a woman's life cycle and across generations. Furthermore, data about men are also required to better understand the role they play from preconception through the stages of pregnancy and beyond. Improved data integration is essential and offers significant richness.

LCT calls for more longitudinal study designs. Prospective cohort studies with appropriate controls, sufficiently large sample size, oversampling among at-risk populations, and adequate duration of follow-up are needed. A study design spanning three generations will enable researchers to begin to investigate the impact of differential early life programming and cumulative allostatic load over the life course, and perhaps even across generations, on health outcomes. Other study designs could be deployed to study three or four generations at a single point in time, connecting data, exposures, health status, and stories. The life course perspective also calls for an integrative approach to disparities research. As outlined by the National Research Council, such an approach integrates research across disciplines to investigate health determinants at multiple levels. This will require improved measurements of life course factors, more sophisticated causal reasoning, and interdisciplinary collaboration among biomedical, behavioral, and social scientists to integrate research on health disparities across multiple disciplines.

Multidisciplinary research networks need to be developed to bridge the existing chasm between biomedical and social–behavioral research on disparities. Long-term, community-linked research collaboration needs to be established. Such collaboration can help ensure that the science addresses relevant life course issues in the communities and that an effective platform to translate scientific research is created. Building community-linked collaboration will be an important first step for doing life course research on disparities.

LCT research calls for well-designed intervention studies to demonstrate what works and what does not in disease prevention and health promotion and optimization across the life course. Although discovery research is still needed, the field cannot get stuck in this phase. For example, despite a growing body of evidence suggesting the critical role that early nutrition plays in developmental origins of health and disease,[58] few intervention studies have been designed with sufficient duration of follow-up to evaluate the benefits of early nutritional interventions for child or adult health outcomes. This leaves an open question as how to best prevent child obesity, early onset type 2 diabetes, or adult metabolic syndrome with early nutrition intervention programs. Such research has its challenges, but the potential knowledge rewards are great. Finally, given the history of inequities and the difference in life trajectories, it is important to oversample at-risk groups and select appropriate controls.

Policy

The life course perspective has far-reaching policy implications for eliminating disparities in birth outcomes and across the life span. As a first step, it calls for greater investments in women's health, including the full array of contraceptive methods. Low-income women and African American women are more likely to lack access to health care than White women and women with financial resources. Rural communities and communities of color also experience access-to-care challenges. Ensuring that all Americans have access to affordable, culturally relevant, quality, coordinated health care services is foundational.

Second, the Life Course Approach calls for greater investments in community health. As long as people of color continue to grow up and reside in neighborhoods and communities that put them at early life disadvantages and under greater cumulative allostatic loads, racial disparities will likely persist, even with the best health care. Eliminating disparities in health outcomes will take more than simply improving individual-level clinical care. Creating the conditions for equitable development requires policy initiatives and investments that build healthy communities. Changing the trajectory of a community requires investments in infrastructure, such as affordable and decent housing, accessible parks and recreation, clean air and water, transportation, quality schools, competent health care, and municipal services. Strengthening communities also requires cross-sectional collaboration.[54] No one group or agency can, by itself, address the multiple factors at multiple levels that contribute to health disparities. MCH leadership needs to engage MCH and non-MCH partners along with community members in a collaborative effort to eliminate health disparities. New partners may include community police officers to double as outreach workers, municipal transportation authorities to map out more accessible bus routes to clinics and major employers, and small convenience store owners to carry healthy groceries. Funders need to include resources for interagency collaborations that would enable a more integrated approach toward health and wellness.

Lastly, LCT calls for greater investments in improving social conditions. Policy actions are needed to support long-term and long-view investments in equity, pushing many MCH practitioners to learn about new sectors and build their policy portfolios. Improving economic access and opportunity is critical, through job training, financial management skill building, higher education, and salaries that not only provide a livable wage but also include benefits. Adequate supports for working parents, including paid parental leave and paid sick leave, foster healthier and more economically secure life courses for families. Practitioners need to ensure that policymakers pay attention to issues that disproportionately affect women's lives, such as taxes on hygienic supplies and diapers and quality, affordable childcare. Men play an important role, positive or negative, in the lives of women and children, and yet they are often treated as an afterthought in MCH. Current policies provide little support, and in some cases great disincentives, for male involvement in pregnancy and parenting, leaving women to bear greater burdens of childbearing and childrearing. For women of color, internalized, personally mediated, and institutional racism contribute to further wear and tear on their body's physiologic systems. By improving social conditions, public policy can help eliminate racial disparities in birth outcomes by protecting women, particularly women of color, against the damaging effects of cumulative allostatic load on their reproductive health.

CONCLUSIONS

The LCT offers the opportunity for practitioners to approach complex health and equity issues with a comprehensive, biopsychosocial perspective. The chapters to follow in this book provide rich examples and strategies for professionals who wish to change their way of work and innovate for change. This approach, as described in Chapter 2, likewise requires attention to equity. Undoing centuries of racism and sexism will not be done during a grant cycle. Yet, it is possible to harness the power of data, the potential of policy, and the moral courage to address deeply ingrained systems of power and privilege—families in this country deserve no less.

KEY POINTS

- The Life Course Approach is essential for improving understanding of how health develops and how disparities are created and perpetuated over time.
- The application of LCT provides practitioners with a platform for exploring new strategies and partnerships to effect change and build equity.
- To advance knowledge about LCT, there is a need for better data integration, more longitudinal designs, well-designed interventions, and multidisciplinary long-term, community-linked research collaborations.
- The 12-Point Plan to Close the Black–White Gap in Infant Mortality developed by Lu et al. offers a multidimensional approach to applying LCT to practice.
- LCT calls for a greater investment in women's health and community health and improving social conditions.

RESOURCES

- The Maternal and Child Health Life Course Research Network (LCRN) is a virtual collaborative network of researchers, service providers, and thought leaders committed to improving health and reducing disease by advancing life course health development research. With funding support from the Maternal and Child Health Bureau, LCRN brings together diverse expertise and perspectives to examine the origins and development of health, and to inform meaningful and evidence-based changes in practice, systems, and policies affecting children and families. To learn more or to join, visit http://www.lcrn.net.
- Halfon N, Forrest CB, Lerner RM, Faustman E, eds. *Handbook of Life Course Health Development.* Springer; 2017. Available at: http://www.springer.com/us/book/9783319471419. Accessed December 7, 2017.
- The MCH Life Course Toolbox is an online resource for MCH researchers, academics, practitioners, policy advocates, and others in the field to share information, innovative strategies, and tools to integrate the life course perspective into MCH work at the local, state, and national levels. The toolbox can be found at http://citymatch.org.
- The Life Course Indicators Online Tool presents measures for 59 life course indicators along with data sources for measuring each indicator. This is a valuable tool for assessing health inequities across a variety of health domains. The life course indicators can be found at http:// www.amchp.org/programsandtopics/data-assessment/Pages/LifeCourseIndicators.aspx.

ACKNOWLEDGMENTS

Thanks are due to Megan Canady for her assistance with the citations for this chapter.

REFERENCES

1. Braveman PA, Kumanyika S, Fielding J, et al. Health disparities and health equity: the issue is justice. *Am J Public Health.* 2011;101(suppl 1):S149–S155.

2. Jones CP. Systems of power, axes of inequity: parallels, intersections, braiding the strands. *Med Care.* 2014;52(10 suppl 3):S71–S75.

3. Wilkinson R, Pickett K. *The Spirit Level: Why Greater Equality Makes Societies Stronger.* New York, NY: Bloomsbury Press; 2010.

4. Halfon N, Larson K, Lu M, Tullis E, Russ S. Lifecourse health development: past, present and future. *Matern Child Health J.* 2014;18(2):344–365.

5. Braveman P. What is health equity: and how does a life-course approach take us further toward it? *Matern Child Health J.* 2014;18(2):366–372.

6. Bronfenbrenner U, ed. *Making Human Beings Human: Bioecological Perspectives on Human Development.* Thousand Oaks, CA: Sage Publications; 2005.

7. Bronfenbrenner U. *The Ecology of Human Development: Experiments by Nature and Design.* Cambridge, MA: Harvard University Press; 1979.

8. Hchokr. Bronfenbrenner's Ecological Theory of Development. Wikimedia Commons. 2012. Available at: https://commons.wikimedia.org/wiki/File:Bronfenbrenner%27s_Ecological_Theory_of_Development_(English).jpg. Accessed December 9, 2017.

9. Fine A, Kotelchuck M. Rethinking MCH: the life course model as an organizing framework. Rockville, MD: US Department of Health and Human Services, Maternal and Child Health Bureau; 2010:7–9.

10. Lu MC, Halfon N. Racial and ethnic disparities in birth outcomes: a life-course perspective. *Matern Child Health J.* 2003;7(1):13–30.

11. Dover GJ. The Barker hypothesis: how pediatricians will diagnose and prevent common adult-onset diseases. *Trans Am Clin Climatol Assoc.* 2009;120:199–207.

12. Sandman C, Davis EP. Neurobehavioral risk is associated with gestational exposure to stress hormones. *Expert Rev Endocrinol Metab.* 2012;7(4):445–459.

13. Bronson SL, Bale TL. The placenta as a mediator of stress effects on neurodevelopmental reprogramming. *Neuropsychopharmacology.* 2016;41(1):207–218.

14. Grizenko N, Fortier M-E, Zadorozny C, et al. Maternal stress during pregnancy, ADHD symptomatology in children and genotype: gene–environment interaction. *J Can Acad Child Adolesc Psychiatry.* 2012;21(1):9–15.

15. Ronald A, Pennell CE, Whitehouse AJ. Prenatal maternal stress associated with ADHD and autistic traits in early childhood. *Front Psychol.* 2010;1:223.

16. Tegethoff M, Greene N, Olsen J, Schaffner E, Meinlschmidt G. Stress during pregnancy and offspring pediatric disease: a national cohort study. *Environ Health Perspect*. 2011;119(11): 1647–1652.

17. Henriksen RE, Thuen F. Marital quality and stress in pregnancy predict the risk of infectious disease in the offspring: The Norwegian Mother and Child Cohort Study. *PLoS ONE*. 2015;10(9):e0137304.

18. Wadhwa PD, Entringer S, Buss C, Lu MC. The contribution of maternal stress to preterm birth: issues and considerations. *Clin Perinatol*. 2011;38(3):351–384.

19. Hauck FR, Thompson JM, Tanabe KO, Moon RY, Vennemann MM. Breastfeeding and reduced risk of sudden infant death syndrome: a meta-analysis. *Pediatrics*. 2011;128(1):103–110.

20. Wang PP. The association between breastfeeding and childhood obesity: a meta-analysis. *BMC Public Health*. 2014;14(1):1267.

21. Bailey DB Jr, Hebbeler K, Spiker D, Scarborough A, Mallik S, Nelson L. Thirty-six-month outcomes for families of children who have disabilities and participated in early intervention. *Pediatrics*. 2005;116(6):1346–1352.

22. Barnett WS. Long-term cognitive and academic effects of early childhood education on children in poverty. *Prev Med*. 1998;27(2):204–207.

23. Bingöl Kızıltunç P, İdil A, Atilla H, Topalkara A, Alay C. Results of screening in schools for visually impaired children. *Turk J Ophthalmol*. 2017;47(4):216–220.

24. Martin EF. Performing pediatric eye exams in primary care. *Nurse Pract*. 2017;42(8):41–47.

25. Yoshinaga-Itano C, Sedey AL, Wiggin M, Chung W. Early hearing detection and vocabulary of children with hearing loss. *Pediatrics*; 2017;140(2):e20162964.

26. Lesnick J, Goerge RM, Smithgall C, Gwynne J. Reading on grade level in third grade: how is it related to high school performance and college enrollment? A longitudinal analysis of third-grade students in Chicago in 1996–97 and their educational outcomes. A Report to the Annie E. Casey Foundation. Baltimore, MD: The Annie E. Casey Foundation; 2010:1–36.

27. McEwen BS, Seeman T. Protective and damaging effects of mediators of stress: elaborating and testing the concepts of allostasis and allostatic load. *Ann N Y Acad Sci*. 1999;896:30–47.

28. Seeman TE, Singer BH, Rowe JW, Horwitz RI, McEwen BS. Price of adaptation—allostatic load and its health consequences. MacArthur Studies of Successful Aging. *Arch Intern Med*. 1997;157(19):2259–2268.

29. McEwen BS. Protective and damaging effects of stress mediators. *N Engl J Med*. 1998;338(3): 171–179.

30. Geronimus AT, Hicken M, Keene D, Bound J. "Weathering" and age patterns of allostatic load scores among Blacks and Whites in the United States. *Am J Public Health*. 2006;96(5): 826–833.

31. Geronimus AT. Black/White differences in the relationship of maternal age to birthweight: a population-based test of the weathering hypothesis. *Soc Sci Med*. 1996;42(4):589–597.

32. Stein JA, Lu MC, Gelberg L. Severity of homelessness and adverse birth outcomes. *Health Psych*. 2000;19(6):524–534.

33. Newsholme A. Report on infant and child mortality. Supplement to the 39th annual report to the local government board, CD5623. London, England: Her Majesty's Stationery Office; 1910.

34. Reidpath DD, Allotey P. Infant mortality rate as an indicator of population health. *J Epidemiol Community Health*. 2003;57(5):344–346.

35. Creanga AA, Berg CJ, Syverson C, Seed K, Bruce C, Callaghan WM. Race, ethnicity and nativity differentials in pregnancy-related mortality in the United States: 1993–2006. *Obstet Gynecol*. 2012;120(2):261–268.

36. Singh GK, Kogan MD. Widening socioeconomic disparities in US childhood mortality, 1969–2000. *Am J Public Health*. 2007;97(9):1658–1665.

37. MacDorman MF, Mathews TJ, Mohangoo AD, Zeitlin J. International comparisons of infant mortality and related factors: United States and Europe, 2010. *Natl Vital Stat Rep*. 2014;63(5): 1–6.

38. National Academies of Sciences, Engineering, and Medicine. *Communities in Action: Pathways to Health Equity*. Washington, DC: The National Academies Press; 2017.

39. Commission on Social Determinants of Health. *Closing the Gap in a Generation: Health Equity Through Action on the Social Determinants of Health. Final Report of the Commission on Social Determinants of Health*. Geneva, Switzerland: World Health Organization; 2008.

40. Centers for Disease Control and Prevention, Division of Reproductive Health. Achievements in public health. 1900–1999: healthier mothers and babies. *MMWR Morb Mortal Wkly Rep*. 1999;48:849–858.

41. Foster HW, Wu L, Bracken MB, Semenya K, Thomas J. Intergenerational effects of high socioeconomic status on low birthweight and preterm birth in African Americans. *J Natl Med Assoc*. 2000;92(5):213–221.

42. Goldenberg RL, Cliver SP, Mulvihill FX, et al. Medical, psychosocial, and behavioral risk factors do not explain the increased risk for low birth weight among Black women. *Am J Obstetr Gynecol*. 1996;175(5):1317–1324.

43. Shiono PH, Rauh VA, Park M, Lederman SA, Zuskar D. Ethnic differences in birthweight: the role of lifestyle and other factors. *Am J Public Health*. 1997;87(5):787–793.

44. Walford HH, Trinh S, Wiencrot A, Lu MC. What is the role of prenatal care in reducing racial and ethnic disparities in pregnancy outcomes? In Handler A, Kennelly J, Peacock N, eds. *Reducing Racial/Ethnic Disparities in Reproductive and Perinatal Outcomes: The Evidence From Population-Based Interventions*. New York, NY: Springer; 2011:151–179.

45. Mathews TJ, MacDorman MF, Menacker F. Infant mortality statistics from the 1999 period linked birth/infant death data set. *Natl Vital Stat Rep.* 2002;50(4):1–28.

46. Singh GK, Yu S. Infant mortality in the United States: trends, differentials, and projections, 1950 through 2010. *Am J Public Health.* 1995;85(7):957–964.

47. Collins JW Jr, Wu S, David RJ. Differing intergenerational birth weights among the descendants of US-born and foreign-born Whites and African Americans in Illinois. *Am J Epidemiol.* 2002;155(3):210–216.

48. David R, Collins J Jr. Disparities in infant mortality: what's genetics got to do with it? *Am J Public Health.* 2007;97(7):1191–1197.

49. Fine MJ, Ibrahim SA, Thomas SB. The role of race and genetics in health disparities research. *Am J Public Health.* 2006;95(12):2125–2128.

50. Fiscella K. Race, genes, and preterm delivery. *J Natl Med Assoc.* 2005;97(11):1516–1526.

51. Johnson K, Posner SF, Biermann J, et al.; CDC/ATSDR Preconception Care Work Group; Select Panel on Preconception Care. Recommendations to improve preconception health and health care—United States. A report of the CDC/ATSDR Preconception Care Work Group and the Select Panel on Preconception Care. *MMWR Recomm Rep.* 2006;55(RR-6):1–23.

52. Ly L, Chan D, Trasler JM. Developmental windows of susceptibility for epigenetic inheritance through the male germline. *Semin Cell Dev Biol.* 2015;43:96–105.

53. Evans RG, Stoddart GL. Producing health, consuming health care. In: Evans RG, Barer ML, Marmor TR, eds. *Why Are Some People Healthy and Others Not? The Determinants of Health of Populations.* New York, NY: Aldine De Guyter; 1994.

54. Hogan VK, Njoroge T, Durant TM, Ferre CD. Eliminating disparities in perinatal outcomes—lessons learned. *Matern Child Health J.* 2001;5(2):135–140.

55. Emmons KM. Health behaviors in a social context. In: Berkman LF, Kawachi I, eds. *Social Epidemiology.* Oxford, England: Oxford University Press; 2000:242–266.

56. Lumley J, Oliver S, Waters E. Interventions for promoting smoking cessation during pregnancy. *Cochrane Database Syst Rev.* 1999(4):CD001055.

57. Lu MC, Kotelchuck M, Hogan V, Jones L, Wright K, Halfon N. Closing the Black–White gap in birth outcomes: a life-course approach. *Ethn Dis.* 2010;20(1 suppl 2):62–76.

58. Barker DJ. Sir Richard Doll Lecture. Developmental origins of chronic disease. *Public Health.* 2012;126(3):185–189.

Appendix 1A: Tobacco Use—A Risk Factor With Intergenerational Impact

Erin K. McClain, MA, MPH

Tobacco use is an issue that cuts across all life stages and affects multiple generations, both in its negative health effects and in the opportunity to intervene and change life trajectories. Tobacco use before and during pregnancy is well known to be associated with immediate poor outcomes for women and infants, including increased risk of infertility, ectopic pregnancy, preterm birth and low birth weight, placental abruption, stillbirth, and infant death.[1] Yet, researchers have also found that in utero tobacco exposure can have lifelong consequences beyond those associated with birth outcomes, including increased susceptibility to tobacco addiction in adolescents, higher levels of nicotine dependence among adults,[2] and increased risk of chronic diseases such as hypertension, diabetes, and hyperlipidemia in adulthood.[3] Researchers have also documented epigenetic changes in fetuses that can affect not only their health but also that of their offspring, such as the increased risk of childhood cancer in the children of women exposed to tobacco when their mothers were pregnant with them.[4]

The health consequences of tobacco use across the life span are well documented and extensive, including increased risk of developing and dying from cancers, respiratory diseases, cardiovascular disease, and diabetes.[1] Tobacco use is also associated with immune system suppression and activation, resulting in increased risk of developing pulmonary infections and autoimmune disorders, such as rheumatoid arthritis, and is associated with an increased risk of developing eye disease.[1] There is no safe level of secondhand smoke (SHS), and it is associated with an increase in low birth weight, impaired lung function, and sudden infant death syndrome in infants exposed to SHS in utero; lower respiratory infections, asthma, and ear infections in children; and stroke, coronary artery disease, and lung cancer in adults.[1]

Emerging research on electronic nicotine delivery systems (ENDS)—the most commonly used tobacco product among youths and young adults—indicates that the aerosol produced by these products is not harmless and contains several chemicals that are known to have adverse health effects, including nicotine, carbonyl compounds, and volatile organic compounds.[5] The nicotine contained in ENDS can harm the developing adolescent brain, and the nicotine delivered by the use of ENDS during pregnancy is associated with increased risk of preterm birth and infant death.[5] In addition, the liquid nicotine solution used in ENDS is a poison hazard if ingested or spilled on skin, especially for young children.[5]

Given that tobacco use is a multigenerational issue that affects people throughout the life span, interventions to address it must be multifaceted and coordinated to truly protect and enhance the life course trajectory of those who use tobacco and their families and communities. Many public health and biomedical interventions focus on ensuring access to and delivery of evidence-based tobacco use screening and treatment for individuals—both in the clinic and community.[6,7] Although this is critical, it is not sufficient. Policies and regulations that provide a system of support that discourage youth initiation of tobacco, encourage tobacco cessation, and protect the larger community from SHS are essential. Evidence-based practices include raising the price of tobacco products by increasing the tobacco tax; policies that require tobacco-free spaces, including public spaces, worksites, and beyond; and high-impact media campaigns, such as Centers for Disease Control and Prevention's Tips from Former Smokers.[1] Other initiatives, such as raising the minimum legal sale age of tobacco products to 21 years to reduce initiation and, subsequently, to decrease prevalence and the burden of tobacco-related disease, are also being explored and implemented by several states and municipalities.[8] Tobacco cessation measures and strategies can span divisions and departments, thus providing a rich opportunity as a starter life course project.

REFERENCES

1. US Department of Health and Human Services. The Health Consequences of Smoking: 50 Years of Progress. A Report of the Surgeon General. Atlanta, GA: Centers for Disease Control and Prevention, National Center for Chronic Disease Prevention and Health Promotion, Office on Smoking and Health; 2014.

2. Oncken C, McKee S, Krishnan-Sarin S, O'Malley S, Mazure C. Gender effects of reported in utero tobacco exposure on smoking initiation, progression and nicotine dependence in adult offspring. *Nicotine Tob Res.* 2004;6(5):829–833.

3. Cupul-Uicab LA, Skjaerven R, Haug K, Melve KK, Engel SM, Longnecker MP. In utero exposure to maternal tobacco smoke and subsequent obesity, hypertension, and gestational diabetes among women in the MoBa cohort. *Environ Health Perspect.* 2012;120(3):355–360.

4. Ortega-García J, Martin M, López-Fernández M, et al. Transgenerational tobacco smoke exposure and childhood cancer: an observational study. *J Pediatric Child Health.* 2010;46(6): 291–295.

5. US Department of Health and Human Services. E-Cigarette Use Among Youth and Young Adults: A Report of the Surgeon General—Executive Summary. Atlanta, GA: Centers for Disease Control and Prevention, National Center for Chronic Disease Prevention and Health Promotion, Office on Smoking and Health; 2016.

6. US Preventive Services Task Force. Tobacco smoking cessation in adults, including pregnant women: behavioral and pharmacotherapy interventions. 2015. Available at: https://www. uspreventiveservicestaskforce.org/Page/Document/UpdateSummaryFinal/tobacco-use-in-adults-and-pregnant-women-counseling-and-interventions1. Accessed September 5, 2017.

7. Fiore C, Jaen CR, Baker TB, et al. Treating tobacco use and dependence: 2008 update—clinical practice guidelines. Rockville, MD: US Department of Health and Human Services, Public Health Service, Agency for Healthcare Research and Quality; 2008.

8. Institute of Medicine. *Public Health Implications of Raising the Minimum Age of Legal Access to Tobacco Products*. Washington, DC: The National Academies Press; 2015.

Appendix 1B: American Indian Community and Life Course

Amy Locklear Hertel, PhD, JD, MSW

This appendix will provide a brief overview as to how Life Course Theory (LCT) may be applied to American Indian populations. A brief discussion of federal Indian policy, the implications of these policies, and a few core concepts are presented. Although it may seem tangential to review federal Indian policy as part of this discussion, it is necessary to deepening an understanding of the health, wealth, and well-being of American Indians (also called Native Americans, Natives, and Indians) today. This understanding is critical to the development of effective and viable social science interventions, research, and policies. In many respects, federal Indian policy has set the life course for an entire population of people.

First, it is important to understand contemporary tribal governments and Native people. The following points should help frame the content. Native Nations (also referred to as tribes, nations, bands, communities, and native villages) are political entities with sovereign governments, which have been reaffirmed by all three branches of the federal government as well as in treaties. Although this appendix may use the term American Indian to refer to a singular group of people, Native America is not a single homogenous population of people. There are more than 560 federally recognized Native Nations in the United States. Although Native Nations are separate political groups, many share similar values and historical experiences. As sovereign governments, Native Nations extend citizenship to individuals meeting enrollment and eligibility criteria as self-determined by each tribal government. Tribal citizens then have certain rights and responsibilities to their tribal communities such as the right to vote, attend ceremonies, and receive certain services. Overall, 0.9% of the total US population identifies as American Indian alone and 1.7% of the US population identifies as American Indian alone or in combination with other races.[1]

FEDERAL INDIAN POLICY

The socioecological model discussed earlier in Chapter 1 addresses the layering of systems that have an impact on health. From a Native perspective, the interplay between the political system and its impact on Native nations, communities, and individuals is profound and complex—so much that it has shaped the health of individuals, families, communities, organizations, and tribal governments for centuries. Table 1B-1 highlights the various federal Indian policy periods from pre-contact to the present.

The oscillating nature of federal Indian policy from removal to assimilation to self-determination has fostered an environment of poor health, discrimination, distrust,

Table 1B-1. Federal Indian Policy Periods From Precontact to the Present

Pre-1492	*Pre-Columbian Period:* American Indian people lived in societies and operated according to their own organized government.
1492–1828	*Colonial Period:* European colonies developed on the East Coast acquiring Indian lands according to the doctrine of discovery and through treaties with tribes for land. Tribal governments were treated as foreign governments.
1828–1887	*Removal, Reservation and Treaty Period:* The US government engaged in the forced removal and migration of tribes from east to west to accommodate the growing US population. Military campaigns relocated tribes to Indian reservations, which were created generally through treaties. During this period, tribes lost access and control of large tracts of land and many people died from starvation and disease. Furthermore, many Native Nations lost control over their local food systems and were forced to maintain a diet of Western food, often lacking in nutritional value.
1887–1934	*Allotment and Assimilation Period:* Settlers' desire for land acquisition and to assimilate American Indians into mainstream America resulted in the General Allotment Act of 1887 (known as the Dawes Act) and the boarding school era. The Dawes Act resulted in the forced conversion of communally held land into small individual parcels for Indian landowners. Millions of acres of tribally controlled land were lost and food systems further devolved. The boarding school was to assimilate Indian children into mainstream society. A common reference to this time is "kill the Indian, save the man." The assimilative practices used during this period proved destructive to Native culture, families, and childhood development.
1934–1945	*Indian Reorganization Period:* The Indian Reorganization Act of 1934 worked to help restore lands to tribes as they reconstituted governments, although often these reconstituted governments were reorganized according to federal government as opposed to traditional standards. The federal government also instituted several programs and projects designed to support tribal autonomy while at the same time forced mainstream values and government structures on tribes. This further dismantled tribal governments and value systems.
1945–1968	*Termination Period:* Congress terminated its federal recognition and assistance to more than 100 tribes. This was an economic disaster for tribes. Millions of acres of land were lost through tax forfeiture sales. Furthermore, the US government instituted a relocation policy, physically relocating Native individuals from reservations to urban areas, cutting them off from their tribal and social support systems. Many urban Indian areas today were populated by federal relocation policies with the intention once again of assimilating and dismantling tribal governments, communities, and individuals.
1968–Present	*Self-Determination Period:* The Indian Self Determination and Education Assistance Act of 1975 has favored tribal control over their futures, including natural resources, land, governance, social service delivery, and other institutions. During this period, tribes are reversing the hardships resulting from the earlier federal policy periods.

Source: Based on National Congress of American Indians.[2]

isolation, and invisibility. Yet Native nations and peoples still exist and have reset their own trajectories through self-determination. Today, many Native nations are thriving, and trends toward improved health, education, and economies are moving in the right direction, yet disparities remain. What is at the heart of this resiliency? Culture. Native culture fuels tribal sovereignty and informs tribal self-determination. For Native people, culture is a strength and it should be fostered to inform practice, policy, and research.

POLICY IMPLICATIONS: HISTORIC TRAUMA, HEALTH DISPARITIES, AND HEALTH TRENDS

The stress associated with historical trauma and discrimination has had a significant impact on American Indians and should be given consideration when one is working with this population. Historical trauma is the "collective experience of violence perpetrated against Indigenous Peoples in the process of colonizing the Americas resulting in an unresolved humanitarian crisis for reservation [and nonreservation tribal] communities."[3] There have been waves of traumas visited on indigenous peoples from land loss, to disease, to boarding schools, to forced relocation onto reservations, to discrimination, and even to the placement of natural gas and petroleum pipelines. These traumas have inhibited health in many tribal communities for centuries, the effects of which are prevalent across Indian Country and Native populations today. Epigenetics (as described earlier in this chapter), historical trauma, adverse childhood experiences, and health disparities are an area of growing exploration among American Indians.

A deeper exploration of the assimilation period may be useful in contextualizing how that era is contributing to the health disparities seen today. Starting in the 1880s, Indian children (as young as 6) were forcibly removed from their homes to live at and attend boarding schools often far from home for long periods of time. There they were taught Christian virtues, the English language, and vocational trades. They were not allowed to speak their language or practice their religion or culture. Their hair was cut and their traditional clothing was forbidden. In many cases, Indian children were harshly punished for trying to maintain their Indian identity. Overall, they were taught that their cultures were inferior and that they should be ashamed for being American Indian. This had a negative impact on their sense of self-worth, their relationships with others, their ability to develop healthy coping strategies, and the transmission of cultural values and norm. By 1887, there were 227 such boarding schools in the United States. This practice continued from 1879 through the 1960s, which resulted in generations of Native children being raised with limited knowledge of their culture, community, family, or how to raise children in their traditional ways.[4] Although not all boarding school experiences were negative, schools that harshly punished Native children left a lasting impression on those children, which has had an impact on the trajectory of their lives and that of their children, family, and community over time.

The impact of historically traumatic events (e.g., boarding schools) on American Indians is evident today. Although the overall population of American Indians in the United States is relatively small compared with that of other populations, the health disparities facing Native people are significant. Native people have significantly higher rates of diabetes (189%), alcoholism (510%), tuberculosis (600%), vehicle crashes (229%), and suicide (62%) compared with other Americans.[5] Furthermore, American Indian youths have the highest rate of suicide in the United States across all other races and ethnicities for those aged 15 to 24 years, with suicide being the second leading cause of death.[5] With respect to education, only 9% of American Indians and Alaska Natives have earned a bachelor's degree and 5% have received a graduate or professional degree compared with 19% and 10%, respectively, for the overall US population.[1]

Even when we consider these disparities, the current policy period has enabled tribes to develop policies, programs, and services that speak directly to their needs and the needs of their citizens. As a result, self-determined initiatives have influenced some promising trends across Indian Country. The tribal college movement has ushered in the creation of tribally controlled colleges and universities that serve the specific needs of American Indians living in geographically remote areas. This policy development enables tribes to offer uniquely tailored educational services. As a result, the number of American Indians awarded postsecondary degrees has nearly doubled over the past 30 years, growing from 7.7% to 14.7% between 1980 and 2013. Today there are more than 35 Tribal Colleges and Universities with more than 75 locations in the United States.

Recent trends across Indian Country to return to sustainable traditional foods and restore self-sufficient traditional food systems will over time shift the diets of Native people away from Western foods that are linked to negative health outcomes toward local, traditional food ways improving individual and community health. Trends reveal that increasing numbers of tribes are growing and harvesting their own food and giving it to tribal citizens and community members, enabling individuals, households, and families to have greater access to healthy foods and saving money on food-related expenses. Data from the Indian Health Service's (IHS's) Special Diabetes Program for Indians showed that obesity and diabetes rates for Native youths have not increased since 2007 and the same is true for adults since 2011. Interestingly, this program is also tribal and community driven; the IHS provides grants to tribes and urban Indian health programs to implement diabetes treatment and prevention services. These trends demonstrate the value of tribal self-determination and benefit of local control over resources.

CORE CONCEPTS: TIME, WELL-BEING, AND THE FOUR Rs

The concept of time is different between Native and non-Native society. Whereas time is viewed linearly in mainstream society, it is viewed as circular in tribal societies. The past informs the present, which in turn informs the future, and so on. There is no end to time, only a new beginning. Furthermore, one should not isolate any time or generation from another—hence the discussion of federal Indian policy and historical trauma at the beginning of this appendix. Building on this understanding of time is the concept of the seventh generation, which holds that every decision a person, family, community, or government makes should be informed by how it will affect descendants seven generations in the future and how it will honor seven generations in the past. The takeaway is that there is great responsibility in decision making, not just for the present but for the past and future as well. Those who live by this traditional value do not take this responsibility lightly.

Another concept worthy of discussion is the medicine wheel. Although tribes may interpret the medicine wheel differently, the image of a circle with four equal quadrants holds significant meaning for most tribes in the United States. The symbol represents many different things; however, most important for the purposes of this appendix are the four aspects of well-being (mental, physical, spiritual, and emotional). The equal quadrants underscore the importance of balance; optimal wellness is achieved through balance, and imbalance produces the opposite result. Some would say that the health disparities of today are attributable (in part) to the imbalance created by historic federal Indian policies including assimilation, removal, and termination that were inflicted on Native Nations.

We can also see LCT expressed through the perpetuation of value systems. La Donna Harris, founder of Americans for Indian Opportunity and a citizen of the Comanche Nation, has identified four core values and obligations that foster indigeneity in tribal communities, known as the four Rs: (1) relationship, (2) responsibility, (3) reciprocity, and (4) redistribution. According to research conducted by Harris and her colleagues at the Center for Interactive Management at George Mason University, these core values cross geography, generation, and tribes in the United States.[6] An understanding of these values and obligations explains the interconnectedness and interdependence of Native people to each other and to their environments. Each is described briefly here:

- Relationship is a kinship obligation, which underscores the communal nature of indigenous societies. The obligation reminds one that maintaining peaceful personal relationships is necessary to reduce conflict and maintain social harmony. Relationship also refers to the belief that everyone and everything is related. This creates a kinship obligation for humans to take care of all things around them. The idea is that we are all related.

- Responsibility is the community obligation and refers to belief that each person has value and something to contribute to the whole of society. If a person is left out of community activities, then society is shortchanged. The implication is that each person has different strengths and with those strengths comes societal responsibilities. Responsibility also creates a personal obligation for individuals to find a meaningful and productive way to make their contribution to community.

- Reciprocity is the cyclic obligation and speaks to the cyclical nature of life, seasons, and relationships. At any given time, an individual is engaged in a reciprocal exchange of obligations and experiences. The belief is that the acts of a person will return to them in their interactions with others.
- Redistribution is the sharing obligation and refers to the continuous balance and rebalance of relationships. The value derived from a good, skill, trait, or talent is not its possession, but in the giving away. Giving is not done with a sense of superiority or charity but in a context in which everyone involved understands that the acts may be reciprocated in the future.

According to LCT, families play a critical role in maternal and child health. An indigenous lens would add elders to the list of critically important individuals to consider when one is developing interventions and policies. In many Native cultures, elders are typically individuals who are older than others in their family or community who are respected for their wisdom and spirituality and recognized for their leadership.[7] Their wisdom and knowledge come from a long life and they use that information to help younger generations understand the present and plan for the future. Therefore, elders are often consulted to inform or make decisions at the individual, community, and tribal government levels. Given their perspective and where they sit in their own life's course, they offer valuable guidance and perspective that only a lifetime of experiences can provide. Another concept that deserves attention is the concept of family. From a Native perspective, family extends well beyond the nuclear family to include grandparents, aunts, uncles, and cousins. The extended family is important and it is the place in which most responsibility for redistribution rests.

LOOKING FORWARD

An indigenous lens would reframe health as well-being, which is a broader concept. The four dimensions of well-being as reflected in the medicine wheel (mental, physical, spiritual, and emotional) are needed to live in balance and to be healthy, comfortable, and happy with life. Again, this is as true for an individual as it is for a community.

Practice

The life course perspective supports intervention strategies that not only address healing from present trauma but also acknowledge and address healing from past historical traumas. The circular concept of time underscores that what happened in the past has an impact on the present and will inform the future. In other words, the traumas visited on past generations have been passed to the present generation and, if left unresolved, will be passed to future generations. For example, instead of addressing a health issue in isolation (e.g., alcoholism), it is useful to (1) determine if the alcoholism existed elsewhere in the family or community, (2) determine why the alcoholism started (i.e., was it a coping mechanism resulting from boarding schools, forced removal, or discrimination?), and (3) help that person work through the historical, political, psychosocial, and economic circumstances that fostered the addiction. Intervening in this cycle of inheriting and bequeathing traumas will not only help present generations of American Indians improve their health and well-being but it will have an impact on future generations as well.

Research

In general, American Indian–specific data are often excluded from biomedical and public health studies. There are many reasons for the exclusion: the population may be categorized as "other" combining American Indians with other small population races and ethnicities; racial and ethnic data may not be consistently collected or recorded in death and medical records; health care providers may make incorrect assumptions about the race or ethnicity of American Indian people; or studies do not oversample for American Indians to combat small populations statistics. However, the inclusion of American Indians in the research process as partners and participants is important, especially during this era of tribal self-determination. Inclusion across the research spectrum (data collection, reporting, dissemination, and intervention) will enable Native Nations and both Native and non-Native practitioners to meet the unique and distinctive needs of this population as they seek to understand American Indian health, reduce health disparities, and improve health outcomes for tribal citizens.

Policy

The life course perspective encourages investments in community health and well-being, which is especially needed across Indian Country. Investments in well-being that benefit entire communities are well suited for tribes given the emphasis placed on relationships. Individuals in relationship (kinship obligation) with each other bear a responsibility (community obligation) to care for and consider each other's well-being. In many tribal communities, this holds true for conventional relationships (i.e., parent–child, spousal, or close friendships) as well as for those living in a community together. Often, individuals or families with an excess of resources (i.e., food or money) will share their excess so none are left without. People are not respected for what they keep but for what they give away. Therefore, policies that invest in community resources will not only foster relationships but will also reduce the responsibility individuals feel to redistribute their own personal resources in the community.

A good model for this investment in the mid-1990s was block grant funding that enabled tribes to design, tailor, and implement policies, services, and programing that best meet the self-determined needs of their citizens. Placing these investments in the hands of those who know the needs and cultures of their people best is good practice and policymaking. Furthermore, it enhances the capacity of communities and governments to determine their future—seven generations forward. In addition, although investments in infrastructure that support physical health are important (e.g., housing, schools, parks and recreation, transportation, quality health care), traditional well-being encourages investments in tribal sovereignty and self-determination, cultural revitalization and sustainability, and capacity building. These types of investments speak to the mental, spiritual, and emotional aspects of well-being, which from a balance perspective is equally as important as physical and mental health.

REFERENCES

1. National Congress of American Indians. Tribal Nations and the United States: an introduction. Available at: http://www.ncai.org/about-tribes. Accessed August 15, 2017.

2. National Congress of American Indians. NCAI: An introduction to Indian Nations in the United States. Available at: http://www.ncai.org/about-tribes/indians_101.pdf. Accessed August 15, 2017.

3. Brockie TN, Heinzelmann M, Gill J. A framework to examine the role of epigenetics in health disparities among Native Americans. *Nurs Res Pract.* 2013;2013:410395.

4. Weaver HN. *Sovereignty, Dependency, and the Spaces in Between: An Examination of the United States Social Policy and Native Americans. Citation Social Issues in Contemporary Native America.* Farnham, England: Ashgate Publishing; 2014.

5. National Congress of American Indians. Indian country demographics. Available at: http://www.ncai.org/about-tribes/demographics#R11. Accessed April 4, 2017.

6. Harris LD, Wasilewski J. Indigeneity, an alternative worldview: four R's (relationship, responsibility, reciprocity, redistribution) vs. two P's (power and profit). Sharing the journey towards conscious evolution. *Syst Res.* 2004;21:489–503.

7. Clark P, Sherman N. The importance of elders and family in Native American culture. Available at: http://blog.nrcprograms.org/wp-content/uploads/2011/05/importance1.pdf. Accessed August 20, 2017.

Appendix 1C: Fatherhood and Life Course

Paul Lanier, PhD

The importance of fathers and other male caregivers to maternal and child health across the life course is often overlooked in research, policy, and practice. Similarly, the importance of becoming a father and engaging in positive parenting to men's physical and mental health is often equally ignored. However, the lens that Life Course Theory brings to understanding maternal and child health outcomes opens a door to include the valuable contribution of male partners and caregivers. Naturally, this broader view of the social conditions that have an impact on women's and children's health should include the men who are part of their lives.

Exploring the role of fathers is timely given important cultural and demographic shifts that are occurring in the United States and many other progressive societies. Over recent decades, Americans have been making improvements in equality between male and female parents in caregiving of young children. In recent years, fathers have experienced a slow but steady transformation in their roles, expectations, and identities. A new generation of young fathers is beginning to shed the traditional primary gender role of "breadwinner," spending more time than ever caring for their children and co-parenting with their partner. These changes reflect broad social progress in women's empowerment, economic demands for labor participation of mothers, and a sharp increase in the number of single-father households. However, the most important factor may be a growing desire among many young men to embrace engaged fatherhood as part of their own emerging adult identity.

This shift toward embracing responsible fatherhood should be welcomed. Studies show that children who experience positive father–child relationships exhibit greater well-being across all stages of child development than those without this experience.[1,2] The positive effects of the father–child relationship extend across a range of outcomes, including healthy socioemotional development, fewer risky health behaviors, and improved academic outcomes.[3,4] Reflecting the societal expectations of the paternal role in caregiving, fatherhood programs and policies have been nonexistent in most communities or have focused solely on financial support. However, the influence of father–child interaction on child well-being extends far beyond economic support.[5-9] The shift toward other important dimensions of father involvement has been highlighted in recent research, such as direct engagement and interaction with the child, availability and monitoring of child behavior, and responsibility for the child's health, mental health, and academic performance.[1,3,10]

Given the importance of the early programming model identified in Chapter 1, focusing on the impact of fathers on early child development is warranted. Although developmental research has been largely dominated by studies of the maternal–infant relationship, recent studies have also uncovered some of the similar and unique benefits of positive father–child relationships. A recent review of studies examining the neurological and hormonal responses to caregiving suggested that, aside from breastfeeding, men appear to be "hard-wired" to take care of children.[11,12] In other words, the variation in male and female caregiving relationships is likely to be more a function of malleable sociocultural pressures than of deterministic biological inputs.

Regardless of the mechanisms driving gender differences in caregiving, there appear to be several unique positive impacts that male caregiving yields.[13] Infants who have engaged fathers in their lives are more likely to explore the world around them with enthusiasm and curiosity.[14] Children with secure relationships with their fathers have higher self-esteem and are less likely to be depressed later in life.[15] Father–child play interactions have been found to be more physical, challenging, and more peer-like compared with mother's play behaviors.[16–20] Recent studies suggest that this type of play contributes to children's social and emotional competence by allowing children to practice reading social cues.[20–22] For example, physical play requires interaction and mutuality, as children must learn to be conscientious of facial expressions, body language, and moods.[23]

Fathers make valuable and unique contributions to their children's cognitive development. Infants with highly engaged fathers demonstrate better cognitive development compared with infants with less-involved fathers.[24] One study of infants born preterm found that those with highly engaged fathers had substantially higher cognitive skills than preterm infants who did not have engaged fathers.[25] Furthermore, sensitive and supportive father engagement was associated with a range of positive outcomes including better language development and higher IQs 3 years later. A more recent study found that four domains of father engagement (cognitively stimulating activities, warmth, physical care, and caregiving activities) were consistently associated with greater cognitive outcomes for infants.[24] Cognitive development sets the stage for early learning and school readiness.

Language development is a critically important aspect of cognitive and social development that is affected by father engagement. A study comparing low-income parents' talk to their toddlers during free play at home found that talk to children did not differ in amount, diversity of vocabulary, or complexity between mothers and fathers.[26] However, fathers produced more questions (where, what, who) and clarification requests, which presented more conversational challenges to children.[26] A similar study examined the differences in talk to 2-year-old children and found that fathers' vocabulary used with children made contributions to later language development beyond the influence of mothers' talk or child care experiences.[27] In a study of low-income families, fathers who engaged in reading books and talking to their toddlers supported their children's cognitive development including the ability to communicate and stronger language at later developmental stages.[24,27,28]

Fathers are important in the preschool years, especially as young children develop skills necessary for later school success. A recent meta-analysis found specific aspects of father engagement (warmth, nurturance, and responsiveness) and the frequency of positive engagement activities (playing with and reading to the child) predicted children's social and academic success.[29] Using a large sample of African American fathers, one study recently found that father participation in home literacy activities (e.g., parent–child reading, singing songs, telling stories, and the number of children's books in the home) was associated with children's reading and math achievement.[30] Recent analysis from the Family Life Project found that fathers' language input during a wordless picture book task in the home before kindergarten entry predicted children's receptive vocabulary and applied problem scores above and beyond mothers' language input.[31]

Father involvement can also have an impact on the health of the mother throughout her life course. Although studies often vary in terms of measuring actual father involvement (as opposed to proxies such as marital status), findings indicate that a partner improves use of prenatal care and reduces unhealthy perinatal health behaviors such as smoking.[32] Paternal involvement is a protective factor against infant mortality and may also be an important leverage point in decreasing racial/ethnic disparities in infant mortality.[33] Although previous research has found a relationship between mothers' depressive symptoms and child problem behaviors, actively involved fathers can buffer this relationship.[34] In other words, parents can compensate for each other's limitations for the benefit of the child.

In many cases, engaging fathers during the perinatal period can be challenging, or even problematic, for a variety of reasons. Fortunately, the early and often tenuous co-parent relationship can be fostered through outside support. Indeed, findings from the Nurse–Family Partnership trials indicate that nurse-visited women had greater involvement with the biological father and better stability in their relationships.[35] A recent enhancement to home visiting, the Dads Matter program, has shown promise in improving father engagement with the mother and infant as well as decreased stress for both parents.[36] Unfortunately, in too many cases, the presence of a man increases the risk of physical and emotional abuse along with associated trauma exposure to the child. Studies suggest that the prevalence of intimate partner violence (IPV) during the perinatal period is in the 4% to 8% range.[37] Involvement in a recent empowerment-based intervention adaptation, Domestic Violence Enhanced Home Visitation, was found to decrease IPV over time in a randomized trial.[38] Strategies to enhance and adapt existing maternal and child health programs to engage fathers in positive ways are available, and many promising strategies exist worldwide to involve men in the prevention of violence.[39]

In addition to expanding the scope of current programs to include fathers, developing programs specifically tailored to fathers is also an important strategy to improve father engagement and improve maternal and child health. Tailoring of a program goes beyond simply limiting participation to male caregivers. New programs should be developed and existing interventions adapted with a specific intention to include fathers in this process. For example, the Coaching Our Acting Out Children: Heightening Essential Skills program (COACHES) uses sports to directly increase the relevance and acceptability of behavioral parent training among fathers.[40] In COACHES, fathers are taught parenting strategies and then practice and receive feedback during the context of a soccer game. Compared with standard classroom-based parent training, fathers demonstrated greater engagement outcomes (e.g., attendance, homework completion, satisfaction). The Dad2K program, a recent adaptation of the behavioral parent training program SafeCare, uses a hybrid home-visitor and computer-based sports-themed coaching model to deliver program content.[41] Clearly, researchers and practitioners across disciplines should work together to develop, test, and scale up effective programs.

In recent years, research on fatherhood and father involvement has broadened understanding of these concepts.[42] Researchers are now beginning to translate this knowledge into programs and policies to improve father engagement and help male caregivers develop the necessary skills to be responsive, reliable, and effective partners and parents. Future efforts to improve maternal and child health should include men and fathers. Although much work is needed to break down long-standing societal norms and expectations that serve as barriers to positive male involvement, the field will likely find many willing men ready to do their part.

REFERENCES

1. Lamb ME, ed. *The Role of the Father in Child Development*. Hoboken, NJ: John Wiley and Sons; 2004.

2. Primus L. Changing systems and practices to improve outcomes for young fathers, their children and their families. Washington, DC: Center for the Study of Social Policy; 2017.

3. Jones J, Mosher WD. Fathers' involvement with their children: United States, 2006–2010. Atlanta, GA: Centers for Disease Control and Prevention, National Center for Health Statistics; 2013.

4. Osborne C, Austin J, Dion R, et al. Framing the future of responsible fatherhood evaluation research for the Fatherhood Research and Practice Network. 2014. Available at: https://goo.gl/35gFhd. Accessed August 1, 2017.

5. Curran L. Social work and fathers: child support and fathering programs. *Soc Work*. 2013;48(2):219–227.

6. Kamerman SB. Fatherhood and social policy: some insights from a comparative perspective. In: Lamb ME, Sagi A, eds. *Fatherhood and Family Policy*. Hillsdale, NJ: Lawrence Erlbaum; 1983:23–35.

7. Lazar A, Sagi A, Fraser MW. Involving fathers in social services. *Child Youth Serv Rev.* 1991;13(4):287–300.

8. Knox V, Cowan PA, Cowan CP, Bildner E. Policies that strengthen fatherhood and family relationships: what do we know and what do we need to know? *Ann Am Acad Pol Soc Sci.* 2011;635(1):216–239.

9. Stahlschmidt MJ, Threlfall J, Seay KD, Lewis EM., Kohl PL. Recruiting fathers to parenting programs: advice from dads and fatherhood program providers. *Child Youth Serv Rev.* 2013;35(10):1734–1741.

10. Cabrera NJ, Tamis-LeMonda CS. *Handbook of Father Involvement: Multidisciplinary Perspectives.* 2nd ed. New York, NY: Routledge/Taylor Francis Group; 2013.

11. Heilman B, Cole G, Matos K, Hassink A, Mincy R, Barker G. *State of America's Fathers: A MenCare Advocacy Publication.* Washington, DC: Promundo-US; 2016.

12. Kuo PX, Carp J, Light KC, Grewen KM. Neural responses to infants linked with behavioral interactions and testosterone in fathers. *Biol Psychol.* 2012;91(2):302–306.

13. Pruett KD. How men and children affect each other's development. *Zero Three J.* 1997;18(1): 3–10.

14. Pruett KD. *Fatherneed: Why Father Care Is as Essential as Mother Care for Your Child.* New York, NY: Free Press; 2000.

15. Dubowitz H, Black MM, Cox CE, et al. Father involvement in children's functioning at age 6 years: a multisite study. *Child Maltreat.* 2001;6(4):300–309.

16. Grossmann K, Grossman KE, Fremmer-Bombik E, Kindler H, Scheuerer-Englisc H, Zimmermann P. The uniqueness of the child–father attachment relationship: fathers' sensitive and challenging play as a pivotal variable in a 16-year longitudinal study. *Soc Dev.* 2002;11(3):301–337.

17. Forbes EE, Buchanan A, Bream V. Adolescents' perceptions of their fathers' involvement: significance to school attitudes. *Psychol Schs.* 2002;39(5):575–582.

18. John A, Halliburton A, Humphrey J. Child–mother and child–father play interaction patterns with preschoolers. *Early Child Dev Care.* 2013;183(3-4):483–497.

19. Lamb ME, Lewis C. Father–child relationships. In: Cabrera NJ, Tamis-LeMonda CS, eds. *Handbook of Father Involvement: Multidisciplinary Perspectives.* New York, NY: Routledge; 2013:119–135.

20. Lindsey EW, Mize J. Parent–child physical and pretense play: links to children's social competence. *Merrill-Palmer Quarterly.* 2000;46(4):565–591.

21. Flanders JL, Leo V, Paquette D, Garcia R, Sequin JR. Rough-and-tumble play and the regulation of aggression: an observational study of father–child play dyads. *Aggressive Behav.* 2009;35(4):285–295.

22. Flanders J, Simard M, Paquette D, Parent S, Vitaro PR, Seguin J. Rough-and-tumble play and the development of physical aggression and emotion regulation: a five year follow-up study. *J Fam Violence.* 2010;25(4):357–367.

23. Cabrera NJ, Tamis-LeMonda C, Bradley RH, Hofferth S, Lamb ME. Fatherhood in the twenty-first century. *Child Dev.* 2000;71(1):127–136.

24. Bronte-Tinkew J, Carrano J, Horowitz A, Kinukawa A. Involvement among resident fathers and links to infant cognitive outcomes. *J Fam Issues.* 2008;29(9):1211–1244.

25. Yogman MW, Kindlon D, Earls F. Father involvement and cognitive/behavioral outcomes of preterm infants. *J Am Acad Child Adolesc Psychiatry.* 1995;34(1):58–66.

26. Rowe M, Coker D, Pan A. A comparison of fathers' and mothers' talk to toddlers in low-income families. *Soc Dev.* 2004;13:278–291.

27. Pancsofar N, Vernon-Feagans L. Mother and father language input to young children: contributions to later language development. *J Appl Dev Psychol.* 2006;27:571–587.

28. Duursma E, Pan BA, Raikes H. Predictors and outcomes of low-income fathers' reading with their toddlers. *Early Child Res Q.* 2008;23:351–365.

29. McWayne C, Downer JT, Campos R, Harris RD. Father involvement during early childhood and its association with children's early learning: a meta-analysis. *Early Educ Dev.* 2013; 24(6):898–922.

30. Baker CE. African American fathers' contributions to children's early academic achievement: evidence from two-parent families from the Early Childhood Longitudinal Study—birth cohort. *Early Educ Dev.* 2014;25:19–35.

31. Baker CE, Vernon-Feagans L. Family Life Project Investigators. Fathers' language input during shared book activities: links to children's kindergarten achievement. *J Appl Dev Psychol.* 2015;36:53–59.

32. Martin LT, McNamara MJ, Milot AS, Halle T, Hair EC. The effects of father involvement during pregnancy on receipt of prenatal care and maternal smoking. *Matern Child Health J.* 2007;11(6):595–602.

33. Alio AP, Mbah AK, Kornosky JL, Wathington D, Marty PJ, Salihu HM. Assessing the impact of paternal involvement on racial/ethnic disparities in infant mortality rates. *J Commun Health.* 2011;36(1):63–68.

34. Chang JJ, Halpern CT, Kaufman JS. Maternal depressive symptoms, father's involvement, and the trajectories of child problem behaviors in a US national sample. *Arch Pediatr Adolesc Med.* 2007;161(7):697–703.

35. Old DL, Kitzma H, Hanks C, et al. Effects of nurse home visiting on maternal and child functioning: age-9 follow-up of a randomized trial. *Pediatrics*. 2007;120(4):e832–e845.

36. Guterman N, Bellamy JL, Banman A, Morales-Mirque. The Dads Matter enhancement to home visiting service: early trends from a multisite randomized clinical trial. Paper presented at: the Association for Public Policy Analysis and Management 37th Annual Fall Research Conference; November 12, 2015; Miami, FL.

37. Sharps PW, Laugho, K, Giangrande SK. Intimate partner violence and the childbearing year: maternal and infant health consequences. *Trauma Violence Abus*. 2007;8(2):105–116.

38. Sharps PW, Bullock LF, Campbell JC, et al. Domestic violence enhanced perinatal home visits: the DOVE randomized clinical trial. *J Womens Health*. 2016;25(11):1129–1138.

39. Tolman RM, Walsh TB, Nieve B. Engaging men and boys in preventing gender-based violence. In: Renzetti CM, Follingstad DR, Coker AL, eds. *Preventing Intimate Partner Violence: Interdisciplinary Perspectives*. Bristol, England: Policy Press; 2017:71–100.

40. Fabiano GA, Chacko A, Pelham WE, et al. A comparison of behavioral parent training programs for fathers of children with attention-deficit/hyperactivity disorder. *Behav Ther*. 2009;40(2):190–204.

41. Self-Brown S, Cowart-Osborne M, Baker E, et al. Dad2K: an adaptation of SafeCare to enhance positive parenting skills with at-risk fathers. *Child Fam Behav Ther*. 2015;37(2): 138–155.

42. Lamb ME. The history of research on father involvement: an overview. *Marriage Fam Rev*. 2000;29(2-3):23–42.

2

Equity

Chad Abresch, MEd, and Kimberlee Wyche-Etheridge, MD, MPH

This chapter examines the potential of Life Course Theory (LCT) to eliminate health disparities and promote fair health outcomes for all people. Although the existence of health disparities is an indication of complex social inequalities, the definition itself is quite simple: *measurable differences in health indicators between groups* (e.g., race, ethnicity, sex). Health disparities have received significant attention in recent years. For example, in 2011, the US Department of Health and Human Services issued a report detailing the goals and actions the department is taking to reduce racial and ethnic health disparities.[1] The federal interagency workgroup, comprising eight US departments and charged with developing and monitoring the Healthy People 2020 objectives, has called upon the nation to "achieve health equity, eliminate disparities, and improve the health of all groups."[2] This call for action from the highest levels of government paired with the continuous unveiling of inequity through current events and social media offers a renewed opportunity for practitioners to press forward for change at a more rapid pace, making the following discussion very timely.

Two things are critically important to recognize when one is discussing health disparities. First, health disparities in the United States are not a new phenomenon—they existed well before data were tracked and reported. Second, health disparities are not improving. In fact, in some cases, they are becoming worse. Consider the following example concerning infant mortality (Table 2-1). In her influential book *Half a Man*, civil rights activist Mary White Ovington noted that in 1908 New York City, 290 Black babies died for every 1,000 born compared with 128 White babies.[3] The most recent data from the Centers for Disease Control and Prevention (CDC) reveals that the number is down to just eight Black infant deaths for every 1,000 births, while the number has come down to just two White babies.[4] These data make it clear that infant mortality has improved remarkably for both groups, yet the disparity has persisted. In fact, the disparity ratio has increased from two- to four-fold. Simply put, for every one White family in New York City that suffers the loss of an infant, four Black families suffer the same.

Infant mortality is not the only health indicator that reveals such a stark and longstanding disparity. In the publication "CDC Health Disparities and Inequalities Report,"

Table 2-1. Black and White Infant Mortality in New York City (Deaths Per 1,000 Live Births)

Year	Black Infant Mortality	White Infant Mortality	Disparity Ratio
1908	290	128	2.27
2013-2014[a]	8.37	2.08	4.02

Source: 1908 data based on Ovington[3]; 2013–2014 data based on US Department of Health and Human Services.[4]
[a]Data reported for non-Hispanic Black and non-Hispanic White in New York County (Manhattan).

data are provided to document nearly 30 disparities across all stages of life, ranging from preterm birth to the expected age of onset for chronic conditions. Among the report's most alarming findings, the authors note that the past decade has seen no improvement in 80% of the disparities while another 13% have actually worsened.[5]

Whenever one considers statistics such as these, it is important to remember the people behind the numbers. For every data point, there is a family who has suffered the real impacts of inequity and understands all too well the pain and loss. Consider the case of an African American woman living in a large Midwestern community. As a child, her father had been arrested on a minor drug charge and sentenced to prison—part of the War on Drugs that "specifically targets people of color."[6] As a result, her mother was forced to hold two and sometimes three minimum-wage jobs to support her and her siblings and was rarely at home with the family. When the young girl became an adult, she began dating a man she hoped would provide the sense of belonging and family she felt was missing from her childhood. By her mid-20s, she had one healthy child and a second on the way. Unfortunately, her partner struggled with addiction and it resurfaced during the pregnancy, spiraling out of control. She spent the final months of her pregnancy wondering where he was and hoping he was OK. Her pregnancy was overshadowed by depression and frequent illness, which her doctor believed was caused by stress. The situation worsened after delivery when she brought her new baby home from the hospital. Despite appearing healthy in the days immediately following his birth, the baby quickly became ill with what seemed to be a normal fever. Unfortunately, his condition was far more serious. Without knowing her now-absent partner had HIV, the young woman had contracted the disease from him and passed it on to her baby. By the time doctors were able to diagnose the real source of the baby's illness, it was too late to save his life.

Stories like this illustrate how social inequalities—including those seen here, such as unfair incarceration practices and inequitable economic systems—unfairly disadvantage some groups and result in health disparities. They further demonstrate how health outcomes often develop over the course of multiple generations. In the following section, these points are explained in greater detail. Then the chapter turns attention to how a Life Course Approach offers unique perspectives and can help promote fair outcomes for everyone.

SOCIAL INEQUALITIES AND HEALTH INEQUITIES

Disparities in population health are known to differ on the basis of social rather than biological factors. As Lu and Halfon note, "While race as a biological concept may have little scientific meaning, as a social construct it may have profound health consequences."[7] Braveman concurs with this perspective:

> Health disparities are differences in health that adversely affect economically or socially disadvantaged groups, such as groups characterized by their wealth, education, or occupational standing; their racial or ethnic identification, religion, language, gender, disability status, sexual orientation, or gender identity; or other characteristics that have often been linked with discrimination, marginalization, or exclusion from economic or social opportunities in a society.[8]

The insights of these authors make clear that, because differences in health exist attributable to unequal social factors, health disparities are better understood as health inequities (i.e., unfair health outcomes). The premise is simple: if society extended the same opportunities to everyone (e.g., educational, economic, health care, housing), population health differences would cease to exist; therefore, health disparities represent a longstanding injustice in a country that proclaims justice as an inalienable right for all. As Braveman succinctly explains, "Equity means justice."[8]

Readers may be familiar with the illustrations included in Figure 2-1.[9] They have been used frequently to depict the difference between equality and equity. The illustration

Source: CityMatCH.[9] Reprinted with permission.

Figure 2-1 . Equality vs. Equity

on the left shows an *equal* distribution of soccer balls, but in this case equal is not fair. Two of the fans cannot see the game. The illustration on the right shows an unequal distribution of soccer balls, but one that is more *equitable*—everyone can enjoy the game.

Although the illustrations in Figure 2-1 are helpful, they may also send the wrong message by depicting the people as unequal in size. The wall, on the other hand, is even for everyone. As a consequence, the smaller sports fans need a boost. The first illustration in Figure 2-2 corrects these problems by depicting all three people as equals.[10] Instead, the wall is the problem. It completely blocks participation for some and makes it difficult for others but fully allows it for a select few. This is our reality today—one in which access to good education, housing, jobs, health care, and so much more are differentially available on the basis of race, ethnicity, and sex. The final illustration on the right shows a picture of what could be—equal access to the benefits of society enjoyed among everyone.

The social inequalities that produce health inequities illustrate the utility of LCT. This is true because if health (good or bad) arose solely from genetic factors shared among certain population groups, their existence would be understood as inherited and preexisting. Apart from medical interventions, nothing could be done to ease the health disparities that some groups suffer. Decades of research, however, have demonstrated that this is not the case. Instead, what happens early in life has profound significance in adulthood. Moreover, what happens in one generation holds significance for future generations.[11] These are the foundational theories of LCT. They indicate that improved social equality will ease health inequities throughout the life span and across generations.

Source: CityMatCH.[10] Reprinted with permission.

Figure 2-2. Social Inequality vs. Equality

While the promise of the life course framework for undoing health inequities is encouraging, some caution is warranted before one examines how best to apply these principles. Larson et al. summarize this point well:

> Overall, knowledge of the complex mechanisms whereby biological, environmental, social, and behavioral factors interact over extended time frames to produce disparities in population health is limited, and many critical questions remain unanswered, such as the ongoing debate about the importance of early vs. later events and the timing and mutability of critical or sensitive periods in human development.[12]

By recognizing health and health inequities as complex and interdependent processes that unfold throughout life spans and across generations, the opportunity arises for a more strategic and manifold response—which also sacrifices simplicity. There are no one-to-one correlations between healthy practices and health outcomes. Diet and exercise, while important, can be thwarted by trauma and economic disadvantage. Similarly, high educational and vocational achievement can be undermined through the microaggressions and overt racism that continue to have an impact on vast segments of the population. Furthermore, for those who live at the nexus of adverse health development, true wellness requires large-scale change. For all of these reasons, LCT represents an important opportunity to restructure approaches to programs, funding, staffing structures, and policy to close gaps.

APPLYING LIFE COURSE THEORY TO ADDRESS HEALTH INEQUITIES

LCT represents a different way of understanding health and illness. It moves away from the traditional medical model to acknowledge the manifold determinants of health and how these determinants either promote or undermine health throughout the life span and across generations. This new perspective holds implications for how health promotion and disease prevention are pursued. Three key factors that practitioners should consider follow next.

Preconception Health Matters

Preconception health suggests that the experiences, exposures, and environments that individuals encounter can cumulatively influence birth outcomes. Nutrition, emotional health, and environmental exposures such as lead and mercury can have profound effects on children if not identified and addressed before pregnancy. For example, when women enter pregnancy with an undiagnosed vitamin D deficiency, the recommended prenatal vitamins do not have concentrations most need to normalize low values. According to research presented in the *American Journal of Obstetrics and Gynecology*, adverse health outcomes such as preeclampsia, low birth weight, neonatal hypocalcemia, poor postnatal growth, bone fragility, and increased incidence of autoimmune diseases have been linked to low vitamin D levels during pregnancy and infancy.[13] Once identified and controlled before conception, the chances of having adverse birth outcomes attributable to vitamin D deficiency decreases or is even eliminated. Vitamin D deficiency in women can result in high blood pressure, lack of endurance, depression, and stress fractures. This example demonstrates how the health of the woman, even before becoming pregnant, shapes the health of her future children just as it impacts hers—health outcomes span multiple generations.

Interconception health, which focuses on the health of women between pregnancies, is also a powerful strategy for improving outcomes and reducing disparities. This is especially true for women who have experienced a previous adverse outcome. The case of the woman with HIV discussed previously is an excellent example. After the pain and loss of her second pregnancy, she sought care for her HIV and was able to reduce her viral load to an undetectable level. In time, she met and married a man who was HIV-negative. When the couple decided they wanted to have a child, they were able to conceive safely because of her undetectable viral load and her partner's use of pre-exposure prophylaxis, known as PrEP. After delivery, the baby received the recommended course of postpartum antiretroviral medication and has shown no indication of infection.[14]

The positive outcome in this case was made possible through combined CDC and Health Resources and Services Administration funding to a local health department that enables population prevention strategies for the whole community and intensive case management for those in need. Public health programs like these show the value of preconception and interconception health and demonstrate how life course trajectories can be positively altered to produce improved outcomes across generations.

Environment Matters

The subject of environmental exposures has many different facets. Environment may refer to the physical, social, or even the psychological environment of a person or group of people. Each of these environments has significant impacts on LCT. The physical environment, for example, has long been associated with cases of neonatal lead poisoning. Too often, however, environmental exposures are thought of only as detriments (e.g., lead, crime, pollutants, abuse) that have been put into the environment and not as assets that have been removed, such as friends, family, parks, or caring teachers.

Consider the case of a young girl growing up in a poor neighborhood with high rates of gang activity. Despite her surroundings, she was an honor student at her local school, arrived early each day, and was always neatly dressed and prepared. When she missed a week of school because of illness, the school sent a home visitor to check on her. The home visitor made several notes about the neighborhood, citing her concern for the young girl's safety. When the home visitor saw a young man involved in what appeared to be an illicit activity, she followed protocol and reported it to local law enforcement.

The next week, after her illness had subsided, the young honor student was again missing from school. Several days passed and still she did not return to class. The home visitor was sent back out to check on the student and learned that the young man she had reported was the girl's older brother who was arrested following her call to law enforcement. The girl explained how her brother had been the one who took her to school every morning, making sure she arrived safely and was early for class. He made sure she had all of the school supplies, uniforms, and lunch money she needed to succeed in school. He was well known and feared in the community and would confront anyone who was a perceived threat to his little sister. He was the one who checked her homework at night for mistakes and made her redo problems when errors were found. When he was removed, her world fell apart. She was afraid to go to school and was too distraught to focus on homework; consequently, her grades fell. Years later, the home visitor continues to wonder if she made the right decision. To be sure, the removal of environmental assets can adversely affect health development as this illustration demonstrates.

Public Systems Matter

One of the grounding theories of LCT concerns differential exposure to risk and protective factors. As Lu and Halfon have noted, population groups experiencing comparatively high levels of protective factors and fewer risks fare better.[7] Risk and protective factors are often thought of as biological and social constructs; however, they very frequently include public policies and systems with broad population impacts. Unfortunately, public systems are not often designed with this perspective in mind. Consider the example of a woman who visits the public health department to recertify her Special Supplemental Nutrition Program for Women, Infants, and Children (WIC) benefits. In many instances, she may never be seen by other areas of the health department that could provide protective services (e.g., home visiting, family planning, immunizations). Unfortunately, this scenario is all too common as preventive health providers often do not communicate with nonmedical service providers in the same department. Not only does such a program-by-program approach drain resources by duplicating processes, it also discourages a comprehensive, person-centered approach to health and wellness.

To adopt a life course perspective, a new paradigm must be established, one in which horizontal integration of services becomes the norm, instead of the exception. This means, in a public health setting, different clinics or services cannot exist in silos but rather must function in an integrative fashion. Realizing this would help to create a public system that better addresses health inequities experienced by disadvantaged groups.

PRACTICAL CONSIDERATIONS

The following strategies can serve as a checklist for practitioners to think through when adopting or further incorporating a life course perspective into practice. Many of these considerations require learning about social power and privilege, which too easily go unnoticed among majority population groups. Public health leaders should continuously pursue trainings for themselves and their staff that help develop personal growth and awareness. Issues to consider include race, ethnicity, gender, sexual orientation, and more. This work will help to ensure and improve these practical considerations.

Review Existing Policies to See Where Inequitable Practices May Exist

Most policies are enacted to address pressing needs and improve the lives of the people they affect. However, the needs of one group are sometimes in direct conflict with the needs of others; when this happens, the effects are often detrimental to minority groups and can serve to further entrench health inequities. In addition, justifications for policy enactment are often laden with assumptions and biases, which can result in policies that do little to address the underlying issue.

To establish public health policies that promote health equity, practitioners should adopt a well-established perspective on racism first promoted by Dr. Camara Jones. In her landmark paper, "Levels of Racism: A Theoretic Framework and a Gardener's Tale,"[15] Jones explores three levels of racism—institutionalized, personally mediated, and internalized:

- Institutionalized racism is defined as "differential access to the goods, services, and opportunities of society by race." Jones explains that "[i]nstitutionalized racism is normative, sometimes legalized, and often manifests as inherited disadvantage. It is structural, having been codified in our institutions of custom, practice and law, so there need not be an identifiable perpetrator." This definition would include policies such as "red lining"—the denial of financing on the basis of race in real estate transactions. It would also include differences noted by researchers in institutional policies that regulate access to pain medication by race and ethnicity.

- Jones defines personally mediated racism as "differential actions toward others according to their race." Examples of personally mediated racism may include attitudes and actions toward patients' timeliness or compliance to unrealistic expectations or health regimens. For example, in many health departments and other clinical settings, offices are open during typical workday hours. For families without flexible work schedules, paid leave, and personal transportation, these hours represent a barrier to care. It is important to keep in mind that personally mediated racism may be expressed in subtle practices such as these, in overt acts of discrimination, or through implicit bias (i.e., automatically activated stereotypes and prejudices), which can lead to differences in care. Overcoming prejudice is like the "breaking of a bad habit," which takes intention, effort, and structural supports.

- Internalized racism is "acceptance by members of the stigmatized races of negative messages about their own abilities and intrinsic worth." Jones notes that internalized racism can result in a sense of hopelessness as well as unhealthy or risky health behaviors.

By way of illustration, recent research has noted that African American women have the lowest rates of breastfeeding initiation and continuation among all US women.[16] The barriers to breastfeeding faced by African American women stem from all three levels of racism discussed by Jones. African American women return to work on average two weeks earlier after giving birth and are more likely to work jobs that do not support breastfeeding (institutionalized racism). African American women also report lower levels of breastfeeding encouragement and education from their health care providers (personally mediated racism). Finally, researchers have noted that negative perceptions of breastfeeding, which date back multiple generations, are common among African American women (internalized racism).[17]

By considering all three levels of racism, public health practitioners are in a better position to enact policies that promote—rather than further marginalize—racial minority groups. Practitioners should also be well aware that policies often discriminate on the basis of issues beyond race, such as gender, citizenship, ethnicity, sexual orientation, and religion. From an LCT perspective, the importance of understanding discriminatory policies cannot be overstated. This is true because policies—whether laws enacted by congressional bodies or procedures used in public agencies—serve either to promote or undermine the health trajectories of population groups, and often have lasting impacts.

Engage Community in a Meaningful Way

Embracing an LCT perspective does not mean overruling community input in favor of life course principles. Too often—and with good intentions—public health practitioners commit this error by designing programs without community representation, request, or buy-in. By doing so, they disenfranchise already marginalized communities and run the risk of doing more harm than good.

Consider the example of a community that was deemed a food desert with virtually no access to healthy food options, including fresh fruits and vegetables. The community became the target population for a Healthy Eating and Active Living grant, which was submitted by the local health department. The grant opportunity was discovered late, and, consequently, the health department was unable to identify the right community partners to participate. Ultimately, the grant application was approved and funded; however, when the plan was shared with community decision makers, the proposed solutions were rejected, leaving the grantee in a precarious situation. Fortunately, the foundation funding the initiative granted permission to alter the proposed program, allowing the grantee and the community to salvage what was felt to be a viable solution.

This example had a positive outcome; however, many other projects have been funded to solve a particular community's health concerns without taking those who will be most impacted into consideration. Communities must be at the table from idea inception to program close out. Most communities, when given the opportunity, will suggest solutions for local challenges but may lack the capital or capacity for execution. Outsiders often assume the lack of progress is representative of a lack of initiative or desire to change. Problems are addressed in deficit-based models that only focus on things that are wrong or going poorly. It is less common to find approaches that are asset-based and focus on things that communities are doing well. These positive approaches can be built upon for sustainable change.

Engaging community is important for LCT because it exemplifies one of the outcomes of optimal health development—thriving. As Halfon et al. note, "Health-development provides a set of resources that organisms draw on in order to pursue goals, such as surviving, achieving a state of physical robustness and resilience, and psychological flourishing."[11] In this way, when communities participate in the design and implementation of public health programs, they are acting as empowered agents of change. They are witnessing, firsthand, their capacity for charting healthier trajectories.

Think Positively

A related implication addresses emerging public health efforts around positive deviance. In this context, positive deviance refers to "uncommon but healthy practices that permit some individuals to thrive when their equally at-risk neighbors do not."[18] Positive deviance honors community participation by searching out examples of healthy outcomes within the community and designing interventions according to the practices of these individuals. In this way, public health interventions are designed "on the street" rather than "in the lab."

The concept behind positive deviance is compelling. In nature, one often sees remarkable images of life flourishing in the harshest of environments. Whether in the depths of the ocean or in the scorching desert heat, life finds a way. Similarly, when individuals and communities are able to flourish in the presence of poverty and civic neglect, it is often the result of unique adaptations that demonstrate their intelligence, creativity, and drive. These positive deviations—outcomes we would not expect—function as a springboard against defeat and despair and offer a model for others who live under the same harsh circumstances.

Positive deviation is more, however, than a compelling notion. In fact, research has demonstrated the effectiveness of positive deviance models in a variety of contexts, and experts now believe the approach may help reduce disparities in important areas such as postpartum weight loss, breastfeeding rates, and overweight and obesity in children. Positive deviance is relevant to LCT because it demonstrates the health trajectories that are possible and the behavioral patterns required to achieve these results.

On the downside, these statements make clear that initiatives utilizing positive deviance strategies may lay additional burdens on communities experiencing health disparities; they must adopt different, sometimes difficult, behaviors to overcome circumstances that other communities do not face. As advocates for the health and well-being of everyone, public health practitioners are understandably more eager to see equitable policies enacted that uplift trajectories for entire communities. Unfortunately, such policies are difficult to realize, and finding examples of positive exceptions helps to fill gaps.

Know the History to Understand the Present

As LCT contends, health is not a point-in-time asset but the cumulative result of lived experience interacting in complex ways with "biological, behavioral, social, and environmental influences."[11] As a result of shared experience, residents of marginalized communities often exhibit similar patterns of health. The community of North Nashville is an alarming example of what happens when a history of discriminatory policy "gets under the skin."[19]

In 1967, the Sixth Circuit Court of Appeals ruled in a controversial case (*Nashville I-40 Steering Committee vs. Ellington*), which cleared the way for construction of a 3.6-mile section of interstate that would cut through the middle of North Nashville, a predominately African American community. Residents of North Nashville argued that building the interstate through their neighborhood would adversely affect the economy and disrupt community cohesion. For the state and the city of Nashville, the interstate was seen as an economic boon that would connect Memphis with Nashville and beyond. Bisecting the North Nashville neighborhood was believed to be the most expedient route, and with the court's approval, the project was set in motion and completed in the early 1970s.

This was not the first setback for North Nashville. In fact, the community had suffered from discriminatory policies and expenditures that stretched over many decades. In response to the Great Depression, the Home Owners Loan Act of 1933 provided relief for nearly 20% of families across the country who owed more on their homes than they were worth. Out of the thousands of families who received aid, only 1% of the funds were granted to African American homeowners. As a result, many African Americans lost ownership of their homes during this time. A decade later, The Federal Housing Act of 1949 set the stage for the leveling of North Nashville's original thoroughfare that encircled—rather than bisected—the growing downtown area. Families displaced by the project were relocated to low standard housing stock farther north, away from the growing downtown area. When pyramidal zoning was instituted to protect suburban landowners from commercial growth and mixed land use, North Nashville was excluded, sanctioning the building of many types of businesses next door to residential properties.

Despite these repeated discriminatory policies, the residents of North Nashville banded together, demonstrating resilience and creating a sense of community pride. In the 1950s, before the construction of the interstate, North Nashville was known as the heart of Nashville's African American community. It was home to a stable population of working-class families as well as many members of the African American elite. Local businesses supplied the community with the goods and services they needed, and the presence of three long-standing institutions of higher education populated the community with college-educated, middle-class residents.

This all changed with the massive disruption caused by the interstate. By 2010, the community had fallen into disarray. Many of the businesses that had flourished in the 1950s closed during and after construction of the interstate. Working families displaced by the construction never returned. Years of neglect, abandoned storefronts, and vacant properties encouraged additional residents that could leave to do so. The social cohesion and collective economics that were once a strength of the community eroded, leaving a cloud of despair, accompanied by poverty, crime, and high rates of chronic illness. Today, more than two thirds of the children in North Nashville live below the federal poverty level. Many of these families struggle to pay rent or keep up with excessively high mortgage rates. The community continues to experience inequitable rates of chronic diseases including asthma, diabetes, obesity, and hypertension, as well as cancer, heart disease, and stroke.

The suppressed health trajectory of North Nashville is no mystery; it is the result of discriminatory policies that have routinely burdened residents for the benefit of others. Knowing this history gives a clearer understanding of the community's less-than-optimal health and allows practitioners to seek real solutions by addressing root causes.

Be Patient But Expect Results

This consideration addressed policy decisions that spanned many decades and negatively affected the community of North Nashville. This illustration demonstrates that, just as the pattern of inequitable health outcomes did not mysteriously appear in that community overnight, more optimal health trajectories are not likely to be achieved quickly. What is needed in communities like North Nashville is a string of supportive policies all working in tandem and spanning many years. Only with this will residents realize the positive health outcomes they deserve.

Given this reality, practitioners who choose to adopt an LCT perspective should realize that the work may be difficult to measure in the short term. Funders, political leaders, and citizens may question the efficacy of public health initiatives that aim to improve outcomes over generations rather than years. In constrained fiscal circumstances and contested political environments, projects able to realize quick wins—even if those wins are unlikely to be maintained—often receive higher priority. Conversely, not all LCT work needs to adopt only the long view. As other chapters in this volume will demonstrate, measurable differences can be achieved in short order with results that continue for years to come. For example, projects that provide housing for pregnant women at risk of homelessness have the opportunity to quickly change life course trajectories for two generations. The bottom line is this: LCT often takes time to fully realize results, but thoughtful practitioners can establish intermediate measures to demonstrate that the work is on track and worthy of continued investment.

CONCLUSIONS

Disparities in population health are long-standing and show little, if any, sign of improving. These disparities are rooted in social inequalities rather than biological determinants. Given their social origins, health disparities represent an unfair and unjust reality of US culture. For this reason, health disparities are more aptly termed health inequities.

Adopting a life course perspective to address health inequities involves several important strategic considerations. For example, LCT encourages practitioners to do the following:

- Understand the importance of environment and lived experiences in shaping disparate health outcomes.
- Consider the earliest pathways of health development, which begin even before conception.
- Redesign public systems, agencies, and policies to support, rather than undermine, healthy trajectories.
- Recall the importance of historical events and traumas in the lives of individuals and communities and seek to empower those individuals with choice and agency.
- Design programs that take positive examples of thriving into account.
- Push for measurable results while recognizing that inequity was built on decades—even centuries—of injustices and will not be undone overnight.

In short, LCT represents an important opportunity to ease, and ultimately erase, health inequities by focusing on the current unjust reality and making clear the need to change circumstances to one day realize a more just society that uplifts the health and well-being of all.

KEY POINTS

- LCT can be used as a tool to understand and address health inequities. Health disparities are measured differences in health indicators and stem from the impact of inequities across generations.
- In addressing health inequities, practitioners should consider preconception health, lived experience, environment, and public systems.
- Strategies for change include these five: review existing policies with an equity lens; engage the community; consider positive deviance; become familiar with history as a means of informing and understanding the present; and remain patient when working toward the long-term goal of closing gaps.

RESOURCES

- "Conversations that Matter: a How-to Guide for Hosting Conversations about Race, Racism, and Public Health": This guide emerged from CityMatCH's Tennessee Racial Healing projects in North Nashville and Orange Mound (Memphis). Both communities have been hard hit by racism and the socioeconomic insults that accompany racism. The Racial Healing projects set out to hold community conversations on these topics and map neighborhood-level connections among race, place, and health. The guide can be found at http://citymatch.org/projects/racial-healing/conversations-matter.
- "CDC Health Disparities and Inequalities Report": The report provides data on 29 health disparities among racial, ethnic, geographic, and socioeconomic groups. The information provided is in service to the goal of reducing disparities and achieving the goals of Healthy People 2020. The report can be found at https://www.cdc.gov/minorityhealth/chdireport.html.
- The Positive Deviance Initiative: This resource includes valuable links to research and literature on the positive deviance approach. Examples of current and past projects are highlighted with several positive deviance evaluations featured throughout. The initiative can be found at http://www.betterevaluation.org/en/resources/tools/Positive_Deviance_Initiative.
- "Going Public. Levels of Racism: A Theoretic Framework and a Gardener's Tale": This article by Camara Jones presents the framework for understanding racism discussed in this chapter. The article can be found in the August 2000 edition of the *American Journal of Public Health: Am J Public Health.* 2000;90(8):1212–1215.
- *Unequal Treatment: Confronting Racial and Ethnic Disparities in Health Care*: This book looks beyond socioeconomic differences that create unequal levels of health care access to consider unequal quality of care. Evidence is presented to confirm quality of care is substantively worse for persons of color. In addition, recommendations are offered for improving care for minority patients to create a more equitable system.

The book can be accessed at https://www.nap.edu/catalog/12875/unequal-treatment-confronting-racial-and-ethnic-disparities-in-health-care.

- "Unnatural Causes" by California Newsreel: http://newsreel.org/nav/title.asp?tc=CN0228.
- "The Raising of America" by California Newsreel: http://www.newsreel.org/video/THE-RAISING-OF-AMERICA.
- The National Center for Education in Maternal and Child Health Library holds a wealth of information on health equity: https://www.ncemch.org/mchlibrary.php.
- Racial Equity Institute: https://www.racialequityinstitute.org.
- People's Institute for Survival and Beyond: http://www.pisab.org.
- CityMatCH Institute for Equity in Birth Outcomes: http://www.citymatch.org/projects/institute-equity-birth-outcomes-0.

Preconception Health and Wellness

- Before, Between & Beyond Pregnancy: https://beforeandbeyond.org.
- Show Your Love Today: https://ShowYourLoveToday.com.

REFERENCES

1. US Department of Health and Human Services, Office of Minority Health. HHS Action Plan to Reduce Racial and Ethnic Health Disparities. National Partnership for Action. 2011. Available at: http://minorityhealth.hhs.gov/npa/templates/content.aspx?lvl=1&lvlid=33&ID=285. Accessed May 12, 2017.

2. Healthy People 2020. Disparities. Available at: https://www.healthypeople.gov/2020/about/foundation-health-measures/Disparities. Accessed May 12, 2017.

3. Ovington MW. *Half a Man: The Status of the Negro in New York.* New York, NY: Schocken Books; 1969.

4. US Department of Health and Human Services, Centers for Disease Control and Prevention, National Center for Health Statistics, Division of Vital Statistics. Linked Birth/Infant Death Records 2007–2014, as compiled from data provided by the 57 vital statistics jurisdictions through the Vital Statistics Cooperative Program, on CDC WONDER On-line Database. Available at: http://wonder.cdc.gov/lbd-current.html. Accessed August 4, 2017.

5. Centers for Disease Control and Prevention. CDC Health Disparities and Inequalities Report—United States, 2013. *MMWR Suppl.* 2013;62(3). Available at: https://www.cdc.gov/mmwr/preview/mmwrhtml/su6203a2.htm?s_cid=su6203a2_w. Accessed May 25, 2017.

6. Alexander M. The New Jim Crow. *Ohio St J Crim L.* 2011;9:7.

7. Lu MC, Halfon N. Racial and ethnic disparities in birth outcomes: a life-course perspective. *Matern Child Health J.* 2003;7(1):13–30.

8. Braveman P. What is health equity: and how does a life-course approach take us further toward it? *Matern Child Health J.* 2014;18(2):366–372.

9. Equality vs. equity. Omaha, NE: CityMatCH; 2017.

10. Social inequality vs. equality. Omaha, NE: CityMatCH; 2017.

11. Halfon N, Forrest CB, Lerner RM, Faustman E, eds. *The Handbook of Life Course Health Development*. New York, NY: Springer; 2017.

12. Larson K, Russ SA, Kahn RS, et al. Health disparities: a Life Course Theory perspective and future research directions. In: Halfon N, Forrest CB, Lerner RM, Faustman E, eds. *The Handbook of Life Course Health Development*. New York, NY: Springer; 2017:1–58.

13. Mulligan ML, Felton SK, Riek AE, Bernal-Mizrachi C. Implications of vitamin D deficiency in pregnancy and lactation. *Am J Obstet Gynecol.* 2010;202(5):429e1–e9.

14. US Department of Health and Human Services. Recommendations for use of antiretroviral drugs in pregnant HIV-1-infected women for maternal health and interventions to reduce perinatal HIV transmission in the United States. AIDSinfo. 2017. Available at: https://aidsinfo.nih.gov/guidelines/html/3/perinatal-guidelines/187/infant-antiretroviral-prophylaxis. Accessed August 15, 2017.

15. Jones CP. Levels of racism: a theoretic framework and a gardener's tale. *Am J Public Health.* 2000;90(8):1212–1215.

16. Jones KM, Power ML, Queenan JT, Schulkin J. Racial and ethnic disparities in breastfeeding. *Breastfeed Med.* 2015;10(4):186–196.

17. Asiodu I, Flaskerud JH. Got milk? A look at breastfeeding from an African American perspective. *Issues Ment Health Nurs.* 2011;32(8):544–546.

18. Walker LO, Sterling BS, Hoke MM, Dearden KA. Applying the concept of positive deviance to public health data: a tool for reducing health disparities. *Public Health Nurs.* 2007;24(6):571–576.

19. Evans GW, Chen E, Miller G, Seeman T. How poverty gets under the skin: a life course perspective. In: Maholmes V, King R, eds. *The Oxford Handbook of Poverty and Child Development*. New York, NY: Oxford University Press; 2012.

3

Looking Back to Move Forward

Milton Kotelchuck, PhD, MPH

Without apology, then, I ask you to use courageously your intelligence, your strength, and your good will toward the removal of economic barriers, which have retarded the full development of children in the past. The important thing is that we should be "on our way" toward adequately meeting their needs. Perhaps you may ask, "Does the road lead uphill all the way?", and I must answer, "Yes, to the very end." But if I offer you a long hard struggle, I can also promise you great rewards. Justice for all children is a high ideal in a democracy . . . We have hardly, as yet, made more than a beginning in realization of that great objective.
                                    –Dr. Grace Abbott, 2nd Chief of the Children's Bureau[1]

The current enthusiasm for Life Course Theory and practice is not new to the 21st century but reflects the long and proud historical legacy of the maternal and child health (MCH) field. The field's progress today reflects the outgrowth of the policy disputes, programmatic history, and increased scientific knowledge over the past hundred years. This history provides inspiration, guidance, and a firm foundation for moving forward with continuing professional and political struggles to achieve optimal and equitable health and well-being for newborns, children, young adults, mothers, fathers, families, and communities.

Historically, the social determinants of health, life course, and equity were not originally articulated as distinctive concepts, nor likely as concepts at all. Having a life span or life course was recognized as a fundamental property of life, the transformation of babies into adults on to old age and death. That childhood or pregnancy had a special significance for one's life course health was a relatively underdeveloped concept. There was, however, no lack of folk traditions emphasizing the importance of early experience, especially during pregnancy, on subsequent health of children or on proper upbringing on adult moral character. There was much practical knowledge of early health-related activities for children that would help them grow into healthier adults. Similarly, the belief that differences in where one lives, grows, works, and plays makes a major impact on health and well-being, while not an explicit concept, was a well-understood reality from people's life experiences throughout the centuries, even if the scientific and epidemiological basis for it was not. The belief that there should be equity of opportunity in life was an area of major conceptual, religious, and political debate in the late 19th and early part of the 20th century. The evolution of these concepts over the centuries is the story of the MCH field, leading to today's Life Course Approach.[2,3]

Illustrated primarily through the lens of infant mortality, this chapter will briefly highlight three distinct eras across the century that have focused on the importance of social determinants, Life Course Approach, and equity for improving reproductive and early life health and well being. The eras are defined as (1) the first decades of the 20th century, (2) the mid-1980s to mid-1990s, and (3) the mid-to-late 2000s onward. The chapter concludes with some historical lessons and inspirations drawn from these periods to guide the current generation of MCH practitioners as they take their place in confronting the long-standing policy and programmatic challenges and seizing upon new opportunities to improve the well-being of women, children, and families across the life span.

ERA 1: THE FIRST NATIONAL PUBLIC HEALTH CAMPAIGN TO REDUCE INFANT MORTALITY

At the turn of the 20th century, infant mortality rates in the United States were greater than 100 infant deaths per thousand births. Maternal mortality rates were up to six per thousand births. Urban areas, especially among the poor, were perceived to have higher death rates than rural areas but information on racial and economic disparities was not well known. High infant mortality rates were one of the main driving forces for the development of the emerging public health fields, as well as the related fields of obstetrics, pediatrics, nursing, nutrition, and social work. The high levels of infant mortality, for the first time, were no longer perceived as a fact of life or as an Act of God but as amenable to social and preventive action.[2-4]

The challenges around infant mortality were part of a larger set of political struggles taking place starting in the late 1800s. During this time, the progressive movement was attempting to address and ameliorate the consequences of the rapid industrialization, urbanization, immigration, the exploitation of workers and immigrants, and the unequal distribution of resources in the country. The progressive movement focused on labor unionization, women's voting rights, immigrant rights, mother's aid (welfare), child labor, and temperance. These efforts directly conflicted with those of people of means who believed that there was an inherent order or ranking among human populations, whether based on social class, slavery/racism, social Darwinism, or politics. The high rates of infant mortality were seen as one brutal indication of the negative effects of the rapid industrialization the United States and its unequal wealth distribution. The struggle for improved maternal and child health began primarily in urban areas with large immigrant populations; it was interwoven with struggles for more equitable and societal resources for women and children, human rights, and equitable services and dignity for families in poverty.[2-4]

The American Association for the Study and Prevention of Infant Mortality (AASPIM) was formed in 1908 and was the first voluntary organization in the United States dedicated solely to infant mortality. It provided a broad national forum to coordinate private individuals, voluntary agencies, and urban health departments. Within AASPIM, there were divergent perspectives about causes of infant mortality and how to address them, often reflective of the emerging health professions of that time. Nutritionists and sanitarians emphasized that infant mortality was primarily a diarrheal disease, which increased dramatically in the summertime, caused by the low-quality, prerefrigeration-era milk consumed by poor children of immigrants. They advocated a number of milk-related interventions, including pasteurization and free milk stations for poor women, a predecessor of today's Special Supplemental Nutrition Program for Women Infants and Children (WIC). The emerging social work and home economics fields viewed infant mortality primarily as a result of the poor hygiene and childcare practices of uneducated immigrant mothers; they launched the Educated Mother's Movement. The AAPSIM also included the emerging new upper-class–oriented medical specialty professions. Pediatricians, lacking other effective interventions in this era before infectious diseases were understood, advocated the use of enhanced infant milk "formulas"— scientifically developed milk substitutes, seen as superior to the milk of lower-class breastfeeding women. Obstetricians, representing a then-small low-prestige field, focused on delivery and neonatal mortality and advocated improvement of obstetric delivery practices. Also active in the AASPIM were advocates of social reform, often social workers, who saw the sources of infant mortality in the poverty of the urban environments and advocated settlement houses as centers for parental education, self-help, and political advocacy for social reform.[3]

Given its broad base of professionals, AASPIM was a very effective advocacy organization, encouraging a series of important initiatives. In 1907, the first Bureau of Child Hygiene was established in New York City, under the leadership of Dr. Josephine Baker, where many of the current MCH interventions were innovatively developed, including nurse newborn home visiting, public supported municipal milk stations linked to maternal education and infant examinations, licensing and training midwives, breastfeeding encouragement, and using detailed birth data to target resources and interventions. In 1909, the first decennial White House Conference on Children was held, which provided the momentum for the establishment of a federal Children's Bureau in 1913. The mandate of Children's Bureau (MCH Bureau/Title V predecessor), however, was initially limited to the study and reporting on problems affecting infant and child health and welfare. Under the inspiring leadership of the first Bureau Chief, Dr. Julia Lathrop, a social worker and the first women appointed to lead a federal agency, it served as a bully pulpit for developing the knowledge base and political will for the nation's first public crusade against infant mortality. The Bureau published *Infant Care*, a free guidebook of scientific instruction for mothers, and fostered the development of motherhood civic clubs. In 1915, the Birth Registration Act was passed, the first national effort to collect standardized birth and death information. By 1918, AAPSIM had encouraged the development of four state and 50 city maternal and child health and hygiene bureaus. The bureaus cultivated widespread support among women's groups, labor unions, parent groups, and philanthropy to create a strong national campaign around reproductive and child health and welfare. However, from the beginning, there was also substantial opposition to any effort on the part of federal (and state) government to provide services to women and children, expressing concerns about the inappropriateness of government intervention into families and a disparagement of the Children's Bureau leadership by women.[2,3]

While this was a period of great programmatic innovation and uptake, it also remained a period of substantial contention and growing divergent perspectives within the AASPIM leadership over strategic approaches to reduce infant mortality. In 1915, Dr. J. Whitridge Williams became the first obstetrician elected to lead this organization, and he advocated a medical model of care for improved clinical care approaches. He argued for the improvements of the obstetric clinical practices, a new form of prenatal medical care, and the reduction of obstetric services by rival and less well-trained midwives, the providers of care for most poor women in the country. His election reflected efforts by the medical field, the American Medical Association, and pediatrics and obstetrics specifically, to improve their clinical practice, enhance professional training and licensure, and increase their political clout.[3]

Countering this medical focus, and reflecting the Children's Bureau's more social/public health orientation and emerging epidemiological evidence, there was simultaneously a growing awareness that infant mortality was not equitably distributed across society—that it was especially elevated among its poorest. In 1913, the Children's Bureau undertook a landmark series of 10 city studies that found that older and younger mothers, multiple deliveries, artificially fed infants, and closely spaced births were linked to infant mortality.[5] Of note, the Georgetown MCH Library has a collection of these studies that may be viewed. The studies also documented the major social inequity in infant mortality distributed by family income; *the poorest families had four-times-higher infant mortality compared with the wealthiest families.* Though the topic of racial disparities was not formally addressed until the late 1920s by the Children's Bureau, the Census Bureau had for decades noted racial disparities in under-one mortality, and several early studies showed disparities by race and immigrant groups, including one by W.E.B. Du Bois (1906) that documented a three-to-one disparity in "Colored" vs. White infant mortality rate in Philadelphia with rates exceeding 300 infant deaths per 1,000 births in the "Colored" community.[6]

In response to the growing awareness of the association of poverty with social disparities, some MCH professionals and progressive political activists developed a set of policy proposals known as Maternity Insurance, which had two principal ideas. The first was that there should be free maternity (clinical) care provided by government for everyone. The second was economic security for pregnant women through "lost wage replacement," nursing coverage, and domestic assistance, thus allowing mothers and infants to have a chance to recover from the delivery and have an optimal start in life.[2,3] They were the central policy platforms in a series of infant mortality improvement legislative proposals introduced in multiple states during the 1920s; all were defeated during this nonprogressive conservative postwar era of limited government. This was the first programmatic and policy effort in the United States to directly address the underlying social determinants of (reproductive) health, and it represented the social welfare pathway ultimately adopted by the MCH community in Europe. Maternity Insurance's two principles represent a strategic policy platform that still can serve as an important guide for practitioners today.

The passage of the Sheppard–Towner Act in 1921, administered by the Children's Bureau, was the most important success of this era.[2–4,7,8] In response to the poor physical conditions of potential recruits to the US military in World War I, and aided by women's suffrage, the Sheppard–Towner Act provided federal grants-in-aid to states to establish state MCH agencies to provide preventive prenatal and well-child care and maternal educational services. This was the first grant-in-aid program with federal funds going to states in history. As the organizational predecessor for Title V, this program operated across 41 states and established 1,594 MCH clinics, largely staffed by women clinicians, many in rural and minority areas; it encouraged the diffusion of many of the innovative MCH programmatic initiatives of this era. The political will for the Sheppard–Towner Act, however, in the conservative postwar 1920s faded, and the legislation was allowed to sunset in 1928. Federal or state support for any clinical or preventive health care had been vigorously opposed by the American Medical Association. Ultimately, the defeat of the Sheppard–Towner Act reflected the defeat of the broader progressive movement in the country. It politically marginalized government provision of health care and established private control over dispensation of medical care to the poor and thus solidified the private medical care model for addressing reproductive health in the United States for the next 50 years.[2,3]

This era established the impact of the social determinants of health on infant mortality and put the United States and Europe on different ameliorative pathways. It reflected the strong historical tension over the government's responsibility for family life. A woman's health in this era focused primarily on her role as a mother, not on her own health for its own sake. This era saw the emergence of separate obstetric and pediatric professions, the Children's Bureau, and the initial state MCH agencies. It highlighted the importance of effective and inspired leaders, especially women leaders; the value of collaboration; the engagement of empowered community groups to gain political will; the synergism of policy and practice; and the importance of accurate data to be translated into effective action.

BETWEEN ERAS 1 AND 2: MEDICAL CARE MODEL FOR REPRODUCTIVE HEALTH

There were no large widespread national movements to address reproductive health or infant mortality during the lengthy period between 1930 and 1980. The medical model of clinical care had become firmly established in the United States for addressing infant and childhood mortality and morbidity. This time period can be divided into two parts: from 1930 to 1965 and from 1965 to 1980.

1930 to 1965

The period from 1930 to 1965 had many important and noteworthy developments, but this was not a substantial period of life course, equity, or policy developments. The Great Depression of the 1930s, accompanied by large social and political movements, raised once again issues of poverty and welfare. Franklin Delano Roosevelt inaugurated the establishment of the Social Security Act of the United States in 1935,[9] and in particular its Title V (Maternal and Child Health Act), a modified re-introduction of the former Sheppard–Towner Act and its Title IV (Child Welfare Act).[9] The scope of the Children's Bureau (Title V), however, was narrowed; it now had to be led by a physician and its programs were to be directed only to poor families (not universally).[2-4,7] This reinforced the split between health and welfare and diminished a focus on social factors' impact on reproductive and child health care.

The infant mortality community under the obstetric profession's leadership fostered much clinical progress during this time period, particularly around improved maternal mortality in the United States. Hospital-based deliveries and prenatal care continued to increase. Infant (especially postneonatal) mortality and childhood morbidity and mortality improvement was especially notable after World War II, with the development of powerful antibiotic drugs and childhood vaccines. The growth of health insurance (initially as an organized labor demand) further institutionalized the medical model of care, and the widespread development of hospitals (Hill–Burton Act, 1946[10]) encouraged the movement toward hospital births. Despite increased access to clinical care, there was virtually no improvement in infant mortality or reduction in racial disparities in birth outcomes after World War II.[2]

1965 to 1980

The vision and action of the civil rights, War on Poverty, antiwar, and women's movements brought to stark attention the fundamental social determinants of racism, class, and gender in the United States and motivated the passage of a profound and outstanding package of federal program and policy legislation starting in 1965. These movements tried to change the role of the federal government vis-à-vis states in ensuring equal political and social opportunities for all citizens independent of race and gender; expanding the Social Security safety net to include health care for the elderly (Medicare, Title XVIII of the Social Security Act) and the poor (Medicaid, Title XIX); addressing the developmental needs of the youngest poor citizens; and creating targeted programs and resources to address specific manifestations of poverty (food stamps, Head Start, community development grants).[11] Affirmative action sought to create a more level playing field and equal opportunities for life.

Medicaid, an insurance program and not a direct provider of medical services, was partially conceived as a limited welfare program to prevent a major source of bankruptcy among poor families and to support single women with children. States managed eligibility and health services coverage. Medicaid can be seen as the beginning of national efforts to secure the first idea of Maternity Insurance—free provision of (maternal) health services. This program also transformed access to care and made it possible to support public clinics and providers willing to care for the poor.

The women's movement achieved several major legislative victories during this period of time, in part because of their political demands for greater control over their own reproductive health and bodies,[12] for unfettered access to contraceptives and abortion, and challenges to patriarchy in homes, work, and society. Policy advances notably included the equal rights assurances based on gender in most War on Poverty legislation and, most importantly, Title X of the Public Health Act,[13] which provided for family planning clinics throughout the United States, premised on the lack of funds for contraceptive services for poor women.[2,4] The women's movement fostered more family-friendly hospital-based obstetric practices, revived midwifery and home birth movements, and raised other challenges to the medical establishment—many of which continue to this day. The Title X programs did not become part of the Maternal and Child Health Bureau, in part because of the lack of enthusiasm at the Bureau and in part because of the concerns of the women's health movement not to be defined solely by their reproductive functions as future mothers.[2,4]

The WIC program was developed (and contested) to address the "special added" nutritional needs of the developing pregnant mother, infant, and child. This program can be seen as a renewal, now with federal support, of the "free milk" programs of the earlier era. The WIC program, directed at women and infants and led by predominantly women nutrition professionals, was placed in the US Department of Agriculture, not the MCH Bureau, which once again did not fight to administer the nonmedical WIC program.[2,4]

The leaders of the War on Poverty understood that poverty was not only the absence of money but also that it influenced the development, spirit, and aspirations of impoverished children and families, and that these early negative impacts on children could be ameliorated and the cycles of poverty broken. The federal government for the first time committed itself to addressing the intellectual and social developmental needs of the nation's poorest children through Head Start and other related programs. In contrast with the reproductive health field, the child development field increasingly focused on the social determinants of health and life course, with the Head Start programmatic "solution" similar to other War on Poverty era initiatives, early compensatory education programs, and with some supplemented maternal training.

The MCH Bureau did not launch any large major new health programs that directly addressed the social determinants of health during this War on Poverty period.

However, they did implement a small series of maternal–infant care demonstration projects. The Improved Pregnancy Outcome program explored the impact of using supplemental health education, nutrition, and social work services to augment clinical prenatal packages in the newly established neighborhood health centers—a return to some of the early 20th century socially influenced services needed by poor pregnant women. This small successful demonstration of a new package of prenatal care services was the pioneer of comprehensive or community-based prenatal care, a model that would be substantially implemented later.[2]

This was a period of major scientific advances relevant to reproductive and child health. The child development field, with its growing interest in cognitive development, disparities, and compensatory programs, flourished in this era. The Head Start program jump-started the program evaluation field and initiated the federal government's requirement for program accountability. Disparities in birth outcomes became a more prominent topic in the MCH epidemiological world, though disparities in race were often subsumed as disparities in class. A new period of environmental health awareness and activism began. And, importantly, this era also began a period of tremendous growth in pediatric neonatology, with the development of neonatal intensive care units (NICUs) and an emerging capacity to keep tiny babies alive.

Overall, the civil rights, War on Poverty, and women's movements of the 1960s and '70s had a dramatic impact on the availability of MCH services and programs and fostered the creation of an important series of targeted compensatory federal programs and policies that directly addressed some of the social deterministic, racist, and gendered roots of poverty. Infant mortality and other poor birth outcomes rates improved substantially after the War on Poverty initiatives, and disparities narrowed slightly.

ERA 2: ACCESS TO COMPREHENSIVE PRENATAL CARE

Over time, the previous civil rights, War on Poverty, and women's movements efforts to address the social and developmental well-being of infants and children were met with increasing political resistance, culminating in part with the election of Ronald Reagan as President in 1980. Similar to the conservative retrenchment in 1920, the Reagan Administration tried to turn back many of the programmatic expansions across class, race, gender, and environment. It proposed to limit the size of the federal government and return social and educational policy back to the states. The federal government imposed more restrictions on abortions and contraceptives in the United States and internationally, actively pursued the War on Drugs with its devastating impact on communities of color, substantially reduced funding for numerous federal health programs, and proposed to cut block grant programs, including WIC and several MCH programs. During this second era between the mid-1980s and mid-1990s, the federal administration began a long period of conservative gains, especially for wealthier and White Americans.

Surprisingly, the Reagan Era proved to be an important positive time for national infant mortality and reproductive health initiatives. Advocates argued that the cutbacks would negatively affect poor communities, raising their infant mortality and malnutrition rates, and further contribute to health and social disparities. The MCH community, in particular, was very active as the proposed cutbacks potentially devastated the Title V agencies and programs of the previous 50 years. Efforts to defend and then expand Medicaid programs in particular became an important focus for the evolving debate between social determinants of health and medical models of care as the principal mode for addressing reproductive health and health disparities.[2]

Infant mortality was seen as the ultimate measure of a society's health. Advocates reported on the impact of health and social program cutbacks on infant mortality, which seemed to level off in the early Reagan years. Controversy over the Reagan Administration actions, especially around infant mortality, served as a rallying point. The unflattering comparison of US infant mortality rates with those of other developed countries and the racial disparities within the country motivated many powerful national professional organizations (e.g., American College of Obstetricians and Gynecologists, American Academy of Pediatrics) to address these professional embarrassments. Second, members of Congress and governors took an interest in the infant mortality issue, with organizations such as the Southern Governors' Association and National Commission on Prevention of Infant Mortality leading the political debates in favor of program and policy improvements.

Third, infant mortality had become a major focus of the MCH community. The March of Dimes shifted its philanthropic focus from infantile paralysis and polio to infant mortality prevention. Fourth, the growing effectiveness of neonatologists, intensive care nurseries, and perinatal regionalization in keeping tiny infants alive showed that interventions in early infancy were effective, though maldistributed. Finally, there was strong growing professional consensus that programmatic and policy initiatives could be effective in improving outcomes, supported by a series of very influential reports from the Institute of Medicine and others that provided the research evidence, cost-savings justifications, and roadmaps for action.[14-16] Key areas for action included increased content and access to prenatal care, regionalization of NICUs, and increased access to family planning. Together, these factors, along with the progressive advocacy communities' protests over the Reagan administration's proposed cutbacks, developed into a massive widespread national movement of mothers, professional groups, the business community, state governors, and progressive advocates.

This time period brought large sustained national public campaigns and movements to address infant mortality in the United States. First, there was professional legitimacy and relatively unified consensus for these efforts. The Southern Governors Association and its Southern Regional Task Force on Infant Mortality (1984), in particular, viewed infant mortality reduction as a major political leadership task, given the high infant death rates throughout the South. Numerous states and cities set up broad infant mortality commissions, often chaired by governors, giving them high political visibility. The Children's Defense Fund engaged in systematic and focused advocacy, creating the first national MCH policy coalition, participating in professional committees, and using an annual data report to drive press, public, and political debates. A very powerful set of grass roots organizations emerged attempting to address reproductive health outcomes and disparities: local March of Dimes coalitions; Healthy Mother, Healthy Child coalitions; and many others, including clergy and business coalitions. These simultaneous professional, political, and popular movements together created a substantial amount of political will and activism around infant mortality reduction.

The key policy achievement of this era was the expansion of Medicaid eligibility and reproductive health service coverage.[2,4] At the start of the Reagan era, roughly 20% of US women were covered, with major geographic disparities (and implicitly race-based disparities, especially in the South). In a series of important legislative victories, there was an incremental successful multiyear effort to increase the number of pregnant women and children eligible for Medicaid and to expand the scope of prenatal (and postnatal and children's) services covered, using each successive year's Omnibus Budget Reconciliation acts as the legislative vehicle. Over time, this allowed increased eligibility, first for two-parent families in which both were unemployed (1984), then expanding coverage to all pregnant women in any types of families below the states Aid for Families with Dependent Children welfare eligibility (1985); and then requiring coverage for all pregnant women and children below 100% of the federal poverty line (1986), making it directly a function of a women's or family's poverty status. Ultimately increasing coverage to 185% of federal poverty levels and providing options for states to choose even higher thresholds increased the number of pregnant women eligible for or covered by Medicaid to about 45% of all births in the United States and higher than 60% in some states. The elimination of most financial barriers to maternity health services was one of the major public health achievements of the 20th century. Maternity Insurance's first proposal for universal access to and provision of maternity health care services has now almost been achieved in the United States.[2]

Simultaneously, the Medicaid expansion legislation also gradually expanded the packages of prenatal care services that could be covered for reimbursement to include health education, social work, and nutrition services as well as case management and home visiting—essentially the MCH Bureau's previous War on Poverty Improved Pregnancy Outcome demonstration project expanded nationally.[2,4] These efforts provided the public health and MCH-associated professional communities the funded ability to address some of the nonmedical care social determinant needs of families, through the politically and professionally acceptable guise of enhanced prenatal care. As a result, a substantial and innovative set of state and local programs were implemented to translate the new Medicaid policy to practice. There were national meetings that encouraged state-to-state information sharing and provided practical programmatic advice to enhance Medicaid enrollment outreach, Title V–Medicaid integrated care case-management programs, co-location of programs, expanded home-visitation programs, and research and evaluation demonstration projects. The Healthy Start Initiative, begun in 1991, the final federal initiative of this second era, fostered local community-based infant mortality and disparities reduction initiatives, initially in mostly urban, very-high-risk communities, and focused on individual comprehensive prenatal services, perinatal systems change, and a required community-based leadership consortium.

Programmatically, this was a time of substantial state and local practice innovations, translating the national policy and professional consensus into programs directly impacting pregnant women and their families. Interestingly, the underlying conceptualization of prenatal care had changed from a narrowly targeted medical care intervention to addressing some of the social factors influencing poor reproductive health. By being framed as an access issue, prenatal care had become conceptualized, in part, as a public health program!

The second era's burst of attention to infant mortality ended rather rapidly in the early 1990s, as infant death and low birth weight rates did not decline noticeably and disparities continued to grow. Given the variations in enrollment processes, quality of care, and the health status of poor women entering pregnancy, Medicaid prenatal expansions did not show consistent results. Perhaps the power of comprehensive prenatal care to enhance birth outcomes and diminish disparities had been oversold, with interventions during pregnancy being necessary but not sufficient. Notably, expansion of family planning coverage during this same period made Medicaid the largest source of public funding for such services.

The second national era addressing infant mortality, like the first era, did re-engage with the impact of the social determinants of health on infant mortality, albeit only indirectly through enhanced prenatal care and increased Medicaid access to that care; the United States and Europe were still on different pathways to improved reproductive health. Women's health in this era still focused primarily on the woman's role as a mother, not on her own health for its own sake. This era highlighted once again the importance of effective and inspired women leaders, the value of multisector collaboration, the engagement of empowered community groups to gain political will, the synergism of policy and practice, and the importance of accurate data to be translated into effective action. The first goal of Maternity Insurance, maternal medical care (insurance), was almost fully accomplished.

TRANSITION TO ERA 3: BUSH TO OBAMA

The period between the first Bush and the beginning of the Obama Administration (mid-1990s to mid–late 2000s) represented a series of conservative and centrist presidents—with the country increasingly polarized by liberal versus conservative social and political positions but without major political grass roots movements. Efforts to expand opportunities on the basis of class, race, gender, sexual orientation, and environmental justice always meet with organized, well-funded resistance. Traditional medical care models, backed by more effective and widespread neonatal intensive care, continued to dominate national health care efforts, but rising costs, need for accountability, health care and insurance industry consolidation, and ongoing poor health outcomes continued to challenge the country.

Three major federal policy initiatives during President Clinton's administration addressed the social determinants of health for children and families. The Health Security Act, a major push to transform the US health care system and make health care a universal right, included a very strong MCH health focus; but that proposal was defeated. The Clinton Administration then focused more on incremental enhancements of access to child health care through the states' Children Health Improvement Program and policy efforts to enhance women's reproductive health rights. The Personal Responsibility and Work Opportunity Reconciliation Act (1996)[17] was a contentious welfare reform effort to improve and limit funds to needy families—a shift from Aid to Families with Dependent Children to Temporary Assistance to Needy Families, which ultimately decreased the number of poor children and families covered by welfare benefits. The Family and Medical Leave Act[18] guaranteed for the first time up to 12 weeks of pregnancy-related leave in the United States, but only for those women working at least half time for companies with 50 or more employees. Critically, however, it did not provide for paid leave. The Clinton Administration did try to financially aid poor working families with children through reform of the tax code, specifically introducing the Earned Income Tax Credit. These efforts reflect tentative policy approaches to addressing important social determinants.

Reproductive health efforts from the 1990s to the mid-to-late first decade of the 21st century reflect four dominant trends. First, there was a shift from broad infant mortality reduction strategic efforts to a narrower focus on very specific topics that were perceived as amenable to interventions, such as sudden unexplained infant death syndrome (safe sleep), folic acid supplementation, enhanced NICU effectiveness, treatment with antiretrovirals to prevent perinatal HIV transmission, or tobacco reduction. Second, a rising use of assisted reproductive technology interventions for infertility, resulting in more multiple births and higher associated rates of poor birth outcomes and increased use of cesarean deliveries, resulted in more premature deliveries.

Third, a new focus on preconception health and health care emerged leading the MCH community to more actively address women's health, both broadly and longitudinally. Preconception health was seen as a way to enhance prenatal care efficacy by starting care before conception, when it may be more effective, as well as a means to have a better impact on women's health before, beyond, and regardless of pregnancy intention. The latter concept rebalances traditional efforts to address the impact of women's health on infant health status, noting the impact of pregnancy on women's health over her life course, thus re-engaging reproductive health to the larger women's health movement.

The Centers for Disease Control and Prevention spearheaded the national effort to define the concept of preconception health and health care through a series of conferences and national meetings, resulting in recommendations published in 2006 in *Morbidity and Mortality Weekly Report*[19] and the launch of the National Preconception Health and Health Care Initiative. Preconception health efforts furthered the growth of women's health within the MCH community.

Fourth, during this time, there was a tremendous growth in the scientific understanding of how social determinants of health become part of the body and their implications on health and development life course. Several lines of critical epidemiological and biological research emerged in this era including pediatric and chronic disease epidemiology (e.g., the Institute of Medicine's *From Neurons to Neighborhood*,[20] the Barker fetal origins of adult disease hypothesis), stress research (e.g., cumulative exposures to stress as an explanatory explanation for the onset of premature birth and racial disparities), and epigenetics. These three exciting areas of research offered new biological basis for the life course and social determinants of health theories emerging in MCH.

ERA 3: MATERNAL AND CHILD HEALTH LIFE COURSE THEORY TO PRACTICE

The third national era to address infant mortality and other poor birth outcomes—and especially their continuing racial and economic disparities—can be seen as beginning in the mid-to-late 2000s. Importantly, this era is still ongoing; MCH practitioners are still creating it. This book and its readers are an important part of that continuing effort and its challenges. In 2007, Drs. Michael Lu and Neil Halfon presented a conceptual paradigm to explain reproductive disparities, the MCH Life Course Theory.[21] Although this idea was not new in other fields such as social work or pediatrics, the significance of the introduction of the Life Course Theory cannot be overestimated. First, it represented a major break from the prevailing emphasis on the medical model of quality prenatal and delivery care services to address disparities and optimize birth outcomes. The role of social determinants of health was returned to prominence both as an explanation and as a potential ameliorative strategy to reduce disparities and optimize reproductive health outcomes.

Second, Life Course Theory places reproductive health squarely in the larger context of multiple longitudinal health models being developed in chronic disease and child development fields. Moreover, by increasing attention to the importance of the earliest life course experiences, it provides a causal starting point and connection with the multiple destructive pathways of poverty on human health and development. By emphasizing social determinants, this model brings the MCH reproductive health field prominently back to the issues of disparities and equity resulting from differential social experiences in life, aligning it with the World Health Organization's emphasis on poverty and its direct amelioration as critical to insuring population health worldwide. Although MCH

Life Course Theory acknowledges the importance of health care interventions, it represents a more balanced social justice model, rather than a health service or medical model, for ensuring equitable and optimal reproductive, child, and women's health.

This life course model has gained substantial traction in the larger MCH community. It has been very appealing to many MCH community constituencies as a causal risk model, which corresponds well with their sense of how the world works and why disparities exist. It brings the MCH field closer to its roots and sense of social justice, which animates so many practitioners. Much effort has been expended in the last few years on educating MCH leaders to adapt Life Course Theory conceptualization and programming into their activities.[22]

Politically, Life Course Theory has influenced several national programmatic and policy initiatives, potentially attributable to the Obama presidency. The Patient Protection and Affordable Care Act[23] (ACA; Obamacare) represents a major victory for the health and health care of MCH communities, and for all Americans—moving the United States closer to the universal ideal of health care as a human right and fully achieving the first component of the Maternity Insurance proposal of the 1920s. The ACA includes numerous specific provisions of direct importance to the MCH communities, including expanded and subsidized health insurance eligibility for Medicaid, the Children's Health Insurance Program, and young adults; assurance of access to women's reproductive and delivery health care, including contraception; and pediatric well-child visits and immunizations as essential benefits without co-pays. The ACA codified most of the developmental social determinants of health–sensitive content of American Academy of Pediatrics' Bright Futures, as well as a major expansion of public health–oriented programs, especially home visitation programs to counter some of the impacts of the social determinants of health on reproductive and early family life.

The Life Course Approach began to shape major new MCH programming and directions in the United States. The US Department of Health and Human Services Secretary's Advisory Committee on Infant Mortality, the federal government's highest advisory body on infant mortality, actively encouraged the application of the life course perspective into governmental programs and policy.[24] The national MCH Bureau, under the leadership of Dr. Peter Van Dyck, was an early and enthusiastic adopter of the Life Course Theory, which was used as the strategic framework for Bureau planning.[25] Virtually all major MCH Bureau programs were revised to be more inclusive of Life Course Theory. Dr. Michael Lu, a known advocate of the life course model, became the next MCH Bureau Administrator. The Bureau strengthened preconception and women's health efforts, oversaw the implementation of Maternal Infant Early Child Home Visiting initiatives, and substantially revised the Healthy Start Initiative (3.0) to make it more programmatically responsive to a life course perspective and better bring a minority community perspective to federal programs.

The Infant Mortality Collaborative Improvement and Innovation Network (IM CoIIN) represents a major new MCH Bureau initiative around infant mortality in this third era.

IM CoIIN is a "multiyear national effort to engage federal, state and local leaders, public and private agencies, professionals, and communities to employ continuous quality improvement, innovation and collaborative learning to reduce infant mortality and improve birth outcomes."[26] Critically, one of its six infant mortality strategic work groups was on social determinants of health—the first time in its history that the MCH Bureau has explicitly supported directly targeted interventions to address the social roots of infant mortality. Overall, the IM CoIIN Workgroup has reinvigorated a broad national conversation and efforts around infant mortality for the first time since the 1980s and 1990s, including a balance of social determinants of health, clinical care, and preventive behavioral strategies. IM CoIIN also fostered important improvements in the timeliness and analysis of MCH population data.

Directly changing the social determinants of health and life course trajectories for population health is significantly harder than introducing a new clinical intervention. There are both conceptual and practical barriers. Many advocates and practitioners are often overwhelmed and do not know where to start. Many areas of the traditional social determinants of health interventions, such as housing, public benefits, home visiting, and adverse childhood experiences, are not traditionally part of most health clinicians' toolbox. Clinicians and other practitioners fear to ask about the social determinants of health, which they recognize are important, when they will not know what to do with the answers. Nor are there many existing successful programs, activities, and social change strategies to learn from. There are often well-entrenched, powerful forces in society that would directly oppose these efforts, who benefit from the unequal social determinants of health and inequalities in society and are not so willing to be transformed, even to improve health outcomes. And the critical question remains, will Life Course Theory improve women's and children's health and reduce disparities? Chapter 13 highlights some strategies and challenges on life course evaluation and impact.

Yet, despite conceptual and practical problems, this third infant mortality era has also been a very innovative period as MCH communities and practitioners try to creatively operationalize Life Course Theory into effective practice—some being inspirations for chapters of this book. Placed-based initiatives, efforts to transform and enhance the environments in which children and families live and thrive, represent a distinctive major set of innovations. The Robert Wood Johnson Foundation's Culture of Health,[27] the Harlem Children's Zone,[28] the Best Babies Zone,[29] and numerous transformative community development and housing efforts are examples; they give meaning to the expression that it takes a village to raise a child. Chapter 5 addresses this theme in greater depth.

Another perhaps less-noticed but most-striking feature of this era is efforts to organize parents and empower families. Verbiest et al. propose the creation of a new reproductive and social justice movement that attempts to blend the reproductive justice, preconception health, and life course initiatives—and then offer practical advice to help develop this movement.[30] The Best Babies Zone initiative explicitly encourages community organizing to create a public health social movement around reproductive health, moving from empowered mothers to empowered communities.[29] In Cincinnati, Ohio, one of its Smart Start community-based parent education groups decided that, beyond learning, they could advise and express their community's voice, and they declared themselves their area's MCH Advisory Board and have functioned that way for a series of area MCH projects. There are several other, perhaps less ambitious, efforts to enhance maternal agency and address social determinants of health factors—such as financial empowerment programs, collective self-help organizations (e.g., the Family Independence Initiative), mothers clubs, peer-to-peer initiatives, and community cafes, or partnering with mothers around health care in groups such as Family Voices, Centering Pregnancy, or parent advisory boards. The community-based participatory research (CBPR) movement strongly endorses community ownership, or agency, over area research and demonstration projects, and CBPR implementation itself can increase parental agency.

Pediatricians, who are often the frontline first responders to child and family poverty in America, have been innovative in developing pediatric poverty-sensitive practice tools and programs. They have made substantial practical progress on creating social determinants of health screening tools to identify family social needs; improving the connections or referrals for parents with needed social resources, often within a practice (co-location with social workers or psychologists); strengthening parenting capacity (e.g., the Reach Out and Read program); and moving slowly toward family-centered, two-generation care and involving fathers in the child's care.[31]

Although the MCH field has focused on mothers and children and their struggles for social justice, the role of men, especially as fathers in families, has remained a tension.[32,33] MCH services often actively excluded fathers, viewing them negatively—for example, as potential abusers. Yet there has been a transition of men's roles and responsibilities in families to one of greater equitable involvement in nurturance, health, and development, beyond their traditional patriarchal roles, in part because of the gains of the women's movement. This era has seen a greater recognition of men as part of the family, of the social environment in which children thrive. Men's health and preconception wellness is important for reproductive outcomes and for their own life course health. Healthy Start, for example, has a major fatherhood involvement and training initiative. There is a growing number of life course–linked initiatives that are beginning to directly and positively involve men in areas such as obesity prevention and postpartum depression treatment. As Lanier describes in Appendix 1C, men's physical and emotional involvement is critical for healthy infant and child development and for men's and family health and well-being.

Traditionally, health policy is often conceptualized as the principal means of righting the negative structural social determinants of health, equalizing opportunities and resources. During this era, three distinct kinds of health policy initiatives have emerged. The first, and newest, recognizes that government processes themselves (e.g., laws, policies, funding decisions) can contribute to disparities by creating differential access to society's economic, health care, environmental, and justice resources (e.g., structural racism supports). To that end, new Health in All Policies approaches to policy assessment for (racial) disparities have been developed, as have Child Health Impact Assessments. These policy approaches as described in Chapter 11 are well suited to the government agencies where many MCH professionals are employed.

The second set of policy initiatives specifically targeted MCH policy issues, such as paid maternity leave initiatives, childhood allowances, or childcare funding support. The United States still has not achieved the Maternity Insurance policy agenda, nor the gains seen by most other European and Canadian social welfare programs and policies that adopted that agenda decades ago. But, for the first time, as part of this era, paid family and medical leave has become part of a political agenda in the United States and is gaining some traction. Currently, some limited forms of paid parental leave exist in four states, and bills are being introduced in several others. It is a policy achievement that might finally be won, 100 years after Maternity Insurance was first proposed! Third, there are still important social justice and structural determinants of health policy battles being fought over racism, economic injustice, environmental degradation, and gender equity, especially around women's reproductive health rights, as well as sustaining and enhancing the Affordable Care Act and ensuring universal access to health care. The War on Poverty legislation successfully addressed and substantially reduced elderly poverty, but redress of family and child poverty continues to linger.

This third historical era of national infant mortality initiatives is notable for its absence of a strong accompanying progressive movement, which was present in both earlier eras. This current era seems to have been more motivated by professional scientific and conceptual developments, but not the demands of an active progressive movement. Therefore, it perhaps is more vulnerable to changes in government funding and political pushback. The election of President Trump, accompanied by Republican control of Congress and most governors, poses a potential challenge to the MCH community, as that administration may not support programs that address the social determinants roots of poor reproductive health and disparities. How this will play out politically and professionally for the infant mortality, reproductive health, women's health, and early childhood communities is not fully clear as this book is being written. Dr. Julius Richmond, the former Surgeon General and cofounder of the Head Start program, noted that when one's party is out of political office and no longer responsible for actual program leadership, that is the time when the new (MCH) program and policy ideas and the creation of political will for the next era are developed!

BRIDGING PAST TO PRESENT

The aspiration and struggles to improve MCH population health are linked to larger political struggles to advance human rights and obtain social justice for all women and children. These larger political struggles empower the creation of public health social and reproductive justice movements and vice versa. But these movements must confront the ongoing tensions about the role of government in family life. Traditionally, conservatives and libertarians believe that government should not have a role in areas that should be private family responsibilities. Gradually there has been an acceptance of the expanding role for government to ensure reproductive and child health care and development.

The 20th century has seen tremendous advances in both maternal health and women's health, against substantial and continuing patriarchal pushbacks. This historical progress has focused on both women's health and mortality as vehicle to ensure healthy children and on women's own health and reproductive autonomy as a civil right. Balancing these two interrelated and independent facets of women's health has been the source of much tension over the century. Life course emphasis on a two-generational model provides new insights to help overcome the long-standing tensions in the MCH field, which often appears to value children over mothers. Preconception health and life course offer new, more holistic approaches to the health of women, as well as to the points in time when the life courses of women and their infants are inextricably interwoven. Similarly, some pediatricians have called for more two-generation family care and parenting supports to ensure healthy life course development for both children and adults. Fathers are still, however, too often left out of these two generational models. Patriarchy still exists and always is a threat to government-supported women's and MCH programs and policies; therefore, a focus on feminism and reproductive justice in their fullest definition remains imperative for practitioners.

Efforts to directly address the social determinants of poor and disparate MCH population health outcomes have been an enduring struggle for past hundred years. MCH Life Course Theory and practice offer a new strategic framework for this long-standing challenge. In this era, for the first time, it fosters specific direct active MCH program and policy efforts to address the underlying social determinants of health factors to optimize reproductive health, linked to similar efforts for child health and development and women's health over the life course.

The tensions and conflict between clinical medical models of care and public health social determinants intervention models have not served the MCH field well. These ultimately are artificial distinctions. Both are needed and must be complementary. Public health and social work practitioners should not abandon clinicians, and clinicians of today and tomorrow need help to promote and advance poverty-responsive health care. Life Course Theory emphasis on prenatal to child health continuity provides new insights to help address the longstanding historical separation of clinical specialty care practices among reproductive health (obstetrics), child health (pediatrics), and women's health (women's primary care). Similarly, programmatic splits between women's health (Title X) and maternal health (Title V) have hindered the unity of MCH field. These divisions have long historical roots (some science, some professional identity, some politics) and they may not easily or quickly coalesce to achieve optimal health. The MCH life course paradigm supports greater unity among these fields and encourages an outcome-focused, not profession-based, orientation.

There continues to be an evolution of the MCH field's understanding of racial disparities, with a greater emphasis on equity itself in this era, as described in Chapter 2 by Abresch and Wyche-Etheridge. With life course having a historical dimension, there is now a growing understanding that racial disparities are not simply another variant of social class disparities but that they have their own historical roots that need attention if racial disparities in reproductive, child, family, and adult health are to be ameliorated.

Historians and political scientists are the scientists of political will, and their insights are critical to the struggles for social justice for women and children. Social determinants of health are not value-free but reflect the historical and political forces that shaped them. The MCH field has spun its wheels too many times and not learned from experiences. Historians can inspire change. Collaboration has been the key to successful MCH practice and policy implementation. Reproductive, women's, and children's health does not happen in a vacuum. Throughout history, advancements occurred when the MCH field collaborated with other professional, community, and political partners to cultivate a culture of health.

Both policy and practice are needed together to address the social determinants of health roots of reproductive, women's, and children's health. Policy alone is insufficient to effect social and community change. MCH history revels several moments of exquisite collaboration—the Sheppard–Towner Act and Medicaid policy expansions are two good examples. Unfortunately, too often there is a disconnect between ground-level experiences and policy. More integrated program and policy efforts are needed, such as enhanced effective bidirectional up–down communication.

Life Course Theory ultimately encourages an expansion of thinking about MCH life course "practice," even given limited resources. New theoretical conceptualizations about interventions and much actual exciting program and policy innovations are ongoing. Focusing on maternal and community agency helps expand the efforts to address the underlying social roots of reproductive health, moving beyond the traditional dual competing medical care or social determinant policy framework. Over the course of MCH history, there have been repeated innovations in engaging and empowering parents and supporting natural community leaders. The concept of individual agency combining to collective or community agency may be the root of social and reproductive justice movements.

CONCLUSIONS

The MCH field has a long and proud history of social justice efforts, with a renewed focus now on addressing the US historical legacy of racism, economic injustice, and gender discrimination that directly influences child, women, family, and community health and development. Although there has been great progress, the disparities in infant mortality by social class and race noted by the Children's Bureau in 1926 are as challenging today as they were then. Advocating optimal health and development and equal opportunity in life for women and children is part of a larger ongoing struggle for social justice and expanded civil rights. There is much hard work ahead, but likewise room for a great deal of optimism. Social justice takes a long time, but the MCH field's legacy and perseverance should inspire continued action. Embracing this new era's focus on Life Course Theory woven with attention to the social determinants of health and equity provides a platform for the field's emerging leaders to step in and up to advance the legacy. MCH foremothers and forefathers struggled professionally and politically for 100 years to ensure social justice and optimal health for women and infants. It is time to take up their mantle.

KEY POINTS

- The MCH field's efforts to address the social determinants roots of poor reproductive, children's, and women's health and disparities has evolved substantially over the past century: first from a conceptual or policy awareness, through indirect initial efforts to enhance access to comprehensive prenatal care, to the current direct programmatic and policy efforts to ameliorate the consequences of poverty, racism, and gender discrimination over the life course.
- It will take a public health social and reproductive justice movement to be able to substantially alter the country's embedded social determinants and existing health care system. Life Course Theory demands active involvement in current political and professional struggles to change pernicious structural inequities.
- The current era is an exciting and challenging period for innovative MCH life course interventions. Initiatives in clinical care, social determinants of health, and maternal/parental agency are needed to make further progress in optimizing health and reducing disparities.
- There is an ongoing need for a better understanding of epidemiological and scientific basis of the social determinants of health and life course science.
- There is a rich legacy of social programs that have successfully tackled improved life trajectories, such as child labor, sanitation, access to health care, and malnutrition. History can offer inspiration for the future.
- Maternity Insurance (universal medical care and lost wage replacement) still provides a strong policy framework for the current era.
- Innovative MCH programs and policy and visions of social justice require leadership, as does the creation and channeling of political will into action. Visionary leadership and collective leadership remain critical.

REFERENCES

1. Health Resources and Services Administration. MCH Timeline. Children's Bureau. 1921. Available at: https://mchb.hrsa.gov/about/timeline/index.asp. Accessed December 1, 2017.

2. Kotelchuck M. Safe mothers, healthy babies: reproductive health in the 20th century. In: Ward JW, Warren C, eds. *Silent Victories: The History and Practice of Public Health in Twentieth-Century America*. New York, NY: Oxford University Press; 2007.

3. Meckel RA. *Save the Babies: American Public Health Reform and the Prevention of Infant Mortality, 1850–1929*. Baltimore, MD: Johns Hopkins University Press; 1990.

4. Margolis L, Kotch JB. Tracing the historical foundations of maternal and child health to contemporary times. In: Kotch JB, ed. *Maternal and Child Health: Programs, Problems, and Policy in Public Health*. Burlington, MA: Jones and Bartlett Learning; 2013.

5. Woodbury RM. *Infant Mortality and Its Causes*. Baltimore, MD: Williams and Wilkins; 1926.

6. Du Bois WEB. The health and physique of Negro Americans. In: *Proceedings of the 11th Conference for the Study of the Negro Problem*. Atlanta, GA: Atlanta University; 1906.

7. Lesser AJ. The origins and development of maternal and child health programs in the United States. *Am J Public Health*. 1985:75(6):590–598.

8. Sheppard-Towner Act (National Maternity and Infancy Protection Act), 42 USC §§161-175 (1921).

9. Social Security Act of 1935, 42 USC ch 7 (1935).

10. Hill-Burton Act (Hospital Survey and Construction Act), 42 USC §§291-291$_o$ (1946).

11. Richmond JB, Kotelchuck M. Political influences: rethinking national health policy. In: McGuire CH, Foley RP, Gorr D, Richards RW, eds. *Handbook of Health Professions Education*. San Francisco, CA: Jossey-Bass Publishers; 1983:386–404.

12. The Boston Women's Health Collective. *Our Body, Ourselves*. Boston, MA: New England Free Press; 1980.

13. Public Health Act, Title X (Population Research and Voluntary Family Planning Programs), 42 USC §§300-300$_{a-6}$ (1970).

14. Institute of Medicine. *Low Birthweight*. Washington, DC: National Academy Press; 1985.

15. Brown SS. *Prenatal Care: Reaching Mothers, Reaching Babies*. Washington, DC: National Academy Press; 1988.

16. Public Health Service. *Caring for Our Future: The Content of Prenatal Care*. Washington, DC: Public Health Service; 1989.

17. Personal Responsibility and Work Opportunity Reconciliation Act, 42 USC §§291-296 (1996).

18. Family and Medical Leave Act, 29 USC §§2601-2654 (1993).

19. Johnson K, Posner SF, Biermann J, et al. Recommendations to improve preconception health and health care—United States. A report of the CDC/ATSDR Preconception Care Workgroup and the Select Panel on Preconception Care. *MMWR Recomm Rep.* 2006;55(RR-6):1–23.

20. Institute of Medicine. *From Neurons to Neighborhoods: The Science of Early Childhood Development.* Washington, DC: The National Academies Press; 2000.

21. Lu MC, Halfon N. Racial and ethnic disparities in birth outcomes: a life course perspective. *Matern Child Health J.* 2003;7(1):13–30.

22. Pies C, Kotelchuck M. Bringing the MCH life course perspective to life. *Matern Child Health J.* 2014;18(2):335–338.

23. Patient Protection and Affordable Care Act, 42 USC §§ 18001 et seq. (2010).

24. Health Resources and Services Administration. Report of the Secretary's Advisory Committee on Infant Mortality: Recommendations for HHS Action and Framework for a National Strategy. 2013. Available at: https://www.hrsa.gov/advisorycommittees/mchbadvisory/InfantMortality/About/about.html. Accessed December 2, 2017.

25. Fine A, Kotelchuck M. Rethinking MCH: The MCH life course model as an organizing framework. Rockville, MD: US Department of Health and Human Services, Health Resources and Services Administration, Maternal and Child Health Bureau; 2010.

26. National Institute for Child Health Quality. Collaborative Improvement and Innovation Network to Reduce Infant Mortality (IM CoIIN). Available at: https://www.nichq.org/project/collaborative-improvement-and-innovation-network-reduce-infant-mortality-im-coiin. Accessed December 2, 2017.

27. Robert Wood Johnson Foundation. Building a Culture of Health, 2017. Available at: https://www.cultureofhealth.org. Accessed December 2, 2017.

28. Harlem Children's Zone. Harlem Children's Zone, 2017. Available at: https://www.hcz.org. Accessed December 2, 2017.

29. Pies C, Barr M, Strouse C, Kotelchuck M; Best Babies Zone Initiative Team. Growing a Best Babies Zone: lessons learned from the pilot phase of a multi-sector, place-based initiative to reduce infant mortality. *Matern Child Health J.* 2016;20(5):968–973.

30. Verbiest S, Malin CK, Drummonds M, Kotelchuck M. Catalyzing a reproductive health and justice movement. *Matern Child Health J.* 2016;20(4):741–748.

31. AAP Council on Community Pediatrics. Poverty and child health in the United States. *Pediatrics.* 2016;137(4):e20160339.

32. Yogman M, Garfield CF; AAP Committee on Psychosocial Aspects of Child Health. Fathers' roles in the care and development of their children: the role of pediatricians. *Pediatrics.* 2016;138(1):e20161128.

33. Kotelchuck M, Lu MC. Father's role in preconception health. *Matern Child Health J.* 2017; 21(11):2035–2039.

4

The Criminal Justice System's Impact on Intergenerational Health

Monica R. McLemore, PhD, MPH, RN, Helen Arega, MA, and Rebecca Bakal, MPH

Life Course Theory attempts to describe and address complex factors that influence health across the life span.[1,2] One of these factors—incarceration—shows the intersections between social determinants of health, health service delivery, and the impact of the criminal justice system on health across generations. A specific focus on the criminal justice system is warranted and essential because of the health and social implications of the overrepresentation of people of color with past or current criminal justice involvement. This system touches individuals, families, communities, and populations with intergenerational ripple effects. Efforts to improve maternal and child health have generally not focused on larger systems such as immigration, child welfare, and incarceration that have an impact on wellness over the life course. Yet these systems play a significant role in perpetuating inequities across the life span.

This chapter will provide a glimpse of not only how race, class, and gender contribute to mass incarceration but also how criminal justice involvement is disparately reflected in low-income communities of color and for women.[3] Incarceration has mostly been examined as an isolated incident that only affects individuals who are currently caught in the carceral system; however, a structural analysis unveils the unbalanced foundation that mass incarceration is built upon and the implications for public health and optimal life trajectories. A life course approach to the carceral system should begin with blighted neighborhoods, with school systems that are designed to not only serve as a pipeline to prison but also as a tool that neglects the fundamental principles of learning and introduces a mechanism of disrespect, rage, and punishment. Furthermore, the placement of drugs and lack of work for young people has been systematically built to reinforce the oppression of Black and Brown individuals.[4] The impact of the carceral system spreads much wider, affecting spouses, parents, children, neighborhoods, and the historical legacies of Black and Brown communities and families.

A clear connection between the system of incarceration and maternal and child health is evident in the fact that during the past 30 years federal and state policies have made it extremely difficult for parents to remain in custody and have autonomy over their children. In 1997, President Clinton signed The Adoption and Safe Families Act, which stripped parents of their parental rights and quickly moved their children out of foster care, permanently placing children with another family.[5] This policy had devastating effects on the child and the parents. Parental rights were dismissed if children had been under foster care for 15 of the past 22 months. Unfortunately, when women are incarcerated, they are likely to spend more than 24 months in prison; thus, the legislation by default automatically removed their rights.[6] The state, however, benefitted because of the financial incentives that were provided because of the increased number of children who ended up in foster care. This is just one of many examples of unintended consequences of drug policies and mandatory sentencing that affect not only the incarcerated person but also the entire family—sometimes across generations.

This chapter advances the idea that mass incarceration is a system that needs reform and, more preferably, dismantling, and that individual behavior change is not sufficient to bring forth the scale of reform to improve quality of life or health of people impacted by incarceration. This system elevates inequities, layers new risk factors on top of already challenged populations, and influences preconception, prenatal, child, adolescent, and adult health. The organization of this chapter begins with an overview of mass incarceration, then describes the health impacts of incarceration. Gender and incarceration is explored. The chapter ends with strategies to decrease recidivism and increase realignment and reentry into communities of people exiting jail and/or prison.

OVERVIEW OF MASS INCARCERATION

The United States leads with the highest incarceration rate in the world at roughly 2.2 million or almost 20% of the world's total population of imprisoned individuals.[7] According to the 2016 Census data, Blacks and/or African Americans comprise 13.3% of the US population and Hispanics and/or Latinos comprise 17.8% of the US population, yet more than half of individuals incarcerated are Blacks and Hispanics/Latinos.[7] The American criminal justice system has 1,719 state prisons, 102 federal prisons, 942 juvenile correctional facilities, 3,283 local jails, and 79 Indian Country jails as well as military prisons, immigration detention facilities, and civil commitment centers.[8] It has been well documented that people who have experienced incarceration tend to be low-income and/or people of color, to be parents to young children, and to have minimal education and/or skills in addition to their incarceration history. These characteristics contribute to challenges in gaining employment, housing, and transportation after release[3-6] and are associated with poverty.

The terms "prisons" and "jails" are often used synonymously; however, there are stark differences between the two. "Jail" is generally defined as a secure facility that houses individuals who are awaiting sentencing, trial, and/or plea agreement. Persons charged with a misdemeanor and sentenced to one year or less can be housed in jails. Finally, persons who are waiting to be transferred to prison or another facility after they have been sentenced can be housed in jails. Jails are governed by the city or county in which the facility is situated.[9]

On the other hand, "prisons" or "penitentiaries" are defined as secure facilities that house persons who have already been convicted of a felony, serving a sentence of a year or more. Typically, the state or federal government controls prisons; thus, the number of persons convicted and entering prison is far less than those entering jails on a daily basis. Individuals going to jail usually do not have much warning in comparison with individuals going to prison who usually get transferred from jail after their conviction or report to prison on a specified date.[9] It is important to note that these definitions are true for most states, but not all. For example, in some states, county jails are known as prison, and in six states there are jails and prisons being operated within the same facility. Some counties allow individuals to serve up to two years in jail as opposed to one. Further complicating this nomenclature is the phenomena of publically funded versus private jails and/or prisons. Entire buildings or specific services (e.g., health, food service) can be contracted to private entities even if a jail or prison is publicly owned or operated.[10]

Mass incarceration was coined and defined by Michelle Alexander as

[A] massive system of racial and social control. It is the process by which people are swept into the criminal justice system, branded criminals and felons, locked up for longer periods of time than most other countries in the world who incarcerate people who have been convicted of crimes, and then released into a permanent second-class status in which they are stripped of basic civil and human rights, like the right to vote, the right to serve on juries, and the right to be free of legal discrimination in employment, housing, access to public benefits.[10]

Wakefield and Wildeman consider mass incarceration to be "an American experiment in incarceration, defined by extreme rates of imprisonment and by the concentration of imprisonment among young, African American men."[4] This system of racial and social control created a pipeline to incarceration by neglecting neighborhoods, removing viable means of income, and allowing dilapidated school systems to exist where Black and Brown families reside.[4]

The US economy was built upon and remains dependent upon free, forced labor— from slavery to the current multileveled prison industry.[7] Specifically, in many rural communities, jails and prisons are the primary employers[11] creating perverse incentives to increase the number of incarcerated persons, particularly when the business model is for profit. The prison phone industry has generated $1.2 billion dollars[12] and has garnered the attention of several organizations that want to see communication reforms in jails and prisons. Finally, the bail bonds industry has been shown to be extremely profitable for the jail and prison industry and detrimental for incarcerated persons and their families.[11] People who are unable to meet bail linger in jails and prisons, creating a two-tiered system for individuals accused of committing crimes—those who can afford to be out and those who cannot. Innocent parents can be kept away from their children because they do not have a few hundred dollars to get out of jail.

The 13th Amendment to the Constitution was carefully phrased as it abolished slavery and involuntary servitude in the United States *except* as punishment for a crime, which codified free and forced labor. This clause was state authorization to use prison labor as a bridge between slavery and paid work.[13,14] The drastic defunding of the social safety net, the War on Drugs, the increased militarization of the police, and the globalization of capital over the last 40 years have contributed to increased rates of incarceration. Over the past three decades, the population of US prisons has increased exponentially, even though crime began to decline before this rise in imprisonment.

Police surveillance and incarceration have become a part of everyday reality for urban communities of color.[10,15] Some scholars have argued that prison is being used as a new way to manage poverty[16] and to perpetuate racism[10,17] and as a tool for economic gain—to generate public jobs in rural areas.[13] Further complicating the issue of criminal justice and communities of color are codified policies such as "stop and frisk," traffic stops, and arrests for minor drug offenses, despite research that people of color are no more likely to commit crimes or use drugs than their White counterparts.[18] This is a burgeoning area of scholarship, and it is likely the case that the rise of mass incarceration is tied to a combination of these factors.

Incarceration and Health

Significant public health implications for incarcerated individuals have been well documented across the United States. People who enter and exit jails and prisons have poorer health than the general population across the life course.[19] Staggering figures have shown that incarcerated individuals suffer from infectious diseases such as hepatitis A, B, and/or C; HIV/AIDS; methicillin-resistant *Staphylococcus aureus* (MRSA); sexually transmitted infections (STIs); and tuberculosis at higher rates than the general population. From an epidemiological standpoint, management of these conditions should be a high priority for public safety, not only for incarcerated individuals but also for their families and other individuals that they will come in contact with while they are incarcerated and once they are released. For example, the proper management of STIs in reproductive-aged individuals is necessary to protect future fertility and prevent transmission.

Many individuals enter carceral systems with a host of chronic diseases such as arthritis, diabetes, high blood pressure, stroke, cancer, heart disease, and asthma that may not be well treated.[20] Currently, jails and prisons do not have the adequate infrastructure, nor have they taken the necessary steps to comprehensively address these complex medical issues. The irony of this lack of infrastructure is that, in the United States, incarcerated individuals are the only people with a constitutionally protected right to health care.[21] The Vera Institute is a research think tank and advocacy and policy organization focused on closing the door to mass incarceration; promoting safety, trust, and justice in America;

and significantly improving the conditions of confinement. According to the Vera Institute, 50% of incarcerated women report having a preexisting medical condition before incarceration compared with 35% of men.[22] Furthermore, 52% report having current medical problems or conditions; 32% report serious mental illness (e.g., bipolar, major depression, and schizophrenia) compared with only 6% of women in the general public; and 82% report drug or alcohol abuse or dependence.[22]

GENDER AND INCARCERATION

As many sectors around the country are highlighting the impacts of mass incarceration, their focus is largely on men, which diminishes the urgency of the growing rate at which women are incarcerated. Although men still lead in the number of those most incarcerated, the number of women in prisons has swelled by more than 700% in the years between 1980 and 2014.[6] Women represent the fastest-growing segment of incarcerated persons in West Virginia, Oklahoma, Kentucky, Alabama, Arizona, Texas, Louisiana, New Mexico, and California.[3] In spite of this increase, comprehensive demographic statistics on incarcerated women are lacking, including limited to no information on pregnancy and reproductive health status. Currently, prisons and jails in the United States confine approximately 206,000 women at a rate of 127 per 100,000.[22,23] With more than 1 million women behind bars or under the control of the criminal justice system, women are the fastest-growing segment of the incarcerated population, increasing at nearly double the rate of men since 1985.[7] Women are now held in jails in every county of the United States—a glaring contrast when compared with the 1970s when the majority of jails did not have any women.[22] Black and Hispanic/Latina women are overrepresented in prisons—Black women representing 44% and Hispanic/Latina women 15% despite the fact that they commit crimes at approximately the same rate as White women.[22]

In the 19th and early 20th century, women were almost exclusively arrested for prostitution, lewd behavior, and vagrancy.[24] Comparatively, contemporary women are still incarcerated for these offenses, which are not violent, as well as for nonviolent drug offenses (29%), property offenses (32%), and public order offenses (21%). Notably, women have less extensive criminal backgrounds than men.[22] It is important to note that a disproportionate number of women are incarcerated because of their failure to make bail for minor offenses (for themselves and others) and the compounding effect that occurs from minor offenses, such as traffic violations and parking tickets.[7, 22]

History of Women in the Penal System

There have been three phases of approaches for how women have been treated while incarcerated compared with how men have been treated. In the first phase (before 1870), women were not treated differently in any way and suffered under the severe policies and practices designed for and by men.[22] The second phase (1870 through 1935) emerged because of significant public outcry and reform efforts. During this time, women's prisons transitioned into facilities that were more appropriate to the specific needs of women and many were developed to exclusively house women. In the third stage (1935 to the present), gender-specific jail and prison programming continues to develop (e.g., classes for women, including reproductive health services); however, they remain variable in providing adequate facilities specific for women.[25] The popular drama series, "Orange Is the New Black," released in 2013, is based on a book by the same name by the author Piper Kerman.[26] This series reflects Kerman's experience in a New York prison. Although the show is dramatic, and many scenes are embellished for television's sake, it gives its audience a relatively accurate glimpse of what women experience during incarceration. In addition, it provides insight to laws, living conditions, and treatment for incarcerated women. What politicians and policymakers fail to fully comprehend is that the majority of women who find themselves in the carceral system are simply trying to survive the harsh realities of poverty, unemployment, and significant physical or behavioral struggles, including those related to past histories of trauma, mental illness, or substance use.[22]

Gender-specific needs for women include comprehensive reproductive health services including menstrual cycle supplies, abortion, family planning, and pregnancy-related services, and mental health, substance use, and other maternal and family bonding supports necessary for success once released from carceral systems. Incarcerated women have gender-specific needs that have not been adequately addressed, including reconnecting with or establishing their roles as mothers, repairing social relationships with family and other sources of support, and healing from trauma-related emotional stressors, along with traditional reentry issues such as finding employment.[27-30] The following section describes these needs in greater detail.

Motherhood and Incarceration

The Sentencing Project and the Vera Institute[6,22] found that there are more than 1.5 million children with parents in prison and 8.3 million children with parents who are under custody. Just over one in five of these children are aged younger than 5 years. In California, two out of three incarcerated women are parents compared with about half of incarcerated men.[3] Several studies have documented the specific needs of previously incarcerated women, which include support to care for their children and other relatives upon release, psychosocial issues related to reunification, difficulty navigating relationships with partners and/or fathers of their children, and the lack of substance use, detox, and trauma recovery services available to women.[3-6] Many women may spend a substantial amount of time apart from their children during the crucial developmental years because of prolonged sentences.[22]

More than two-thirds of incarcerated women have children aged younger than 18 years and approximately 5% are pregnant upon incarceration.[22] Pregnant women, despite the fact that many professional organizations have identified shackling as being a harm to laboring individuals, are constrained during labor and immediately after delivery. Many postpartum women and babies are separated at birth. In addition, many facilities do not allow birthing women to have outside family or friend social support during labor except for the supervising sheriff or guard. More than half of incarcerated women lived with their children before they started serving time.[31] Mothers are often placed more than 500 miles from their home, making it difficult to receive visits from family and friends. In fact, more than half of women who are both incarcerated and mothers have never had a visit from their children.[22,27] Upon release, mothers face a unique set of issues: in addition to gaining job skills and employment, mothers must reconstruct their relationships with their children and with their children's caretakers. Women with criminal histories are disproportionately likely to be poor and of color, thereby facing compounded barriers to employment and housing security and being able to provide for their children.[27] Correctional facilities also rarely take into account that women are the gatekeepers of their families and communities and that their parental stressors occur more frequently and uniquely compared with men.

Mental Health and Trauma

The rate of victimization for women incarcerated is astounding; for example, 86% of women experienced sexual violence, 77% of women experienced partner violence, and 60% experienced caregiver violence, all which have not been explored or noted when demonizing incarcerated women.[22] Individuals who have been incarcerated experience high rates of sexual assault,[32] trauma,[32-34] and violence[32-34] throughout their lives, which has deleterious impacts on their health.

The traumatization of women in jails has not been widely discussed or investigated, but it is estimated that women are far more likely to experience sexual violence from other incarcerated individuals (27%) and jail staff (67%).[22] According to Bloom et al., "Correctional procedures such as searches, restraints, and use of solitary confinement, do not take into account the violence, trauma, and mental illness the majority of incarcerated women have experienced outside of jail and can reactivate trauma in women who have suffered abuse."[22] The high-stress nature of the carceral environment invokes posttraumatic stress disorder, unsafe and triggering spaces that punish women for reacting, defending, and protecting themselves from the abuse, which gets misinterpreted as their being defensive and combative.[22] Incarceration creates a tremendous impact on a women's life course, amplifying existing depression, shame, and trauma.[22]

Access to Care

The majority of women who are incarcerated in the United States are of reproductive age with a mean age of 36 years.[22,27] Many women are also impacted by the incarceration of their partners who are of reproductive age. Understanding the effect of poor reproductive health services in jails and prisons has been the focus of understanding the specific needs of incarcerated women.[15,22,23,27–30] Comprehensive statistics on reproductive health services, specifically abortion, family planning, and pregnancy-related care, are not routinely collected[22,23,27–30]; however, it is known that carcerally involved women in prisons have better access to health services than women in jails. The quality of care women receive, however, is extremely varied. Research has shown that these services are not adequate, timely, or routine.[22] For example, comprehensive reproductive health services such as access to contraception—whether used to prevent pregnancy or other reasons—are not available.[15,35] Further complicating the matter of women's health service provision and access is that jails are generally county-run and therefore dependent on county-level funding, which often results in limited financial resources.[22] In turn, women who become incarcerated may receive limited reproductive health services.

Reproductive Health and Rights

The lack of availability of menstrual hygiene products, contraceptive care, and access to abortion services, and forced sterilization are critical reproductive justice issues that are intricately linked to incarceration. Reproductive rights and incarceration further expose America's historical practices of forced incarceration (slavery) and racial bias. Jails often fail to meet even the most basic hygiene needs of the women in their custody. Many incarcerated women across the nation have reported being denied menstrual hygiene products, toilet paper, and clean underwear. In many instances, jails do not have a sufficient supply or are very selective on how they distribute products. Failure to provide adequate menstrual products poses significant health risks (e.g., yeast infection, urinary tract infection, rash); not only does it cause harm to the body but it also causes embarrassment. Policymakers around the country have begun to file complaints and lawsuits to address this issue (e.g., New York and Wisconsin).[21,35]

The Vera Institute has found that although many incarcerated women take interest in starting contraceptive care, it is not readily accessible to them. For example, a survey of women detained at New York City's Rikers Island jail found that although New York City Department of Health and Mental Hygiene policy requires the facility to offer all jailed women family planning services, they rarely received contraceptive counseling or services during their stay or before release.[22] For women who do receive family planning services, it is imperative that they have full access (i.e., affordable, close proximity to their residence) to care in their communities upon being released to prevent complications, screen for infectious diseases, and ensure efficacy of method. A seamless transition to clinical care upon release, however, is not a guarantee. Surveys that have been conducted throughout California have revealed that many women are unable to see a doctor for about 30 days upon their release. Essentially, access to contraceptive care is rarely available, accessible, or affordable for women in the carceral system.[15,21,35]

Access to pregnancy termination care for incarcerated women is extremely convoluted and almost nonexistent in many jails or prisons throughout the nation. Lack of quality, timely, and unbiased clinical care reduces women's access to information and thereby strips of them of their right to choose how they would like to move forward in their pregnancy. Despite the fact that the US Supreme Court has ruled that any regulation restricting abortion access cannot place an undue burden on women seeking abortions, in practice, the ability of a pregnant woman who is incarcerated to access an abortion varies widely depending on the jurisdiction and facility in which she is housed.[15,22] Although there are some laws and policies in place, they are not enforced, so women often receive information too late, which has devastating physical, emotional, and spiritual effects on the mother for a lifetime.

Forced sterilization is a procedure that makes persons unable to reproduce without their true informed consent.[15,28] Although most people think about this practice as something that happened historically, this practice is still a current threat on incarcerated people's reproductive lives. For example, more than 100 women incarcerated in California were sterilized by tubal ligation surgery between 2006 and 2010 in a setting that was not conducive to informed consent, although informed consent to any surgery is both ethically and legally required.[15,24]

THE IMPACT OF INCARCERATION ON THE LIFE COURSE OF FAMILIES

Incarceration has an impact on more than just the individual who is imprisoned—it has a ripple effect across generations. Approximately 12% of African American children reside with their grandparents, where neither parent lives in the home.[32-34] The implications of mass incarceration and the lifelong sequelae of having incarcerated parents has been shown to have an impact on their behavioral and mental health across the life course. The most significant (and most studied) is readiness for school; children who have incarcerated parents are known to have delays in their educational progression, to have delinquency, and to be at higher risk for incarceration themselves as youths and as adults.[32-34]

Children with incarcerated parents are less likely to meet developmental milestones, to complete vaccine schedules, and to receive preventive health services, and often have delayed progression through school.[32,34] In addition to decreased parental bonding and inconsistent social support, children of incarcerated parents can cycle through the foster care system and are subject to complete disconnection from parents across the life span.

These impacts are significant given many of these children are also disproportionately affected by the social determinants of health that contribute to poorer health outcomes. Mass incarceration has devastating impacts on entire families and communities because of the compounded effects of poverty, neighborhood, and interpersonal violence, and carcerally involved individuals experience decreased access to social safety net services.

STRATEGIES TO REDUCE RISKS AND ADD PROTECTION

Health care, human service, and public health practitioners cannot overlook the significant impact that the carceral system has on the communities they serve. The criminal justice system represents a failure on the part of communities and country to support conditions that allow everyone to thrive. Policies at many levels reflect the entrenched racism that fuels this pipeline, which then derails the life trajectories for the people impacted—disproportionately people of color. Leaders, advocates, and practitioners can and must respond to this crisis if they wish to improve maternal and child health for those at greatest risk for harm. Life Course Theory offers an excellent tool for advancing this response. There are strategies throughout this book that practitioners can consider and deploy to begin to address the conditions that layer risks on certain communities as well as to examine their own lens and mental frames on incarceration.

Fortunately, there are multiple strategies that can be used to prevent incarceration, to improve the experiences of those in the system, and to decrease recidivism:

1. Provide jobs and training opportunities for previously incarcerated individuals.
2. Provide peer-to-peer support.
3. Provide trauma-informed care including wraparound services for families.
4. Provide prison nurseries and other programs to keep mothers and babies together.
5. Use restorative justice approaches to keep people who commit crimes out of jails and prisons.

The final section of this chapter describes these opportunities for intervention.

According to the Bureau of Justice Statistics, recidivism among released prisoners in a 5-year period was documented to be between 68% and 77%, with just under half convicted of a new crime within a year after their initial release.[19] "Reentry" is defined as exiting jail or prison and returning to their communities. "Realignment" is a specific term used within the criminal justice system in California that seeks to coordinate care, services, and funds from statewide prisons to county jails, with potential applications in other states. Realigning incarcerated individuals with community resources after release is a key factor in the reduction of recidivism. Providing employment and vocational opportunities to recently released individuals has been well recognized as an important strategy for reducing recidivism by building self-esteem and giving responsibility in the legal workforce, which has the potential to improve their chances of successful reintegration.[23,27–30]

Provision of vocational opportunities has been one of the most successful strategies to reduce recidivism by incarcerated individuals.[22,27–30] Consistent employment has been shown to be one of the most important factors for preventing a return to prison or jail. In addition, efforts to ensure greater employability of previously incarcerated individuals such as "ban the box" initiatives—in which job seekers are not required to disclose their carceral history—have also been successful in supporting people to find consistent employment.

Peer-to-peer support is crucial and offers space to share stories and provides structured opportunities for real-time support. Gender-specific groups have been tested and shown to improve parenting skills and birth outcomes and to decrease recidivism. Models grounded in harm reduction and risk mitigation have resulted in innovative public health and community-based programs that allow previously incarcerated people to support others who have experienced incarceration to improve their lives.

Trauma-informed care approaches[3,27–29] with co-located social services decreases the burden for previously incarcerated individuals and allows for a "one-stop shop" approach, which increases service utilization and recovery. This approach that acknowledges the trauma women have experienced is valuable across services—vocational, clinical, upon release, and while incarcerated. An example specific to women that has shown superior outcomes is prison nurseries[6,7,27] for breastfeeding rates, family bonding and attachment, and drug treatment and recovery.

Successful prison nurseries have clinical staff who provide breastfeeding support, well-baby visits, and other preventive health services for moms and babies. There are ethical issues that need to be addressed when one is evaluating these programs, particularly because children who begin their lives in jail or prison are exposed to the same hazards as adults (i.e., communicable diseases, violence). Key questions should be addressed, such as should infants and/or children who have not committed crimes be incarcerated because of the actions of their parent(s)? Do the bonding benefits outweigh the potential costs? Who should determine where newborns are placed if one or more of their parents is incarcerated? Do policies around foster care and adoption placement need to be amended to not penalize parents who are in prison? What resources could and should be provided to families providing kinship care to children while parents are incarcerated? And, most importantly, can innovative programs be developed to achieve the goal of family bonding and restorative justice outside the prison walls?

Restorative justice approaches[3,6,27] have been suggested as a solution to decrease mass incarceration and to dismantle the separation caused by incarceration. These approaches posit that if alternatives to jail and prison were available, such as drug treatment (including for pregnant women, families, and as an alternative to jail), peer-to-peer courts, alternative sentencing, and other noncarceral options (e.g., policy changes that shift approaches to enforcing or prosecuting low-level crimes), much of the disruption caused by mass incarceration could be avoided. Local policies, judges, and advocates along with engaged residents can support change in their communities in terms of how courts approach sentences for pregnant women, alternative programs to avoid prison, and bail for low-income individuals that can unnecessarily prolong separation from children, home, and employment.

Practitioners and maternal and child health advocates can make incremental changes to address the complex needs of incarcerated individuals particularly by mapping care provision between carceral and secular health care systems to improve the transition for families. For example, local health departments may be responsible for providing services to jails in their communities. What is the quality of that care? What role can health departments play in assessment, assurance, and surveillance? How can coalitions come together to provide transitional services? Hospitals that provide services to pregnant women who are in the carceral system can advocate patient rights and policies that provide equitable, quality care. They can also provide training to their staff around their bias about women in the system, offer specially trained doulas to support laboring and postpartum women, and deploy highly trained social workers and nurses to be on care teams for these patients while hospitalized.

Other key activities could include ensuring potential for parental visitation and connection at all levels of the criminal justice system, designing programs that support family activities, supporting community resources for family-based clinical services, offering home-visiting services to families, ensuring that women leaving the carceral system have access to reproductive and mental health services, connecting children of incarcerated individuals with other family members, and providing counseling and support to families across the process. Future work should evaluate the effectiveness and success of programs designed to restore families within communities.

CONCLUSIONS

The rise of mass incarceration provides a prime opportunity for a bold call for action for practitioners from all disciplines. A Life Course Approach to the criminal justice and carceral system presents an opportunity to develop new programs, test novel interventions, build new partnerships, and engage on a policy level to improve the life course trajectory of justice-involved individuals and their families. Carceral-involved individuals require support to restore them to their family and community. To act, it is necessary to learn about the local carceral system and policies in a person's state and county. Practitioners should assess the services being provided to individuals at all stages of the process, including bail, awaiting trial, sentencing, restorative justice, short-term stays, transitions into and out of the carceral system, maternity care, and clinical care. Efforts should focus on women who are the most vulnerable and impacted by mass incarceration—whether they are parents or partners of incarcerated men or if they themselves are incarcerated.

To engage in work to address the carceral system, practitioners should build relationships with key stakeholders—namely, community activists, clinicians, health departments that provide care, social services, philanthropists, researchers, community-based programs, and individuals who have been impacted by the system. Similarly, practitioners need to learn from sheriffs, wardens, and others who are responsible for the care and keeping of individuals during incarceration to understand their goals, perspectives, resources, and needs. Convening groups of diverse individuals such as these requires skillful facilitation but collectively much work can be accomplished.

Life Course Theory underscores the importance of understanding the larger system of incarceration with the history of oppression and racism it represents along with related power and economic impacts. Organizing agency and community viewings and discussions of documentary films such as "13th" can prompt important conversations.[14] Practitioners can host book discussions at work, in the community, and in their own social circles to learn about the system and how to deconstruct it. Advocacy for greater community oversight of carceral decision making is essential and can be fostered as more and diverse professionals participate in community fora and community advisory boards to carceral programs.

Finally, a life course perspective insists that maternal and child health practitioners pay special attention to people involved in the criminal justice system who are at risk for unintended pregnancy, wish to become pregnant, are pregnant, and/or are parenting by adapting, deploying, and testing programs such as home visiting; group prenatal care; prenatal, labor, and postpartum doulas; reproductive health education and services; and life coaching to ensure optimal health outcomes across the life course. Efforts to close disparities in health outcomes cannot ignore the impact of the experience of incarceration on maternal and child health populations, elevating the risks that track individuals toward incarceration and the doubled risks that follow them when released. Ultimately, Life Course Theory creates a platform that can launch significant efforts to interrupt systems of oppression, such as mass incarceration, and bring new perspectives and a greater sense of urgency to this critical issue.

KEY POINTS

- Mental health services and substance use services need to be readily available to people—as a preventive and/or alternative to incarceration.
- Advocacy for restorative justice approaches is crucial. Criminal justice is grounded in deterring crime, while mental health and substance use problems should be clinically and/or medically managed to include harm-reduction strategies.
- Gender-specific needs exist when one is considering populations with current or previous carceral involvement—practitioners should be documenting and addressing these needs.
- The intergenerational needs of families (children, parents, grandparents) should be considered in the development of interventions.

- Community-based programs should be developed to facilitate this relationship as well as to provide support for successful and permanent transitions from incarceration to the community. Public health and social work practitioners should serve as a bridge between the carceral and traditional health and social service providers.
- Mass incarceration is one system that has an impact on the life course of individuals and communities. Practitioners can no longer assume that others are working to dismantle this system—everyone must engage to interrupt this system.

RESOURCES

Books

These books provide historical and current perspectives on mass incarceration:

- Alexander M. *The New Jim Crow: Mass Incarceration in the Age of Colorblindness.* New York, NY: New Press; 2010. This well-researched book maps the connections between slavery and coined the term "mass incarceration": http://newjimcrow.com/about.
- Wakefield S, Wildeman C. *Children of the Prison Boom: Mass Incarceration and the Future of American Inequality.* New York, NY: Oxford University Press; 2014. This book documents one of the most comprehensive studies of children impacted by mass incarceration: https://global.oup.com/academic/product/children-of-the-prison-boom-9780199989225?cc=us&lang=en&.
- Sufrin C. *Jailcare: Finding the Safety Net for Women Behind Bars.* Oakland, CA: University of California Press; 2017. This book, written by a physician and anthropologist, documents the unique needs of incarcerated women: http://www.ucpress.edu/book.php?isbn=9780520288683.
- Stevenson B. *Just Mercy: A Story of Justice and Redemption.* New York, NY: Penguin Random House; 2014. This true story documents movement through the criminal justice system in the United States. It is written by one of the most accomplished contemporary legal scholars working to bring equity to the system: http://bryanstevenson.com/the-book.
- Davis A. *The Prison Industrial Complex.* Chico, CA: AK Press; 2001. This book gives a full picture of what the term "prison industrial complex" means: https://www.amazon.com/Prison-Industrial-Complex-Angela-Davis/dp/1902593227.
- Foucault M. *Discipline and Punish: The Birth of the Prison.* Paris, France: Vintage Books/Gallimard; 1977. This historical book documents the role of jails and prisons in society: https://monoskop.org/images/4/43/Foucault_Michel_Discipline_and_Punish_The_Birth_of_the_Prison_1977_1995.pdf.
- Jamal AM. *Have Black Lives Ever Mattered?* San Francisco, CA: City Lights Books; 2017. This book provides a historical timeline of police brutality throughout the

decades and the rise of the Black Lives Matter movement: https://www.amazon.com/
Black-Lives-Mattered-Lights-Media/dp/0872867382.

- Shakur A. *Assata: An Autobiography.* Chicago, IL: Lawrence Hill Books; 1987. The true
story of Assata Shakur and her a life as a Black Panther activist: https://www.amazon.
com/Assata-Autobiography-Shakur/dp/1556520743.
- Richie BE. *Arrested Justice: Black Women, Violence, and America's Prison Nation.* New
York, NY: NYU Press; 2012. This book documents the impact of violence, rape, incest,
and poverty that Black women in America face: http://www.jstor.org/stable/j.
ctt9qghqn.

Documentaries

Most of these films are available free online at the links provided or are available in
public libraries:

- Duvernay A. *13th.* Distributed by Netflix: http://www.avaduvernay.com/#/13th.
- Garbus L, Wilbert R. *The Farm: Angola USA:* http://www.imdb.com/title/tt0139193.
- *The Biggest Prison System in History:* http://topdocumentaryfilms.com/biggest-
prison-system-history.
- Pillscher M. *Broken on all Sides:* http://brokenonallsides.com.
- *In the Land of the Free:* http://www.imdb.com/title/tt1297923.
- Lynch S. *Free Angela Davis and All Political Prisoners:* https://sholalynch.wordpress.
com/about/free-angela-2013.

Additional Items

- This article discusses incarceration as a social determinant of health for maternal
health outcomes: https://www.ncbi.nlm.nih.gov/pmc/articles/PMC4161663.
- American Psychological Association statement about ending shackling: https://www.
apa.org/about/gr/issues/women/shackling-incarcerated-women.pdf.
- American Congress of Obstetricians and Gynecologists' recommendations for
perinatal health care for incarcerated women: https://www.acog.org/Resources-And-
Publications/Committee-Opinions/Committee-on-Health-Care-for-Underserved-Women/
Health-Care-for-Pregnant-and-Postpartum-Incarcerated-Women-and-Adolescent-
Females.
- National Council on Incarcerated and Formerly Incarcerated Women and Girls:
https://nationalcouncil.us.
- The Vera Institute: http://vera.org.
- National Resource Center for Justice Involved Women: http://cjinvolvedwomen.org.

REFERENCES

1. Lu MC, Halfon N. Racial and ethnic disparities in birth outcomes: a life-course perspective. *Matern Child Health J.* 2003;7(1):13–30.

2. Wise PH. Framework as metaphor: the promise and peril of MCH life-course perspectives. *Matern Child Health J.* 2003;7(3):151–156.

3. INCITE! Women of Color Against Violence. *The Revolution Will Not Be Funded: Beyond the Non-profit Industrial Complex.* Cambridge, MA: South End Press; 2007.

4. Wakefield S, Wildeman C. *Children of the Prison Boom: Mass Incarceration and the Future of American Inequality.* New York, NY: Oxford University Press; 2014.

5. Adoption and Safe Families Act of 1997 (HR 867), Pub L 105-89 (1997).

6. The Sentencing Project Research and Advocacy for Reform. Fact sheet: Incarcerated women and girls. 2015. Available at: http://www.sentencingproject.org/publications/incarcerated-women-and-girls. Accessed May 21, 2017.

7. National Association for the Advancement of Colored People. Criminal justice fact sheet. 2017. Available at: http://www.naacp.org/criminal-justice-fact-sheet. Accessed May 21, 2017.

8. Wagner P, Rabuy B. Mass incarceration: the whole pie 2017. Prison Policy Initiative. 2017. Available at: https://www.prisonpolicy.org/reports/pie2017.html. Accessed May 21, 2017.

9. Clem Information Strategies. What is the difference between prison and jail? 2017. Available at: http://cleminfostrategies.com/whats-the-difference-between-prison-and-jail. Accessed May 21, 2017.

10. Alexander M. *The New Jim Crow: Mass Incarceration in the Age of Colorblindness.* New York, NY: New Press; 2010.

11. Kearney MS, Harris BH, Parker EJL. The Hamilton Project Report: Ten economic facts about crime and incarceration in the United States. Available at: http://www.hamiltonproject.org/papers/ten_economic_facts_about_crime_and_incarceration_in_the_united_states. Accessed May 21, 2017.

12. Federal Trade Commission. WC Docket No. 12-375. Available at: https://apps.fcc.gov/edocs_public/attachmatch/FCC-13-113A1.pdf. Accessed May 21, 2017.

13. Gilmore K. Slavery and prison—understanding the connection. *Soc Justice.* 2007;27(3):1–10.

14. Duvernay A. *13th.* Distributed by Netflix. Available at: http://www.avaduvernay.com/#/13th. Accessed May 21, 2017.

15. Sufrin C, Kolbi-Molinas A, Roth R. Reproductive justice, health disparities and incarcerated women in the United States. *Perspect Sex Reprod Health.* 2015;47(4):213–219.

16. Wacquant L. *Punishing the Poor: The Neoliberal Government of Social Insecurity.* Durham, NC: Duke University Press; 2009.

17. Forman J. Racial critiques of mass incarceration: beyond the New Jim Crow. *SELA (Seminario en Latinoamérica de Teoría Constitucional y Política) Papers*. Yale Law School. 2010: 110. Available at: http://digitalcommons.law.yale.edu/yls_sela/110. Accessed May 21, 2017.

18. Hart C. *Drugs, Society, and Human Behavior.* 16th ed. New York, NY: McGraw-Hill; 2015.

19. Durose MR, Cooper AD, Snyder HN. Recidivism of prisoners released in 30 states in 2005: patterns from 2005 to 2010. US Department of Justice, Office of Justice Programs, Bureau of Justice Statistics. 2014. Available at: https://www.bjs.gov/index.cfm?ty=dcdetail&iid=270. Accessed May 21, 2017.

20. Centers for Disease Control and Prevention. Correctional health data. 2016. Available at: https://www.cdc.gov/correctionalhealth/health-data.html. Accessed May 21, 2017.

21. Kajstura A, Immarigeon AK. States of women's incarceration: the global context. Prison Policy Initiative. Available at: https://www.prisonpolicy.org/global/women. Accessed May 21, 2017.

22. Vera Institute of Justice. Overlooked: women and jails in an era of reform. 2016. Available at: https://www.vera.org/publications/overlooked-women-and-jails-report. Accessed May 21, 2017.

23. Carson EA, Anderson E. Prisoners in 2015. US Department of Justice, Office of Justice Programs, Bureau of Justice Statistics. 2016. Available at: https://www.bjs.gov/index.cfm?ty=pbdetail&iid=5869. Accessed May 21, 2017.

24. Pishko J. *A History of Women Prisons.* 2015. Available at: https://daily.jstor.org/history-of-womens-prisons. Accessed May 21, 2017.

25. Rafter NH. Prisons for women, 1790–1980. *University Chicago Press J.* 1983;5:129–181.

26. Kerman P. *Orange Is the New Black: My Year in a Women's Prison.* New York, NY: Spiegel and Grau; 2010.

27. Bloom B, Owen B, Covington S. Gender responsive strategies. Research, practice and guiding principles for women offenders. National Institute of Corrections. 2013. Available at: http://nicic.gov/library/018017. Accessed May 21, 2017.

28. Garcia M, Ritter R. Improving access to services for female offenders returning to the community. *J Natl Inst Justice.* 2012;269:18–23.

29. Stanley D, Sata N, Oparah JC, McLemore MR. Evaluation of the East Bay Community Birth Support Project, a community-based program to decrease recidivism in previously incarcerated women. *J Obstet Gynecol Neonatal Nurs.* 2015;44(6):743–750.

30. McLemore MR, Warner Hand Z. Making the case for innovative reentry employment programs: previously incarcerated women as birth doulas—a case study. *Int J Prison Health.* 2017;13(3-4):219–227.

31. Greenfeld LA, Snell TL. Women offenders. 2000. US Department of Justice Office of Justice Programs Bureau of Justice Statistics. https://www.bjs.gov/index.cfm?ty=pbdetail&iid=568. Accessed May 21, 2017.

32. Hanlon TE, Carswell SB, Rose M. Research on the caretaking of children of incarcerated parents: findings and their service delivery implications. *Child Youth Serv Rev.* 2007;29(3): 362–384.

33. Kruttschnitt C. The paradox of women's imprisonment. *Daedalus.* Summer 2010:32–42.

34. Travis J, McBride EC, Solomon AL. Families left behind: the hidden cost of incarceration and reentry. Washington, DC: Urban Institute Justice Policy Center; 2005.

35. Sufrin C. *Jailcare: Finding the Safety Net for Women Behind Bars.* Oakland, CA: University of California Press; 2017.

5

Place-Based Initiatives

Monica Y. B. Braughton, MPH, Megan K. Calpin, MPH, MCP,
Denise Pecha, LCSW, and Cheri A. Pies, DrPH, MSW

During much of the 20th century, maternal and child health (MCH), like many sectors, focused on clinical interventions to improve health outcomes.[1] Over the past two decades, researchers and practitioners have both recognized and voiced the limitations of this medical approach to health and well-being. An opening for initiatives that address the social determinants of health, including the risk factors, protective factors, and health equity issues that influence outcomes for women, children, and their families, emerged. Life Course Theory (LCT) has served as a theoretical framework and a paradigm to support revitalization of this approach,[2] and the resurgence of interest in "place-based" initiatives has provided a focus. This chapter provides a brief overview of the development of place-based initiatives, a discussion of their intersection with LCT and MCH, and key strategies and considerations for practitioners who may wish to align their work with this approach.

THE EVOLUTION OF PLACE-BASED INITIATIVES

For this discussion, place-based initiatives are described as collaborative endeavors to direct resources to neighborhoods to improve the social, economic, and/or built environments. Though there is renewed interest in place-based initiatives today, they have a long history in the United States tracing back to the settlement houses of the late 19th century.[3] These early attempts at alleviating poverty focused on addressing the needs of individuals within the crowded neighborhoods of a growing urban America.[4]

Modern place-based initiatives are based on antipoverty theory developed in the 1960s, as America entered a period of civil unrest solidified by decades of housing segregation and the loss of industrial jobs in major cities. Between 1964 and 1966, the Ford Foundation became the first to fund in broad-scale community development through its Gray Areas program investments in Boston, Massachusetts; Oakland, California; New Haven, Connecticut; Philadelphia, Pennsylvania; and Washington, District of Columbia.[3] These programs sought to spur "community action" through citizen participation and local institutional change, ultimately focusing on reforming service delivery systems to reduce poverty.[5]

President Lyndon B. Johnson's administration took lessons from the Ford Foundation's pilot cities to spread place-based ideas as a strategy of the War on Poverty. Johnson's community action programs were predicated on the "maximum feasible participation" of communities, in which resident decision making on local antipoverty programs was seen as a crucial part of aligning the work of local agencies to local needs.[6] This bottom-up approach has largely lived on in the community development programs of the 21st century.

In the 1970s and 1980s, the federal government retreated from funding broad networks of place-based initiatives. State and local governments, as well as community-based organizations, stepped in to replace more coordinated federal policy with varied success.[4] Municipal governments relied on tax credits to encourage corporations to relocate (or stay) in urban, high-unemployment Enterprise Zones; however, these Zones created few lasting or quality jobs for low-income residents.[7] Nonprofits and faith-based investment programs also began working to expand access to financial resources in some urban and rural communities; these efforts resulted in community development corporations and community development financial institutions, many of which continue to support affordable housing and locally driven small businesses today.[4]

By the 1990s, heightened federal oversight of financial institutions was improving fair lending in neighborhoods where banks had previously refused to loan,[8] and local grass roots initiatives were flourishing in the absence of a federal place-based antipoverty effort. These initiatives became increasingly multi-issue in their approaches.[9] For example, the Harlem Children's Zone, which started in the mid-1990s in New York City, focused not just on improving educational outcomes but also on community violence, affordable housing, homelessness, and other factors in its work.[10]

In the first two decades of the 21st century, a renaissance in community change initiatives (now known as "place-based" initiatives) was spurred by a renewed focus on the interconnected causes and effects of poverty and a philanthropic interest in a more "holistic" grant-making approach that intentionally focused on these complexities.[3] As a result of this interest, these initiatives now encompass a wide range of projects, including multisite initiatives funded by health foundations such as The California Endowment and the Robert Wood Johnson Foundation (among many others), and federal place-based initiatives started under the Obama Administration, such as Promise Zones. Together these programs represent billions of dollars of investment in affordable housing, loans and grants to small businesses, community improvements, and support for organizations to guide the work.[4]

DEFINING CHARACTERISTICS OF 21ST CENTURY PLACE-BASED INITIATIVES

As evidenced in this brief history, the drivers, strategies, and goals of place-based initiatives have evolved over time. Given these changes, what unites current place-based initiatives? A few common features—as well as the ways in which they continue to vary—are described here. First, all place-based initiatives are rooted in the recognition that a person's opportunities and challenges are influenced not just by their personal choices but also by their social and physical surroundings. Examining an experience such as pregnancy can help to illustrate this principle. In California, all low-income pregnant women are eligible for pregnancy-related Medicaid coverage, allowing them to attend regular prenatal visits, access labor and delivery care, and attend postpartum visits at no cost.[11] Assuming that a woman chooses to enroll in this coverage, many factors in her environment still influence the likelihood of a healthy birth outcome. These factors include the availability of transit options so she can visit her doctor; social support from her partner, family, and community; and/or the stressors she faces if she does not have steady employment or stable, safe housing. Place-based initiatives recognize that an intervention focused on the person (such as education about prenatal care or health care coverage) can only be successful when they are supported by efforts that address the infrastructure, economy, and community around her.

Second, place-based initiatives focus on improving complex conditions in communities influenced by concentrated, long-standing, and interconnected disinvestment. These communities are characterized by lack of access to quality jobs, underfunded schools, or poorly maintained infrastructure of which the community does not have ownership. While some initiatives may focus on addressing several of these interconnected issues at once, others have elected to organize around a single issue, either as a primary concern or as an entry point into beginning to address other root causes or related outcomes. The complexity of these challenges motivates many place-based initiatives to make multiyear commitments to communities.

Third, as the name implies, place-based initiatives are focused on specific geographic areas. This geographic area is often described as a "neighborhood"; however, the definition and scale of neighborhood can vary widely. Some initiatives may focus on a single census tract or a few city blocks, whereas others focus on much larger swaths of a city. There is often an emphasis on defining the neighborhood as residents themselves define it; therefore, the neighborhood may not align with political, census, or other administrative boundaries.[12] The boundary of the neighborhood may also be influenced by the outcomes the initiative hopes to achieve. For example, initiatives focused on improving job opportunities may choose to work within both a residential neighborhood and the regional labor market where most residents seek employment.[13] Place-based initiatives recognize that work within the neighborhood's boundaries encompasses not just residents of the community but also anyone who works, plays, learns, or otherwise spends time in that space.

The interconnected root causes of these problems necessitate the fourth key aspect of place-based initiatives: collaboration among organizations, experts across disciplines, and residents of the community. As illustrated earlier, the barriers to a healthy pregnancy that a woman may encounter—such as unreliable transportation, fragmented social support, inadequate housing, or lack of job opportunities—point to the number of actors needed to make lasting change in birth outcomes. While place-based initiatives necessitate the involvement of a diversity of organizations, partners can vary greatly depending on the initiative's focus, the lead organization's sector and expertise, and the history of cross-sector collaboration in the community and among the partners involved.

Community residents are critical partners in the success of a place-based initiative. Their historical perspective and lived experience make them experts on the origins of a community's current conditions and key stakeholders in implementing solutions. Community participation has long been seen as critical for the design and implementation of comprehensive community development.[3] In theory, place-based efforts are able to amplify local residents' voices and emphasize their ideas in ways that other efforts may stifle. In practice, resident participation in place-based initiatives has varied widely over time, ranging from top-down structures that have tokenized community members and focused on "fixing" individuals, to grass roots, resident-driven, and resident-owned efforts.[4] Engaging residents as key partners is a core value of modern place-based initiatives.

Although these key characteristics demonstrate basic similarities, modern place-based initiatives remain highly variable in their focus, implementation, and resources. The following sections further detail how place-based initiatives have emerged in the specific field of MCH, as well as how these principles operate in practice.

PLACE-BASED INITIATIVES AND LIFE COURSE THEORY

The principle that "place matters" has been interpreted and operationalized differently depending on the time, place, and discipline within which it is applied. In the field of MCH, the reemergence of place-based initiatives coincided with an increased focus on the concept of LCT. LCT suggests that a complex interplay of biological, behavioral, psychological, and social protective and risk factors contribute to health outcomes across the span of a person's life. This approach also suggests that these protective and risk factors accumulate over generations and have their greatest effects during critical periods of growth, including preconception, pregnancy, early childhood, and adolescence.

In 2003, Lu and Halfon brought attention to LCT as a way to understand disparities in birth outcomes, positing that persistent racial inequities in preterm birth, low birth weight, and infant mortality were the result of underlying social, economic, and environmental factors.[14] Applying this theory to the field of MCH requires greater investments in women's health across the life span and concerted efforts to address broader social conditions such as racism, poverty, and discrimination. For MCH practitioners, place-based strategy has become a way to apply LCT to practice. Place-based initiatives recognize the environmental factors that influence health outcomes and the importance of supporting both the individual and the community where that individual resides. Because of the shared focus on the social determinants of health, structural causes of poor health, and the intergenerational effects of community conditions, the synergy between these two frameworks is useful for remediating racial inequities in MCH outcomes.

CASE STUDY: BEST BABIES ZONE INITIATIVE

One example of a place-based initiative that has emerged from the MCH sector is the Best Babies Zone Initiative (BBZ), based at the University of California, Berkeley. In 2012, building on the work of Dr. Michael Lu, the School of Public Health at the University of California, Berkeley, received funding from the W.K. Kellogg Foundation to apply LCT at the neighborhood level in three geographic "zones" to improve reproductive and perinatal outcomes. In its first phase, BBZ launched in three neighborhoods in US cities: Price Hill (Cincinnati, Ohio), Hollygrove (New Orleans, Louisiana), and Castlemont (Oakland, California). Three additional neighborhoods joined BBZ in 2017, participating in technical assistance and peer-learning opportunities that support their community's efforts to reduce infant mortality. The following section provides a case study of BBZ's work in one neighborhood.

Hollygrove is a working-class, predominantly African American neighborhood on the western edge of Orleans Parish in Louisiana. This part of New Orleans had historically dealt with poverty and high crime rates and was still recovering from Hurricane Katrina when BBZ launched in 2012. In that year, US Census data showed that 30% of housing in the neighborhood was vacant, and the majority (56%) of residents struggled with high housing burden.* In addition, residents faced factors common to many low-resource communities, including lower-than-average educational attainment, high rates of unemployment, and intergenerational poverty.[15] Like those in all three participating BBZs, Hollygrove families experienced racial inequities in poor birth outcomes. In 2013, infant mortality in Hollygrove was 14.2 per 1,000 live births, 70% higher than the rate in Orleans Parish (8.2 per 1,000 live births) and more than double the national rate (6.2 per 1,000 live births). Nearly one in five births were preterm (19%) or low birth weight (18%), compared with approximately one in eight in the parish overall.[15]

Hollygrove was selected to participate in the BBZ Initiative because of these identified health and economic inequities, as well as the interest of local champions—Louisiana State University, the City of New Orleans Health Department, and Healthy Start New Orleans—in using place-based strategies to improve community conditions. As a health organization with expertise focusing on birth outcomes, Healthy Start New Orleans

---

*Housing and rental burden is defined as households spending more than 30% of monthly income on rent or mortgage payments.

acted as a "backbone organization,"[16] with dedicated staff who could convene partners, guide cross-sector solutions, and track progress on a set of shared measures for all partners working in the zone.

In addition to these core partners, Hollygrove had an existing social infrastructure to catalyze the work. The neighborhood was home to many long-term residents who were deeply knowledgeable about the community's history, and many of whom were involved in a neighborhood association. A large senior citizen population also had its own active association, despite being displaced from its senior community center following Hurricane Katrina. Finally, a well-established and respected faith-based organization called Trinity Christian Community was already offering community services to Hollygrove residents and was interested in partnering with Healthy Start New Orleans to cultivate community engagement.

BBZ Hollygrove centered its work on the idea of a "public health social movement" in which community members could guide, execute, and sustain a long-term effort to improve health by addressing the conditions that they identified as most salient to their community. Therefore, BBZ Hollygrove focused on community outreach during its first year to gain an understanding of resident needs, build trust, and encourage the participation and leadership of community residents. Key strategies included conducting weekly door-to-door outreach, hosting community conversations to discuss priority issues, and establishing a regular presence in the zone.

On the basis of these early conversations, BBZ Hollygrove identified several key factors that contributed to high levels of community stress, which have been linked to poor birth outcomes. These community priorities included the following:

- Economic opportunity: The lack of well-paying jobs in the community was recognized as a key cause of economic instability, stress, and intergenerational poverty. Residents wanted to accelerate economic development and link residents to available jobs in Hollygrove and throughout the city.
- Education: Residents identified that, to improve their employment opportunities, they needed to address barriers to completing or continuing their education, such as inadequate childcare options and disempowerment.
- Blight: Flooding caused by Hurricane Katrina had increased the number of blighted properties in the community, some of which raised safety concerns because they were being used for illicit activity in key areas of the neighborhood. Residents and staff wanted to track blighted property in the neighborhood and empower residents to advocate to the city for blight reduction and removal.
- Environmental exposure: Hollygrove is bounded to the northwest and northeast by an interstate highway and is traversed by a heavy rail line. Residents raised concerns about their daily exposure to car and train pollution, which increased their risks of immediate health challenges including asthma, and long-term effects such as poor birth outcomes.

To respond to these priorities, BBZ staff and partner organizations began to implement activities not traditionally pursued by MCH organizations. These activities included the following:

- Partnering with the YMCA to bring a high-school equivalency test preparation class to Hollygrove to reduce barriers to attaining additional education.
- Connecting with citywide job training programs to bring job skills support to community residents.
- Training residents to advocate for improvements to the neighborhood's built environment, including how to bring attention to blighted properties.
- Partnering with Tulane University to measure particulate matter in Hollygrove's air and soil, in support of efforts by residents and grass roots organizers to prevent the redirection of additional heavy rail traffic through Hollygrove.
- Hosting community events such as Wellness Days and Back to School Fairs to offer regular health and wellness opportunities, engage other local programs, build community, and reclaim public space.
- Offering healthy food vouchers to community residents through a partnership with the local farm and market.

In addition to these activities, leadership from Healthy Start New Orleans continued to implement "traditional" MCH programs, including reproductive health outreach events, parenting groups, and breastfeeding support.

KEY STRATEGIES

In this case study and other place-based initiatives, several key strategies have been critical for effectively fostering work that improves social and physical environments in communities. This section examines a sample of these strategies (including examples of their deployment in a cross-section of place-based initiatives) and early successes to which they have contributed.

Involve Community Residents Early and Often, With Roles Ranging From Participant to Leader

Actively engaging residents in place-based work contributes to an initiative's sustainability and alignment with community priorities. For example, residents in Hollygrove identified blighted properties as a major community concern. Without talking to the community, BBZ efforts may have missed this community stressor and the existing momentum around this issue. Furthermore, attempting to transform a community from the outside is not only difficult to sustain but also can reproduce harms by reinforcing power dynamics. For example, residents and government agencies in Hollygrove have historically had tense relationships. Although resident engagement does not reverse this history, failing to involve residents at all would have jeopardized the initiative's prospects by continuing to build on already-shaky ground.[17]

While engaging residents throughout the life of a place-based effort is crucial, so too is honoring the capacity of residents to engage. Understanding the various roles that community members can play[18] and creating opportunities to increase participation, leadership, and ownership over programs creates space for resident leaders to engage more deeply in the work. Some residents will only want to be involved as learners or participants in programs designed to meet identified community needs. Regardless of whether residents serve as community experts, partners, or leaders, respecting their time with financial compensation whenever possible shows that their participation is valued as work and that they are crucial to the success of the initiative.

Hire Staff With Diverse Experience to Guide the Work

Seeking out staff and consultants with expertise in other fields—and with the ability to build bridges between the ideologies and networks of these disparate sectors—is paramount to a place-based initiative's success. Many place-based initiatives have begun to make this a more regular part of their hiring criteria. For example, CelebrateOne is an initiative in Columbus, Ohio, that focuses on reducing infant mortality in several key neighborhoods throughout the city.[19] Recognizing the need to address the social and economic causes of health inequities, the initiative employs professionals with backgrounds that span transportation planning, business, public health, and health care, knowing that a diverse range of skills and thinking is important for implementing complex community change efforts that address infant mortality (Patrice Brady, MCRP, and Teresa Long, MD, MPH, oral communication, March 2017).

Identify and Cultivate Shared Values With Cross-Sector Partners

As residents begin to identify priority issues in their neighborhood, they will also begin to highlight the broad array of actors—including nonprofits, businesses, government, and service providers—who influence those issues. Although many (if not all) of these entities may see the importance of each other's work and may even recognize that sector silos inhibit their success, engaging in meaningful cross-sector work still requires a significant investment of time to develop partnerships and begin to speak the same language. Therefore, identifying the shared values that bring organizations together is a critical strategy for place-based initiatives.

One example of this strategy can be found in the CityMatCH Institute for Equity in Birth Outcomes (Equity Institute), a multisite initiative focused on reducing inequities in birth outcomes.[20] As part of their foundational work, each participating city incorporates trainings that discuss race, racism, and the impacts of racism on birth outcomes. Dedicating time to these trainings has helped each Equity Institute to build shared understanding of these principles, gain clarity on the root causes of poor birth outcomes in their communities, and create a touchstone that all partners can return to when orienting their work. Once these common values are established, agreeing on shared goals can begin to propel the direction of a place-based initiative's work.

While starting with clear shared values can guide an initiative's work, they must also accurately reflect the interests of the communities and partners involved to be effective. The California Endowment's 10-year Building Healthy Communities (BHC), for example, began with 10 key outcomes intended to guide cross-sector partners in the planning phase for 14 California place-based initiatives. These outcomes spanned a broad range of factors that influence community health, including health access, community violence, environmental well-being, and economic development. At the five-year mark, however, BHC acknowledged that this approach had been too prescriptive and had required additional work to identify a new set of systems change strategies that better represented these diverse communities, their partners, and their priorities.[21] This key lesson learned demonstrates that a strong foundation for partnership and place-based work is not determined by the sole *existence* of a set of core values but rather by the participatory *process* of identifying, deliberating, and agreeing upon these values.

Build in Opportunities for Early Wins

Because of their emphasis on social determinants of health, place-based initiatives that use LCT acknowledge that change can take years to achieve. This is a product of the focus on addressing entrenched systems of inequity and the challenges that can arise along that path. For practitioners, this slow progress can be trying. However, place-based initiatives do begin to exhibit early evidence of positive change within the first few years, and creating opportunities for these early wins is a key way to keep all parties engaged.

One example of an early win is the "mom's club" formed through the work of the BBZ team in Cincinnati, Ohio. Mothers in the Price Hill neighborhood had expressed interest in having a space for pregnant and parenting women to come together, exchange advice, and find support. In response, BBZ staff at Cincinnati Children's Hospital partnered with an early care and education organization to launch a "mom's club" in Price Hill. Together, these partners hired a resident mom to help facilitate monthly meetings and worked with other local organizations to secure space, guest speakers, and other resources for participants. Over the course of 18 months, this group grew to include dozens of parents (including fathers) and eventually evolved into a "parent council" focused not just on health and social support but also on community activism and parent advocacy. Although it is not a unique project, the success of the "mom's club" helped to build relationships between organizations, created a tangible example of how partners could work together to build protective factors in the community, and energized community residents about ways that they could be involved with projects that contributed to community change.

CHALLENGES

Place-based initiatives have led to neighborhood-scale successes and built resident buy-in and leadership. At the same time, practitioners engaged in these initiatives will openly share that this type of work is challenging and dynamic. Some challenges are not unique to place-based initiatives but can be particularly pronounced given the strategies employed by these efforts. For example, nonprofits often face high turnover because of relatively low salaries, temporary funding, or limited advancement opportunities. Government positions, on the other hand, can be more stable for employees, but may take longer to fill. Both of these human resource issues can interfere with the need to build strong relationships with community residents and partner organizations. Place-based initiatives can plan for this inevitable turnover by creating strong relationships with residents and partners at all levels of the initiative and actively acknowledging the time required to rebuild partnerships when staff leave.

Securing adequate funding is also a perpetual challenge for many community-based organizations. Because place-based initiatives often make a long-term commitment to the community, they face the added challenge of securing stable funding that is also flexible enough to allow for their evolving work. Some foundations have modified their funding models in response to this work; although this has resulted in grants that last 10 or more years, there are few—if any—grants that currently fund place-based initiatives for long enough to witness intergenerational change. Furthermore, the history of place-based initiatives shows that these funding shifts may not be permanent. At the same time that long-term funding is critical, short-term funding is also an important resource for experimenting with early projects that build trust and momentum. Leveraging short-term grants to achieve early wins is one way to build strong relationships with partner organizations and pave the way for future opportunities to apply for grants together, or share grants between key members of the collaborative.

Similarly, coordinating a collaborative of partners is not unique to place-based initiatives but is nonetheless part of what makes place-based work difficult. Deciding on shared goals and managing shared projects requires a significant investment of time, trust, and communication; working with cross-sector partners with different practices or jargon can further complicate this process. Though time and trust may be the solutions to this challenge, they do not come easily to the work. Even when all parties have genuine intentions and committed staff, trust will develop slowly and will likely stumble, and time will always be in short supply. While initiatives are encouraged to be intentional in how they establish trust and shared understanding among partners, they are also advised to remember that maintaining these key elements is an ongoing process.

In addition to these implementation challenges, many place-based initiatives are still determining how to evaluate change. A place-based initiative may be interested in several different issues that all take many years to change and can be difficult to measure at the neighborhood scale. Collaborative projects applying LCT, for example, have struggled with how to measure progress toward reducing racial inequities in birth outcomes. Because LCT posits that birth outcomes are influenced by cumulative exposures over one's lifetime, it can be difficult to settle on a small set of metrics that indicate positive movement. One strategy to address this has been to acknowledge that many measures are tied to place-based work and to focus on a few that are key to a particular initiative. For example, BBZ has identified 13 community-level indicators associated with its broader objectives for community transformation, including preterm birth rates, income inequality, employment opportunities, and high-school graduation rates. Although a zone may not focus on each indicator equally over time, having these indicators—and recognizing that some will improve more rapidly than others—helps to establish the initiative's scope. Incorporating measures across sectors can also be a useful way of creating space for non-MCH partners and respecting the work already occurring in those sectors.

Focusing on the "upstream" causes of poor birth outcomes can also make it challenging to measure the immediate results of an initiative's work. In BBZ Hollygrove, for example, drawing a line between birth outcomes and resident advocacy to prevent pollution is challenging, if not impossible. As a result, collecting and emphasizing qualitative data is a critical part of place-based evaluation. While quantitative indicators will continue to remain important, qualitative methods capture progress on indispensable aspects of a place-based initiative such as partnership development, capacity building, and shifting paradigms.

Finally, it can be challenging to break with a status quo, wherein grant-funded organizations receive "credit" for a discrete number of clients served that they can include in grant reports. For example, a grant-funded community-based organization may be a key partner in a collaborative effort that has a positive impact in the community. While this effort requires the organization's grant-funded resources, the organization may find it difficult to quantify how many people benefited, or how much of this benefit can be "attributed" to one particular grant. By definition, place-based initiatives rely on collaboration and must continue to grapple with explaining to funders and other key stakeholders how their investment bolsters the success of the entire collaborative.

SUCCESSES

Despite these persistent challenges, place-based initiatives have also produced early successes that point to their continued potential to effect sustainable change at the community level. Notably, the emphasis on community organizing has contributed to resident activism. For example, BBZ Hollygrove's collaboration with Tulane University produced data that helped staff and residents understand current exposure to air and soil pollution. The timing of this data collection was particularly opportune, as other local organizers were rallying opposition to a proposed increase in Hollygrove's heavy rail traffic from two trains per day to 27 trains per day. Resident activism that incorporated data on the link between Hollygrove's particulate matter and poor birth outcomes was used by city council members to advocate—and eventually vote—against this additional rail traffic.

Initiatives that have had more time to mature have also seen long-term successes. Atlanta, Georgia's East Lake community, part of the Purpose-Built Communities initiative, has worked for more than 20 years to transform housing, improve schools, bolster social cohesion, and disrupt cycles of poverty. Over this time period, the community has seen decreased violent crime, increased employment, and early signs that children growing up in the community will have greater economic and educational opportunities.[22] Other initiatives, such as the Harlem Children's Zone (HCZ), have seen improved health outcomes associated with their work. In the case of HCZ, efforts to improve the screening and diagnosis of children with asthma led to decreased incidence and severity of asthma attacks among children in the zone.[9]

In addition to these changes at the local level, place-based initiatives have been a useful tool for continuing to shift the national public health paradigm from medical and behavioral interventions to systems change solutions that address the root causes of health inequity. For maternal and child organizations in particular, they have created space to test interventions that might otherwise be considered "non-MCH" or even "non–public health." In New Orleans, for example, Healthy Start New Orleans was able to try its hand at addressing educational attainment as part of BBZ. Furthermore, place-based initiatives have pushed other organizations to see where their work fits into public health. In MCH, focusing on the neighborhood and expanding the conversation to the entire life course has helped partners to see the connections between their work, community opportunity, and birth outcomes. Bringing these stakeholders together yields better short-term solutions and builds a foundation for future partnerships that address the root causes of poor health.

CONSIDERATIONS FOR PRACTITIONERS

The groundswell of interest in place-based initiatives has been accompanied by literature that explores the communities and practitioners leading this work, including those focused specifically on MCH issues. This chapter only scratches the surface of the experiences, results, and insights gained in this field. A number of practical steps and resources for practitioners interested in learning more about these efforts or bringing these strategies to their own work are provided in this section.

Connect With Other Local and National Place-Based Initiatives

Practitioners have found success by communicating with other efforts within or across cities. Sharing challenges, successes, and ideas for new directions with like-minded professionals both normalizes the dynamic nature of place-based work and provides a learning network to spread effective ideas and build support across initiatives or sites.

Place-based initiatives should start by becoming familiar with other initiatives in their own city. Establishing these positive relationships can mitigate tensions that may arise from working on the same "turf" and can create room for shared local learnings. Reaching out to local networks to find out about other initiatives is the first step to getting connected to this work.

Nationally, many multisite initiatives have learning networks, such as the PolicyLink's Promise Neighborhoods Institute or University of California Berkeley's BBZ Technical Assistance Center. Many other online and in-person forums—such as FSG and the Aspen Institute's Collective Impact Forum—also host lively conversations about place-based work. Engaging with these forums will expose practitioners to others undertaking similar work across the country.

Beyond connecting with other place-based initiatives, practitioners are encouraged to forge partnerships with other local and national efforts focused on social change. For example, BBZ has increasingly positioned its own pursuit of a "public health social movement" within the larger national context for political and social change. While efforts such as Black Lives Matter or the Fight for $15 do not label themselves as place-based initiatives, connecting and aligning with these and other similar movements can offer additional opportunities to strengthen local successes.

Explore Examples of Successful Cross-Sector Collaboration

While the opportunity to forge new partnerships and engage in innovative work can be exciting for some organizations, it can feel daunting to others. Drawing on previous examples of cross-sector collaboration (both contemporary and historical) can help to guide organizations as they explore possibilities and gives them models that allow them to practice their cross-sector skills. Given the renewed interest in this arena, many organizations—including the Build Healthy Places Network, The Intersector Project, and the Robert Wood Johnson Foundation—have created libraries of cross-sector collaboration case studies, guidance, and lessons learned that MCH practitioners can turn to when contributing to their own cross-sector efforts.

Establish a Framework and Infrastructure to Support Collaboration

Because collaboration is integral to the success of a place-based initiative, practitioners are encouraged to identify a guiding framework that helps partners to understand what the process will look like and what role they might be expected to play. Some initiatives have found success by using the Collective Impact framework, a structured approach in which a "backbone organization" guides multiple partners in activities that support a common agenda measured by shared indicators.[16] This framework does not work for all collaboratives or place-based initiatives; however, identifying similar guiding principles for the specific partners and organizations involved can help to set expectations for the collaborative process.

Regardless of the framework, strong collaboration infrastructure can help to facilitate successful partnerships for a place-based initiative, particularly among organizations that are forging new relationships. Taking steps to define this infrastructure—such as identifying a governance structure or establishing memoranda of understanding—can clarify roles and provide a touchstone to return to if and when conflict arises. For example, when the Near Eastside neighborhood of Indianapolis, Indiana, joined BBZ in 2017, partner organizations established data-sharing agreements among themselves. These agreements established parameters that help the group move toward shared metrics and indicators and have been crucial for creating clear guidelines for ethical and responsible data sharing.

Seek Out Expertise Across Disciplines

As described in this chapter, place-based initiatives draw from a long history that spans disciplines as diverse as city planning, public health, social work, microfinance, education, community organizing, and critical race theory. As a result, a wealth of knowledge and experience can be used to inform implementation. Literature specific to place-based initiatives or community change initiatives can be found in almost all of these disciplines and can be a natural starting point for learning more. Practitioners are also encouraged to seek out in-depth expertise in these disciplines. BBZ has done this by convening an annual advisory board composed of cross-sector leaders whose perspectives help staff to guide implementation and provide context to their work. Other initiatives have taken steps to hire staff with academic or practical experience from fields outside public health. Circulating job openings through non–public health networks, partners, or venues can increase the likelihood of finding strong candidates with cross-disciplinary skills. Alternatively, encouraging staff to participate in trainings offered by local partner organizations or national affinity groups can expand an organization's exposure to other fields. Although these trainings may not be a solution unto themselves, they can open the door to better understanding, deeper engagement, and stronger partnerships that support an organization's ability to participate in a place-based initiative.

Furthermore, seeking out staff who have experienced similar circumstances to those in the community—by virtue of their racial, cultural, geographic, religious, or economic backgrounds—can expand the lens through which a place-based initiative views its possible community engagement, program, and partnership strategies. Actively striving for diversity in a place-based initiative's workforce not only strengthens the initiative's work but also reinforces the larger mission of achieving equity. Place-based initiatives benefit immensely from valuing lived experience on equal footing with academic credentials or professional experience whenever possible, whether at the organizational level or within the hiring committee's decision-making process. By backing these hiring practices with professional development opportunities that fully support staff in their roles, place-based initiatives can improve their prospects for retaining staff, building long-term relationships with the community, and fostering strategies with the best chances of success.

Build on Previous Monitoring and Evaluation Work

Mirroring the growth in place-based initiatives, common practices for evaluating these complex initiatives have also taken shape over the past 20 years. Although no gold standard in place-based evaluation exists, many initiatives have turned to similar frameworks, timelines, and indicators to monitor their work. For example, developmental evaluation has gained popularity as a framework because of its ability to respond to the evolution of complex, innovative initiatives.[23] Place-based initiatives also tend to rely heavily on a mixed-method approach that helps to capture data on quantitative changes in community indicators and qualitative changes in momentum, voice, and political visibility, as well as the steps that helped to achieve those changes.

Many initiatives, including BBZ, have also created evaluation timelines that clarify the multiple stages of progress and highlight short-, mid-, and long-term outcomes. Compilations of life course indicators can inform what outcomes are appropriate for the initiative and where they fit into this long-term trajectory.[24] Practitioners embarking on new place-based initiatives can benefit from these methods and lessons, even as they continue to evolve.

Incorporate Elements of Place-Based Practice That Advance the Work

Although practitioners may see the need for a place-based approach in their community, implementing a place-based initiative may not always be feasible. For example, CityMatCH's Equity Institute works specifically with city and county health departments, who may find it politically untenable to focus resources on one particular neighborhood rather than the entire city. When a place-based initiative is not the right approach, elements of place-based practice can still inform and advance an organization's efforts. Practitioners are therefore encouraged to incorporate elements and strategies of place-based practice—such as a focus on resident engagement, cross-sector collaboration, or the links between people and place—that are best suited to their organization and approach to community change. For example, although many of the Equity Institute participants do not consider themselves place-based, they do focus on mapping their city's birth outcomes data. This process highlights the concentration of poor birth outcomes in specific neighborhoods and builds the case for a "targeted universalism" that improves a city's overall goals by making additional resources and supports available for residents experiencing the greatest inequities.[25]

Given the resources, time, and dedication required for a place-based initiative, practitioners, residents, and partners are encouraged to work together to explore whether a place-based initiative is the appropriate approach for their community. Understanding the different components, barriers, and potential successes will shed light on which strategies work best for a particular community and whether individual elements of a place-based approach can be used to strengthen existing work.

Keep Striving to Address the Structural Causes of Inequity

Place-based initiatives emerged to address poverty, violence, and poor health outcomes in communities across the United States. Although the root causes of these conditions vary from place to place, it must be acknowledged that they emerged from a history of policies and institutionalized racism that systematically limited opportunity for certain communities. Practitioners must understand that partners will come to this work with different awareness of these structural inequities and varying degrees of readiness or comfort to discuss these histories. Educating leaders on institutional and organizational equity is an ongoing process that will need to be continually revisited as leadership changes, as political opportunities shift, and as organizations become more willing to discuss and address the structural causes and resulting traumas of inequity. Place-based initiatives are encouraged to seek out organizations and resources that can facilitate these conversations about racial equity.

CONCLUSIONS

Place-based initiatives have taken many forms over the past century, from nascent community development efforts, to federally driven tax incentives in urban areas, to the diverse and wide-reaching initiatives seen today. The components that overlap with LCT—including the focus on a broad spectrum of risk and protective factors, the recognition of the accumulation of health and wealth over generations, and the emphasis on addressing persistent racial inequities in health outcomes—make place-based initiatives particularly promising for MCH practice.

Beyond these theoretical underpinnings, place-based initiatives and MCH have another similarity: they continue to tackle some of the same problems that brought them into existence. Just as MCH practitioners are still determining how to eliminate racial inequities in birth outcomes, place-based initiatives are still searching for the best solutions for decreasing poverty and improving economic opportunity. Signs of success— early, small, or large—can be used to shape the ways that place-based initiatives are implemented and the ways that MCH practitioners can utilize place-based principles in their work. As more organizations experiment with elements of place-based work, the knowledge about what works and what is possible will keep growing. By building on these histories, lessons, and best practices, practitioners can continue working to support healthy families, neighborhoods, and communities.

KEY POINTS

- Place-based initiatives are collaborative endeavors to direct resources to neighborhoods to improve the social, economic, and/or built environments.
- Place-based initiatives have a long history in the United States and have evolved since the 1960s into a field focused on advancing a broad portfolio of community improvements.
- Strategies of life course–informed place-based initiatives include the following:
  o Involving community residents early and often,
  o Hiring staff with diverse experience to guide the work,
  o Identifying and cultivating shared values with cross-sector partners, and
  o Building in opportunities for early wins.
- The following are recommendations for practitioners interested in learning or doing more:
  o Connect with other local and national place-based initiatives.
  o Explore examples of successful cross-sector collaboration.
  o Establish a framework and infrastructure to support collaboration.
  o Seek out expertise across disciplines.
  o Build on previous monitoring and evaluation work.
  o Incorporate elements of place-based practice that advance the work.
  o Keep striving to address the structural causes of inequity.

RESOURCES

To learn from other local and national place-based initiatives:

- Best Babies Zone: http://www.bestbabieszone.org.
- CityMatCH: http://www.citymatch.org.
- FSG and the Aspen Institute's Collective Impact Forum: http://www.collectiveimpactforum.org.

To explore examples of successful cross-sector collaboration:

- County Health Rankings and Roadmaps What Works for Health series: http://www.countyhealthrankings.org/roadmaps/what-works-for-health.
- The Intersector Project's case studies library: http://www.intersector.com/case-library.

To learn about Collective Impact as a framework for collaboration:

- Stanford Social Innovation Review's roundup of articles on Collective Impact: https://ssir.org/articles/entry/collective_impact.

- Mark Cabaj and Liz Weaver's reflections on Collective Impact's evolution and a vision for Collective Impact "3.0":
http://www.tamarackcommunity.ca/library/collective-impact-3.0-an-evolving-framework-for-community-change.

To build on previous monitoring and evaluation work:

- The Federal Reserve Bank of San Francisco and the Nonprofit Finance Fund's Investing in Results: http://www.investinresults.org.
- Improving the Outcomes of Place-Based Initiatives: http://www.frbsf.org/community-development/publications/community-investments/2010/march/place-based-initiatives-outcomes-improvement.

To keep striving to address the structural causes of inequity:

- Customized racial equity resource guide: W.K. Kellogg Foundation's Racial Equity Resource Guide: http://www.racialequityresourceguide.org.
- Free online course on health inequity: National Association of County and City Public Health Officials Roots of Health Inequity: http://www.rootsofhealthinequity.org.
- Tools and resources on racial equity for government institutions: Local and Regional Government Alliance on Race and Equity tools and resources:
http://www.racialequityalliance.org/tools-resources.
- Findings from the Aspen Institute and the Jacobs Center's Connecting Communities Learning Exchange:
https://www.aspeninstitute.org/publications/resident-centered-community-building-what-makes-it-different.

REFERENCES

1. Lantz PM, Lichtenstein RL, Pollack HA. Health policy approaches to population health: the limits of medicalization. *Health Aff (Millwood)*. 2007;26(5):1253–1257.

2. Pies C, Kotelchuck M. Bringing the MCH life course perspective to life. *Matern Child Health J*. 2014;18(2):335–338.

3. The Center on Philanthropy and Public Policy, Sol Price Center for Social Innovation, Sol Price School of Public Policy, University of Southern California. *Place-Based Initiatives in the Context of Public Policy and Markets:Moving to Higher Ground*. 2015. Available at: https://socialinnovation.usc.edu/files/2014/12/Prioritizing-Place-Moving-to-Higher-Ground.pdf. Accessed November 11, 2017.

4. von Hoffman A. The past, present and future of community development in the United States. In: Andrews N, Erickson D, eds. *Investing in What Works for America's Communities*. San Francisco, CA: The Federal Reserve Bank of San Francisco and Low Income Investment Fund; 2012:10–54.

5. O'Connor A. Community action, urban reform, and the fight against poverty: The Ford Foundation's Gray Areas program. *J Urban Hist*. 1996;22(5):586–625.

6. Adler G. Community action and maximum feasible participation: an opportunity lost but not forgotten for expanding democracy at home. *Notre Dame J Law Ethics Public Policy*. 2012; 8(2):547.

7. Bondonio D, Engberg JB. Enterprise Zones and local employment: evidence from the states' programs. *Reg Sci Urban Econ*. 2000;30(5):519–549.

8. Benjamin L, Rubin JS, Zielenbach S. Community development financial institutions: current issues and future prospects. *J Urban Aff*. 2004;26(2):177–195.

9. Kubisch AC, Auspos P, Brown P, Dewar T. Community change initiatives from 1990–2010: accomplishments and implications for future work. *Community Invest*. 2010;22(1):8–12.

10. Harlem Children's Zone. History: The beginning of the Children's Zone. Available at: http://hcz.org/about-us/history. Accessed May 29, 2017.

11. Covered California. Health coverage options for pregnant women. Available at: http://www.coveredca.com/individuals-and-families/getting-covered/pregnant-women. Accessed May 29, 2017.

12. Coulton C, Chan T, Mikelbank K. Finding place in community change initiatives: using GIS to uncover resident perceptions of their neighborhoods. *J Community Pract*. 2011;19(1): 10–28.

13. Teitz M. Neighborhood economics: local communities and regional market. *Econ Dev Q*. 3(2):111–122.

14. Lu MC, Halfon N. Racial and ethnic disparities in birth outcomes: a life-course perspective. *Matern Child Health J*. 2003;7(1):13–30.

15. Pies C, Barr M, Strouse C, Kotelchuck M; Best Babies Zone Initiative Team. Growing a Best Babies Zone: lessons learned from the pilot phase of a multi-sector, place-based initiative to reduce infant mortality. *Matern Child Health J*. 2016;20(5):968–973.

16. Turner S, Merchant K, Kania J, Martin E. Understanding the value of backbone organizations in Collective Impact. *Stanf Soc Innov*. July 2012. Available at: https://ssir.org/articles/entry/understanding_the_value_of_backbone_organizations_in_collective_impact_1. Accessed May 29, 2017.

17. *Best Babies Zone Year 5 Evaluation Report*. Best Babies Zone, UC Berkeley School of Public Health. 2017. Available at: http://www.bestbabieszone.org/data. Accessed November 21, 2017.

18. Arnstein SR. A ladder of citizen participation. *J Am Inst Plann*. 1969;35(4):216–224.

19. City of Columbus City Council. *Greater Columbus Infant Mortality Task Force Final Report and Implementation Plan*. 2014. Available at: http://celebrateone.info/wp-content/uploads/2015/06/IMTF-2014-Final-Report-FINAL.pdf. Accessed May 29, 2017.

20. CityMatCH. Institute for Equity in Birth Outcomes. Available at: http://www.citymatch.org/projects/institute-equity-birth-outcomes-0. Accessed May 30, 2017.

21. The California Endowment. *A New Power Grid: Building Healthy Communities at Year 5.* 2016. Available at: http://www.calendow.org/wp-content/uploads/BHC_Halftime_Report_2016.pdf. Accessed May 28, 2017.

22. Naughton C. An outcomes-based approach to concentrated poverty. In: *What Matters: Investing in Results to Build Strong, Vibrant Communities.* San Francisco, CA: The Federal Reserve Bank of San Francisco and Low Income Investment Fund; 2017. Available at: http://investinresults.org/book. Accessed May 31, 2017.

23. Parkhurst M, Preskill H, Lynn J, Moore M. The case for developmental evaluation. *FSG Blog.* March 2016. Available at: http://www.fsg.org/blog/case-developmental-evaluation. Accessed May 29, 2017.

24. Callahan T, Stampfel C, Cornell A, et al. From theory to measurement: recommended state MCH life course indicators. *Matern Child Health J.* 2015;19(11):2336–2347.

25. Powell J. Race, place, and opportunity. *Am Prospect.* September 21, 2008. Available at: http://prospect.org/article/race-place-and-opportunity. Accessed May 29, 2017.

6

Integrating Life Course Into Evidence-Based Home Visiting

Carol Brady, MA, and Faye Johnson, BS

Evidence-based practice and its application to service delivery models have shaped health and social services for at-risk families for more than a decade. Driven by increased scrutiny of public expenditures and pressure to demonstrate that interventions actually work, more public and private funders have prioritized the use of evidence-based interventions to address identified needs at both the family and community level.[1] Nowhere has this been more apparent than in the field of home visiting, in which public policy, funding, and advocacy by model developers have contributed to the spread of a set of home visiting models and positioned them as the gold standard of early childhood interventions.[2-4]

How does the focus on evidence-based practice and its application to service delivery programs align with a Life Course Approach? Expanded use of evidence-based models in the home visiting sector offers an opportunity to examine this question and, in the process, provide insight into how well Life Course Theory (LCT) is integrated into service delivery and the potential for increasing its impact.

Evidence-based home visiting models offer structured, prescriptive interventions that have demonstrated, through research and evaluation, positive effects on maternal and child health and wellness for enrolled families. Reflecting a key tenet of the LCT, these programs aim to decrease risks and boost protective factors for vulnerable families.[5] In addition, these programs have an impact on women and their children at a critical period of time: pregnancy and the early years of rapid infant brain development following birth. Moreover, the National Academy of Medicine and others have cited home visiting as a promising strategy for addressing the social determinants of health and health disparities on an individual level.[6] Bolstering services and resources as well as reducing barriers and risks can help close disparities and optimize health and wellness over a person's life.

Home visiting programs also offer the opportunity for multigenerational impact—serving mothers and infants with effects that may ripple out to grandparents. Evidence-based home visiting models, however, have encountered challenges with scaling their impact and consistent replication of results, particularly on a population level.[7] Are there ways home visiting models could be enhanced to better align with LCT and achieve a greater impact? Experience suggests that the answer is yes and that consumer voice and community-driven services are key.

This chapter reviews the evolution and growth of home visiting and its role in supporting a Life Course Approach to maternal and child health. Inherent challenges in implementing evidence-based home visiting models at both the individual and population level are examined. This chapter draws from the work of researchers and thought leaders, as well as the authors' extensive experience in implementing both evidence-based and community-driven programs for women and children in high-need, low-resourced neighborhoods. Finally, the chapter provides examples of how life course strategies have been used to expand the impact of home visiting and offers recommendations for practitioners who may wish to foster change.

HOME VISITING: GROWTH AND CURRENT STATUS

Home visiting is a service delivery strategy that provides direct support and coordination of services to families in their homes. Program components vary but generally include (1) education in effective parenting and childcare techniques; (2) education on child development, health, safety, and nutrition; (3) assistance in gaining access to support networks through group activities; and (4) assistance for parents in obtaining education, employment, and access to community services.[8] Depending on the home visiting model, services are delivered by a range of health and social service staff trained to deliver a structured intervention at a meaningful intensity and duration.

Home visiting as a strategy for providing public health and early education dates back to the 19th century in the United States. Early efforts, part of the Settlement House movement, were supported by wealthy philanthropists who sought to provide immigrants and the urban poor with social support and a "mentor/model" to help lift them out of poverty.[9] Interest in home visiting as an antipoverty strategy grew during the 1960s as part of the War on Poverty.[10] Efforts to increase educational opportunities and "level the playing field" for poor children during this period led to investments in programs such as Head Start, as well as a renewed interest in home-based services as a strategy for supporting low-income parents in raising children who entered school ready to learn.[11] A decade later, public health experts embraced home visiting as a strategy to prevent child abuse and neglect.[12] Research by David Olds and preliminary outcomes from the Hawaii Healthy Start program[13-15] added credence to home visiting as an effective prevention approach. This research also introduced the concept of using a defined "model" to consistently achieve desired outcomes. As a result, home visiting became more structured and less flexible as an intervention, with "model fidelity" a dominant concern. Less attention was paid to broader community factors or individual family characteristics. A "model" program was expected to deliver the same services and achieve the same outcomes regardless of location or participants. Flexibility and significant variations in implementation were viewed as a problematic to achieving desired results.

Buoyed by research and evaluation results, the US Advisory Board on the Prevention of Abuse and Neglect in 1993 recommended the adoption of federal legislation to provide universal, voluntary home visiting with a goal of supporting positive family interaction.[16] The recommendation stimulated small investments in home visiting by a variety of federal agencies over the next decade. The focus of home visiting was subsequently broadened to include child development and school readiness with the introduction of the Education Begins at Home Act in 2004.[17]

In 2008, at the request of the George W. Bush Administration, the Agency for Children and Families (ACF) launched the first significant national Home Visiting Initiative and provided 17 states with $10 million in competitive funding to encourage investment of existing funding streams into evidence-based home visiting models. Many states embraced this approach and invested tobacco settlement dollars and other funding into home visiting programs.

With its emphasis on "evidence-based home visiting models," ACF funding represented a significant shift for the sector. Home visiting moved from a service delivery strategy to a reliance on a set of specific models that offered more structured, manual-centered interventions based on extensive research and evaluation. Key examples include the Nurse–Family Partnership and Healthy Families America. These and other home visiting models established national offices and created infrastructure to support local replication sites. Community service providers interested in implementing one of these models were required to demonstrate need and capacity and to receive approval from the model developer. Model developers, in turn, generally provide required training and ongoing technical assistance to local affiliate sites, charging fees for these services. The relationship between local sites and the national office of the model developer is not unlike a franchise model in the business world. Model developers also require periodic reporting of service delivery data at least annually to maintain affiliate status. Some models, such as Nurse–Family Partnership, require use of the model's data system, which facilitates monitoring and reporting on key required elements. The model developer has an ongoing relationship with sites and works with local implementing agencies to ensure "model fidelity"—that is, program implementation that adheres to specific requirements demonstrated through research to produce desired outcomes.

Before the ACF initiative was fully implemented and evaluated, federal investment in evidence-based home visiting was expanded significantly in 2010 as part of the Patient Protection and Affordable Care Act (ACA).[18] The Maternal, Infant, and Early Childhood Home Visiting Program (MIECHV) was established in the federal legislation and significant resources—originally authorized and funded for $1.5 billion over five years—were provided to states to implement selected models that were deemed "evidence-based" in "high-need" communities. Although home visiting as a service delivery strategy was already a part of multiple public health initiatives, including the federal Healthy Start program and many state birth outcome improvement efforts, what distinguished the

MIECHV program was its focus on supporting a specific set of models that demonstrated an impact on key outcomes of child well-being specifically defined in federal legislation. This focus aligned with ACF's efforts and the ACA's emphasis on evidence-based clinical care.

Similar to the Healthy Start program and other federal initiatives, MIECHV focuses on providing services in communities defined as "high-need" on the basis of an assessment of multiple factors that have an impact on outcomes for children. Communities experiencing significantly higher rates of infant mortality and disparities in birth outcomes are priority for federal Healthy Start, while high-need areas for MIECHV are determined on the basis of multiple indicators of maternal and child health, abuse and neglect, domestic violence, crime, educational attainment, poverty, and unemployment. The federal MIECHV legislation also targets specific priority populations for services on the basis of their elevated risk for adverse child outcomes. These include eligible families living in state-designated high-need communities, low-income eligible families, pregnant women aged younger than 21 years, families with a history of abuse or neglect, families affected by substance abuse, families using tobacco in the home, families impacted by low student achievement, families with children who are developmentally delayed or disabled, and military families.[18] It is important to note that home visiting services funded by MIECHV are not limited to these priority groups. However, the federal government closely tracks the population receiving services on the basis of these legislatively mandated priorities and annually reports this information to Congress.

To determine models that qualified for state funding and implementation under MIECHV, in 2009, the US Department of Health and Human Services established the Home Visiting Evidence of Effectiveness (HomVEE) review, which examined published literature and set criteria for assessing the evidence of effectiveness for home visiting programs that target families with pregnant women and children aged birth to 5 years.[19]

On the basis of a comprehensive, multitiered review, home visiting models were determined to be eligible for MIECHV funding if, according to rigorous evaluation, they demonstrated improved outcomes in a minimum number of specific domains, including maternal and child health, child development, prevention of child abuse and neglect, parenting, and economic self-sufficiency. Initial review efforts identified 45 home visiting programs for consideration. Of these, only 16 initially met criteria for inclusion on the Health Resources and Services Administration's (HRSA's) list of evidence-based models eligible for MIECHV funding. This list is dynamic with models included or excluded on the basis of updated research and evaluation results. By 2017, the initial list had grown to 20 home visiting models.[20]

The federally approved list of models includes widely implemented programs such as Healthy Families America, Nurse–Family Partnership, Early Head Start, Home Instruction for Parents of Preschool Youngsters, and Parents as Teachers, as well as programs with more limited dissemination such as Early Start (New Zealand–based), or targeted eligibility such as Family Spirit (Native American families) and the Early Intervention Program for Adolescent Mothers.[20] All of the programs use home visiting as their primary service delivery mechanism and endeavor to reduce social, developmental, and cognitive risk factors experienced by children living in low-income families by assessing their needs, providing education and support, and linking them to services available in the community. Eligibility varies according to model, with some targeting specific groups such as teenagers or first-time mothers. The models vary on when services are initiated with some beginning in pregnancy and others after delivery. There are also differences in staffing, ranging from professional staff such as nurses and mental health counselors to paraprofessionals. Nurse–Family Partnership and Family Connects, for example, employ bachelor's-level registered nurses as home visitors, whereas Healthy Families America and Early Head Start–Home Visiting focus on the knowledge and life experience of a home visitor rather than level of educational attainment. Enrollment by families is voluntary, and model-trained home visitors generally provide services at least monthly for two or more years.

Federal MIECHV legislation requires states to implement evidence-based home visiting models in communities identified as high-need on the basis of a state needs assessment. By law, states are required to report on specific programmatic performance and outcome measures annually to the federal government in six legislatively defined domains: maternal and child health, childhood injuries and abuse and neglect, school readiness, domestic violence, family economic self-sufficiency, and coordination of services.[18]

Home visiting models determined to be evidence-based for the MIECHV program vary in their focus and have an impact on specific risk factors and domains.[21] None of the currently approved home visiting models demonstrate an impact across all six domains, and some affect only one or two outcomes.[20] This is not surprising because MIECHV, through the HomVEE review process, attempted to categorize research and evaluation findings for a diverse group of programs that use home visiting as a primary service delivery strategy into a set of legislatively mandated domains. Model creators generally aimed to address one or more of these domains in developing their programs but had no way of anticipating the breadth of expectations included in MIECHV legislation.

As part of the requirements for receiving MIECHV funding, states must show improvement in a specified number of performance measures and domains annually. States that fail to meet improvement thresholds face additional federal reporting and the imposition of a compliance plan and risk potential loss of funding. With this federal investment, home visiting is positioned as a key strategy for changing the health, social, and economic trajectory of a family through its demonstrated success in resolving individual risks and mitigating adverse community factors.

In 2016, the evidence-based home visiting programs funded by MIECHV provided services to approximately 160,000 parents and children annually in 893 counties in all 50 states, the District of Columbia, and five territories. Nearly three-fourths of participating families had household incomes at or below 100% of the federal poverty guidelines ($24,300 for a family of four), and 44% were at or below 50% of those guidelines ($12,150 for a family of four). The number of children and parents served annually has increased nearly five-fold since 2012, and the number of home visits provided annually reached nearly 1 million in 2016.[22] This growth was in addition to the estimated 400,000 to 500,000 families, or about 3% of all families with children aged younger than 6 years, served by other home visiting programs through other local, state, and federal funding streams.[23] Federal reports to Congress document meaningful achievements by MIECHV-funded implementation sites in identifying developmental delays, intimate partner violence, and maternal depression, with the overwhelming majority (98%) of states demonstrating improvement in at least four of the six benchmark areas previously identified.[24] MIECHV reporting requirements allow the program to report participant- and service-specific information in aggregate across models and states. Few other home visiting efforts have this capacity, at least on a national level.

HOME VISITING THROUGH A LIFE COURSE LENS

Despite this growth and promising results, states and communities have encountered challenges in scaling evidence-based home visiting models, yielding consistent outcomes, and achieving gains at the population and community levels.[25] These challenges are not unique to home visiting and encompass issues commonly experienced when one is moving from research to practice.[26] A life course framework offers insight into some of the challenges experienced in scaling evidence-based home visiting programs and how their implementation could be enhanced to achieve even greater impact. In the following discussion, a life course lens is utilized to examine three challenging areas for the programs: replicating outcomes, family engagement and retention, and missed opportunities for promoting equity.

Implementation Challenges

Interventions deemed evidence-based gain this imprimatur after rigorous study and evaluation that demonstrate a positive effect on specific outcomes. Adherence to model fidelity is a cornerstone of evidence-based interventions and home visiting is no different in this respect. Model fidelity is supported in a variety of ways including staff training provided by model developers; careful supervision to ensure staff compliance with core practices, standards, and principles; detailed service protocols; and model-specific data systems to monitor implementation.[27] Despite a rigorous effort to standardize implementation, models can produce inconsistent and uneven results.[28]

From a life course perspective, differential outcomes are not only expected but also predictable because context matters.[29] The environment—that is, the community—in which home visiting and other evidence-based programs are delivered to families can profoundly alter both the short- and long-term impact of an intervention, regardless of adherence to a program model. In the life course framework, environment encompasses both health and social service systems, as well as broader social determinants such as poverty, housing, transportation, education, racism, and violence.[29] These risk and protective factors underscore the importance of community fit and engagement in both model selection and service delivery.

Experience indicates that the selection of a particular home visiting model for implementation in a community is driven by a variety of considerations, including state priorities, the needs and capacity of local implementing agencies, and marketing by model developers. Most states offer eligible communities an option to choose from a limited number of specific models on the basis of needs identified in the federally required needs assessment. The process for selecting models, however, is often top-down or driven by the capacity and interests of local providers seeking to implement these programs. A Life Course Approach would elevate input by the community, particularly from families potentially eligible for services, in this process.

Ideally, consumers should have a say in determining community needs and deciding what services should be available to address them. The rush to embrace evidence-based home visiting programs, however, has resulted in implementation challenges similar to those experienced in other health, education, and social service arenas.[30] Experience demonstrates that solutions, even if they are data-driven and evidence-based, have a better chance of success if the communities they seek to serve are actively engaged in their selection and implementation. The perils of using a top-down approach are illustrated in recent efforts to reform the Newark, New Jersey, school system. Note Barnes and Schmitz, "Instead of generating excitement among Newark residents about an opportunity to improve results for their kids, the reform plan . . . sparked a massive public outcry. At public meetings, community members protested vigorously against the plan."[30]

The perception that solutions were being imposed without actively involving the community in their development was a key factor contributing to the plan's failure. The authors call for "patient urgency," balancing the desire to quickly put into place programs with a demonstrated impact on family outcomes with the need to engage the community as active partners in selecting and implementing an intervention. Although home visiting is less of a hot-button issue than school reform, the need for community engagement is no less important to achieving change at both the individual and community level. This view is supported by home visiting researchers, who note that local leadership, program champions, and alignment with trusted organizations in a community have an important influence on program acceptance and use.[31,32]

Context also encompasses the resources available in a community, which can have a profound impact on the effectiveness of home visiting. Assessment of individual risk factors and linkage to services are core components of evidence-based home visiting models. Most high-need communities, however, are underresourced and struggle with both availability and access to the services needed to address many of the risks identified by home visitors.[32] For example, if home visitors screen participants for perinatal depression, there must be a provider in the community who can treat mothers identified as depressed. Referral to a provider with limited capacity, cultural competence, payment options, or scope of services is not only ineffective but also could have detrimental impacts on future resource seeking.

Furthermore, the adverse environments in which families live can limit impact and even undo early gains produced by program participation.[32] LCT underscores that interventions focusing solely on individual behavior change will fall short if they fail to take into account the broader social and environmental context in which people live.[29] Yet, addressing broader community factors that have an impact on vulnerable families is well beyond the scope and, some would say, the role of an evidence-based intervention like home visiting. While these programs can successfully affect the trajectory of individual families, they are unlikely by themselves to produce meaningful and sustained change at the community level. Home visiting is an individual, time-limited intervention and its long-term success depends on how effectively it functions as part of a larger public health effort that addresses social determinants at a broader community level.[32]

Engagement

Family engagement and retention are critical to achieving desired outcomes in home visiting and other evidence-based programs. Participation in these programs is voluntary—that is, the family has to agree to enroll, be present for, and actively participate in the required number of home visits and continue through program completion, which usually lasts two or more years. Dosage, the intensity or frequency of contact, and duration in service are associated with program impact on outcomes.[25]

As implementation of evidence-based home visiting models becomes more widespread, programs frequently struggle with missed appointments and families who drop out before completing the prescribed intervention.[31,33] Studies indicate that families generally receive 50% of visits expected by the program model (range of 38% to 56%) with many families (range of 20% to 80%) dropping out of programming early.[25,34] Low engagement and retention is particularly problematic in the highest-risk families who could benefit the most from early intervention, education, and support.[31] Family engagement and retention clearly affects the impact of evidence-based home visiting programs as well as their cost-effectiveness.[32]

Multiple factors influencing family engagement and retention have been identified at the participant, program, and community levels.[31,33] These include how well the model and staff reflect race, culture, and beliefs of the families enrolled; family priorities, attitudes, and previous experiences with services; staff and participant matching; perceived value of the service; and community context.[31,33] Strategies to improve family engagement and retention focus on cultivating and improving referral networks, staff training, and encouraging flexibility in model implementation, such as adapting the content or frequency of required visits, to respond to the preferences and needs of families.[31,33,34]

Family engagement and retention was among the topics addressed in 2014 by MIECHV implementation sites participating in the HRSA-funded Home Visiting Collaborative Improvement and Innovation Network (HV CoIIN). With technical support provided through a cooperative agreement with the Educational Development Corporation, local home visiting programs created and tested actionable strategies to address many of the identified factors that have an impact on family participation.[35] The experience and results of local programs are highlighted in an HV CoIIN toolkit.[36]

While the HV CoIIN included a focus on parent involvement, LCT suggests an additional dimension to consider: family choice. The Life Course Approach underscores the importance of organizing and delivering services in ways that build resiliency and social capital while reducing dependency.[28] Consumer empowerment, in guiding their own care as well as leading change in their communities, is critical to improving outcomes across generations. However, efforts by service providers to cultivate referrals, as well as to recruit and engage potential participants, are frequently influenced by programmatic rather than participant needs. Experience shows that providers often recruit families to fill caseloads and meet the requirements and expectations of funders. Less attention is given to the role of family choice and the importance of developing systems that support consumer-driven services. Competition for resources and market share as well as strongly held beliefs by program providers about model efficacy (e.g., "We're the best!") contribute to this orientation.

As noted previously, evidence-based home visiting models differ in their focus, staffing, programmatic approaches, and impact on specific domains. One size—or a single home visiting model—does not fit all. The common performance measures used by MIECHV to gauge all models, regardless of their focus, has contributed to misunderstandings about differences in program services and their impact on specific risks and populations. Rather than duplicating services, the availability of multiple programs in a community affords families a choice of interventions that could better meet both their needs and preferences. Ensuring families are offered options, in both home- and community-based programs, requires coordination and accountability at the community level and a recognition by funders and policymakers of the unique contributions of different home visiting programs. This requires a systems-based approach for ensuring that families have options and access to services that meet their preferences and needs, while avoiding duplication of effort by multiple programs in a community.

Coordinated Intake and Referral

The Maternal and Child Health Bureau of the US Department of Health and Human Services has challenged states and communities to provide families with access to services in a coordinated manner. The Title V Program, Federal Healthy Start Program, and MIECHV, among other federal programs, include a focus on systems development and a mandate for community- and consumer-driven services. Ideally, community systems of care should be in place to identify at-risk families, assess their needs, and connect them with services. Programs should work together to avoid duplication, facilitate enrollment, and share resources to address gaps in care. Families who seek help should have a role in deciding the services they receive on the basis of both their preferences and needs.

As part of MIECHV, states have started to explore the development of centralized or coordinated intake and referral (CI&R) systems.[37] The goal is to make services more accessible to families by standardizing assessments, streamlining referral processes, reducing duplication, and creating efficiencies for both programs and the families they seek to serve. The level and scope of CI&R varies among states that have attempted to implement systems. Several have developed a state-level system of centralized intake, administered by a state agency, while others have focused on the development of regional or local systems, coordinated by a public health or nonprofit agency, to account for local characteristics and resources. Some states limited CI&R to home visiting or MIECHV-funded programs, while others included a broader range of health, social, and support services.[37] Regardless of level and scope, states testing this approach have followed a similar process, including engagement of program partners, cataloging available services and programs with information about eligibility and capacity, designing a decision tree for referrals, tracking referrals and their disposition, and establishing staff and other infrastructure to sustain and refine CI&R processes.

In a 2016 brief, the National Evidence-Based Home Visiting Model Alliance, which includes representatives from six models, identified three approaches to centralized or coordinated intake: the triage model, the shared decision-making model, and the market model.[38] The first two models are primarily provider- or program-driven, whereas the market model offers the family the most choice. The market model requires all early childhood service providers, including home visiting models, to come together and develop shared material for use in outreach and recruitment efforts. Families are then able to choose which program might be most appropriate to their needs and enroll directly. Providing this choice requires significant collaboration and trust among participating programs, as well as a commitment to engaging consumers in designing processes from the beginning. It requires service providers to intentionally elevate the role of families and acknowledge their centrality in decision making.

Florida adopted the market approach in 2015 when the MIECHV program and other state partners worked in 10 communities to develop and pilot locally driven CI&R systems. The Florida initiative leveraged an established system of maternal and child health service delivery, the state Healthy Start program, which includes statewide universal prenatal and infant risk screening.[39] This screening process had been used since the program's inception in 1991 to identify at-risk pregnant women and infants. Its use was subsequently expanded in 1998 with the implementation of Healthy Families Florida to include identification of families at risk for abuse and neglect. The new project explored how communities could use the Healthy Start infrastructure—which includes community-based nonprofit organizations responsible for developing local systems of care (Healthy Start coalitions)—to more effectively link at-risk families with all available services in their communities.

Family choice, rather than program needs, was prioritized as a central principle of the proposed CI&R process. This focus was driven by the advice of Tana Ebbole, an early childhood leader in the state responsible for designing the Healthy Beginnings system in Palm Beach County.[40] In remarks at the first meeting of the group, Ebbole advised community teams to "focus on families" when encountering competition, mistrust, and other common challenges. Ebbole strongly promoted the concept that honoring family needs, preferences, and choice was key to successful engagement in services. Acknowledging that different programs met different needs for families at different times, she highlighted that families were in the best position to determine "fit" with services. Communities were encouraged to include family representatives on their CI&R planning team and to solicit participant input throughout the development and implementation process.

Although some communities struggled with incorporating the family voice and choice in their efforts, many communities were successful. Most of the pilot sites produced community decision trees, public awareness and outreach material highlighting eligibility requirements and services offered by all programs, and referral and follow-up processes that created true opportunities for family choice. One community even developed a CI&R app for families seeking services. Metrics are being collected to track referrals and enrollment, as well as 90-day retention, to guide community teams in testing and refining their CI&R systems. A forthcoming evaluation will examine the impact of family choice on engagement and retention in home visiting and other early childhood programs. Clearly, however, CI&R looked significantly different in communities that used this approach and required substantially more planning, communications, transparency, and trust among participating agencies.

Equity

Equity is a core concept in LCT. The life circumstances experienced by different population groups contribute to disparities in outcomes and health status. Eliminating these disparities requires action beyond individual interventions or programs; rather, action must address risks and protective factors at the population level and the community changes needed to optimize health and social status across generations.

Home visiting was cited as a key strategy for addressing inequity in the 2010–2015 Health and Human Services Action Plan to Reduce Racial and Ethnic Health Disparities.[41] The plan notes that the program "aims to meet the diverse needs of children and families in at-risk communities, particularly underserved minority women and their families with limited social support networks" by providing "services—including coordination and referrals to other community services—that can lead to improved outcomes in prenatal, maternal, newborn, and child health and development; parenting skills; school readiness; and family economic self-sufficiency."[41]

Yet, home visiting programs have failed to consistently reach and retain the groups most affected by inequity. Racial and ethnic minority participants, for example, typically enroll for shorter periods and receive fewer home visits than nonminorities.[31] Similarly, younger, more economically disadvantaged, unmarried participants and families with limited English language proficiency are difficult to engage and tend to leave programs earlier.[31] Moreover, participants living in especially distressed and chaotic communities are less likely to accept and enroll in program services, according to a MIECHV brief on family enrollment and engagement.[25]

For HRSA and MIECHV administrators, LCT underscores the importance of "using an 'equity lens' to continually assess the potential for differential impact of public health interventions, even those that are evidence-based."[27] Overcoming the challenges of engaging families experiencing the greatest disparities requires intentional efforts on the part of models and local implementation agencies. These include adhering to best practice standards, demonstrating a respect for local cultural norms and customs, and matching home visitors and families by race and parenting status,[31] in addition to understanding the social determinants of health.

Staff training, workforce development, and strengthening cultural competency and humility at the organizational and individual home visitor levels are necessary but insufficient for addressing equity through evidence-based home visiting. By using a life course frame, a deeper dive would acknowledge and develop strategies through home visiting to address the impact of racism in all its forms on allostatic load, as well as individual and multigenerational trauma and stress.[42] There is a growing recognition of the need to expand work to reduce adverse childhood experiences (ACEs) to include racism and racial trauma, as well as community factors that have a disproportionate impact on people of color and other minority groups.[43] The Philadelphia Urban ACE study demonstrated the differential impact of experiencing racism, witnessing violence, and living in unsafe neighborhoods on Blacks and Hispanics, which were added to original ACE questions focusing on physical and emotional abuse and neglect.[44] Efforts to integrate trauma-informed care into home visiting across program models, such as the Neuroscience, Epigenetics, ACEs, and Resilience (NEAR@Home) Toolkit created by MIECHV grantees in HRSA Region X, represent a major step in translating key tenets of the science behind LCT into practice.[45] To fully realize the potential of home visiting, however, efforts like NEAR@Home (available free of charge online) must be expanded to address not only trauma related to physical and emotional abuse and neglect but also trauma attributable to racism.

Although selected home visiting programs have demonstrated an impact on individual life course factors related to the social determinants of health,[46] opportunities remain for strengthening the role these interventions play in promoting equity. Building partnerships between home visiting programs and organizations that address economic security and family self-sufficiency beyond mere referral agreements creates capacity for better serving low-income families.

A unique partnership between Goodwill of Central and Southern Indiana and the National Service Office of Nurse–Family Partnership demonstrates the value of meaningful collaboration in addressing social determinants and improving outcomes for both children and parents. With support from the Aspen Institute, the organizations started working together in 2016 to expand their services in ways that offer greater collective impact for families. Their partnership enables each organization to reach additional families with unique services while also scaling across programs to ensure families have access to wider array of services. The initiative leveraged support and education provided through home visiting to first-time mothers by the Nurse–Family Partnership with adult education, childcare, and wrap-around economic development services provided by Goodwill with a goal of breaking the cycle of intergenerational poverty experienced by the families served by both organizations. Initial work in Indianapolis offers a potential model for replication nationally.[47]

EXPANDING THE LIFE COURSE POTENTIAL OF HOME VISITING

Enhancing the focus of current evidence-based home visiting models on two additional areas would also contribute to better alignment with the Life Course Approach and increase their impact on the trajectory of vulnerable families. Home visiting programs are uniquely positioned to expand interventions as part of a two-generation approach and to contribute to the development of social capital in high-need communities.

Two-Generation Approach

Home visiting programs strive to meet the needs of children and parents together, helping them to achieve economic security through education, increased economic assets, and health and well-being. Strengthening this focus is critical to maximizing the life course potential of home visiting. Both children and parents benefit from equal attention in home visiting programs. Federal MIECHV benchmarks and performance measures ensure all home visiting programs screen caregivers for perinatal depression and intimate partner violence to reduce the child's exposure to trauma and promote healthy child development. MIECHV-funded programs are also measured on their success in promoting family self-sufficiency through parental education and workforce training. Yet, home visiting models could do more, particularly during the interconception period when most attention shifts to the child's health and development. While acknowledging the importance of child outcomes, a stronger focus on supporting parents to plan their next pregnancy, support their relationships, and achieve their life goals, as well as raise healthy and secure children, would better align current home visiting programs with a Life Course Approach.

Unintended pregnancy and short birth intervals, in particular, have profound intergenerational impacts on social determinants of health and equity. Low-income women are more than five times as likely as higher-income women to have an unintended birth.[48] Unintended and mistimed childbearing is associated with higher rates of poverty, less family stability, and worse outcomes for children, contributing to inequality across generations.[49] At least one study has suggested that coupling more effective prebirth interventions such as family planning, good nutrition, and weight loss with postbirth interventions such as parenting support could contribute significantly to the elimination of disparities in adult outcomes.[50]

Revision of federal performance measures in 2016 eliminated measures on interconception intervals and preconception health. The unintended consequence of these changes was to reduce MIECHV's focus on reproductive life planning and interconception health, both important life course strategies for reducing disparities and social inequity.[49] Few interventions, especially those that are clinic- or center-based, provide services to the mother for two years after birth at the intimacy and intensity of a home visiting program. Opportunities abound for an increased emphasis on family planning, parental education and training, relationship building, and other life course issues. These include effective and ongoing contraception counseling; linkage to ongoing women's health services, including mental health care; development of a reproductive life plan; and strong referral relationships to facilitate child care and other supports critical to parental employment and completion of education.

Social Capital

A Life Course Approach has an impact on both the content of interventions and how services are delivered. This includes providing more opportunities for strengthening social supports and relationships beyond the one-to-one relationship between the participant and home visitor. Social connections—the relationships formed with other adults that offer a circle of support—are a critical component of the protective factors framework.[51] High-need, impoverished neighborhoods, in particular, are characterized by higher rates of social isolation.[52-54] Social connections offer critical supports on the individual level and, if expanded, can contribute to upward mobility in low-income families.[51,55]

Selected home visiting models, such as Parents as Teachers (PAT), incorporate group activities in addition to individual interventions. Group Connections is one of four PAT model components and is intended to support positive parent–child interaction through group learning, as well as to improve family functioning by building social connections.[56] Group activities provide an opportunity to promote inter- and independence while building friendships and connection in the community. This can extend to reproductive social capital, which means that community members can better advocate and support policies and programs to improve women's and men's health, the health of their children, and the health of any children they wish to conceive in the future.[57] All home visiting and other early childhood programs should take advantage of opportunities to incorporate group activities into their services consistent with a Life Course Approach.

Home visiting and other early childhood programs also have a unique opportunity to leverage their long-term relationships with families to build the social capital needed to create change at the community level. These programs encourage and support the innate resiliency and motivation of families during the critical period around birth and early childhood. Some parents graduate from home visiting programs empowered and motivated to do more. They recommend the program to others, start alumni groups, serve on community advisory groups—in other words, their leadership has been sparked. Cultivating this leadership spark is not the focus of most home visiting models, although parent leadership is an important component of early childhood and early intervention programs such as Head Start and Title V Children with Special Health Care Needs.[58,59] This is a missed opportunity to transition from individual to community-level interventions, which are key to achieving equity. With support, self-advocacy can evolve into community advocacy, which is critical to ameliorating environmental and social determinants in communities that threaten the health and economic success of families.

The Magnolia Project, a federal Healthy Start project in Jacksonville, Florida, offers an example of how this approach might be operationalized. The project has created a Leadership Academy to build the capacity of residents in a high-need community to effectively participate and create social change. The Leadership Academy is designed for individuals to gain knowledge of the community's impact on poor birth outcomes and to develop leadership skills to mobilize and take action.[60] The 16-week program uses a grass roots leadership curriculum developed by the University of Arizona's Cooperative Extension Service–Arizona Community Training program.[61] Participants are nominated by social service agencies and recruited from Magnolia Project clients. The curriculum was adapted to include a discussion of infant mortality, local icons, the social determinants of health, the roots of inequality, LCT, and racism.

Group discussion and didactic instruction is led by a trained facilitator, which includes interactive sessions. Community field trips are incorporated into the program, including visits to the Kingsley Plantation and La Villa Museum of African American Arts and Culture to broaden their understanding of their community—now characterized primarily by its deficits—and its historic underpinnings and contributions. Participants also attend various city government and civic meetings. Leadership Academy participants develop a community action plan and undertake a year-long community-improvement project. Projects are presented during Leadership Academy graduation ceremonies. Community projects have addressed bullying, neighborhood beautification, father involvement in schools, relocation of unsafe school bus stops, and increasing access to healthy foods. Leadership Academy graduates have been nominated to serve as community representatives on school organizations and nonprofit boards, including the Northeast Florida Healthy Start Coalition and Magnolia Project Community Action Network.[62]

In terms of community and participant engagement, the home visiting sector has much to learn from the federal Healthy Start program and place-based initiatives. Healthy Start is recognized for implementing community-led and consumer-driven strategies to reduce infant mortality.[63] Federal guidance requires Healthy Start projects to organize Community Action Networks (CANs), which serve as "backbone organizations" to address the social determinants of health on a community level.[64] CANs comprise program participants, partner organizations, and other groups that commit to sharing a common goal and agenda and work collectively to ameliorate community conditions that contribute to disparities in birth outcomes. CANs represent an effort to move beyond services for individual program participants into neighborhood-level interventions—a bottom-up approach as opposed to the common top-down approaches. In addition to the CAN, Magnolia has also integrated the life course model throughout its core programming, providing individual-, group-, and community-level services in a women's clinic and through case management that address the social determinants of health.

As Healthy Start moves toward implementing a standard set of core services across sites and MIECHV continues to expand its focus on collective impact, there are opportunities to build on the strengths of both initiatives and achieve even greater impact at both the individual and community level.

KEY STEPS FOR CHANGE

In the previous sections, the use of evidence-based home visiting models was examined to provide insight into how well LCT is integrated into service delivery and how it could be applied to further strengthen interventions in this sector. Many of the points highlighted in this discussion are not unique to home visiting but are also relevant to other early childhood services and settings. The following recommendations are offered for incorporating LCT—specifically focusing on consumer- and community-driven strategies—into home visiting as well as a broader array of health and human services for families.

Engage the Community and Families Who Will Receive Services Early, Starting With the Selection of the Program or Intervention

Practice "patient urgency" when responding to opportunities to develop or expand services in a community. Invest time in engaging community leaders and potential program participants in identifying and prioritizing needs. Obtain ideas and input on how best to address the needs identified. The best way to ensure this happens is to leverage an established relationship—do not wait until there is a request for proposals or funding opportunity! Shared decision making and community buy-in are critical to successful implementation. *Start by* reviewing the Centers for Disease Control and Prevention's *Principles of Community Engagement*[65] and performing an assessment of your organization's readiness[66] to develop meaningful collaborations with families and community leaders.

Elevate the Family Voice in Governance and Service Delivery

Recognize that families are experts in their own care and are more likely to utilize services that are responsive to their needs and concerns. Families are in the best position to provide feedback on what works and what does not work. They are essential partners in ensuring your program or services are culturally appropriate and reflect the values and priorities of the community. Optimize the role of families and their input by making them part of your organization's governance and leadership. *Start by* learning more about the strategies used by the federal Head Start program to involve families in all aspects of their services—from governance to volunteers and employees. In 1967, Head Start became the first child development program to elevate the family voice. It has created a formal framework, which serves as a road map to guide its efforts.[67,68]

Embed Evidence-Based Models and Programs Such as Home Visiting Into Larger Systems of Care and Strengthen Partnerships With Organizations Addressing Social and Economic Determinants

Complex problems experienced by families and communities require multisector, multiagency solutions. Collective Impact takes collaboration to the next level by facilitating systems development and implementation of effective cross-sector strategies. Programs and services have the greatest impact when they leverage other resources and work systematically to create change. Collective Impact is built on a common agenda, shared measurement, mutually reinforcing activities, continuous communication, and backbone leadership. Key concepts of LCT—equity, empowerment, and engagement—form the foundation of Collective Impact. It takes more than one program to change the trajectory of a family or a community. *Start by* exploring the principles of Collective Impact practice and its potential for creating meaningful, lasting change.[69]

Intentionally Focus on Equity and Opportunities to Build Reproductive Social Capital in High-Need Communities

The first step in addressing inequity and disparities is to build a culturally competent and diverse workforce. Enrollment, retention, and performance data by race and ethnicity is critical to gauging success in reaching high-need populations that experience the greatest disparities. Trauma-informed care should explicitly deal with racism and discrimination, in addition to violence and neglect. Group activities and other opportunities to reduce isolation and cultivate peer support contribute to the social capital of a community. Lasting efforts to address social determinants require increasing knowledge across all sectors of the community and the involvement, advocacy, and leadership of residents; organizations serving high-need areas have a key role to play in building leadership skills in program participants. *Start by* assessing the cultural competency and training needs of your organization. Ensure that cultural competency also explores subcultures. The National Center for Cultural Competence has assessment tools and other resources to assist in this process.[70] Consider strategies like those outlined in the Community Tool Box developed by the University of Kansas that your organization can use to strengthen the leadership potential of program participants.[71] Take the next step by deepening the understanding of staff and program participants of racism and its contribution to poverty, trauma, and health inequity. Workshops offered by organizations such as the Racial Equity Institute in North Carolina[72] and the People's Institute for Survival and Beyond in New Orleans, Louisiana,[73] can help both staff and program participants begin this critical journey.

CONCLUSIONS

The use of evidence-based models is an important but partial solution for changing the trajectories of families and communities. The impact of MCH programs such as home visiting can and should be enhanced by applying a Life Course Approach. Aligning strategies to better support the health and well-being of parents, addressing community context, building family leadership, connecting young families with each other, and increasing parent choice reflect life course principles. A laser focus on advancing equity across all home visiting programs would lead to a shift in outcomes on many levels. The strong foundation that home visiting programs provide offers an excellent launching point for innovation and interconnection to improve the trajectory of generations.

KEY POINTS

- Life course and the social determinants of health can be used to contextualize the limitations of evidence-based programs and to suggest ways to enhance the long-term impact of home visiting programs.
- Community and family engagement is critical to the effective implementation of home visiting and other evidence-based programs.
- Home visiting programs offer a two-generation strategy for building reproductive social capital in families and, potentially, communities—provided they are part of a collective impact approach.

RESOURCES

- National Home Visiting Resource Center: https://www.nhvrc.org.
- Home Visiting Evidence of Effectiveness: https://homvee.acf.hhs.gov.
- Home Visiting Collaborative Improvement and Innovation Network: http://hv-coiin.edc.org.
- Nurse–Family Partnership: http://www.nursefamilypartnership.org.
- Parents as Teachers: http://parentsasteachers.org.
- Early Head Start: https://eclkc.ohs.acf.hhs.gov/hslc/tta-system/ehsnrc/about-ehs.
- Healthy Families America: http://www.healthyfamiliesamerica.org.
- The Maternal, Infant and Early Childhood Home Visiting Program: https://mchb.hrsa.gov/maternal-child-health-initiatives/home-visiting-overview.
- Healthy Start: https://mchb.hrsa.gov/maternal-child-health-initiatives/healthy-start.
- THRIVE Washington: https://thrivewa.org/nearhome-toolkit-guided-process-talk-trauma-resilience-home-visiting.
- Zero to Three: https://www.zerotothree.org.
- Center for the Study of Social Policy:http://www.cssp.org/reform/strengtheningfamilies/about.
- Robert Wood Johnson Foundation: https://www.cultureofhealth.org/en/what-were-learning/sentinel-communities.html.
- Ascend at The Aspen Institute: http://ascend.aspeninstitute.org.
- Collective Impact Forum: https://collectiveimpactforum.org.

REFERENCES

1. Johnson MI, Austin MJ. Evidence-based practice in the social services: implications for organizational change. *J Evid Based Soc Work*. 2008;5(1-2):239–269.

2. Karoly LA, Kilburn MR, Cannon JS. Early childhood interventions: proven results, future promise. Santa Monica, CA: RAND; 2005.

3. Boller K, Strong DA, Daro D. Home visiting: looking back and moving forward. Washington DC: Zero to Three; July 2010:4–9.

4. Cole P. The research case for home visiting. Zero to Three. February 2014. Available at: https://www.zerotothree.org/resources/144-the-research-case-for-home-visiting#downloads. Accessed May 20, 2017.

5. Minkovitz CS, O'Neill KM, Duggan A. Home visiting: a service strategy to reduce poverty and mitigate its consequences. *Acad Pediatr*. 2016;16(3 suppl):S105–S111.

6. Adler NE, Cutler DM, Fielding JE, et al. Addressing social determinants of health and health disparities: a vital direction for health and health care. National Academy of Medicine. September 2016. Available at: https://nam.edu/wp-content/uploads/2016/09/Addressing-Social-Determinants-of-Health-and-Health-Disparities.pdf. Accessed February 16, 2017.

7. Goldberg J, Bumgarner E, Jacobs F. Measuring program- and individual-level fidelity in a home visiting program for adolescent parents. *Eval Program Plann*. 2016;55:163–173.

8. The California Evidence-Based Clearinghouse for Child Welfare. Definition for home visiting programs for child well-being. Available at: http://www.cebc4cw.org/topic/home-visiting. Accessed February 16, 2017.

9. Home Visiting. Historical summary. Available at: http://homevisiting.org/history. Accessed February 16, 2017.

10. Park J. A family impact analysis of home visiting programs. Family Impact Analysis Series. University of Wisconsin, Madison, Policy Institute for Family Impact Seminars. 2003. Available at: https://www.purdue.edu/hhs/hdfs/fii/wp-content/uploads/2015/06/fia_analyses_fphvp.pdf. Accessed February 16, 2017.

11. Weiss HB. Home visits: necessary but not sufficient. *Future Child*. 1993;3(3). Available at: https://www.princeton.edu/futureofchildren/publications/docs/03_03_05.pdf. Accessed July 29, 2017.

12. Kempe CH. Approaches to preventing child abuse: the health visitor concept. *Am J Dis Child*. 1976;130(9):941–947.

13. Olds DL, Henderson CR, Tatelbaum R, Chamberlin R. Improving the delivery of prenatal care and outcomes of pregnancy: a randomized trial of nurse home visitation. *Pediatrics*. 1986;77(1):16–28.

14. Olds DL, Henderson CR, Tatelbaum R, Chamberlin R. Preventing child abuse and neglect: a randomized trial of nurse home visitation. *Pediatrics*. 1986;78(1);65–78.

15. Duggan AK, McFarlane EC, Windham AM, et al. Evaluation of Hawaii's Healthy Start Program. *Future Child.* 1999;9(1):66–90.

16. Krugman RD. Universal home visiting: a recommendation from the US Advisory Board on Child Abuse and Neglect. *Future Child.* 1993;3:185–191.

17. S.2412 Education Begins at Home Act. 108th Congress. Available at: https://www.congress. gov/bill/108th-congress/senate-bill/2412. Accessed December 3, 2017.

18. Congressional Research Service. Maternal and Infant Early Childhood Home Visiting (MIECHV) Program: background and funding. February 15, 2017. Available at: https://www. everycrsreport.com/reports/R43930.html#fn10. Accessed May 23, 2017.

19. US Department of Health and Human Services, Office of Planning, Research, and Evaluation. Home visiting programs: reviewing evidence of effectiveness. June 2014. Available at: http://homvee.acf.hhs.gov/HomVEE-Brief2014-13.pdf. Accessed March 20, 2017.

20. US Department of Health and Human Services, Administration for Children and Families. Home visiting evidence of effectiveness. Available at: https://homvee.acf.hhs.gov. Accessed March 20, 2017.

21. Osborne C. Home visiting programs: four evidence-based lessons for policymakers. *Behav Sci Policy.* 2016;2(1):29–36.

22. The Maternal, Infant, and Early Childhood Home Visiting Program: partnering with parents to help children succeed. Washington, DC: US Department of Health and Human Services, Health Resources and Services Administration, Administration for Children and Families; 2017. Available at: https://mchb.hrsa.gov/sites/default/files/mchb/MaternalChildHealthInitiatives/ HomeVisiting/pdf/programbrief.pdf. Accessed December 3, 2017.

23. Congressional Research Service. Home visitation for families with young children, February 3, 2010. Available at: https://www.everycrsreport.com/reports/R40705.html. Accessed February 10, 2017.

24. Demonstrating improvement in the Maternal, Infant, and Early Childhood Home Visiting Program: A report to Congress. Washington, DC: US Department of Health and Human Services, Health Resources and Services Administration, Administration for Children and Families; March 2016. Available at: https://mchb.hrsa.gov/sites/default/files/mchb/MaternalChildHealthInitiatives/ HomeVisiting/pdf/reportcongress-homevisiting.pdf. Accessed December 3, 2017.

25. Maternal, Infant, and Early Childhood Home Visiting Technical Assistance Coordinating Center. MIECHV issue brief on family enrollment and engagement. July 2015. Available at: https://mchb.hrsa.gov/sites/default/files/mchb/MaternalChildHealthInitiatives/HomeVisiting/ tafiles/enrollmentandengagement.pdf. Accessed March 10, 2017.

26. Suplee LH, Metz A. Opportunities and challenges in evidence-based social policy. *Soc Policy Rep.* 2015;28(4):3–11.

27. Daro D. Replicating evidence-based home visiting models: a framework for assessing fidelity. Evidence based cross-site evaluation. Issue Brief 3. Available at: http://supportingebhv.org/crossite. Accessed May 23, 2017.

28. Daro D, Hart B, Boller, K, Bradley MC. Replicating home visiting programs with fidelity: baseline data and preliminary findings. US Department of Health and Human Services, Administration for Children and Families. December 2012. Available at: http://www.chapinhall.org/research/report/replicating-home-visiting-programs-fidelity-baseline-data-and-preliminary-findings. Accessed May 1, 2017.

29. Fine A, Kotelchuck M. Rethinking MCH: the life course model as an organizing framework concept paper. US Department of Health and Human Services, Health Resources and Services Administration, Maternal and Child Health Bureau. November 2010. Available at: https://www.hrsa.gov/ourstories/mchb75th/images/rethinkingmch.pdf. Accessed December 3, 2016.

30. Barnes M, Schmitz P. Community engagement matters (now more than ever). *Stanford Social Innovation Review*. Spring 2016. Available at: https://ssir.org/articles/entry/community_engagement_matters_now_more_than_ever. Accessed March 10, 2017.

31. Daro D, McCurdy K, Nelson C. Engaging and retaining parents in voluntary new parent support programs. Chicago, IL: Chapin Hall Center for Children at the University of Chicago; 2005.

32. Daro D, Dodge K. Strengthening home visiting intervention policy: expanding reach, building knowledge. In: Haskins R, Barnett WS, eds. *Investing in Young Children New Directions in Federal Preschool and Early Childhood Policy*. Washington, DC: Brookings Institution; 2010:79–88.

33. Institute for Child and Family Well-Being. Issue Brief: Engaging families in home visiting. University of Wisconsin, Milwaukee. April 2016. Available at: http://uwm.edu/icfw/wp-content/uploads/sites/384/2016/04/Engaging-Homes-in-Family-Visiting.pdf. Accessed December 3, 2017.

34. Gomby DS, Culross PL, Behrman RE. Home visiting recent program evaluations: analysis and recommendations. *Future Child*. 1999;9(1):4–26.

35. The Home Visiting Collaborative Improvement and Innovation Network. Available at: http://hv-coiin.edc.org. Accessed July 29, 2017.

36. The Family Engagement Toolkit. Home Visiting Collaborative Improvement and Innovation Network. Available at: http://hv-coiin.edc.org/resources/family-engagement-toolkit. Accessed July 29, 2017.

37. Maternal, Infant, and Early Childhood Home Visiting Technical Assistance Coordinating Center. MIECHV issue brief on centralized intake systems. October 2014. Available at: https://www.greatstartgeorgia.org/sites/default/files/miechv_issue_brief_centralized_intake.pdf. Accessed February 16, 2017.

38. C-Intake: lessons learned and recommendations. Washington, DC: National Home Visiting Model Alliance; 2016.

39. Florida Department of Health. Healthy Start. Available at: http://www.floridahealth.gov/programs-and-services/childrens-health/healthy-start. Accessed May 24, 2017.

40. Bjerke E, Fleischman L, Scuello M, Wilkens D. Client engagement and attrition: lessons learned from a Palm Beach, FL system of care. Issue Brief. Palm Beach, FL: The Children's Services Council of Palm Beach County; August 2015.

41. US Department of Health and Human Services, Office of Minority Health. HHS Action Plan to Reduce Racial Disparities: a nation free of disparities in health and health care. 2010. Available at: https://minorityhealth.hhs.gov/npa/files/Plans/HHS/HHS_Plan_complete.pdf. Accessed February 17, 2017.

42. Lu MC, Kotelchuck M, Hogan V, Jones L, Wright K, Halfon N. Closing the Black-White gap in birth outcomes: a life-course approach. *Ethn Dis*. 2010;20(1 suppl 2):62–76.

43. Lieberman L. More evidence that racism and discrimination are ACEs. ACEs Connection: A Community of Practice Social Network. 2015. Available at: http://www.acesconnection.com/blog/more-evidence-that-racism-and-discrimination-are-aces. Accessed May 20, 2017.

44. Institute for Safe Families. Findings from the Philadelphia Urban ACE Survey. 2013. Available at: https://www.rwjf.org/content/dam/farm/reports/reports/2013/rwjf407836. Accessed May 20, 2017.

45. Zorrah Q. NEAR@Home Toolkit: A guided process to talk about trauma and resilience in home visiting. Thrive Washington. 2015. Available at: https://thrivewa.org/nearhome-toolkit-guided-process-talk-trauma-resilience-home-visiting. Accessed May 20, 2017.

46. Williams DR, Costa MV, Odunlami O, Mohammed SA. Moving upstream: how interventions that address the social determinants of health can improve health and reduce disparities. *J Public Health Manag Pract*. 2008;14(suppl):S8–S17.

47. White R, Delgado B, Severson L. Scaling up scaling out: white paper on lessons from Goodwill of Southern and Central Indiana and the Nurse–Family Partnership. Aspen Ascend Institute. 2016. Available at: http://b.3cdn.net/ascend/9364017b55cf90431f_w4m6iby1z.pdf. Accessed April 20, 2017.

48. Guttmacher Institute. Unintended pregnancy in the United States: fact sheet. September 2016. Available at: https://www.guttmacher.org/sites/default/files/factsheet/fb-unintended-pregnancy-us_0.pdf. Accessed April 20, 2017.

49. Sawhill I, Venator J. Reducing unintended pregnancies for low-income women. In: Kearney MS, Harris BH, eds. *Policies to Address Poverty in America*. Washington, DC: Hamilton Project; 2014:37–44.

50. Sawhill I, Karpilow Q, Venator J. The impact of unintended childbearing on future generations. The Brookings Institution. 2014. Available at: https://www.brookings.edu/wp-content/uploads/2016/06/12_impact_unintended_childbearing_future_sawhill.pdf. Accessed May 2, 2017.

51. Harper CB. The Strengthening Families approach and protective factors framework. Washington, DC: Center for the Study of Social Policy; 2014. Available at: http://www.cssp.org/reform/strengtheningfamilies/branching-out-and-reaching-deeper. Accessed May 3, 2017.

52. Rankin B, Quane JM. Neighborhood poverty and the social isolation of inner-city African American families. *Soc Forces*. 2000;79(1):139–164.

53. Tigges LM, Browne I, Green GP. Social isolation of the urban poor: race, class, and neighborhood effects on social resources. *Sociol Q*. 1998;39(1):53–77.

54. Reeves RV, Cuddy E. Poverty, isolation and opportunity. Social mobility memo. Brookings Institution. 2015. Available at: https://www.brookings.edu/blog/social-mobility-memos/2015/03/31/poverty-isolation-and-opportunity. Accessed May 3, 2017.

55. Florida State University, Institute for Family Violence Studies, College of Social Work. *The Protective Factors: An E-Book Series for Supervised Visitation Programs—Supportive Social Connections*. Available at: http://familyvio.csw.fsu.edu/wp-content/uploads/2010/05/2014Protective-Factor-4-forDCFFINAL.pdf. Accessed May 17, 2017.

56. Parents as Teachers. Evidence-based model. Available at: http://parentsasteachers.org/evidence-based-model. Accessed May 3, 2017.

57. Jones L, Lu MC, Lucas-Wright A, et al. One hundred intentional acts of kindness toward a pregnant woman: building reproductive social capital in Los Angeles. *Ethn Dis*. 2010; 20(1 suppl 2):36–40.

58. US Department of Health and Human Services, Administration for Children and Families. Head Start, Early Childhood Learning and Knowledge Center. Available at: https://eclkc.ohs.acf.hhs.gov/school-readiness/article/pfce-interactive-framework. Accessed May 17, 2017.

59. US Department of Health and Human Services, Health Service and Resource Administration, Title V Maternal and Child Health Services Block Grant to States Program: guidance and forms. 2017. Available at: https://mchb.hrsa.gov/sites/default/files/mchb/MaternalChildHealthInitiatives/TitleV/508CompliantMCHBGtoStatesGuidanceApr2017.pdf. Accessed May 17, 2017.

60. Brady C, Johnson F. Integrating the life course into MCH service delivery: from theory to practice. *Matern Child Health J*. 2014;18(2):380–388.

61. Waits JO, Stuart ME. Arizona community training: grassroots leadership. Tucson, AZ: University of Arizona Cooperative Extension Service; 2001. Available at: http://www.ila-net.org/Members/PublicationFeatures/View_Publication_Feature.asp?DBID=4. Accessed May 17, 2017.

62. Northeast Florida Healthy Start Coalition. Make a Difference! Leadership Academy. Available at: http://nefhealthystart.org/community-initiatives/make-a-difference-leadership-academy. Accessed May 17, 2017.

63. Howell E, Devaney B, McCormick M, Raykovich KT. Back to the future: community involvement in the healthy start program. *J Health Polit Policy Law*. 1998;23:291–317.

64. Healthy Start EPIC Center. Achieve Collective Impact. Available at: http://healthystartepic. org/healthy-start-approaches/achieve-collective-impact. Accessed May 12, 2017.

65. *Principles of Community Engagement.* 2nd ed. Washington, DC: The National Institutes of Health, Centers for Disease Control and Prevention, Health Resources and Services Administration; 2011.

66. Minnesota Department of Health. Assessing readiness to engage the community: linking principles to practice. Available at: http://www.health.state.mn.us/communityeng/intro/linking. html. Accessed May 22, 2017.

67. *The Head Start Parent, Family, and Community Engagement Framework: Promoting Family Engagement and School Readiness, From Prenatal to Age 8.* Washington, DC: US Department of Health and Human Services, Administration for Children and Families, Office of Head Start; August 2011.

68. US Department of Health and Human Services, Administration for Children and Families, National Center on Parent, Family, and Community Engagement. *Families as Advocates and Leaders.* 2013. Available at: https://eclkc.ohs.acf.hhs.gov/hslc/tta-system/family/docs/advocates-pfce-rtp.pdf. Accessed May 22, 2017.

69. What is Collective Impact? Collective Impact Forum. Available at: http://collectiveimpactforum. org/what-collective-impact. Accessed May 22, 2017.

70. The National Center for Cultural Competence. Georgetown University Center for Child and Human Development. Available at: https://nccc.georgetown.edu. Accessed May 23, 2017.

71. University of Kansas, Work Group on Community Health and Development. Building leadership. In: Community Tool Kit. Available at: http://ctb.ku.edu/en/building-leadership. Accessed May 23, 2017.

72. The Racial Equity Institute. Available at: https://www.racialequityinstitute.org. Accessed July 29, 2017.

73. The People's Institute for Survival and Beyond. Available at: http://www.pisab.org. Accessed July 29, 2017.

7

Housing

Deborah Allen, ScD, and Jessica Wolin, MPH, MCRP

Life Course Theory compels practitioners to recognize the impact of the social determinants of health on outcomes for the people they serve. Transportation, education, employment with livable wages, and housing are all factors that can either support or inhibit a person and/or family's well-being over time. All of these issues are challenging for practitioners to address. Housing in particular poses a significant dilemma for maternal and child health (MCH) practitioners. On the one hand, safe, secure housing has long been recognized as a predictor of population health. On the other hand, it is the most expensive item in many families' budgets, a stark reflection of inequality between rich and poor in the United States, and the only basic need for which this country has no entitlement program. While agencies at local, state, and national levels provide some relief for low-income residents, increasingly squeezed housing markets make it difficult to meet this basic need for many families. The assumption that the private market, the government, and charitable resources will effectively meet the housing needs of most families drives the system. Unfortunately, there are few jurisdictions in the United States where that assumption matches reality.

The experience of clinical, social service, and public health practitioners who work with low-income families is that housing can be an ongoing cause of economic hardship and psychosocial stress for families. Recent events, including the bank foreclosure crisis of 2008, the shift toward construction of high-end housing as an investment rather than housing for the consumer market, along with stagnant incomes among the lower four quintiles in the economy, have expanded the challenge. It is even more difficult for programs that serve low-income women, children, and families to address the underlying causes of adverse health outcomes that are linked to housing.

This chapter examines the relationship between housing and the health of low-income families. It explores the nation's response to housing families and how housing inadequacy and homelessness undermine the health of women and their children. This chapter also looks at current efforts to effectively address the impact of inadequate housing on health including a case study of one Boston, Massachusetts, program specifically designed to meet housing needs of the MCH population. The intent of this chapter is to strengthen MCH practitioners' understanding of housing as a social determinant of family health. The content models how readers can learn more about systems such as this one and can envision how they might adapt their work and focus to better address these basic needs.

HOUSING AS A SOCIAL DETERMINANT OF MATERNAL AND CHILD HEALTH

The physical quality of the homes in which one lives is the most visible link between housing and health. Homelessness, which may mean life on the street or residence in a form of shared shelter, brings heightened physical risk in terms of exposure or lack of safety. More subtly, housing inadequacy and homelessness are profound stressors, posing direct risks to mental health and adding to physical insult through the biological effects of extreme and persistent stress.[1-3] Over the past decade, the Life Course Theory has heightened MCH practitioners' understanding of the mediating role of stress, linking social factors that include housing to both mental and physical health.

Unsafe and hazardous housing has been recognized as a cause of poor health since the 19th century, when reformers began to call for improved conditions in urban areas. In 1842, Edward Chadwick, who was known at that time as a harsh enforcer of Britain's punitive poor laws, documented disease mortality in sections of Glasgow and Edinburgh, ascribing the endemic diseases he saw to the "general condition of the residences of the laboring classes, where disease is found to be the most prevalent."[4] His report based its case for reform on the cost to business of disease outbreaks in the workforce. As noted in the history section of *The Future of Public Health*[5] conditions in US cities at the time were similar to those in England. In 1865, in New York City, "'the filth and garbage accumulate[d] in the streets to the depth sometimes of two or three feet.'"[5] In a 2-week survey of tenements in the 16th ward of New York inspectors found more than 1,200 cases of smallpox and more than 2,000 cases of typhus.[6] In Massachusetts in 1850, deaths from tuberculosis were 300 per 100,000 population and infant mortality was about 200 per 1,000 live births.[7]

Moving forward a century and a half, although the causes and rates of death may differ, the link between inadequate housing, poor health, and premature death is still evident. The National Center for Health in Housing State of Healthy Housing Report of 2013 estimated that 35 million, or 40%, of homes in metropolitan areas in the United States had one or more hazards that could have an impact on resident health and safety.[8] The hazards most commonly seen included water leaks, roofing problems, damaged interior walls, and signs of mice—conditions associated with a range of adverse health outcomes. These, of course, are the hazards that families with housing face; however, homelessness adds a further dimension of risk to the housing–health equation.

Housing and Inequality

Discrimination in housing is both a consequence and a cause of inequality in the United States. Long-term policies, some at the level of the financial institution and some shaped by federal, state, and local laws, have blocked access of people of color to subsidies and loans that enabled White families to become home owners from World War II forward.[9]

Explicit policies also closed off some neighborhoods to residents of color regardless of their ability to pay (an example of "red lining"). In addition to limiting access to home ownership, racist housing policies have resulted in the now commonplace residential segregation in cities, towns, and suburbs across the United States.[10] In San Francisco, California, for example, a city with a history of displacement and gentrification and a dwindling African American population, the majority of African American residents live in segregated public housing.[9,11,12] The well-documented correlates of segregation in majority-Black communities have been disinvestment and neglect resulting in deterioration in the built environment, heightened exposure to adverse environmental conditions, and diminished access to quality schools, health care, and community services.[10,13,14]

Restriction of home ownership and choice of neighborhood by people of color has, in turn, become a major factor in long-term income inequality. Home ownership is the primary means by which working- and middle-class Americans acquire and pass on equity across generations.[13] Lack of opportunity in this regard means that the upward mobility experienced by successive waves of White immigrants to the United States in the 19th and early 20th century has largely been closed off to Black families and other populations of color, forcing each generation to make its own way without the cushion of even modest inherited wealth.[9] Social disparities, driven by institutionalized racism, underlie health inequities and preventable differences in health outcomes for African Americans in the United States. The consequences for African American families are severe with a high proportion of childbearing African American women living in hyper-segregated areas[15] with limited accessibility of resources necessary for maternal and fetal health and increased stress over time.[14]

THE IMPACT OF HOUSING ON THE HEALTH OF FAMILIES

Housing Instability

The United States is in the midst of an affordable housing crisis, making access to housing severely limited for low-income families across the country. Waitlists for housing assistance programs are years long, even more than a decade in some places, with thousands of people waiting for rental assistance if waitlists are even open at all. According to the National Coalition for Low Income Housing's Spotlight report, "The private and subsidized rental markets only make 3.2 million affordable homes available for the nation's 10.4 million Extremely Low Income (ELI) renter households resulting in a national shortage of 7.2 million rental homes."[16] The result is that 75% of the poorest households, with incomes below 30% of the median for a given geographic area, pay more than half of family income on rent.[16,17]

Most low-income families in the United States do not live in subsidized housing— only one in four households that qualify receive rental support. The families that go without help are forced to rent in the private market where the rates are increasingly unaffordable. For many families, this makes housing instability a harsh reality. Unfortunately, there is not a uniform standard definition of housing instability. Features often cited are difficulty paying rent, paying more than 50% of income on rent, living in overcrowded conditions, moving frequently, and being at risk of losing housing because of eviction.[18]

It is no surprise that not having a secure home is associated with poor health outcomes for women and their families with stress a major contributing factor.[19] The disproportionate allocation of income to housing forces many families to forgo other critical, health-related expenditures such as medicine and healthy food. Families that live in overcrowded conditions have additional risks including fire, excessive noise, and exposure to communicable diseases.[11] For children, overcrowding is associated with significant adverse impacts on school achievement, behavior, and physical health.[20] Frequent moves, for instance, a result of housing instability, is associated with adverse birth outcomes. Carrion et al. demonstrated that for a sample of young mothers living in New York City, housing instability was a significant predictor of low birth weight after they adjusted for clinical, behavioral, and demographic factors.[21] Similarly, frequent moves are associated with impairments in child cognitive development and behavior.[22] Housing instability is also associated with vulnerability to several forms of violence. A woman may stay with an abusive partner when her only alternative is living on the street.[23] Furthermore, families are often forced to live in neighborhoods with elevated levels of community violence when options are limited.[24]

The common denominator across all of these correlates of housing insecurity is stress. Fear of eviction, foreclosure, discovery of residents who are "off lease," conflicts with landlords, rent increases, and ultimately risk of homelessness, all contribute to a high level of stress experienced by families living with housing insecurity.[11] This in turn can make it difficult for families to follow clinical treatment plans and public health recommendations, as the more immediate need of shelter takes precedence over other important needs.

Homelessness

Housing and Urban Development defines family homelessness as follows:

> Families with children or unaccompanied youth who are unstably housed and likely to continue in that state . . . . [I]t applies to families with children or unaccompanied youth who have not had a lease or ownership interest in a housing unit in the last 60 or more days, have had two or more moves in the last 60 days, and who are likely to continue to be unstably housed because of disability or multiple barriers to employment.[25]

Families living in shelters, single-room-occupancy hotels, transitional housing, abandoned buildings, public indoor spaces, the homes of strangers, cars, or outdoors are all considered homeless. Homelessness affects low-income, single mothers disproportion-ately. The typical homeless family includes a young mother, children aged younger than 6 years, and an income below the federal poverty level.[26] Many families and many preg-nant women without children end up in shelters having first experienced periods of housing instability, which can include frequent moves and doubling up with family and friends.[27] For most families, homelessness is a short-lived or episodic situation, but for a small number, it is a chronic situation.[28]

The overall rate of homelessness has dropped in recent years, largely because of poli-cies discussed at the end of this chapter, as have the rates for virtually all subgroups (e.g., veterans, single adults, families) within the homeless population. The rate of "unshel-tered homelessness"—people who fit the previous definition and who are not sheltered in a government or privately funded facility—has fallen as well.[29] However, the propor-tion of the homeless population made up of families with children has increased. In 2015, families with children comprised 37% of the US homeless population. In cities with extremely high housing costs, the rate was even higher. In Boston, families, for example, made up 55% of the city's homeless population in 2015, up 25% from 2010.[30]

A body of literature has emerged on the association between homelessness and a variety of adverse health conditions. Researchers in this area face the challenges of distinguish-ing cause from effect (e.g., does homelessness cause illness or does illness lead to home-lessness?) and controlling for social determinants other than housing associated with both poor health and homelessness. However, there is evidence linking homelessness to poor health for pregnant women and to poor birth outcomes such as preterm birth[31]; in some cases, it is linked to related behaviors such as substance use.[32] Similarly, homeless children struggle with negative health outcomes and challenges to their physical and emotional well-being and development.[33] Family homelessness is increasingly recog-nized as a national issue of critical importance.

Pregnant women face particular challenges with securing homeless services because of restrictions on who can live in shelters and single room occupancy units. Pregnant women without children are not considered eligible for family housing, and pregnant women with children are not welcome in environments for single adults. In many com-munities, pregnancy is viewed as a temporary condition and, thus, pregnant women are not appropriately prioritized for homeless services or permanent housing.

Pregnancy adds still another dimension to the housing–health linkage. The so-called nesting instinct, while widely ascribed to women in the final stages of pregnancy, has not had firm scientific support until 2013, when a study found that women exhibit nesting behaviors, including space preparation and social selectivity, which peak in the third trimester of pregnancy.[34] As is the case with nonhuman mammals, nesting in women may serve a protective function.[34] The specific behaviors included selecting, cleaning, and organizing a living space and striving to limit social contacts to trusted individuals, all related to the future well-being of the expected child.

Homelessness clearly poses a profound threat to the drive for securing a safe place to nurture and to the drive for limiting social contact to trusted individuals during the third trimester.[21] This phenomenon may explain, at least in part, research findings showing a strong association between homelessness and adverse pregnancy outcomes[35] and baseline findings of the project described in the section that follows showing high levels of depression and posttraumatic stress disorder among Boston women who were homeless or at imminent risk of homelessness during pregnancy.[36] In fact, the data indicate that women who are homeless are less likely to receive adequate prenatal care or take prenatal vitamins, more likely to smoke and be over- or underweight, and, ultimately, more likely to experience a preterm or low–birth-weight birth.[21,24,35]

Public Housing

The history of public housing in the Unites States traces back to the Great Depression and the United States Housing Act of 1937 that aimed to provide affordable housing for low-income people.[37] In the mid-1960s, the US Department of Housing and Urban Development (HUD) was created. HUD oversees public housing across the United States with local housing authorities managing the actual public housing sites and determining eligibility of residents. Public housing is designed for low-income residents often with specific sites or units designated as family housing or senior housing. Eligibility is determined by the local housing authority and is based on annual gross income, citizenship status, age, disability, and family composition. Local housing authorities follow income eligibility standards set by HUD.[37] Families or individuals with an income that is 80% of the median income for the local area may be eligible for housing and are considered in the lower income limits while those with an income of 50% of the median income are considered in the very-low-income limits.[37] As a result, income limits vary across the United States and a family or individual who might qualify in one community might be ineligible in another. In 1969, the Brooke Amendment established a cap on the percentage of a person's income to be paid toward rent for a public housing unit. Originally set at 25%, it was then raised to the 30% standard in place today.[37]

As of 2014, approximately 789,211 children (ages 0–17 years) live in public housing and make up 37% of all residents.[38] Thirty-five percent of public housing families are female-headed with children and nearly 50% of residents remain in public housing for five years or more.[38] Families who live in public housing are exceedingly poor with the average annual household income less than $14,000, well below the federal poverty line.[38] Today, public housing sites are often in distressed communities with high concentrations of poverty, elevated violence, hazardous living conditions, isolation, racial residential segregation, and lack of access to resources and services.

As public housing across the United States has fallen into disrepair and sites have become locations fraught with social and economic hardship, efforts to "transform" public housing have arisen. In the mid-1990s, the HOPE VI program was initiated to promote resident self-sufficiency, support the development of mixed-income communities, and leverage resources.[39] When HOPE VI was terminated in 2009, it was followed by the Choice Neighborhoods program that also promoted the development of mixed-income housing, services for youth and families, and investments in neighborhood resources.[40] These large scale federal initiatives have facilitated the rehabilitation and rebuilding of public housing across the United States and the implementation of numerous programs for residents. At the same time, they are not without controversy as one significant consequence is often the displacement of low-income residents from their homes and communities. In cities such as San Francisco, this displacement has resulted in families moving far away from their support and service providers; the disintegration of social networks; and, in some cases, the erasure of entire communities.

Health issues and disability may be significant contributing factors to why individuals and families move into public housing in the first place. Furthermore, living in public housing may also exacerbate or in fact cause new health problems. Regardless, the adults and children who live in poorly maintained public housing have been shown to experience adverse physical and mental health conditions at rates higher than their peers living in housing provided on the private market.[41] Chronic health conditions such as arthritis, asthma, diabetes, hypertension, and obesity are seen more often in adults living in public housing[41] while children struggle with school attendance, trauma, and related mental health conditions.[42] In many public housing sites, the physical environment as well as concentrated poverty with high levels of community violence take a toll on the physical and mental health of families.

Degraded housing structures and neglected, or even hazardous, surrounding environments common to public housing sites impact the mental and physical health of women and children. Living in substandard housing and unhealthy environments has been shown to result in high levels of depression and other mental health conditions.[43] Indoor and outdoor pollutants such as lead, solvents, and pesticides are common in old and poorly maintained public housing sites can have adverse effects on physical health. Family emotional health suffers as they feel a lack of control of their environment and exposure to toxins.[44] Furthermore, the spatial layout of public housing neighborhoods can also lead to fear and anxiety as residents are unable to monitor their physical safety due to a poorly constructed physical environment.

Unique to public housing are a set of restrictive rules governing the lives of tenants and exacerbating tenant stress. These rules include policies that prevent former drug offenders from qualifying for public housing, contributing to the common phenomenon of "off-lease" residents. As a result of such restrictions, a large number of the male residents of family public housing sites are not officially allowed to live there, and when they do, are considered "off-lease" and prohibited. This "hiding in plain sight" is stressful for all involved but it is the only course of action for families trying to stay together despite the rules. In addition, some "off-lease" residents contribute income to a family that, if it were accounted for, would make them ineligible for federally subsidized housing. For women living in public housing, seeking out resources including domestic violence services, parenting support, or even health care can result in calling attention to their "off-lease" family members, putting their housing at risk.

OPPORTUNITIES FOR CHANGE

The first systematic residential building code was passed in England in 1844. Like those that followed elsewhere in Europe and in the United States, it emphasized sanitation and safety—protection from sewage and fire in particular. In the 20th century, housing codes retained their focus on sanitation and safety but expanded to cover exposures to lead paint, toxic building materials, and asthma triggers. Today, responsibility for preventing or mitigating environmental exposures attributable to degraded, poorly maintained, or otherwise hazardous housing conditions resides most importantly with the federal Department of Housing and Urban Development. State and local housing agencies, local housing authorities and other government agencies, housing developers, the construction and banking industries, and, of course, consumers are key stakeholders in relation to housing policy. Housing policy is made at all levels of government, thus local and national level advocacy groups play a critical role in ensuring access to affordable high-quality housing for families. Community leaders and advocates work to ensure that pregnant women and families are not overlooked in initiatives to address chronic homelessness often focused on single adults.

Given the clear influence and impact of housing on health across the life course, finding innovative ways to connect the housing industry with MCH programs is important. In particular, Life Course Theory challenges the view that stages in a person's life (e.g., pregnancy, the neonatal period, and early childhood) are temporary, time-bound periods. Life Course Theory brings to the foreground the reality that quality housing is the foundation of health across the life course and can influence well-being across generations. Innovative work in Boston offers one approach to addressing this long-standing challenge, as described in the Healthy Start housing case study later in this chapter. Lessons and strategies that may be applied to advancing this work in other communities are offered.

INNOVATION AT WORK

While this is still an emerging area for partnership, there are programs across the country that are addressing issues around housing and health with a life course view. In San Francisco, the Homeless Prenatal Program (HPP), founded 25 years ago, is a model for serving low-income women and families who face housing instability and homelessness. Their mission is to end childhood poverty, and they view pregnancy as a moment full of opportunity to support and enable women. They provide access to housing, prenatal and parenting support, child development resources, family finances and stability services, access to technology, domestic violence and substance abuse counseling, family unification assistance, and emergency support of basic needs. They have pioneered the practice of hiring former clients as program and case managers and now more than half of HPP's program staff members are former clients or come from the community they serve.[45]

Supportive housing is a model of housing that recognizes the health and social needs of residents. For families, supportive housing provides an opportunity to live in a stable, secure environment while addressing pressing issues that undermine family development and well-being. The Corporation for Supportive Housing leads the Child Welfare and Supportive Housing Resource Center in partnership with US Department of Health and Human Services, Administration on Children, Youth, and Families, and four private foundations: the Robert Wood Johnson Foundation, the Annie E. Casey Foundation, Casey Family Programs, and the Edna McConnell Clark Foundation. The Resource Center provides support for two significant initiatives testing strategies and effectiveness of supportive housing for families including the federally funded Partnerships to Demonstrate the Effectiveness of Supportive Housing for Families in the Child Welfare System and the Robert Wood Johnson Foundation–funded Keeping Families Together initiative, which uses supportive housing to offer stability to families with children who are at risk of recurring involvement in the child welfare system.[46] These projects are bringing supportive housing to homeless families in communities across the country. Their work is proving the impact of this innovative approach and its value as a key strategy for uniting housing and health.

The report Innovative Models in Health and Housing, produced by the Low Income Investment Fund and Mercy Housing, with support from the Kresge Foundation and the California Endowment, was released in summer 2017.[47] Although the report does not focus specifically on families, the work does present innovative models of how the health care system in a growing number of communities is coming forward to address housing needs. There are lessons to be learned about how health systems can play a role in creating access to affordable housing and, in the process, improve health outcomes. The authors conclude that successful models use three main investment strategies: (1) use of shared savings, reserves, or increased financial flexibility within a capitated health care delivery system (either a managed care or accountable care organization) in partnership with a local housing authority; (2) use of a hospital community benefits obligation that requires hospitals to spend resources on community health to maintain tax-exempt status; and (3) local or state investment built upon resources from an expanding health care sector.[45] By leveraging the power of health care financing, housing has become more accessible—a key step toward better health outcomes.

Finally, whole-family clinical service models help to improve the health of low-income families living in public housing.[48] These programs usually intervene simultaneously with different generations of the family unit. Family models have been used to deliver on-site primary care and behavioral health and support services in public housing.[49] Clinical services that target two generations have seen promising results among public housing residents.[48]

The Housing Opportunity and Services Together (HOST) program establishes a model for whole-family service delivery in mixed-income communities.[48] Currently being piloted in Chicago, Illinois, Portland, Oregon, New York City, and Washington, DC, the HOST program provides intensive wraparound services to support families in public and mixed-income communities.[48] Primary care services are placed with social- and community-based interventions to incorporate the family in a wraparound of services.[50] In Chicago, the HOST program provides intensive case management services to heads of household while at the same time providing after- school activities and job training to youths in those homes.[50] In Portland, HOST focuses on providing income and rent management services to heads of household and providing primary care, behavioral health case management, and academic monitoring for youths.[50]

Case Study: Healthy Start in Housing, Boston

Healthy Start in Housing (HSiH) grew out of a long-term relationship between the Boston Public Health Commission (BPHC) and the Boston Housing Authority (BHA) around programs to support chronically homeless Boston residents and to improve environmental quality in public housing. The latter focused on asthma control via elimination of triggers in the home environment and elimination of exposure to secondhand smoke. BPHC leadership raised the idea of a focus on pregnant women in response to long-term frustration of BPHC and other perinatal home visitors with the intransigence of homelessness and housing insecurity among the women they served. On the basis of the view that averting homelessness during pregnancy could provide long-term, intergenerational benefits, the housing authority offered BPHC the opportunity to design a program using up to 75 units of housing at a given time to promote healthy birth outcomes and reduce birth outcome inequality in Boston. This meant that 75 women at risk of adverse outcomes could avoid a 5-year, 40,000-person waiting list for public housing in Boston and their newborns could enter a world in which their fundamental need for shelter was met.

Setting parameters for program eligibility was the greatest challenge. If women were defined as eligible simply on the basis of pregnancy status and housing insecurity, demand would have exceeded supply two-fold because of the shortage of low-rent housing in Boston. If eligibility were limited to women who were homeless, it would have been too narrow, excluding women in insecure situations at imminent risk of homelessness. Ultimately, eligibility was defined in terms of (1) pregnancy status, (2) pregnancy risk, (3) housing risk, and (4) ability to meet BHA requirements. Later, women with a previous child diagnosed with serious special health care needs were included.

Once determined eligible, women were required to participate in three workshops, which covered tenant rights and obligations and provided a brief training on budgeting, among other topics. To ensure adequate support for program participants, HSiH enhanced traditional home visiting, expanding to include night and weekend shifts, so that clients would not be forced to choose between employment and other daytime obligations. Program staff received training on the BHA application process and other matters related to tenancy. They were also trained in Problem-Solving Education, a form of brief, cognitive–behavioral therapy aimed at providing tools to assist clients with tenancy and related challenges.

The Boston University School of Public Health evaluation team collected demographic characteristics, measures of emotional well-being and social functioning, and information on health behaviors, birth outcomes, housing history at baseline and then 4, 8, and 12 months later. Evaluation findings included statistically significant differences between HSiH participants and comparison group members on social functioning, emotional well-being, and re-initiation of smoking after delivery. HSiH clients experienced no very-low-birth-weight births and no infant deaths; although both adverse outcomes occurred among comparison-group women, numbers were too small to achieve statistical power. Differences found in social functioning were limited to HSiH participants who came to the program following some period of homelessness. In sum, the HSiH model is feasible and replicable, relying on resources, public housing, and home visiting, which are found to some degree in large and even midsize US cities. Effective implementation, however, requires care and nurturing of partnerships, specialized training of staff, and active monitoring and evaluation.

This program is always evolving to adapt and improve. In 2017, for example, five of the housing units were made available to provide shelter for men who were caring for their young children. Criteria and guidelines continue to be adapted as well.

NEXT STEPS

Housing issues not only have an impact on young adults and families but they also can cause significant stress for practitioners who are trying to provide quality care on a shoestring budget up against broken systems. Home visiting programs in general are challenged to meet the needs of families who are frequently in transition and/or who are forced to live in residences that are unsafe. Likewise, clinicians and case managers can spend a fair amount of time keeping up with the frequent relocation of their low-income patients. Although the Boston case study and lessons described in the next paragraphs tend to focus on pregnant women, housing has an impact on the life course of many populations not described here, including children with special health care needs, fragile seniors, individuals struggling with substance use issues, veterans, individuals leaving the criminal justice system, and young adults who are trying to be independent with jobs that do not pay a livable wage. Taking on public health challenges such as obesity and stress reduction are extremely difficult when clients' basic needs are not being met. At the same time, policies such as tobacco-free public housing may support healthier lifestyles.

Reorient Housing Policies and Programs Toward Maternal and Child Health Populations

Life course science provided the justification for giving pregnant women special consideration for housing in the HSiH program. Policymakers were convinced to change structures and policies by demonstrations that provision of housing would have an impact on future generations. Furthermore, in an era of "two-generation" and "multi-generation" strategies, the Life Course Approach holds particular resonance. Pregnant women are the literal embodiment of these generational strategies—holding current and future generations in one physical being. A Life Course Approach reorients discussion of pregnant women to the current and future impacts of housing and its context for child development. For many policymakers, providing housing to pregnant women is seen as low priority as pregnancy is viewed as a temporary situation. Educating policymakers about the negative health consequences of housing instability to birth outcomes, infant health, and child development is a critical step toward meaningful policy change.

Partnerships Between Health and Housing Agencies Are Possible and Needed

Linking public health and housing agencies to provide housing to pregnant women who are homeless or at imminent risk of homelessness to sustainable tenancy is feasible. The relationship between BPHC and BHA has been the backbone of HSiH implementation in Boston. It has depended on strong relationships at both leadership and frontline levels, which have been dependent, in turn, on regular communication of challenges, transparency, and acknowledgment of the respective contribution of each partner. Public health, social work, and other practitioners can begin to engage with colleagues in the housing sector by first learning their vernacular (see glossary in Appendix 7A at the end of the chapter). Consider attending a local housing conference or event or participate in public meetings that address housing issues. Take time to fully understand the challenges clients face in obtaining housing—particularly the policies—and use that as an opportunity to meet with people who work in housing agencies to learn more.

Remember that communities often have innovating nonprofit or other types of housing programs that might prove to be interesting new partners for MCH programs. There are also some fields of study such as urban planning and community development that have a growing alignment with life course perspectives and an interest in promoting equity. Emerging professionals from those sectors, joining with new professionals in public health, social work, and health care, could align their efforts and create new and exciting approaches to reducing risks and elevating protections for families.

Data, Monitoring, and Evaluation Matter

Given the complexity of the program, the extent to which it affects the lives of participants and the value of the resource it provides, there is no room for sloppiness. Ongoing monitoring and evaluation are needed to ensure fidelity to program guidelines, prompt identification and response to client struggles and program lapses, and regular reinforcement of program goals among managers, staff, and clients. There is a need for more in-depth studies of the health effects of housing intervention. For example, one of the women enrolled in the HSiH program shared that she had felt a palpable drop in her blood pressure when she came home to her own apartment after having been homeless for a time. Another woman spoke of dropping from 350 pounds to a healthy weight after placement. These personal stories point to the possibility of health improvement for both mothers and babies that would make larger-scale, proactive investment in interventions of this type cost-effective.

Maternal and Child Health Staff Training

Home visiting and other perinatal and family support programs must grapple with the housing needs of clients to the extent possible. This includes ensuring program expertise in regard to all housing and housing support options available. States may, for example, have housing programs targeted to individuals with disabilities that may be unfamiliar to perinatal case managers but useful to a subset of clients who are eligible or who could have children who are eligible for such programs. Leaders should recognize the profound impact of homelessness and housing insecurity on maternal stress and offer enhanced support to help women cope. Case managers do not like to dwell on problems they cannot solve. Training for staff on trauma awareness and strategies to help clients recognize and deal with stress are not substitutes for meeting basic needs, but they are tools that may help staff help clients whose problems are intransigent.

Enhancing the skills of home visitors to support the transition of clients from insecure housing to sustainable tenancy is critical. Many of the women referred to HSiH since its inception have had histories of eviction that made them ineligible for the program. Ensuring that those women who do receive housing will continue to do well in their new homes requires more intensive, adaptable, client-centered approaches to case management than is typical.

Public health and social work professionals can be a voice for expanded housing options. For example, BPHC issued a report making the health case for a raised minimum wage, which pointed to housing as one of the key intervening variables between income and health. The need for a high level of sensitivity on the part of staff poses practical challenges for MCH programs, which may rely on professional staff who have been trained to deliver health education in a one-way, didactic manner that assumes a receptive listener or on paraprofessionals whose own experiences of hardship or cultural norms about self-sufficiency may make patience with "noncompliant" clients hard to muster. Social determinants and Life Course Theory are not abstractions to the women served; they may impede trust, lead to anger at programming that feels intrusive, and, in general, create distance between programs and clients. Overcoming these barriers requires close examination of how programs operate and how staff is trained. Staff training on trauma is a first step toward supporting women in these circumstances, but assessment of mental health needs and protocols for referral to trauma-informed mental health services should be an element in all programs designed to address life course issues.

CONCLUSIONS

Life Course Theory provides an opportunity to elevate the impact of housing on MCH, illuminating that safe, affordable, and stable housing creates a supportive physical and emotional context for development and nurturing of families. Housing instability, segregated communities, hazardous living conditions, and homelessness create relentless stress that has a negative impact on the life course trajectory. Economic decisions associated with housing often force families to make choices regarding the food they purchase, the medical care they access, and how they manage anxiety and stress. For housing policymakers, an understanding of life course can change the way the housing commodity is viewed for young families. New partnerships among sectors, innovative ideas that bridge disciplines and industries, and different ways of approaching long-standing housing challenges for families are required to close gaps in outcomes for women, infants, and families. Today, public health and social work professionals can be a voice for expanded housing options and ensuring health through stable, affordable, quality housing for women and their families.

KEY POINTS

- Housing insecurity, lack of access to housing, low-quality housing, and residential racial segregation all undermine the health of women and families. Stress is a common pathway by which these factors compromise well-being along with environmental hazards and overcrowding.
- Innovative collaborations between housing and health point to ways in which family homelessness and housing insecurity can be addressed while improving outcomes across generations.
- Educating policymakers about the negative consequences of housing instability to birth outcomes, infant health, and child development is a critical step toward meaningful policy change.

RESOURCES

- American Planning Association (https://www.planning.org) focuses on helping planners shape the building of healthier and safer communities, addressing commutes, housing options, and lasting value. The Plan4Health links public health and planning practice.
- Shapiro TM. *Toxic Inequality: How America's Wealth Gap Destroys Mobility, Deepens the Racial Divide, and Threatens Our Future.* New York, NY: Basic Books; 2017.
- Corporation of Supportive Housing (http://www.csh.org) promotes supportive housing as a solution to family homelessness.
- Homeless Prenatal Program (http://www.homelessprenatal.org) provides innovative, community-based services for homeless and low-income pregnant women and their families.
- Knight K. *Addicted. Pregnant. Poor.* Durham, NC: Duke University Press; 2015.
- National Alliance to Prevent Homelessness collects and publishes data on trends in housing and homelessness and advocates preventive strategies.
- National Safe and Healthy Housing Coalition focuses on education and outreach to national stakeholders and federal public decision makers.
- Urban Institute's Metropolitan Housing and Communities Policy Center (https://www.urban.org/policy-centers/metropolitan-housing-and-communities-policy-center) examines how housing and place shape people's lives.

ACKNOWLEDGMENTS

Both authors contributed equally to this work. Thank you to Megan Canady for her assistance with the citations for this chapter.

REFERENCES

1. National Health Care for the Homeless Council. Homelessness & health: what's the connection? *National Health Care for the Homeless Council.* 2011:11–13.

2. Wasserman JA. Stress among the homeless. In: Cockerham C, Dingwall R, Quah S, eds. *The Wiley Blackwell Encyclopedia of Health, Illness, Behavior, and Society.* Hoboken, NJ: Wiley; 2014:2295–2298.

3. Roman CG, Knight C. An examination of the social and physical environment of public housing residents in two Chicago developments in transition. Washington, DC: The Urban Institute; 2010:1–31.

4. MacNalty AS. Report on the sanitary condition of the labouring population of Great Britain. *Br Med J.* 1965;2(May):926. doi:10.2105/AJPH.56.1.143-a.

5. Institute of Medicine. A history of the public health system. In: *The Future of Public Health.* Washington, DC: National Academies Press; 1988:56–72. Available at: https://www.ncbi.nlm. nih.gov/books/NBK218224. Accessed November 27, 2017.

6. Winslow CEA. The evolution and significance of the modern public health campaign. An address. New Haven, CT: Yale University Press; 1935:65.

7. Hanlon G, Pickett J. *Public Health Administration and Practice. St. Louis, MO:* Times Mirror/ Mosby; 1984.

8. *Baltimore–Washington Rail Intermodal Facility Health Impact Assessment.* National Center for Healthy Housing. 2013. Available at: http://www.nchh.org/Portals/0/Contents/Baltimore-Washington-Intermodal-Facility-HIA_Final-Report.pdf. Accessed November 10, 2017.

9. Rothstein R. *The Color of Law: A Forgotten History of How Our Government Segregated America.* New York, NY: Liveright Publishing Corporation; 2017.

10. Landrine H, Corral I. Separate and unequal: residential segregation and Black health disparities. *Ethn Dis.* 2009; 19(2):179–184.

11. Promoting housing security and healthy homes for families served by maternal, child and adolescent health programs. San Francisco, CA: Children's Environmental Health Program, San Francisco Department of Public Health; 2017.

12. Hirsch A. Choosing segregation: federal housing policy between Shelley and Brown. In: Bauman J, Biles R, Szlvian K, eds. *Tenements to the Taylor Homes: In Search of an Urban Housing Policy in Twentieth Century America.* University Park, PA: Pennsylvania State University Press; 2000.

13. Williams DR, Collins C. Racial residential segregation: a fundamental cause of racial disparities in health. *Public Health Rep.* 2001;116(5):404–416.

14. Nyarko K, Wehby G. Residential segregation and the health of African-American infants: does the effect vary by prevalence? *Matern Child Health J.* 2012;16(7):1491–1499.

15. Osypuk T, Acevedo-Garcia D. Are racial disparities in preterm birth larger in hypersegregated areas? *Am J Epidemiol.* 2008;167(11):1295–1304.

16. Emmanuel D, Yentel D, Errico E, et al. Housing Spotlight Fall 2016. 2016;6(1):1–3. Available at: http://nlihc.org/sites/default/files/HousingSpotlight_6-1_int.pdf. Accessed November 17, 2017.

17. Desmond M. How homeownership became an engine of income inequality. *New York Times Magazine.* May 9, 2017. https://www.nytimes.com/2017/05/09/magazine/how-homeownership-became-the-engine-of-american-inequality.html. Accessed November 27, 2017.

18. Kushel MB, Gupta R, Gee L, Haas JS. Housing instability and food insecurity as barriers to health care among low-income Americans. *J Gen Intern Med.* 2006;21(1):71–77.

19. Stahre M, VanEenwyk J, Siegel P, Njai R. Housing insecurity and the association with health outcomes and unhealthy behaviors, Washington State, 2011. *Prev Chronic Dis.* 2015;12:E109.

20. Solari CD, Mare RD. Housing crowding effects on children's wellbeing. *Soc Sci Res.* 2012; 41(2):464–476.

21. Carrion BV, Earnshaw VA, Kershaw T, et al. Housing instability and birth weight among young urban mothers. *J Urban Health.* 2015;92(1):1–9.

22. Fowler PJ, McGrath LM, Henry DB, et al. Housing mobility and cognitive development: change in verbal and nonverbal abilities. *Child Abuse Neglect.* 2015;48:104–118.

23. Domestic violence and homelessness. Administration for Children and Families. 2015. Available at: https://www.acf.hhs.gov/domestic-violence-and-homelessness. Accessed August 22, 2017.

24. Evidence matters. US Department of Housing and Urban Development. 2016. Available at: https://www.huduser.gov/portal/periodicals/em/summer16/highlight2.html. Accessed September 15, 2017.

25. Changes in the HUD definition of "homeless." US Department of Housing and Urban Development. January 18, 2012. Available at: https://endhomelessness.org/resource/changes-in-the-hud-definition-of-homeless. Accessed January 14, 2018.

26. Homeless families with children. National Coalition for the Homeless. 2009. Available at: http://www.nationalhomeless.org/factsheets/families.html. Accessed September 15, 2017.

27. Evidence matters. US Department of Housing and Urban Development. 2014. Available at: https://www.huduser.gov/portal/periodicals/em/fall14/highlight3.html. Accessed September 15, 2017.

28. Duffield B. Are we creating chronic homelessness? Institute for Children, Poverty, and Homelessness; New York, NY. 2016:1–8.

29. Unshelter homelessness: trends, causes, and strategies to address. National Alliance to End Homelessness. 2017. Available at: https://endhomelessness.org/wp-content/uploads/2017/07/unsheltered-brief-final-7.26.pdf. Accessed November 27, 2017.

30. City of Boston 35th Annual Homeless Census. Boston, MA: Boston Public Health Commission; 2015:1–3.

31. Cutt DB, Coleman S, Black MM, et al. Homelessness during pregnancy: a unique, time-dependent risk factor of birth outcomes. *Matern Child Health J.* 2015;19(6):1276–1283.

32. Kramer MR, Cooper HL, Drews-Botsch CD, Waller LA, Hogue CR. Social science and medicine metropolitan isolation segregation and Black–White disparities in very preterm birth: a test of mediating pathways and variance explained. *Soc Sci Med.* 2010;71(12):2108–2116.

33. McCoy-Roth M, Mackintosh B, Murphey D. When the bough breaks: the effects of homelessness on young children. *Child Trends.* February 2012;3(1):1–7.

34. Anderson MV, Rutherford MD. Evidence of a nesting psychology during human pregnancy. *J Evol Hum Behav.* 2013;34(6):390–397.

35. Stein JA, Lu MC, Gelberg L. Severity of homelessness and adverse birth outcomes. *Health Psych.* 2000;19(6):524–534.

36. Allen D, Feinberg E, Mitchell H. Bringing life course home: a pilot to reduce pregnancy risk through housing access and family support. *Matern Child Health J.* 2014;18(2):405–412.

37. HUD's public housing program. US Department of Housing and Urban Development. January 18, 2012. Available at: https://www.hud.gov/topics/rental_assistance/phprog. Accessed January 14, 2018.

38. Demographic Facts, Residents Living in Public Housing. National Center for Health in Public Housing. New York, NY. 2010.

39. About HOPE VI. US Department of Housing and Urban Development. January 18, 2012. Available at: https://www.hud.gov/program_offices/public_indian_housing/programs/ph/hope6/about#4. Accessed January 14, 2018.

40. Choice neighborhoods. US Department of Housing and Urban Development. January 18, 2012. Available at: https://www.hud.gov/program_offices/public_indian_housing/programs/ph/cn. Accessed January 14, 2018.

41. Carlos M, Popkin SJ, Guernsey E. Poor health: the biggest challenge for HOPE VI families? HOPE VI: Where do we go from here? Brief 5. Washington, DC: The Urban Institute; 2005.

42. Jordan R, Mireles A, Popkin SJ. HOST Youth: the challenges of growing up in low-income housing. Urban Institute Brief 4. Washington, DC. October 2013.

43. Gallagher M, Bajaj B. Moving on: Benefits and challenges of HOPE VI for children. Washington, DC: The Urban Institute; 2007.

44. Krieger J, Higgins DL. Housing and health: time again for public health action. *J Info.* 2002;92(5).

45. Homeless Prenatal Program. 2015. Available at: http://www.homelessprenatal.org. Accessed August 22, 2017.

46. Corporation for Supportive Housing. 2012. Available at: http://www.csh.org. Accessed August 22, 2017.

47. Bamberger J, Bluestein R, Latimer-Nelligan K, et al. Innovative models in health and housing acknowledgements. San Francisco, CA: Low Income Investment Fund; 2017.

48. Popkin SJ, Scott MM, Parilla J, Falkenburger E, McDaniel M. Planning the housing opportunity and services together demonstration: challenges and lessons learned. Brief. Washington, DC: Urban Institute; 2012.

49. Popkin SJ, Getsinger L. Tackling the biggest challenge: intensive case management and CHA residents' health. Brief 3. Washington, DC: The Urban Institute; 2010.

50. Popkin SJ, McDaniel M. Can public housing be a platform for Change? Washington, DC: Urban Institute; 2013.

Appendix 7A: Glossary of Housing Terms

Deborah Allen, ScD, and Jessica Wolin, MPH, MCRP

Affordable Housing—Under the Housing and Urban Development Act of 1969, Congress passed the Brooke Amendment, which established a limit on the percentage of income a public housing resident could be expected to pay for rent. This limit was originally set at 25% of income and was eventually raised to 30% of income in 1981. Today, housing is considered "affordable" when residents pay no more than 30% of their total income for housing costs including rent or mortgage payment, insurance, taxes, and utilities.

Daily Rent Hotel or Single-Room Occupancy (SRO)—A residential property of multiple single-room units. Bathroom and kitchen spaces (if available) may be shared among residents. These units are generally not intended for families and may be called a "hotel."

Housing Advocates—Community members and organizations who recognize adequate housing as a critical economic, social, and cultural right and who work on issues related to homelessness, affordability, safety, and tenant's rights.

Housing Authority—A local agency funded by the federal government that manages local public housing units, determines who is eligible to reside in the units, and administers rental assistance programs such as Section 8 vouchers.

Market Rate Housing—Housing that is rented or sold at any price the owner can get for the property. There are no subsidies for the housing.

Mixed Income Housing—A development made up of housing with differing levels of affordability, generally including some market-rate housing and some affordable units.

"Off Lease"—Residents of public housing who are not officially on a lease and are not actually supposed to be living in a unit. Many "off-lease" residents are living in public housing despite rules that are supposed to restrict their access or because of limits on the number of allowed residents.

Private Developers (For-Profit and Nonprofit)—Private developers finance and build housing. Increasingly, private developers are engaged with public housing projects. Created under the Obama administration, the Rental Assistance Demonstration program converts public housing units into Section 8 program units with private developers taking over the leasing and management of the units. Private developers are able to leverage capital and loans that local housing authorities cannot and can apply those funds to improving or rebuilding the units. These units are to remain permanently affordable and residents who remain through the conversion are to pay no more than 30% of their income toward rent.

Property Managers and Landlords—Responsible for the daily operations of rental units and properties including leasing, maintenance, and other residential community needs. Some property management companies specialize in managing public and/or supportive housing communities.

Public Housing—Subsidized housing administered by federal and state governments, managed by more than 3,300 local housing authorities for residents who are eligible low-income families, elderly people, and people with disabilities. More than 1.2 million households live in public housing of some type in the United States. Many sites are highly concentrated blocks of low- and high-rise apartments; however, increasingly, public housing is built in a variety of settings and formats including mixed-income communities built by private developers. Federal funding for these sites flows from the US Department of Housing and Urban Development to local housing authorities.

Rent Control—Rules that determine how much an owner can charge tenants for their rental housing. How much the rent can be raised is often regulated.

Residential Treatment—A live-in health care facility focused on treating individuals, and sometimes families, who are working to stabilize substance use.

Section 8—Established in the mid-1970s as a voucher program that provides rental assistance to low-income individuals and families to use in the private rental market.

Shelter—A type of temporary overnight housing for those who are homeless. Many shelters operate on a first-come, first-served basis with no guarantee of space the following night. Some shelters are designated specifically for single adults, youths, and families.

Supportive Housing—An intervention that combines housing (or financial assistance for housing) with supportive services for people who have experienced homelessness as well as people with disabilities. Supportive services vary but could include job training, life skills development, substance use programming, and case management. The housing environment may be concentrated in a single shared site or spread out among mixed-income units.

Transitional Housing—A housing environment with or without adjacent supportive services whose goal is to provide temporary support to individuals and families as they work to increase stability, safety, and/or wellness. Programs tend to operate as nonprofit organizations, with some focusing specifically on issues such as substance use, domestic violence, workforce development, and transition from foster care.

8

Partnerships: Building Blocks for Change

Dorothy Cilenti, DrPH, MPH, MSW, and Gibbie Harris, MSPH, BSN

Taking a Life Course Approach to programs and change necessitates new partnerships. This may be building relationships within an organization, such as cross-pollinating via divisions or departments, as well as building relationships with unexpected partners, such as business, housing, and city planning. Collaboration is hard work and requires ongoing attention. Development of multisector partnerships through collaboration, however, is necessary to transform and align the various systems that have an impact on the health of populations across the life span. A body of research continues to demonstrate how health is a result of many social and environmental factors in addition to access to medical care.[1] Extending the health system's connection with communities is critical given that key drivers of risk are often nonclinical in nature. Moreover, with an emphasis on smaller government and decreasing funding for health and human services, the role of nontraditional partners is more important than ever.

Today's complex and dynamic environment requires a systems-thinking approach. For individuals and communities to achieve optimal health throughout the life course, it is necessary for health systems, governmental public health, hospitals, primary care providers, behavioral health agencies, social services, the business community, and community-based organizations to come together in true partnership to change the status quo in their communities. This approach to health improvement will be key to public health, social work, and related human service agencies as they continue to work to improve the conditions in which people live and the ways they are served.

This chapter will enable the reader to build expertise in establishing and sustaining partnerships and collaboration. Readers will be exposed to the skills needed to achieve successful partnerships through examples described throughout the chapter. Content includes the role of partnerships, community engagement, description of a variety of key elements that are part of partnerships, and challenges and opportunities that partnership presents. As Dr. Paul Farmer of Partners in Health has noted, "With rare exceptions, all of your most important achievements on this planet will come from working with others—or in a word, partnership."[2]

THE ROLE OF PARTNERSHIPS

A partnership happens when two or more parties commit to joint action and/or the sharing of resources.[3] Simply put, it is an agreement to do something together that will benefit all involved. Partnerships are embraced when individuals or organizations agree that working together will yield more effective results than working in isolation. Partnerships can build on what is already being done and ensure that certain activities are not duplicated or fragmented. They allow parties to share goals, decision making, resources, benefits, risks, and responsibilities. As a result, each party is more efficient and can afford to take on greater risk.

People form partnerships for many different reasons. They might be striving to

- Find solutions to challenging problems;
- Make efficient use of limited resources;
- Integrate ideas or activities;
- Improve a service or program;
- Develop a more holistic, systemic approach to an issue;
- Promote communication and dissemination of information;
- Increase their power or influence;
- Improve relationships between diverse stakeholders; or
- Gain expertise.[3]

Internal and External Partnerships

In approaching this work, it is important to bear in mind that partnership building and community engagement can happen within the organization as well as between the organization and outside groups. Before stepping outside the doors of the primary care practice to build an external partnership, for example, it is important to first look internally to see if the practice is doing what it can to coordinate and expand services within the practice walls. The Nemours Children's Health System, like many health systems, was inwardly focused for many years. As they engaged in efforts to improve the health of all children, Nemours learned how to partner effectively within their organization among their multiple departments. They assessed organizational capabilities and defined roles that departments would fill. They identified areas that would be enhanced through expanded collaboration. Moreover, they provided a structured, strategic approach to working together. This work built their skills in collaboration and allowed them to model their true commitment to partnership when moving outside their walls.

Nemours first started developing external partnerships by providing data to the education sector showing how healthy eating and physical activity affect academic achievement. Health system leadership recognized that a healthy community does not result only from treating one patient at a time; they now work with many community partners that share their vision of wellness. Currently, Nemours uses health expertise not only to address medical challenges but also to identify, prevent, and address root causes that hinder optimal health and have the potential to negatively influence future well-being. Nemours strives to address health at all levels—individual, interpersonal, organizational, community, state, and national.[4]

Another example of these internal and external partnership efforts centers on local health departments. Most health departments engage a number of programs within the department as well as partners in the community to address maternal and child health issues. An illustration of internal efforts within the department are services that address infant mortality, which can involve family planning, maternity care, home visiting services, nutrition and breastfeeding support, immunizations, well-child care, and care management. Ideally, these services are well coordinated through internal partnerships among staff leaders to provide easy, one-stop access for women and children and make limited funds stretch as far as they can. Through external partnerships, a health department might bring together numerous organizations on a child fatality prevention task force or perinatal health coalition, for example, to tackle larger issues of infant mortality such as reimbursement for services, transportation, and breastfeeding-friendly policies.

Types of Partnerships

A partnership is an agreement between two or more stakeholders to coordinate with each other. Partnerships are a type of strategic relationship or alliance. In some cases, the relationship is about an exchange—resources, skills, know-how, access to a certain population. At other times, partners have a common end goal and agree to work with each other to achieve this. Partnerships can increase efficiencies or increase effectiveness—save costs, become better at what one does, and/or achieve something together that cannot be done alone.

The work of health and human services may be accomplished by a simple partnership with another agency. While having a variety of partners and perspectives at the table is compelling, keeping the goal in mind along with an understanding of the root causes of the problem is important to build the partnership appropriately. Some efforts require a few organizations to work together over time. Others are short-term and may require a work group to focus intensely on a specific issue. Government-appointed task forces usually address a specific topic (e.g., child fatality) with membership that often changes with elections. Sometimes if the challenge is complex, it may be best addressed with a coalition. Although there is a variety of ways groups come together, this section describes three partnership types—coordinating councils, coalitions, and collaborative partners—and when they are best deployed.

Coordinating Councils

Coordinating councils are appropriate for initiating the alignment of the work of different partners toward a shared goal. These councils are usually self-organized and self-governed groups that enable critical partners to work on a range of strategies, policies, activities, and issues that address specific goals. Membership reflects the unique composition of each sector, often including agencies that are already working with a specific population or issue. For example, the education sector may engage the juvenile justice system in an effort to address lagging high-school graduation rates in its district. A related example of a coordinating council is a planning body for addressing underage use of alcohol at the community level. Members of these councils are usually volunteers representing public schools, treatment, social services, and law enforcement. Some councils include organizations with similar roles, such as behavioral health agencies, with the goal of better coordinating their work or referrals, addressing unmet needs, or working collectively on policy issues that have an impact on them all. A council may be an effective approach to bringing people with mutual interests together to better understand contributing factors to a problem and to generate ideas to address the problem. Networking and information exchange are benefits for participants. Councils do not necessarily take steps as a group, however, to effect change.

Coalitions

Coalitions tend to be action-oriented and more diverse, thus requiring more attention and coordination. Given the complexity of coalitions, practitioners should be thoughtful in convening such a group. If there is a sense of urgency to address an important problem, with resources and invested stakeholders available, a coalition may be an effective mechanism to make significant improvements in policies, programs, and systems. For example, to prevent gun violence and advocate gun control, several groups, unions, and nonprofit organizations banded to form the Coalition to Stop Gun Violence. The goal of the coalition is to help communities become free from gun violence. Through advocacy and education, they have successfully helped states pass gun violence restraining orders that allow law enforcement and family members to temporarily remove firearms from loved ones in crisis.[5]

The Community Coalition Action Theory developed by Butterfoss and Kegler[6] suggests that coalitions form because of a threat, opportunity, or mandate. A lead agency or convening group recruits additional coalition members to ensure diverse community representation. Coalitions base their confidence in gaining credibility on inviting unlikely partners who wish to attain the same end goal, but their reasons for achieving these goals may differ.

Coalitions or partnerships that involve numerous organizations often begin with intention and much effort to figure out how they are going to work together. Issues that need to be addressed include governance, decision-making processes, membership responsibilities, resource sharing, and program focus. Coalition leadership and staff develop operating procedures and structures to facilitate member engagement in the work of the coalition and to ensure that the benefits of participation outweigh the costs. To maintain coalition momentum and effectiveness, engaged members pool their diverse individual and organizational resources, which creates the collaborative synergy that results in comprehensive strategies to improve policies, programs, and practices to achieve community health outcomes of interest. Ultimately, stakeholders can choose to work in their own way while agreeing on the partnership's end goal.

The challenge for coalitions is to maintain the intensity and engagement needed as the work moves forward. Without a deliberate focus, these partnerships will eventually become ineffective and cease to exist. Unfortunately, this can lead to negative feelings in a community or reduced credibility for the convening organization. Coalitions should be launched with careful thought and investment. Likewise, the disbanding of a coalition—whether the work has been accomplished or interest has waned—should be done with appropriate recognitions, communication, and even debriefing so as to learn for future endeavors.

Collaborative Partnerships

If one considers the drivers that are impacting the health system and the opportunities that they create, the development of true collaborative partnerships is the strategy that will create the synergy to ensure health improvement. Collaboration is a new level of partnership as stakeholders agree to exchange information and work toward a common goal and agree to share resources and decision making. Whereas councils and coalitions tend to be focused on a single issue, these partnerships address many challenges through well-organized, long-term coordination and evaluation of partner activities. Alignment of partner activities to prioritized strategic initiatives ensures that agencies and staff with the right capabilities to advance the mission are included—knowledge is a priority over titles and roles. Dedicated program staff provides a seamless experience for partners. Standardized processes structure partner relationships from the outset, enabling staff from participating organizations to concentrate on achieving stated goals. Clear and strong leadership is essential for setting the tone and elevating the importance of work and participation over time. Effective multisector partnerships engage a range of residents and other stakeholders in community-driven social change. Partnership members build capacity by making connections with people across sectors and using a shared language. Creating a cohesive group may be more difficult with diverse membership, but the rewards can be great.

Many clinics, community organizations, and health care systems are implementing best practices in the hopes of ensuring positive outcomes for individuals, families, and communities. Improved health throughout the life span will require the development of multisector partnerships, a focus on the social determinants of health, and a fundamental change in mental models of what creates "good health" in a community.

COMMUNITY ENGAGEMENT

Defined as the process of working collaboratively with and through groups of people affiliated by geographic proximity, special interest, or similar situations to address issues affecting the well-being of those people,[7] community engagement is fundamental to establishing and sustaining partnerships. The goals of community engagement are to build trust, enlist new resources and allies, create better communication, and improve overall health outcomes as successful partnerships evolve into lasting collaborations. Engagement of the community affected by the issue or problem that is being addressed must happen from the beginning of the process if the effort is to be successful. Recognizing and addressing power differences between community members and leaders, government officials, and other formal leaders is essential and practitioners must learn how to engage communities differently.

Often the types of invitations to community organizations and leaders to participate in building a relationship (e.g., emails) are not sufficient to engage community residents. A number of strategies can assist in improving successful engagement. Phone calls and in-person conversations are often effective methods for recruiting partners and can be essential when one is reaching out into the community. Consider having meetings at times and locations that are convenient for working community members. Providing transportation, food, childcare, and even stipends often makes participation in coalition work more appealing and possible for community members. Offering leadership training for key residents to increase their capacity to participate fully is beneficial. Education and thoughtful orientation can help them feel more comfortable and less self-conscious about being at the table with "professionals." Other members of the coalition must make sure that community representatives are included as full members of the group whose ideas are just as important as those offered by others.

Participants' mental models should also be explored. These models are personal beliefs, ideas, images, and verbal descriptions that consciously or unconsciously form from experiences and that (when formed) guide thoughts and actions within narrow channels.[8] These representations of perceived reality explain cause and effect and lead to expectations of certain results, give meaning to events, and predispose individuals to behave in certain ways. Although mental models provide internal stability in a world of continuous change, they also blind people to facts and ideas that challenge or defy deeply held beliefs. They are, by their very nature, fuzzy and incomplete. Moreover, individuals have different models (that differ in detail from everyone else's) of the same concept or subject, no matter how common or simple.

For example, tobacco prevention work typically requires bringing people together with very different mental models regarding the role of government in regulating use of tobacco products. People who have mental models in support of individual rights may resist efforts on the part of government agencies to limit secondhand smoke exposure. Other individuals may favor government intervention to ensure that the public is protected from secondhand smoke exposure. Actively exploring these models not only helps the members of the group understand how everyone is thinking about the issue at hand but it also helps explain perceived barriers to ideas and limitations on actions. Changing mental models about the way things are and should be takes conscious effort on the part of all partners and requires skilled facilitation to make the process productive instead of potentially destructive. When done effectively, it can make the difference between a success or failure in the collaborative process. Resources are provided at the end of the book to help practitioners improve their skills with mental models.

The rationale for community-engaged prevention work is largely rooted in the socioecological model, which recognizes that lifestyles, behaviors, and the incidence of illness and health are all shaped by social and physical environments.[9] The growing commitment to community engagement is beginning to encourage health professionals, community leaders, researchers, social workers, and policymakers to consider this approach. There are different levels of community involvement, with increasing involvement, impact, trust, and communication.[7] While achieving shared leadership is clearly a very desirable state, each step in the continuum moves the needle forward in terms of bridging communication and working together. Furthermore, the level of engagement may also be determined by the scope of the problem and the issues to be addressed. Some issues may require a short term "fix" or need less involvement to change. Others may be deeply rooted in a community and influenced by a wide variety of entrenched social issues. Regardless, all efforts need to start at the beginning and take steps forward one at a time.

Developed by the University of Wisconsin Population Health Institute, the Action Wheel (Figure 8-1) demonstrates the cyclical nature of this work in a community as well as the numerous multisector partnerships that are required to change the health outcomes of a community.[10] Efforts typically start with the collection and analysis of data and resources, working with community members to define their most pressing concern. Information about needs and/or gaps helps collaborators focus their work through the development of a plan that includes action steps. Implementation of plans requires agreement of those involved and the availability of resources. Finally, no process is complete until the success of the effort is determined through an evaluation, complete with predetermined measurements. Ongoing alignment of efforts and communication are mandatory to accomplishing the goals of a collaborative effort.

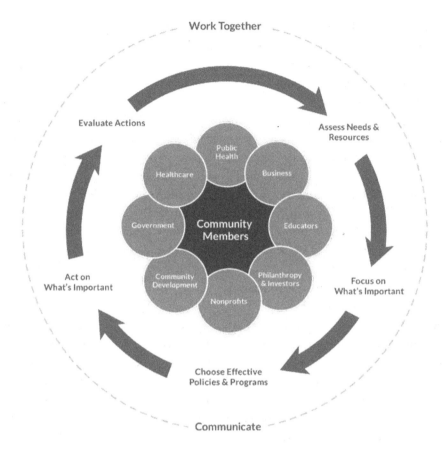

Source: University of Wisconsin Population Health Institute.[10] Reprinted with permission.
Figure 8-1. The Action Wheel.

PARTNERSHIP ELEMENTS

Several core elements are necessary to build sustainable partnerships:

- A shared vision, mission, and goals to provide focus;
- Effective partner recruitment;
- Boundary-spanning leadership;
- A governance structure for joint decision making;
- An organization to shepherd the process;
- Effective communication; and
- Sustainable funding.

Evaluation of the process of partnership development and the outcomes of the partnership work is critical.[11]

Shared Goals, Vision, Mission

Naming the problems or goals that have brought together multiple organizations in common purpose is an important first step in creating and maintaining strong partnerships. This may be more complex than it seems, as different partners will bring their own agendas to the table. Collecting, assessing, evaluating, and disseminating data on the needs of specific populations is critical to mobilizing community partners around improved health for individuals, families, and communities. Community assessments provide a nice model for this step in building strong partnerships. A number of entities at the local and regional levels are engaged in community needs assessments—whether as a requirement for the Title V Block grant, or by health departments, hospital systems, and federally qualified health centers or community health centers. This work engages many entities and individuals in an effort to include broad perspectives on the needs of the community. The community benefit requirements for hospitals offer a good example.[12]

Under current Internal Revenue Service requirements, nonprofit hospitals are required to conduct a community needs assessment every three years describing how the health care needs of the community (or the hospital catchment area) are being addressed. They need to describe how they are leveraging their community benefit resources to address these needs and provide justification for any unmet needs. Hospitals also have to document a true community need for the activities they are conducting. Furthermore, the community needs assessment process must engage a broad range of perspectives. Hospital administrators and health leaders have an opportunity to collaboratively develop implementation strategies that bring the best evidence to the field to achieve health improvements for individuals, families, and communities across the life span. Organizations should examine how to best use this requirement by coordinating the alignment of the data-collection process, pooling resources, and advocating a common agenda for health improvement efforts.

Partner Recruitment

In identifying and recruiting members, the goal, vision, and mission of a partnership should drive the invitation for partners and agencies. Leaders should consider readiness, alignment, and resources (e.g., human, funding, space) in this process, and utilize existing relationships and networks to identify individuals who will bring the needed energy and connections to the work at hand. There needs to be sufficient relationships with those sectors of the community with whom the partnership needs to work to accomplish goals. Often the identified individuals are serving on various community partnerships and may be overextended. In addition, the amount of work generated by the partnership may expand significantly while membership levels may not. One strategy to engage and maintain members is to offer varying levels of involvement (e.g., members may serve on a committee or serve as a committee chair). Position descriptions for members and the various roles they fill will ensure that leadership and members have a shared understanding of the requirements and expectations.

Leadership

Partnerships need boundary-spanning leaders who understand and appreciate partners' different perspectives, can bridge diverse experiences, and are comfortable sharing ideas, resources, and power. Traditional leaders typically have a narrow range of expertise, are used to being in control, and speak a language that may not be understood by a broad range of individuals. Boundary-spanning leaders understand systems thinking and have the ability to help others understand the importance of thinking broadly about issues and all of the forces that affect them.

Partnerships may involve a number of people assuming leadership, in both formal and informal leadership roles. This can be challenging, and leaders who are convening the group should be able to articulate what the partners may accomplish together and how the collaborative work will benefit not only children, families, and the community but also each individual organization represented in the partnership. They must be able to help everyone involved stay focused on the big picture, while assisting each individual partner to recognize that their participation in the collaborative process is an advantage to their individual organization. That advantage will be different for each organization and can fluctuate over time. Benefits for collaboration for partners may include the following:

- An enhanced ability to address an issue that is important to them,
- The acquisition of additional funds,
- New competencies,
- Useful knowledge to support their own activities,
- Increased exposure to and appreciation by other groups in the community,
- A strengthened capacity to meet performance goals and the needs of their clients,
- Valuable relationships, and
- An opportunity to make a meaningful contribution to the community.[13]

Participants may not agree on all dimensions of the problem, but they must agree on the primary goals for the partnership as a whole. Leaders of partnerships need strong relationship skills to foster respect, trust, and openness among partners. They need to be able to frame the important issues and keep those issues front and center. In addition, strong leaders will be able to support and fuel action and recapture learning from action.

Finally, communicating and celebrating progress is essential. For example, the CEOs of Detroit Medical Center, Henry Ford Health System (fiduciary), Oakwood Healthcare System, and St. John Providence Health System commissioned the Detroit Regional Infant Mortality Reduction Task Force in 2008 to develop a plan of action to help more babies survive to celebrate their first birthdays. After a year of having no infant deaths in a very-high-risk area, the Detroit Regional Infant Mortality Reduction Task Force received numerous awards and recognitions including being featured in the University of Kentucky's national study on successful partnerships, the Detroit Wayne County Health Authority's "Best of the Safety Net Award," and a variety of journal, newspaper, and television features.[14] The effort put into elevating the success of the coalition paid off in spades, both for the current work and for future endeavors.

To enact change at various levels, the partnership must have legitimacy, or "authority to lead." There are multiple ways to gain authority, including being a trusted source of information, acting as a neutral convener, identifying resources to bring to the table, and receiving support from elected officials, community organizations, residents, and others. As grass roots support is often important when one is trying to influence conditions that affect diverse populations, engaging community-based organizations and residents in leadership positions is critical. Leaders need to help partners develop a common language without jargon or acronyms so that they may communicate meaningfully with each other. The effective leader synthesizes partners' different ideas, stimulates partners to be creative and look at things differently, and identifies effective ways to combine the partners' resources and in-kind contributions.

Governance

A governance structure for joint decision making is crucial to the success of collaborative efforts. True partnerships are equal and require shared ownership. Through procedures that determine how partnerships make decisions and do their work, governance influences the extent to which partners' perspectives, resources, and skills can be combined. The formalization of these procedures sustains the way a partnership works beyond the engagement of any particular leader or staff person.

Forms of governance vary and may reflect the partners' comfort level with the decision-making process, the degree to which members support partnership decisions, and the timeliness of the partnership's decisions. Consensus decision making is one example of a group decision-making process in which group members develop and agree to support a decision in the best interest of the whole. Consensus typically results in an acceptable resolution, or one that can be supported, even if it is not the preferred decision of each individual. A less desirable but sometimes necessary approach to decision making is majority rule (i.e., the decision is supported by the majority but there may be a minority of members opposed to the decision).

Integrator: Backbone Agency Role

Most successful partnerships need an organization or leader to serve in a convening role.[15] This role provides support and structure to collective efforts. Unique roles for the agency that assumes this responsibility include consensus building, prioritizing competing issues, and ensuring long-term commitment to shared goals among partners. With respect to resources, the integrator can determine what gaps need to be filled and where duplication of resources may be minimized. They promote innovation by helping organizations in different systems make connections rather than working in traditional silos. The integrator disseminates evidence and best practices to various partners to spread promising approaches. Lead agencies may explore opportunities to leverage new sources of funding or work with payers to develop innovative financing and payment systems. They may share data across systems to identify and bridge gaps that often result when work is not aligned. Integrators also serve as neutral conveners, providing a table where everyone can come together and participate with an equal voice and vote. They must be good facilitators. Although integrators are often initially funded with grants, identifying other sustainable financing streams is key so that they can focus on the supports and systems changes needed to continuously innovate and address community needs.

Communication

Effective communication in a collaborative environment requires the following:

- Understanding the ground rules,
- Developing strong listening skills,
- Learning positive behaviors that immediately gain the respect and trust of others,
- Working to make everyone on the team feel involved and valued in the collaboration process, and
- Developing "bridge-building" techniques for working with all types of people.

Effective communication strategies and mechanisms to coordinate partner activities are needed to facilitate synergistic thinking and action. Determining with the group in advance how they want to receive communication (e.g., emails, newsletters, social media) is necessary to increase the likelihood that information will be received and read. Analysis and documentation capacities may also be critical to provide partners with supports that synthesize their ideas, help them make timely decisions, and evaluate the functioning and progress of the partnership.

Funding

Sustainable funding is necessary to ensure that the partnerships evolve into strong collaborations. There will need to be resources to continue the programmatic efforts of the collaborative and to support the integrators who invest time and energy in supporting the work. Long-term financial planning is a chief challenge for nearly all partnerships. Most groups operate without a robust financial infrastructure and do not have dependable resources to deliver their full potential value. The most commonly used financing structures tend to be those that are short-term in nature, such as small grants, small gifts, or pooled funding. There may be tensions related to sharing funding and staff, so it is important to have well-executed memoranda of understanding specifying how resources will be allocated. Having multiple leaders representing various sectors in the governance role of the partnership may contribute to greater transparency and diversification in funding sources. Finally, should partnership efforts pave the way for larger grants or contracts, tensions could again intensify if leaders need resources and wish to compete for them.

Evaluation

Those involved in the provision of all levels of health services, from prevention to chronic care, continue to improve their ability to measure and evaluate the impact of the programs and efforts targeting improvement in health outcomes. However, as these entities join with each other and with community in partnership to approach health outcomes in new and different ways, it is critical that the process of those partnerships be evaluated as well as the programmatic efforts that come from the partnerships. These types of collaborations cannot stagnate, and continued effort is necessary for them to evolve as the needs change. Not understanding and improving the process of partnering will lead to less-than-optimal outcomes and usually the eventual death of the partnership.

While partners have many efforts that demand their limited resources, being able to demonstrate measurement of success is a requirement not only for programs but also for partnerships. A collaborative that cannot demonstrate effectiveness will not receive ongoing attention from partners. Social network analysis, described in Chapter 13, is one strategy for evaluating the strength of partnerships. Other measures contributing to partnership effectiveness include the following:

- Commitment and visibility,
- Positive climate for decision making,
- Human and social capital,
- Visionary leadership,
- Strategic thinking,
- Membership diversity,
- Formal structure and membership development, and
- Effective communications.[16]

The Wilder Collaboration Factors Inventory is a free tool to assess how a collaboration is doing on 20 research-tested success factors.[17]

There are many existing data sources, indicators, and interactive tools that are relevant to meeting the information needs that drive partnerships; however, many communities are unaware that such tools exist, and often the data are available at the national, state, or county level. The Agency for Healthcare Research and Quality's Area Health Resources files house health data resource products that draw from an extensive county-level database assembled annually from more than 50 sources and can be accessed at http://ahrf.hrsa.gov.[18] More tools are needed, however, that provide interactive access to data at the community level.

CASE STUDIES OF PARTNERSHIPS AND COLLABORATION

Collaboration can happen in numerous settings at various levels, such as clinical practices, neighborhoods, communities, and states. These partnerships can involve individuals interacting with their medical providers, health professionals working with community support agencies, multiple entities in a community coming together around a shared goal, and funders and policymakers agreeing to support a specific effort. The case studies that follow offer some examples of collaborations. Additional examples of successful collaborative partnerships may be found through the Robert Wood Johnson Foundation's Culture of Health website.[19]

Case Study 1: Regional Health Initiative in North Carolina

Leaders in a local health department (Buncombe County Health and Human Services in Asheville, North Carolina) and nonprofit hospital (Mission Health) worked together to complete their required health assessments and to develop community health improvement plans to address priority health needs. Assessment activities included data analysis, interviews, and community forums. The assessment clearly demonstrated a significant and detrimental impact of interpersonal violence on the community. Their work resulted in a broad engagement of organizations in the community (beyond traditional partners), development of shared goals, and improvements in health outcomes. The two agencies provided the support and infrastructure to this regional health improvement initiative now comprising more than 20 community and clinical partners. The joint leadership of these organizations facilitated multisector alliances through a shared governance process.[20] The commitment and involvement of key leaders, county government leadership, and hospital leadership as part of the alliance led to a sense of urgency and willingness to come to the table, leaving individual agency priorities at the door and sharing resources for the success of the effort.

Because of the availability of data and community interest in the issue of domestic violence and its impact on mothers and their children, the timing was right for a call to action that leveraged significant resources in creative ways to engage community partners and transform current service delivery systems for vulnerable women, children, and families. One result of this multisector partnership has been the development of a Family Justice Center to offer one-stop, multidisciplinary services to victims of domestic violence and sexual assault. The collective work has resulted in healthier behaviors, increased access to services, and new approaches to address social determinants.

Case Study 2: Family Success Alliance

In response to large disparities in opportunities for children and families in Orange County, North Carolina, the Family Success Alliance (FSA) was formed to bring together community members, local government agencies, nonprofits, and other community leaders.[21] The mission is to reduce the effects of poverty on development and academic achievement by implementing evidence-based practices that are responsive to the priorities and needs of children and their families. The work is modeled on the Harlem Children's Zone/Promise Neighborhood effort.[22]

FSA is currently working in two zones within the county. The zones were selected through a community-driven data process, which included the creation of a countywide poverty index that identified six zones where families were struggling to meet their financial demands. After an intensive community engagement process, the Advisory Council selected two zones to pilot the work. A gap analysis done in partnership with the two zones identified community priorities, including affordable, high-quality childcare; school readiness; and meeting basic family needs.

A core group of staff located at the Orange County Health Department, the backbone organization, facilitates the work. Memoranda of understanding have been put in place to identify ways in which each partner will prioritize programming in the zones, create common measures, create data-sharing agreements, participate in regular zone meetings, and commit to Collective Impact training and work. Within its first few years, the FSA partnership achieved its initial goals for important "quick wins." These included establishing the infrastructure to support collaboration, forming a productive partnership, launching community-based programming, designing and conducting a formative evaluation, and seeking additional funding for the partnership and its programs. The partnership continues to explore ways to spread its programs to other low-income zones in the county.

CHALLENGES

The ability of a partnership to achieve high performance is influenced not only by leadership but also by factors in the external environment, which may be outside the scope of the partnership's influence. Recruiting and retaining partners may be more difficult in communities where there is little history of cooperation and trust or significant competition for resources. Moreover, there may be numerous partnerships in place involving many of the same agencies. In these circumstances, leaders must communicate their value to other stakeholders, with a specific focus on life course development and strategies to synergize policies across multiple generations. Competition throughout a health system and in communities with many issues that affect health must be considered and linkages with programs working on the root causes of other issues will be necessary. For example, previously separate sectors must be aligned to integrate services, and networks of partners are needed to create a culture of health at the local and state levels.

Most partnerships struggle with fragile infrastructure, which can include limited staff capacity or strained capabilities for important functions such as continuous quality improvement, evaluation, communications, operations, and strategic financial management. In addition, nearly all partnerships find long-term financial planning a major challenge. Most partnerships do not have dependable resources and tend to use financing structures that are short-term in nature, such as grants. Strained infrastructure is a common barrier for all partnerships, especially those just starting out. Paying attention to building staff capacity, establishing essential operational functions, and setting expectations for resource sharing across participating organizations can help sustain a partnership in the long run.[23]

OPPORTUNITIES FOR COLLABORATION

While there are certainly challenges given the current economic and political environment, there are also many opportunities for health and human service organizations to achieve their goals to improve the health and well-being of individuals, families, and communities through working collaboratively across sectors. In addition, there is more attention being given to the social and environmental factors that influence health, such as poverty, education, employment, access to healthy foods, smoke-free places, and opportunities for physical activity—all well aligned with a life course perspective. There have been many demonstrations and small-scale programs supporting the critical role of place-based interventions and upstream approaches to create optimal health.[24] Communities now need to move to a culture of health to ensure that these strategies are brought to scale and are sustainable.

The National Prevention Strategy provides a roadmap to move health from a system of sick care to one based on wellness and prevention.[25] It builds upon the state-of-the-art clinical services in place in this country and the progress that has been made toward understanding how to improve the health of individuals, families, and communities through prevention. The goal of the National Prevention Strategy is optimal health for everyone at all stages of life. There is growing recognition that the health and social issues affecting the well-being of communities and the health of specific populations cannot be addressed sufficiently by any one organization. Population health as a concept is driving all sectors to think about outcomes. A frequently cited definition for population health is "the health outcomes of a group of individuals, including the distribution of such outcomes within the group."[26] The group of individuals may be defined in many different ways—a patient panel in a primary care practice, a hospital catchment area, or a specific geographical entity, for example. Regardless of the focus, achieving health outcomes for any population requires collaborating with others. Therefore, health and human services practitioners will need to align with others who are in a strategic position to address the social and environmental factors contributing to the health of individuals, families, and communities.

The National Prevention Strategy encourages partnerships among federal, state, tribal, local, and territorial governments; business, industry, and other private-sector partners; philanthropic organizations; community and faith-based organizations; and everyday Americans to improve health through prevention. Through these partnerships, the National Prevention Strategy seeks to improve America's health by helping to create healthy and safe communities, expand clinical and community-based preventive services, empower people to make healthy choices, and eliminate health disparities. Preventing disease before it starts is critical to helping people live longer, healthier lives and keeping health care costs down. Poor diet, lack of physical activity, tobacco use, depression, trauma, and alcohol misuse are just some of the challenges or risk factors faced. Many of the strongest predictors of health fall outside the health care setting. Housing, transportation, education, worksites, and environment are major elements that affect the physical and mental health of Americans—across generations.

CONCLUSIONS

As health across the life span moves beyond the scope of what any individual organization can accomplish alone, multisector partnerships play an increasingly important role. Leaders across the nation view cross-sector collaboration as vital to achieving their visions for population health and health equity. Whereas some partnerships have existed for many years, many more are just beginning and are continuously evolving. They may start out informally but often become more formal over time, through letters of commitment, memoranda of understanding, and/or bylaws to clearly articulate roles and responsibilities. Partnerships can be supported in a variety of ways, including in-kind contributions, grants, membership fees, or a combination of approaches. Community engagement is key to addressing social determinants of health. Community priorities may sometimes differ from data-identified priorities and should be given due consideration. Data sharing can be challenging when one is working across sectors such as housing, education, and law enforcement, making documentation of outcomes difficult. Effective internal and external communications, while challenging, are key to success. Finally, leaders need to be attuned to critical issues such as power dynamics, organization/sector "personalities," and the need for partners to be seen, heard, and supported. The investment of time, talent, and resources will pay off in improved life trajectories for many people.

KEY POINTS

- Create a shared vision and identify mission alignment.
- Consider nontraditional partners and seek out existing partnerships.
- Identify someone to manage the collaborative with the skills to do the work.
- Define clear roles and responsibilities.
- Develop a process to measure and evaluate success.
- Communicate, communicate, communicate.
- Make sure everyone brings resources to the table and leaves with a common goal to improve population health.

RESOURCES

- To learn more about mental models, check out Peter M. Senge et al.'s *The Fifth Discipline Fieldbook: Strategies and Tools for Building a Learning Organization*. New York, NY: Currency, Doubleday; 1994.
- The National Maternal and Child Health Workforce Development Center has resources on leadership and change management, systems integration, and evidence-based decision making. You can find more information at https://mchwdc.unc.edu.
- The MCH Navigator provides online modules and other distance-based learning resources at https://www.mchnavigator.org.
- The Robert Wood Johnson Foundation Culture of Health website highlights how communities are working toward health through multisector partnerships. More information is available at https://www.cultureofhealth.org.
- FSG helps communities find new ways to achieve results. Their website, http://www.fsg.org/tools-and-resources, provides ideas for action, publications, toolkits, and opportunities to participate in virtual learning communities.
- Video and transcript: Community Impact Forum, *Complementary or in Conflict? Community Organizing and Collective Impact*: http://collectiveimpactforum.org/blogs/1/video-and-transcript-complementary-or-conflict-community-organizing-and-collective-impact.

REFERENCES

1. Braveman P, Gottlieb L. The social determinants of health: it's time to consider the causes of the causes. *Public Health Rep.* 2014;129(suppl 2):19–31.

2. Goodreads. Paul Farmer Quotes. Available at: https://www.goodreads.com/author/quotes/6684.paul_farmer. Accessed March 3, 2017.

3. Frank F, Smith A. *The Partnership Handbook*. Minister of Public Works and Government Services Canada. 2000. Available at: http://publications.gc.ca/collections/Collection/MP43-373-1-2000E.pdf. Accessed December 5, 2017.

4. National Forum on Hospitals, Health Systems and Population Health. Partnerships to build a culture of health. Available at: http://www.healthyamericans.org. Accessed May 30, 2017.

5. The Coalition to Stop Gun Violence. Available at: https://www.csgv.org. Accessed August 22, 2017.

6. Butterfoss F, Kegler M. Toward a comprehensive understanding of community coalitions: moving from practice to theory. In: DiClemente RJ, Crosby RA, Kegler MC, eds. *Emerging Theories in Health Promotion Practice and Research: Strategies for Improving Public Health.* San Francisco, CA: Jossey-Bass; 2002:194–227.

7. *The Principles of Community Engagement.* 2nd ed. Bethesda, MD: Clinical and Translational Science Awards Consortium Community Engagement Key Function Committee, Task Force on the Principles of Community Engagement; June 2011. DHHS NIH Publication No. 11-7782.

8. BusinessDictionary. Mental models. Available at: http://www.businessdictionary.com/definition/mental-models.html. Accessed November 26, 2017.

9. Centers for Disease Control and Prevention. The social–ecological model: a framework for prevention. Available at: https://www.cdc.gov/violenceprevention/overview/social-ecologicalmodel.html. Accessed March 3, 2017.

10. University of Wisconsin Population Health Institute. The Action Wheel. County Health Rankings & Roadmaps. 2015. Available at: http://www.countyhealthrankings.org. Accessed December 5, 2017.

11. Kania J, Kramer M. Collective Impact. *Stanford Soc Innov Rev.* 2011;9(1):36–41.

12. Internal Revenue Service. New requirements for 501(c)(3) hospitals under the Affordable Care Act. Available at: https://www.irs.gov/charities-non-profits/charitable-organizations/new-requirements-for-501c3-hospitals-under-the-affordable-care-act. Accessed March 3, 2017.

13. Lasker RD, Weiss ES, Miller R. Partnership synergy: a practical framework for studying and strengthening the collaborative advantage. *Milbank Q.* 2001;79(2):179–205.

14. Women-Inspired Neighborhood Network: Detroit. 2014. Available at: http://healthyamericans.org/health-issues/wp-content/uploads/2015/09/Wisdom.pdf. Accessed June 3, 2017.

15. Nemours. Integrator role and functions in population health improvement initiatives. 2012. Available at: http://www.improvingpopulationhealth.org/Integrator%20role%20and%20functions_FINAL.pdf. Accessed March 3, 2017.

16. Barnes PA, Erwin PC, Moonesinghe R. Measures of highly functioning health coalitions: corollaries for an effective public health system. *Front Public Health Serv Syst Res.* 2014;3(3):1–7.

17. Amherst H. Wilder Foundation. Wilder Collaboration Factors Inventory. Available at: https://www.wilder.org/Wilder-Research/Research-Services/Pages/Wilder-Collaboration-Factors-Inventory.aspx. Accessed August 5, 2017.

18. Health Resources and Services Administration, Data Warehouse. Area Health Resource Files. Available at: https://datawarehouse.hrsa.gov/topics/ahrf.aspx. Accessed November 26, 2017.

19. Robert Wood Johnson Foundation. Culture of Health. Available at: https://www.cultureofhealth. org. Accessed June 1, 2017.

20. Harris G. Transforming health through multisector partnerships. *N C Med J.* 2016;77(4):1–4.

21. Orange County North Carolina. Family Success Alliance. Available at: http://www. orangecountync.gov/departments/health/FSA.php. Accessed June 3, 2017.

22. Harlem Children's Zone: A national model for breaking the cycle of poverty. Available at: https://hcz.org. Accessed June 3, 2017.

23. The Rippel Foundation. ReThink Health. Understanding multi-sector partners for health: the basics. Available at: https://www.rethinkhealth.org/the-rethinkers-blog/understanding-multi-sector-partnerships-for-health-the-basics. Accessed April 19, 2017.

24. Public Health 3.0: A call to action to create a 21st century public health infrastructure. Available at: https://www.healthypeople.gov/sites/default/files/Public-Health-3.0-White-Paper. pdf. Accessed March 3, 2017.

25. National Prevention Council. *National Prevention Strategy: America's Plan for Better Health and Wellness.* June 2011. Available at: https://www.surgeongeneral.gov/priorities/prevention/ strategy/report.pdf. Accessed March 3, 2017.

26. Kindig D, Stoddart G. What is population health? *Am J Public Health.* 2003:93(3):380–383.

9

Human-Centered Design

Rachel L. Berkowitz, MPH, Jessica Vechakul, PhD, MPH, MS, Bina Patel Shrimali, DrPH, and Thea Anderson, MPH, MSW

Life Course Theory (LCT) suggests that social factors influence individual well-being over a lifetime and subsequently have an impact on birth outcomes from generation to generation.[1] There are a variety of ways in which LCT can be translated into action.[2] Human-Centered Design (HCD) is a process and set of methods for exploration of challenges and possible solutions, driven by a deep understanding of the potential beneficiaries (those who would use or benefit from the developed solutions, such as a patient or program participant).

Use of the HCD process to generate innovative approaches to maternal and child health (MCH) work aligned with LCT is relatively new. This chapter introduces readers to HCD and provides two case studies to illustrate its application in relation to the LCT. The chapter explores the strengths and challenges involved in the application of HCD and offers recommendations for practitioners who might consider using this process in their own work. Although the two case studies in this chapter highlight the use of HCD in a place-based life course–focused initiative (an initiative working to effect change in a specific neighborhood), this process could be applied in diverse contexts, such as clinical settings, intervention planning meetings, and programs.

OVERVIEW: HUMAN-CENTERED DESIGN FOR SOCIAL IMPACT

Design is described by Robert Buchanan as "the plan, project, or working hypothesis which constitutes the 'intention' in intentional operation."[3(p8)] As defined, design permeates every conceivable aspect of life, from the materials used on a day-to-day basis to the structures through which society operates. HCD, also called "design thinking," channels the concept of design through a lens focused on potential users.[4] With roots in architecture, urban planning, and engineering and often associated with the creation of innovative products in the commercial sector, HCD is an iterative process for problem solving in which the priorities, needs, and behaviors of end-users (the potential beneficiaries or users of a given product or solution) serve as a driving force throughout a product's conceptualization, development, and distribution.[4-7] Creating a product or program based on a deep understanding of the needs and desires of intended beneficiaries is applicable to public health's complex challenges.[7]

As described in 2010 by Tim Brown and Jocelyn Wyatt of IDEO, a global innovation and design firm that applies HCD to social sector challenges around the world,

> Design thinking incorporates constituent or consumer insights in depth and rapid prototyping, all aimed at getting beyond the assumptions that block effective solutions. Design thinking—inherently optimistic, constructive, and experiential—addresses the needs of the people who will consume a product or service and the infrastructure that enables it.[7(p32)]

HCD processes are fundamentally context-specific, relying on local knowledge and perspective to determine what problems are really important to explore and what solutions may be uniquely tailored to that context. HCD encourages creative thinking to tackle difficult problems. HCD also allows movement through multiple iterative cycles to test, refine, and evolve programs or products, starting simple and scaling up. Iteration offers opportunities for continuous improvement and adaptation on the basis of new information or a deeper understanding of beneficiaries or the challenge.

The Human-Centered Design Process

The HCD process, presented in Figure 9-1, illustrates the main phases for moving from problem to solution. The three main phases (Understanding, Ideation, and Experimentation and Implementation) are presented linearly (left to right), but iteration among phases is

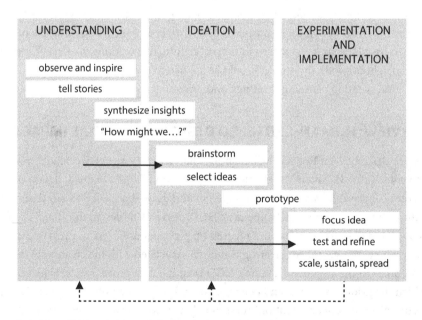

Source: Vechakul et al.[5] Adapted with permission from Springer and the authors.
Note: This visual generally describes the Human-Centered Design process utilized by the Best Babies Zone initiative.

Figure 9-1. Human-Centered Design Process

also a natural part of the process (e.g., being inspired to return to understanding or ideation as a result of experimentation). The HCD process is usually driven by a design team, made up of individuals with diverse backgrounds, perspectives, and expertise (including individuals trained in conducting HCD) to encourage innovative thinking and synergistic collaboration. As will be described in the case studies, this design team may also include the beneficiaries themselves or other partners. Regardless of whether such individuals are a part of the design team itself, the phases of HCD are focused on understanding the priorities of beneficiaries and other stakeholders and grounding the development of solutions in that perspective. In this way, engagement with beneficiaries and stakeholders is always key to the HCD process.

Throughout the HCD process, as new information is uncovered, the design team deepens its understanding of the problem and develops shared understanding of and empathy for the key stakeholders (including potential beneficiaries, community members, clinicians, and family members). The design team strives to embrace ambiguity as exploring new perspectives and ideas may be opportunities for innovation. Key activities within each phase are presented (white boxes). Details about each of the three phases are provided. The approach to HCD described in this chapter is based on the process used by the Gobee Group,[8] a social innovation design consultancy that served as an advisor and collaborator for both case studies. An example of using the HCD process within a home visiting program will be incorporated into some phase descriptions to illustrate the process more concretely.

Mindsets

IDEO.org, the nonprofit that was launched by IDEO in 2011,[9] describes seven core "mindsets" in its *Field Guide to Human-Centered Design*.[10] The mindsets are key to the HCD process and are summarized in Table 9-1: empathy, optimism, iteration, creative confidence, making, embracing ambiguity, and learning from failure. These mindsets can effectively encourage creative collaboration and shared decision making with multidisciplinary partners and key stakeholders. In addition, HCD, as guided by these mindsets, offers methods to help the design team thoroughly understand a problem, generate ideas, and evaluate ideas in relation to the priorities and perspectives of key stakeholders. For example, sharing stories builds empathy for stakeholders by capturing complexities and nuances that hard facts cannot. Maintaining optimism through processes of solving serious public health problems is not always easy, but it can help the team identify resources and opportunities rather than focusing on negatives.

The uncertainty inherent in embracing ambiguity in an iterative HCD process may feel at odds with linear and directed approaches often undertaken in the planning of public interventions. However, embracing ambiguity creates the space for innovations to arise, and iteration mitigates risks through small-scale tests. Creative confidence encourages the design team to believe in everyone's ability to solve problems and to value

Table 9-1. Mindsets From IDEO.org's *Field Guide to Human-Centered Design*

Empathy	"Empathy is the capacity to step into other people's shoes, to understand their lives, and start to solve problems from their perspectives. Human-centered design is premised . . . on the idea that the people you're designing for are your roadmap to innovative solutions. All you have to do is empathize, understand them, and bring them along with you in the design process." (p. 22)
Optimism	"Optimism is the embrace of possibility, the idea that even if we don't know the answer, that it's out there and that we can find it . . . optimism makes us more creative, encourages us to push on when we hit dead ends, and helps all the stakeholders in a project gel." (p. 24)
Iteration	"By continually iterating, refining, and improving our work, we put ourselves in a place where we'll have more ideas, try a variety of approaches, unlock our creativity, and arrive more quickly at successful solutions . . . We iterate because it allows us to keep learning." (p. 25)
Creative confidence	"Creative confidence is the belief that everyone is creative . . . the belief that you can and will come up with creative solutions to big problems . . . Creative confidence will drive you to make things, to test them out, to get it wrong, and to keep on rolling, secure in the knowledge that you'll get where you need to go." (p. 19)
Making	"We build our ideas so that we can test them, and because actually making something reveals opportunities and complexities that we'd never have guessed were there . . . the goal is always to convey an idea, share it, and learn how to make it better." (p. 20)
Embracing ambiguity	"Human-centered designers always start from the place of not knowing the answer to the problem they're looking to solve . . . By embracing that ambiguity, and by trusting that the human-centered design process will guide us toward an innovative answer, we actually give ourselves permission to be fantastically creative." (p. 23)
Learning from failure	"[F]or human-centered designers, sorting out what won't work is part of finding what will. Failure is an inherent part of human-centered design because we rarely get it right on our first try . . . The point is to put something out into the world and then use it to keep learning, keep asking, and keep testing." (p. 21)

Source: Based on IDEO[10] and Nevarez.[11]
Note: Quotes are from IDEO.[10]

everyone's ideas, input, and expertise. Making ideas tangible allows the design team to test and engage with ideas viscerally to learn from failure and small-scale tests before investing significant resources.

Building a design team and organizational culture based on these mindsets as part of the HCD process is critical. For example, before beginning an HCD process, agreeing to these mindsets and acknowledging the discomfort they might cause is an important part of ensuring that the design team shares the same foundation. Moreover, returning to these mindsets at appropriate times in the process and discussing how they benefit the team when moving through each of the three phases described in Figure 9-1 will keep the process grounded in these core values. Even when individuals are unfamiliar with the process, engagement with HCD is most effective when the design team "trust[s] the process"[10(p13)] and creates the space for new and innovative ideas to evolve. Encouraging a culture wherein design team members support one another in maintaining these values creates an environment ripe for creativity and innovation.

Phase 1: Understanding

The HCD process begins with Understanding (Figure 9-1). During the Understanding phase, the goal is not to focus on solutions, but rather to understand the depth and complexity of a particular problem as well as the potential resources available to address it. Often the process will begin with an overarching charge, such as "improve the outcomes for home visiting clients." This charge is typically broad and open-ended, and does not yet fully underscore the key needs of the potential beneficiaries, but rather serves a good starting point for further inquiry. The activities and tools used during this phase are then meant to increase empathy for and understanding of the needs and context of the end user (e.g., home visiting clients). There is no specific timeline for the Understanding phase. While more time spent in this phase may result in the discovery of more insights, strategic use of activities and methods tailored to the context at hand could yield enough information in a short amount of time. The iterative nature of HCD as seen in Figure 9-1 also allows for a return to the understanding phase to learn new information or clarify existing knowledge if necessary. The ultimate goal of the Understanding phase is to ensure that the design team practitioners are asking a question that grapples with a key concern of the beneficiary.

Early in the phase, the development of a project brief can provide useful context for the design team before engaging with beneficiaries directly. The brief should consist of a description of the parameters, perspectives, and realities of the key theme of interest.[7] For instance, summarizing the strategies used within the home visiting program, the outcomes that have been recorded, and the strengths and challenges noted by previous programmatic reports could be a useful brief for the home visiting example. Development of this project brief may draw from review of scholarly and gray literature, results from previous research or program monitoring and evaluation, or a community needs and asset assessment (depending on the focus of the HCD process). This strategy is not unique to HCD; in fact, most project development and planning would benefit from such a document. Although this context is important, the brief only captures what is known from the lens of specific sources (e.g., the program, reports, or literature). The truth of the end-user's experience may contradict, explain, or amplify information within the brief; therefore, the primary focus of the Understanding phase is engagement with the beneficiaries and stakeholders.

Techniques such as interviews, in-context observations, user or peer documentation through photos or prose, and asset mapping are examples of the variety of methods that may be used in the Understanding phase to connect with and learn from the end user.[10,11] These same methods may be used with other stakeholders who are critical for the success of the project. While information is being gathered, the design team should also begin synthesizing insights from what has been learned. "Insights" can be thought of as "aha moments," which indicate something important or surprising that may have deepened or shifted the team's understanding of the problem or users.

As an example, an activity with home visiting staff to document through drawing the experience of a typical day for staff revealed that many home visitors did not have a "home base" to use between home visits with clients (to use the bathroom, write client notes, and generally take a break in the midst of a busy day). Staff relied on their cars and sought out public bathrooms, making the day more chaotic. This insight helped program managers consider how they might leverage existing spaces throughout the county for home visitors to use between visits. Using a creative method such as drawing elicited clear and specific insights that may not have arisen from typical communication methods and helped staff to feel better understood by managers.

The process of gathering of information and synthesis of insights requires a variable amount of time; the design team may share stories from different Understanding experiences with each other, inspire ideas with respect to what has been observed, and channel those conversations into the development of a list of insights. These insights can then be further discussed, debated, and explored in an effort to refine the key question of the design challenge and identify a core need or problem for the end user.

The problem statement is often phrased in the form of a "How might we" question.[10] Rather than a question focused solely on understanding an issue (e.g., "Why don't home visiting clients have better outcomes?"), the intentional phrasing of a "How might we" question focuses on inspiring solutions (e.g., "How might we support the comfort and well-being of home visitors between client visits?"). The "How might we" question focuses on a core problem derived from the insights and lessons learned within the Understanding phase but should not contain a solution within the question. The way in which the problem is framed is meant to inspire ideas during phase 2.

Phase 2: Ideation

The focus of the Ideation phase is to think of solutions to the problem statement generated during the Understanding phase. The design team begins by brainstorming as many ideas as possible to address the problem statement without critiquing or censoring any ideas at this stage. Though beneficiaries and stakeholders may not be a part of the design team (and so may not be participating directly in brainstorming ideas), their voices, priorities, and perspectives are at the center of idea generation—design team members' ideas should be motivated by the engagement with end users and the insights derived from the Understanding phase.[7,10,11] Design team members can also use techniques such as reflecting on analogous situations and bouncing ideas off each other to generate additional ideas during brainstorming. The use of sticky notes on which individuals write ideas and post them on a wall so that the ideas may be moved and grouped into themes is a popular tool for brainstorming; other tools can also be used to organize the brainstorming process.[10,11] Ensuring the design team itself contains diverse voices, perspectives, and areas of expertise becomes particularly important in this phase to enable the generation of a wide variety of ideas. Ground rules for brainstorming help ensure a conducive environment for creative and innovative exploration; Figure 9-2 includes the ground rules adapted for the case studies from IDEO.org's *Field Guide*.[10]

With many ideas to choose from, the team selects the most promising ideas for the Experimentation and Implementation phase. The team will consider the parameters from the brief and the insights from the Understanding phase to ground the selection process in the realities of the issue. The team will sort, group, and evaluate the ideas to identify two or three ideas that best fit the limitations and priorities of the problem.[10,11] One tool that can be used to help with organizing ideas is the 2 × 2 matrix.[12] In such a matrix, two lines are drawn in a plus sign shape on a surface such as a poster or a white board to create four equal squares. Each line represents the extremes of the characteristics (e.g., quick to implement vs. time intensive, low-cost vs. high-cost), those the team decides are important for prioritizing ideas. Two extreme pairs are selected, and the opposite extremes are then placed at each end of a line. Each resulting quadrant thus represents two characteristics (e.g., quick to implement and high-cost, time intensive and low-cost). The design team, according to the priorities identified during the Understanding phase and the available resources and parameters of the design team itself, may then select which ideas would be best to prototype (a tangible way to test each idea and learn from small-scale experiments[7]) to determine which idea should ultimately be implemented. For example, if the project needs a quick win with few resources, the team may select three easy-to-implement, low-cost ideas for prototyping in phase 3. Ultimately, the ideas selected should be in line with the insights learned from the beneficiaries and be feasible to prototype with beneficiaries in phase 3.

Phase 3: Experimentation and Implementation

The Experimentation and Implementation phase encompasses as many cycles of test, review, and refinement as project constraints allow and as the design team deems necessary. This phase includes both initial prototyping to determine which ideas will progress and full-fledged action plans for the implementation and subsequent iterations of piloting and scaling a program or product.[7] The goal of this phase is to make the ideas tangible and to receive feedback from the end users to refine the idea to better meet the users' needs. "Making things tangible" could involve making a poster with a storyboard to describe a service. It could mean making small-scale paper or foam models to represent the idea in a physical way that users can interact with and modify. For a program, making an idea tangible might mean role playing or testing out portions of the program.

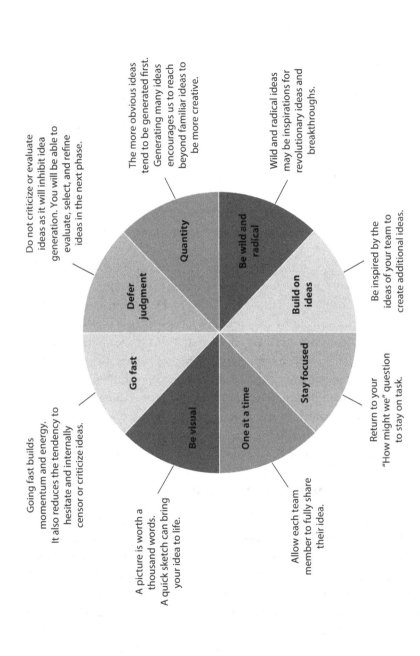

Source: Based on IDEO.[10]

Figure 9-2. Ground Rules for Ideation Brainstorming

For example, training a small number of home visitors to use a specific communication technique during their visits, observing the visits, and speaking with both clients and home visitors afterward could serve as a prototype for a communication strategy. By starting small, with concrete, structured opportunities to test or prototype aspects of the idea, the team can quickly learn how to adapt and improve to make the best use of resources when the program or product is implemented to scale.

The first round of prototyping can serve to focus the work on one idea to pursue for broader implementation.[11] Depending on capacity, the design team may decide to initially pursue multiple ideas from the Ideation phase, conducting several rounds of prototyping for each. Each prototype may be geared toward answering a particular question or different aspects of the solution. For example, when designing a home visiting program, one prototype may focus more on the experience of clients whereas another may focus on the experience of the home visiting staff. The methods used to prototype will depend on resources and time, and the value of a simple, rapid prototyping approach should not be underestimated.[10,11] The more quickly the design team can learn while minimizing cost, the better the product will be when it is ready to move into larger and more resource-intensive implementation. On the basis of feedback from beneficiaries and stakeholders, the design team may decide that none of the ideas protoyped is best for moving forward, and a return to the Ideation phase may be deemed necessary on the basis of new insights learned.

Once an idea has been identified for broader implementation, project planning with thorough monitoring and evaluation strategies will be key. Throughout all components of this phase, one core feature remains: the design team is always seeking new information and user feedback to incorporate into the next iteration. Revisiting the insights from the Understanding phase throughout this process will ground the work in findings about the users and the challenge; building in opportunities for dialogue with beneficiaries during this phase will enhance the ultimate result; and returning to earlier phases of HCD on the basis of information learned is a viable option and should be embraced.

Human-Centered Design in Public Health Research and Practice

The HCD process has similarities and differences in relation to other approaches used in public health research and practice, including community-based participatory research (CBPR) and the Plan–Do–Study–Act (PDSA) quality improvement methodology. Within a CBPR process, the goal is to engage potential beneficiaries or participants as equitable partners throughout the process of identifying, developing, and implementing research opportunities and resulting actions.[13,14] CBPR projects often focus on the development of deep relationships between universities (or other entities developing research or programs) and communities over time to ensure that community members are genuine partners in research endeavors and the translation of knowledge into change.[14] In contrast to CBPR, HCD processes do not always involve beneficiaries on the design team itself.[4,15,16] However, at its core, HCD is committed to the development of ideas according to end user priorities and so engagement with beneficiaries throughout the HCD process is a prominent feature. In addition, through its potentially rapid process, HCD may allow for nimbler and action-oriented engagement with end users in creating and testing interventions or products than a full CBPR process might be able to do in the same amount of time. Bringing the principles of CBPR into the HCD process can also be a useful way to engage beneficiaries as part of the design team itself and forge deeper partnerships with communities in the process.

The PDSA methodology is a popular quality improvement approach in the health care field.[17] PDSA provides an iterative approach to designing, testing, and revamping an intervention. HCD and PDSA share a consideration of beginning implementation at a small scale, testing possible solutions early and often, and adapting in response to lessons learned.[17,18] The HCD process differs from PDSA in the explicit commitment of the HCD process to beneficiary-centered understanding and empathy to develop solutions. In this way, the HCD process can be complementary to PDSA, adding complexity and a user-centered lens to the "Plan" stage so that the project that makes up the "Do," "Study," and "Act" phases is grounded in key challenges as identified by beneficiaries.[18,19]

Given the multilevel and multifaceted issues with which fields such as public health and social work grapple to address health inequities,[20] the HCD process is uniquely suited to advancing intervention efforts; it centers innovative ideas around the people most affected by an issue and allows rapid testing and reflection before bringing an idea to scale. In spaces where evidence-based interventions are not working as expected, the HCD process may be helpful for reexamining the challenge at hand and considering ways to adapt efforts more effectively.

HCD has been used to address a wide array of public health and health care issues. For example, HCD has been used to support the global scaling of antiretroviral therapy treatment programs,[21] examine anxiety triggers for patients going through radiotherapy treatment for cancer,[22] and improve how service changes are implemented in a hospital system.[23] This methodology has also been used in addressing challenges to community well-being, in line with the LCT's emphasis on the impact of experiences throughout life affecting birth outcomes over time. For instance, HCD has been used to guide the placement of new emergency obstetric and newborn services within a village,[24] create improved sanitation systems,[25] and develop a comprehensive messaging campaign for parents around supporting children's brain development.[26] The next section provides an overview of the HCD process, the application of which will be illustrated through two case studies.

USING HUMAN-CENTERED DESIGN IN LIFE COURSE WORK

Building on the overview of the HCD process, this section focuses on two case studies to illustrate the application of HCD in LCT-based work. HCD is best learned by using the process. Each case study is followed by a reflection on the strengths, challenges, and recommendations for future efforts. The case studies also serve as a foundation for discussing what MCH practitioners might consider when applying HCD in their own life course work. The authors were each involved in one or both of the projects described in the case studies. Though both case studies focus on the use of HCD in place-based work, the HCD process could be applied in any setting (e.g., clinics, health departments, advocacy organizations) in which practitioners are seeking to approach problems in an innovative way and address challenges that affect women and families throughout the life course.

Background for Case Studies: The Best Babies Zone in Castlemont (Oakland, California)

In 2009, the Alameda County Public Health Department (ACPHD) in California launched Building Blocks for Health Equity to help advance health equity efforts within the Department and Alameda County more broadly.[27] In 2012, ACPHD continued to expand this work within the Family Health Services Division by joining a W.K. Kellogg–funded life course project led by the University of California, Berkeley, called the Best Babies Zone initiative (BBZ). BBZ's vision is that "every baby is born healthy, into communities that enable them to thrive and reach their full potential"[28] with a specific focus on community transformation in six neighborhoods across the United States. ACPHD selected the 7-by-12-block area of Oakland, California—the Castlemont neighborhood—for its BBZ work.[5]

According to Census estimates, Castlemont has a population of 5,431 residents, of whom 48.9% identify as Hispanic or Latino and 42.3% identify as Black or African American.[29] Castlemont residents face some notable challenges: one in four residents lives below the poverty level, including nearly 40% of children aged younger than 5 years. Based on 2009 to 2013 averages, 13.3% of the approximately 100 annual births in Castlemont were premature (compared with 9.2% and 11.8% in Alameda County and the country, respectively) and 11.4% of births were low birth weight (compared with 7.3% and 8.1% in Alameda County and the country, respectively).[30] Despite its challenges, Castlemont also has unique strengths: it is home to active community organizations and resident leaders, and there is a strong sense that people in the area are creating positive change. For these reasons, Castlemont was selected as the site for the BBZ in Oakland. BBZ Castlemont has collaborated with residents and partners to effect change in the neighborhood in relation to four community-identified priority areas: safety and violence, community building, education, and the local economy.

Recognizing the challenges of developing effective interventions to address complex systemic issues that affect the health of Castlemont's residents, BBZ staff identified the need for innovative approaches.[5] Staff identified HCD as a promising practice to develop small, concrete ideas in the neighborhood that would move beyond traditional service-oriented solutions to increase momentum for broader community transformation. Funding was obtained from The California Wellness Foundation to work with the Gobee Group[8] to

Table 9-2. Two Human-Centered Design Approaches and Best Babies Zone Pilot Examples

	HCD With Partners	HCD With Residents
BBZ Pilots	*The Design Sprint (2013)*	*The East Oakland Innovators (2014)*
	Program length: 3 months **Number of team members:** 14 **Number of HCD facilitators/coaches:** 2 **Team participants:** Alameda County Public Health Department, East Bay Asian Local Development Corporation, East Bay Sustainable Business Alliance, Federal Reserve Bank of San Francisco, the Gobee Group, Mandela MarketPlace, Social Services Agency of Alameda County, Y&H Soda Foundation, Youth UpRising **Focus area:** Local economy	**Program length:** 8 months **Number of team members:** 9 **Number of HCD facilitators/coaches:** 3 **Team participants:** Alameda County Public Health Department, East Oakland residents, the Gobee Group **Collaborator organizations:** Brighter Beginnings, Lotus Bloom-Room to Bloom, Youth UpRising **Focus areas:** Local economy, education, community building
Overview	1. Worked with community to identify priority area of challenge and opportunity. 2. Identified a group of stakeholders, including topical "experts" and partners to participate in the team. 3. Moved through HCD process, engaging with residents strategically to center and enhance the work. **Results:** Following the HCD process, implemented the resulting project, starting small, testing, and working to scale.	1. Identified a group of residents committed to community development in their neighborhood. 2. Moved through an initial structured process of learning by doing HCD to familiarize residents with HCD model. 3. Supported residents to use the HCD process to address areas of challenge and opportunity within their community while strengthening personal leadership skills. **Results:** Supported residents to pilot the resulting projects from the HCD process and consider ways to sustain efforts moving forward.

Source: Based on Vechakul et al.,[5] Vechakul,[31] and Anderson.[32]
Note: BBZ=Best Babies Zone; HCD=Human-Centered Design.

assist with applying HCD to identify early-stage projects. Two different pilot programs involving two different strategies for applying the HCD process emerged from this work. Table 9-2 summarizes the two strategies. Case study 1 presents the Design Sprint, an example of HCD with partners on the design team; case study 2 presents the East Oakland Innovators (EOI), an example of HCD with residents on the design team. Both case studies are presented to demonstrate the versatility of HCD's application and to inspire readers to consider what approaches might be best suited to their needs.

Case Study 1: Human-Centered Design With Partners Through the Design Sprint

Staff first practiced HCD in 2013 through the 12-week Design Sprint with 14 partners from 9 different organizations focused on economic development (Table 9-2).[5] A "Design Sprint" typically refers to a more condensed and rapid design process.[33] The Design

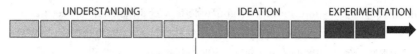

UNDERSTANDING   IDEATION   EXPERIMENTATION

How might we work with community members and leverage
existing assets and resources to support a visible small win to
build a vibrant local economy in the Castlemont neighborhood?

Source: Based on Vechakul et al.[5] and Vechakul.[31]

Note: Each block represents a week in the Design Sprint process, shaded with reference to the Human-Centered Design process described in Figure 9-1. The formal Design Sprint concluded with focusing on one idea (and so did not move into initial implementation); the arrow indicates the ongoing work of implementation and iterative testing and refining, which continued through Best Babies Zone's and partners' efforts with the Castlemont Community Market.

Figure 9-3. Overview of 12-Week Design Sprint Process

Sprint was used to orient the BBZ work around "small, visible wins" and to train staff in the use of HCD for future efforts. The Design Sprint brought together a design team representing community development, government, economic development, and design fields to participate in a facilitated HCD process lead by trained ACPHD staff and the Gobee Group. The focus of this effort was on engaging partners, getting to know the Castlemont community, and identifying first steps for strengthening economic vibrancy in the neighborhood.[5] The rapid timeline was intentional: long enough to be fully engaged in a productive process while still being respectful of the busy design team participants' time commitment. Each week, the group would meet for two hours (most often in Youth UpRising, a youth-focused community development organization in Castlemont) to learn about HCD and move through the process by implementing specific activities or discussions (Figure 9-3).[5,31]

The 6-week Understanding phase consisted of neighborhood walks and conversations with local residents, leaders, and current and former business owners to understand the needs, strengths, and challenges of the community. Insights from the Understanding phase revealed that many people were giving back in the Castlemont community, neighbors and business owners strived to help each other, and many expressed interest in visible positive opportunities to build community as a countermeasure to feelings of being unsafe from community violence. There is a thriving arts community in East Oakland, and many people were engaged in cottage industries—making and selling items to make ends meet. The "How might we" question of focus for the group was ultimately "How might we work with community members and leverage existing assets and resources to support a visible small win to build a vibrant local economy in the Castlemont neighborhood?"[31] A "small win" is a project focused on making an impact on a smaller level that has the potential to be scaled if successful.

The 4-week Ideation phase consisted of a structured brainstorming process consisting of sticky notes and drawings, narrowing of ideas, and using methods to collectively assess ideas for further refinement and development. The Design Sprint team selected the most promising four ideas: youth murals, local newsletters, child-friendly spaces in business, and a community arts market. The 2-week Experimentation phase included developing storyboards and gathering feedback on the top four ideas at the local school and church. Following these prototyping sessions, the community market was selected as the idea to pursue for ongoing implementation.[5]

The monthly Castlemont Community Market launched in December 2013 as a collaboration among BBZ, Youth UpRising, and Castlemont High School.[34] The market aims to showcase the strengths and talents of local artists and enterprises, to encourage neighbors to buy from one another to keep money circulating within the local economy, and to work with economic development partners to provide support for entrepreneurs who want to expand their businesses. BBZ has continued to spearhead the ongoing evolution of the market in Castlemont, incorporating lessons learned, testing out new ideas to build on successes and learn from challenges, and supporting broader economic development efforts in conjunction with the market.[5]

The Design Sprint Strengths and Challenges

The Design Sprint is an example of an HCD process in which partners and staff learned HCD by implementing the process as part of the design team in a real-world setting (in contrast to a model in which consultants move through the process to develop solutions on behalf of clients).[4,5,9] Table 9-3 summarizes the strengths and challenges of the Design

Table 9-3. Key Strengths and Challenges From the Design Sprint

Strengths	• Learn-by-doing style enhanced understanding of HCD for participants.
	• Bringing together organizations to move through HCD process strengthened collaborative bonds.
	• HCD's focus on asking key questions and moving toward tangible, small-scale action made tackling a large problem seem doable.
	• Commitment from ACPHD to move forward after the Design Sprint for implementation allowed participants to focus on learning the process knowing their work would proceed afterward.
	• The empathy-building focus of HCD and being out in the community allowed participants to gain deeper understanding of the Castlemont community.
	• Rapid prototyping provided very useful feedback from residents at minimal cost.
Challenges	• As a pilot effort with a focus on building HCD capacity, residents were integral parts of the Understanding phase and prototyping but were not a part of the HCD team itself as originally intended.
	• The need to have specific activities and times to walk around Castlemont and connect with residents based on the schedules of participants limited which residents had the opportunity to communicate their thoughts.
	• Concern that engaging with residents during an ambiguous process with no guaranteed outcome can lead to false hope or mistrust in the community.

Source: Based on Vechakul et al.[5] and Vechakul.[31] The reflections in this table are drawn both from the results of the qualitative evaluation of the Design Sprint and from additional notes from the authors involved in the Design Sprint (Shrimali and Vechakul).

Note: ACPHD = Alameda County Public Health Department; HCD = Human-Centered Design.

Sprint. In contrast to other project planning experiences, the design team appreciated the focus on developing a problem statement based on a deeper understanding of the community and identifying a tangible, small-scale action based on feedback from residents in the face of a large issue—community economic vibrancy. The process strengthened bonds among partners and deepened their understanding of Castlemont.

Design team participants highlighted several challenges during the Design Sprint. The busy schedules of team members resulted in sporadic attendance, challenging the continuity of the HCD learning experience. Engaging with residents (the intended beneficiaries) during the design process was also challenging. Working to have meetings of the design team during regular business hours (as partners were participating as part of their professional work) limited resident engagement—while the design team was in the neighborhood, residents may have been at work or away from their homes. The flexible and discovery-focused nature of HCD created the concern among the design team members that if nothing productive resulted from the HCD experience, relationships between design team members and residents could be damaged. Staff and time constraints limited the capacity of the team to include residents as team members. The team decided to pilot the HCD process with organizational partners to gain familiarity, paving the way for future opportunities in which residents would act as co-designers.

Case Study 2: Human-Centered Design With Residents Through the East Oakland Innovators

In this project, BBZ staff engaged residents as part of the design team in the EOI program to strengthen resident capacity to drive innovation in Castlemont (Table 9-2). The Innovators were a group of residents who were using HCD to develop "small-win" projects around key community priorities. Interested residents learned of the program through partner organizations and publicity fliers, submitted applications, and were interviewed to join the EOI program. Building on the efforts of and lessons learned from the Design Sprint, the EOI program was designed to train residents as HCD practitioners and then to support residents to move through their own HCD process as design team members and implement projects in their own community.[31,32]

The EOI program included nine resident Innovators who lived in, worked in, or otherwise had a connection to the Castlemont neighborhood for an intensive 8-month program in 2014. During the program, Innovators learned about and moved through their own HCD process with support from coaches (Figure 9-4). Three coaches served as facilitators and guides with the goal of supporting the Innovators in developing sustainable projects that were grounded in Castlemont realities. One of the three coaches had expertise in HCD and was affiliated with Gobee Group. The EOI program included monolingual Spanish-, monolingual English-, and bilingual English- and Spanish-speaking residents, in keeping with the demographic representation of the neighborhood.

1. How might we demonstrate the value of the individual and power of the community as an engine of change?

2. How might we motivate adults in the community to participate in educational and productive programs?

3. How might we provide more oversight for local businesses, including what happens around businesses, what happens in businesses, and what businesses are associated with?

QUICK WIN

UNDERSTANDING

IDEATION

EXPERIMENTATION AND IMPLEMENTATION

How might we address the challenges of city infrastructure as it affects problems of trash and dumping?

Note: Each block represents a week in the East Oakland Innovators (EOI) program, shaded with reference to the Human-Centered Design (HCD) process described in Figure 9-1 along with the addition of the EOI Quick Win. The formal EOI program concluded following a short implementation phase for each EOI team; the arrow indicates the ongoing work carried out by two of the EOI teams to continue adapting and implementing their projects. The timeline also indicates how the focus of the design challenge evolved by noting the "How might we . . ." questions guiding the HCD process at various stages in the program.

Figure 9-4. Overview of 8-Month East Oakland Innovators Program

Accordingly, an English–Spanish interpreter was a part of the coaching staff. The group met one to two times a week at times convenient for the Innovators (evenings or weekends) in or near Castlemont. Childcare, food, a monthly stipend, and additional support (such as transportation) were always provided.

The EOI program began with a 12-week "Quick Win" training (a rapid, guided engagement with HCD similar to a Design Sprint; Figure 9-4). During the Quick Win, the coaches preselected a relevant problem in the Castlemont neighborhood (trash and dumping) and guided the Innovators through Understanding, Ideation, and Experimentation and Implementation phases. Each Quick Win phase introduced specific methods along with an HCD toolkit[11] with additional resources. Though a project was piloted as a result of the Quick Win (a community party that included education around civic dumping services), the primary purpose of the Quick Win was to support the Innovators to become the drivers of the HCD process for the "Big Win" when they would drive the HCD process.

For the Big Win, the Innovators divided into three design teams, each with a coach. Design teams formed around a common interest area of importance to the community: parent education, citizen empowerment, and local business development. The design teams moved through each phase of the HCD process using methods from the toolkits, which each design team identified as relevant to its work. The 5-week Understanding phase included activities such as neighborhood walks to speak with neighbors and observe how people interacted with each other, interviews and surveys with residents as they picked up children from school, and observations of how individuals shopped in a neighborhood store.

On the basis of their insights, each design team refined a "How might we" question tied to the team's topic (Figure 9-4). During the 2-week Ideation phase, each design team used sticky notes to record individual ideas (each team generated more than 50 ideas) and organized ideas on according to similarity. Design teams then identified methods to narrow their topics on the basis of time, feasibility, and the lessons learned from the Understanding phase. The 13-week Experimentation and Implementation phase included initial prototyping of identified ideas with residents, which resulted in further development of ideas. For example, the local business development team created a rating system for local corner stores according to how healthy their products were that would be displayed in store windows. The goal was to promote stores with healthier products and increase their business in the community. The design team spoke with store owners about participating in the rating system and with shoppers about the impact of the idea; the store owners refused to participate, and the shoppers said the rating would not change their shopping habits. Based on these findings, the team revisited their Understanding and Ideation phase results to identify a new direction.

Following Experimentation, three projects were piloted: (1) a Sister Circle meeting focused on the power of women and connectedness, (2) a series of parent self-care classes to promote personal education and well-being, and (3) a publicity campaign focused on increasing the availability of healthy food in a local store. To support the piloting of these projects during the Experimentation and Implementation phase, the coaches provided additional training on project planning, budget management, and monitoring and evaluation. Each pilot project was implemented with support from collaborator organizations, and each design team member received a small financial award at the end of the program, which could be applied to further refining the pilot. Two of the three teams continued their programs. One design team partnered with a local early childhood center to extend their parent self-care classes, and a second design team continued to engage with the local store to explore other business promotion activities. Several Innovators remained involved with BBZ in different leadership capacities, and BBZ has begun to implement additional rounds of the EOI program.

The East Oakland Innovators Strengths and Challenges

The EOI program is an example of an HCD process with residents (the Innovators) as members of the design team. Table 9-4 summarizes the strengths and challenges of the pilot program, based on a mixed-method evaluation of the EOI program and its

Table 9-4. Key Strengths and Challenges From the East Oakland Innovators

Strengths	• Participants felt the HCD framework provided a good structure for organizing thoughts and moving toward potential impacts.
	• The learn-by-doing approach was a useful way to understand and feel confident in HCD.
	• Participants developed a deeper connection to and understanding of Castlemont.
	• Moving through the HCD process together built trust and a sense of connection among participants.
	• The HCD process and leadership programs increased confidence and experience with HCD and leadership skills for all participants.
	• Participants felt motivated to continue engaging with community work as a result of the program.
Challenges	• The program evolved as it was happening and was the first time BBZ had developed and implemented a resident-based HCD program.
	• Challenges with attendance and attrition delayed and complicated the program overall, resulting in uneven understanding of HCD across the participants and less time for project planning and implementation.
	• The limited scope and reach of project implementation during the program was disappointing to participants.
	• Facilitating in both English and Spanish added time and confusion to the process at times, particularly when the interpreter had to serve simultaneously as a coach.
	• Coaches were more directly involved in driving the HCD process than originally intended, acting as participants in the Big Win teams rather than as more removed facilitators.

Note: BBZ = Best Babies Zone; HCD = Human-Centered Design. The reflections in this table are drawn both from the results of the quantitative and qualitative evaluation of the East Oakland Innovators and from additional notes from the authors involved in the program (Berkowitz, Vechakul, Shrimali, and Anderson).

impact on the Innovators. Innovators appreciated the team building and engagement with Castlemont and learning HCD through its application. They were inspired to continue their work in the community, a result of the intentional resident leadership skill-building emphasis. The focus on ensuring that residents were the drivers of the process resulted in unique challenges. Implementing the program and teaching HCD in multiple languages was difficult. While this was vital for ensuring residents from throughout Castlemont could participate, additional resources (a separate interpreter who was not also a coach) were necessary. The transition between the coaches' roles during the Quick Win (leaders and teachers of the HCD process) and during the Big Win (supporters and thought partners for the Innovators' process) was difficult and unclear for some Innovators. Ultimately, the residents still relied on the coaches for guiding aspects of HCD during the Big Win. Innovators felt different levels of confidence in their HCD skills moving into the Big Win (because, in part, of attrition and absenteeism) and coaches were sometimes called on to take more of a lead role than was intended. In addition, the Innovators wanted to make more of an impact in their community than was feasible; more time for implementation with support from the coaches was desired.

Recommendations

Though derived from the Design Sprint and EOI experiences, these recommendations represent important points of consideration for any HCD process (Box 9-1). A design team must ensure that all members are invested, clear on the parameters and time commitment of the process, and represent diverse sectors and levels of expertise relevant to the topic. Including beneficiaries as part of the design team is an important consideration, as they will bring different and meaningful perspectives and expertise to the design process overall. Investing resources to support all design team members to participate fully in the process (transportation support, childcare, additional trainings, flexible meeting times, dedicated team building opportunities) is important. Ensuring that the design team is available to engage with beneficiaries at the times most convenient for them is crucial for building empathy and trust. If members of the design team are new to the HCD process, having a facilitator with HCD expertise will ensure the process moves forward as design team members are learning.

Considerations of power dynamics between the facilitators/coaches and the design team members is a key part of developing the team dynamic; reflecting on the mindsets that guide the HCD process can support this effort. Ensuring sufficient time and resources to support implementation following the experimentation process is ideal. Neither the Design Sprint nor the EOI was able to identify funds to support implementation at the outset, but the programs were committed to finding a way to move forward and were fortunate to ultimately identify opportunities. Being transparent at the start about what resources are available is important for building trust and group understanding.

It is important to note that these case studies are only two examples of using the HCD process in MCH LCT–based work. Both case studies were pilot efforts of BBZ Castlemont, were not developed with comparison groups to determine how the effect of using the HCD process might compare with other program development strategies. They were created within the context of a public health department that is supportive of innovative approaches to MCH work. An HCD process in a different context may include a design team with different groups of stakeholders, including partners and beneficiaries, and individuals from other relevant fields (e.g., government representatives, medical professionals, academic researchers). An HCD process may be longer or shorter than the case studies' time periods and may be more iterative (involving a return to previous phases during the process to further clarify the work). The key takeaway is that the HCD process can allow a program to think differently about the challenges being addressed and may inspire new ideas and strategies centered on the intended beneficiaries. The final section of this chapter provides some guidance for considering the use of the HCD process in the reader's own work.

Box 9-1. Recommendations From Case Studies

- Incorporate representation from different fields with a commitment to the community of beneficiaries or the general topic to allow diverse perspectives; consider bringing together both organizational partners and beneficiaries as part of the HCD team.
- Ensure full buy-in from participants (and their organizations, if applicable) to engage fully in the process.
- Consider potential challenges with scheduling and retention before and during recruitment, communicate commitment at the outset with participants, and recognize that some will still need to leave regardless.
- Ensure that all coaches feel confident in HCD to guide the process of participants learning by doing HCD and communicate specific plans for coaches' roles with teams, including considerations of power sharing and project responsibility.
- Identify the priorities, capacity, and limitations of the HCD team and the lead organization while organizing the process.
- For multilingual programs, ensure sufficient resources for interpreters to serve that key role without additional responsibilities.
- Consider how to best schedule opportunities for interaction with the community and residents to ensure a diversity of voices is incorporated.
- Ensure there is sufficient time for project implementation with support from coaches and additional resources, whether during or after the formal program.
- Dedicated, flexible resources that can be brought to bear on whatever outcome results from HCD are key to identify as soon as possible.

Source: Based on Vechakul et al.[5] and Vechakul.[31] The reflections in this box are drawn from the results of the qualitative evaluation of the Design Sprint, the results of the quantitative and qualitative evaluation of the East Oakland Innovators, and additional notes from the authors.
Note: HCD = Human-Centered Design.

BRINGING HUMAN-CENTERED DESIGN INTO PRACTICE

Ultimately, HCD is a process best learned by doing. The goal of this chapter was to serve as an introduction to how HCD can be applied in MCH work. As the reader considers the HCD process, the authors recommend keeping the following pieces of advice in mind.

Trust the Process

HCD inherently involves ambiguity. Though each process begins with a key theme or issue area of focus, the specific solution or end result is not decided at the beginning of the process. By starting from a more open and exploratory place, the HCD process allows the perspectives and priorities of end users and stakeholders to really drive the development of innovative solutions. This is distinct from a more typical experience of receiving funding to implement a specific, predefined solution, and, as such, the process may feel chaotic. The iterative nature of HCD means that the process is adapting and evolving on the basis of new insights into the challenges and priorities of the intended beneficiaries. The temptation may be to avoid these periods of discomfort by keeping a solution in mind throughout. However, rushing to define something concrete or specific negates the potential for HCD to create the space for innovation. HCD practitioners are encouraged to embrace the discomfort and uncertainty of the process throughout to maximize creativity and possibility.

Consider Goals and Capacity Before Beginning the Process

The HCD process necessitates a commitment to the HCD mindsets (Table 9-1) and an ability to put those mindsets and the process of HCD into practice. The ability to convene relevant stakeholders for the design team, build in time to engage in a new way with end users, and truly build on what is learned from the process are important for the potential impact of the process's results. Reflection on the goals of an effort and the capacity of an organization to support an HCD process before diving in will help in deciding how best to utilize this approach. The scale of the process can be adjusted to fit the needs of the organization and its current work.

Bring Human-Centered Design Into Work in Incremental Ways

The HCD process is not only useful for ongoing program planning. HCD activities, mindsets, and processes on a small scale internally can also help spark innovation in the workplace. Utilizing an HCD process for internal planning with staff may be a productive way to bring innovation into an organization. For example, in a team meeting to plan an event, the HCD process can be used to hone in on the challenges of the event, brainstorm creative solutions, and prototype ideas to help determine how best to address those challenges. Thinking creatively and reflecting on the needs and capacities of an organization can inspire new ways to incorporate HCD and familiarize staff with the process.

Invite Different Voices to the Design Team

Diverse voices bring unique perspectives, ideas, and insights to the HCD process, creating an environment for richer brainstorming, questioning, and understanding. A design team can include organizational partners, community stakeholders, beneficiaries, patients, clinicians/direct service providers, and field experts. Even if the design team cannot incorporate this diversity of members, it is important to consider different ways through which such stakeholders could engage with an HCD process. For example, an expert may be invited to participate in a few meetings as part of the Understanding phase on the basis of identified design team interest. Focus groups could be held with patients or with consumers to engage their ideas.

Keep Coming Back to the Key Question and Insights

The value of developing a key question that gets to the root of a problem as described by beneficiaries cannot be overstated. A well-targeted question honed during the Understanding phase and insights identified in response to that question can inspire the types of solutions that address key problems in innovative ways. Public health practitioners bring a wealth of experiences and training to their work and it may be difficult to shake the feeling that a business-as-usual solution is the only possible option to address a difficult challenge. The way to reflect on whether that might be the case is to return to the key question and the insights provided by beneficiaries and stakeholders during the HCD process. Does the business-as-usual solution really address what end users say is most important? If so, why has that solution not been successful to date according to end users' and stakeholders' insights? Is the business-as-usual solution really answering the key question? What are other possible answers according to the insights of beneficiaries? Such reflection can inspire different ways of thinking about possible solutions and create a space for developing answers that are more fully grounded in the priorities and key concerns of beneficiaries.

Allow "Crazy" Ideas to Be the Seeds of Innovation

Relatedly, the Ideation phase, in which judgment is deferred and no idea is shut down (Figure 9-2), can be as frustrating as it is freeing. It is tempting to feel that the solution is already known, and this can bias a design team member against considering other possibilities. Let the brainstorming process happen as openly and inclusively as possible, building on ideas of others, returning to insights from the Understanding phase for inspiration, and pushing the design team members to think about ideas they may ordinarily reject for being too outlandish. For some, this opportunity to brainstorm without limits may feel natural and exciting. For others, this may feel uncomfortable, overwhelming, or futile. For the latter, trusting the process once again comes into play. The Ideation phase occupies a specific part of the process, which is bound by the narrowing of ideas to select those that will be prototyped. Even if this phase feels too open-ended, design team members can be comforted by the HCD process overall, which seeks to move toward concrete action.

Support the Implementation Process as Much as Possible

Unless the HCD process is being used as a way of learning the methods without intention of implementation, it can feel very frustrating to get to the exciting point of experimentation and be unable to continue. This is especially true if beneficiaries have not only been engaged during the HCD phases but also have been members of the design team itself. If, for example, there are limited funds and time to support implementation, this should be shared at the beginning of the process so that the team can incorporate these parameters into the process of selecting ideas for prototyping. Always remain transparent about what can be done and consider if or how it may be possible to test, refine, and implement the idea resulting from the HCD process.

Developing a project centered around the perspectives of beneficiaries and using the iterative process of HCD to start small and adapt before scaling may ultimately be more fiscally responsible than implementing a top-down project. Limited funding may also inspire more creative solutions. Transparency and reflection in relation to funding parameters with design team members, stakeholders, and beneficiaries will be an important early step in the process. Though different from seeking funding for the implementation of a predefined intervention, the use of the HCD process and the commitment to grounding work in the perspectives of end users may be attractive to funders who are willing to support innovative solutions. Highlighting the potential of HCD to identify innovative and beneficiary-centered solutions as you seek funding can ultimately be a strength.

Seek Support While Learning the Process

HCD is best learned by doing. For early engagement with the HCD process in an organization, it can be very useful to collaborate with an experienced HCD practitioner. This type of assistance can allow team members to learn while still feeling confident that the HCD process is being effectively implemented. If identifying an HCD expert or consultant is not feasible for the organization, online materials do exist to introduce an individual or group to HCD and, in some cases, support movement through a full HCD process. IDEO U (listed in the Resources) is one example, and online course sites such as Coursera[35] and +Acumen[36] also include courses in HCD. Local colleges or universities may include HCD classes as well; although courses may be geared toward product design (as befitting the origins of HCD for such endeavors), an introduction to the approach may be translated to social issues and public health challenges within an organization. The authors cannot endorse a specific course, but organizations are encouraged to read reviews, reach out to individuals who practice HCD, and reflect with their organization to determine whether any of these resources might be best suited for the project at hand.

CONCLUSIONS

HCD provides a valuable, innovative, and creative approach for understanding and endeavoring to address complex challenges in MCH work seeking to actualize the LCT. The unique human-centered focus ensures that efforts will be grounded in the beneficiaries' individual needs and assets. The solutions generated through HCD-based work can move MCH efforts closer to creating environments that support healthy infants, children, adolescents, fathers, mothers, and communities.

KEY POINTS

- The HCD process is a useful approach for developing and enhancing public health program planning efforts as driven by the priorities and perspectives of potential beneficiaries (e.g., patients, clients, community members).
- The HCD process consists of iterative phases (Understanding, Ideation, and Experimentation and Implementation) that support the creation of innovative solutions to difficult problems and is led by a design team, which can include partners and beneficiaries.
- In using the HCD process, design team members are encouraged to trust the process, allow "crazy" ideas to be the seeds of innovation, and always return to the needs, experiences, and priorities of beneficiaries to drive the work.
- Action strategies for practitioners
  - Consider how the HCD process might support MCH life course work.
  - Learn HCD by using it in different aspects of MCH life course work.
  - Explore ways of engaging with partners and beneficiaries throughout the HCD process to strengthen your relationships and your impact.

RESOURCES

- IDEO.org's Design Kit: a collection of guides, resources, and online methods to support your HCD process (http://www.designkit.org).
- IDEO U: online courses in HCD for individuals and groups (https://www.ideou.com).

- Stanford University's d.school methods: resources, videos, and methods to support an HCD process (http://dschool.stanford.edu/use-our-methods).
- The Innovation Learning Network: organizations and resources that support the use of design for healthcare innovation (http://www.innovationlearningnetwork.org/#aboutus).
- MIT D-Lab Publications: a collection of research, guides, and frameworks from the MIT D-Lab with a focus on use of HCD in communities around the world to address global poverty challenges (http://d-lab.mit.edu/node/1502).
- Coursera: an online course site for university-based classes that offers HCD courses (https://www.coursera.org).
- +Acumen: an online course site focused on social change that offers HCD courses (http://www.plusacumen.org).
- Best Babies Zone's East Oakland Innovators Design Thinking Toolkits (http://www.acphd.org/building-blocks/projects/bbz/east-oakland-innovators.aspx).

ACKNOWLEDGMENTS

This chapter would not have been possible without the hard work and dedication of the BBZ Castlemont team, past and present, who developed and supported the Design Sprint and the East Oakland Innovators projects and whose current efforts continue to push BBZ Castlemont forward: Kiko Malin, Jessica Luginbuhl, Mariela Uribe, Deja Kono, Zachary Fernandez, Mariela Nevarez, Silvia Guzman, Ivey Williams, Nakia Woods, Tanya Rovira-Osterwalder, Simone Saldanha, Atmaja Aswadhati, Jevon Cochran, Aaron de la Cerda, Flor Chavez, Jose Caballero, Jacqueline Belloso, and Niko Martinez. Special thank you to Mariela Uribe, manager of BBZ Castlemont, for reviewing the chapter. Thank you to Jaspal Sandhu for his thoughtful review and recommendations to strengthen the chapter and to the Gobee Group for all their support throughout both projects. The work represented in this chapter would not be possible without BBZ Castlemont, the funders who have supported the BBZ Castlemont work in the past and present (including The San Francisco Foundation, The California Wellness Foundation, The California Endowment, the Kaiser Northern California Community Benefit Programs, and The W.K. Kellogg Foundation), the national team of the BBZ Initiative, and organizations who partner with BBZ Castlemont. And, thank you especially to the Design Sprint design team members and East Oakland Innovator design team members for all their tremendous work with these efforts, and the Castlemont community members whose insight, participation, and drive made this work possible and meaningful.

The authors held the following former affiliations in relation to the case studies described in this chapter. Rachel Berkowitz was the community engagement coordinator with the Best Babies Zone Castlemont project and a coach for the East Oakland Innovators. Jessica Vechakul was an evaluator for the Design Sprint and a Design

Thinking consultant and coach for the East Oakland Innovators. Bina Patel Shrimali was the director of the Best Babies Zone Castlemont project and the manager of the Building Blocks for Health Equity Unit. Thea Anderson was an evaluator for the East Oakland Innovators.

REFERENCES

1. Lu MC, Halfon N. Racial and ethnic disparities in birth outcomes: a life-course perspective. *Matern Child Health J.* 2003;7(1):13–30.

2. Pies C, Kotelchuck M. Bringing the MCH life course perspective to life. *Matern Child Health J.* 2014;18(2):335–338.

3. Buchanan R. Wicked problems in design thinking. *Des Issues.* 1992;8(2):5.

4. Vechakul J. Human-centered design for social impact: case studies of IDEO.org and the International Development Design Summit. 2016. Available at: http://search.proquest.com/dissertations/docview/1834819858/abstract/8DE27B5E34D044E7PQ/1. Accessed January 20, 2017.

5. Vechakul J, Shrimali BP, Sandhu JS. Human-centered design as an approach for place-based innovation in public health: a case study from Oakland, California. *Matern Child Health J.* 2015;19(12):2552–2559.

6. Gasson S. Human-centered vs. user-centered approaches to information system design. *J Inf Technol Theory Appl.* 2003;5(2):29.

7. Brown T, Wyatt J. Design thinking for social innovation. *Stanf Soc Innov Rev.* Winter 2010:31–35.

8. Gobee Group. Home. Available at: http://www.gobeegroup.com. Accessed January 20, 2017.

9. IDEO.org. Our approach. Available at: http://www.ideo.org/approach. Accessed February 1, 2017.

10. *The Field Guide to Human-Centered Design: Design Kit.* 1st ed. San Francisco, CA: IDEO; 2015.

11. Nevarez M. EOI design thinking toolkits. East Oakland Innovators. Alameda County Public Health Department. 2014. Available at: http://www.acphd.org/building-blocks/projects/bbz/east-oakland-innovators.aspx. Accessed January 23, 2017.

12. Stanford University d.school. 2X2 Matrix. The K12 Lab Wiki. Available at: https://dschool-old.stanford.edu/groups/k12/wiki/29e5a/2X2_Matrix.html. Accessed August 16, 2017.

13. Israel BA, Schulz AJ, Parker EA, Becker AB. Review of community-based research: assessing partnership approaches to improve public health. *Annu Rev Public Health.* 1998;19(1):173–202.

14. Wallerstein NB, Duran B. Using community-based participatory research to address health disparities. *Health Promot Pract.* 2006;7(3):312–323.

15. International Development Innovation Network. Home. Available at: https://www.idin.org. Accessed January 27, 2017.

16. Sanders EB-N, Stappers PJ. Co-creation and the new landscapes of design. *CoDesign*. 2008;4(1):5–18.

17. Taylor MJ, McNicholas C, Nicolay C, Darzi A, Bell D, Reed JE. Systematic review of the application of the Plan–Do–Study–Act method to improve quality in healthcare. *BMJ Qual Saf*. 2014;23(4):290–298.

18. Ungar T, Knaak S, Szeto AC. Theoretical and practical considerations for combating mental illness stigma in health care. *Community Ment Health J*. 2016;52(3):262–271.

19. Reed JE, Card AJ. The problem with Plan–Do–Study–Act cycles. *BMJ Qual Saf*. 2016;25(3): 147–152.

20. Marmot M. Social determinants of health inequalities. *Lancet*. 2005;365(9464):1099–1104.

21. Gobee Group. Optimize ARV. Available at: http://www.gobeegroup.com/optimizearv. Accessed May 18, 2017.

22. Mullaney T, Pettersson H, Nyholm T, Stolterman E. Thinking beyond the cure: a case for human-centered design in cancer care. *Int J Des*. 2012;6(3). Available at: http://search.proquest.com/openview/0a3ee7412fe288d5d39d47a8e321895e/1?pq-origsite=gscholar&cbl=466416. Accessed May 18, 2017.

23. Lin MC, Hughes BL, Katica MK, Dining-Zuber C, Plsek PE. Service design and change of systems: human-centered approaches to implementing and spreading service design. *Int J Des*. 2011; 5(2). Available at: http://search.proquest.com/openview/e4d74962d04fb45646803d45f0fb8bab/1?pq-origsite=gscholar&cbl=466416. Accessed May 18, 2017.

24. Concern USA. PlanWise—a data-driven tool for placing help where it's needed. 2016. Available at: http://www.concernusa.org/story/planwise-a-data-driven-tool-for-placing-help-where-its-needed. Accessed May 18, 2017.

25. IDEO.org. Clean team. Projects. Available at: https://www.ideo.org/project/clean-team. Accessed May 18, 2017.

26. IDEO.org. Vroom: a human-centered take on early childhood development. Available at: http://www.designkit.org/case-studies/2. Accessed May 18, 2017.

27. Shrimali BP, Luginbuhl J, Malin C, Flournoy R, Siegel A. The Building Blocks Collaborative: advancing a life course approach to health equity through multi-sector collaboration. *Matern Child Health J*. 2014;18(2):373–379.

28. Best Babies Zone. Home. Available at: http://www.bestbabieszone.org. Accessed February 1, 2017.

29. US Census Bureau. 2011–2015 American Community Survey 5-year estimates—Census Tract 4097. Available at: https://factfinder.census.gov/faces/nav/jsf/pages/searchresults.xhtml?refresh=t. Accessed January 31, 2017.

30. Harder+Company Community Research. Best Babies Zone Secondary Data Dashboard, 2009–2013 Averages. 2013. Available at: http://www.bestbabieszone.org/content/common/common.download_file.php?action_special=download_file&sid=1297e13a8ea5f670a51d945adadf2852&download_file_id=763945. Accessed January 31, 2017.

31. Vechakul J. Design sprint evaluation. 2014. Available at: https://jessvech.files.wordpress.com/2014/05/bbz-design-sprint-evaluation-report.pdf. Accessed January 27, 2017.

32. Anderson T. *Evaluation of the East Oakland Innovators: Resident-Led Design Thinking Project in the Best Babies Zone—Oakland* [master's thesis]. Berkeley, CA: University of California Berkeley School of Public Health; 2015.

33. IDEO. A sleek, seamless Apple Watch Camera band. 2016. Available at: https://www.ideo.com/case-study/a-sleek-seamless-apple-watch-camera-band. Accessed May 18, 2017.

34. Best Babies Zone. Castlemont Community Market. Available at: http://www.acphd.org/media/350131/castlemont-community-market.pdf. Accessed February 2, 2017.

35. Coursera. Online courses from top universities. Available at: https://www.coursera.org. Accessed November 23, 2017.

36. +Acumen. +Acumen, the world's school for social change. Available at: http://www.plusacumen.org. Accessed November 23, 2017.

10

Putting Life Course Into Practice

Christina (Kiko) Malin, MPH, MSW, Deborah B. Ehrenthal, MD, MPH,
Belinda Pettiford, MPH, Elizabeth A. Smulian, MPH, CHES,
and Quinton Cotton, MSW

Once exposed to the principles underlying the life course perspective, many practitioners become immediate converts to this new way of understanding how social and neighborhood conditions can influence health outcomes over generations. Equally compelling is the theory's elucidation of how social inequality drives disparities in health outcomes, especially among racial/ethnic groups.[1] However, the challenge often lies in determining how to redesign public health programs, policies, and services in a way that not only reflects life course principles but also has a measurable impact on population health. Life Course Theory (LCT) clearly details how transgenerational poverty, residential segregation, institutionalized racism, and other deeply rooted social problems have an impact on individual and community health.[2,3] The rationale is clear but the translation into practice seems daunting. How do public health, social work, and other practitioners fix poverty or end racism?

Many organizations across the country have begun to develop and test new strategies for addressing social conditions across the life span in a bid to achieve optimal health and well-being for the women, men, children, and families they serve. This chapter will highlight the varied approaches that different states and local organizations have undertaken to reframe their work along a life course continuum and will offer concrete examples of how practitioners can achieve small wins that may have some impact on the social conditions affecting the populations they serve, despite the deep inequities inherent in the broader societal context. Challenges to change are described, as are strategies for advancing this work and directions for the future.

The chapter also offers an in-depth exploration of the experiences of three states in translating life course principles into practice. These examples were chosen because all three states found unique ways to address disparities in birth outcomes, which in some of the sites are among the worst in the country. The methods chosen and implemented in these states are currently among the best examples illustrating the effectiveness, the challenges, and the efficacy of the LCT and the collaborative process needed to fully realize its benefits.

FINDING A LIFE COURSE APPROACH THAT WORKS

Successful strategies to integrate a life course perspective into one's work may differ depending on the size and reach of the organization. An organization operating at the state or regional level may play the role of a catalyst and convener through the development of broad statewide plans or centralized coordination of intensive work at the local level. Locally focused organizations may also serve as initiators and coordinators but have the opportunity to forge closer relationships with communities that may spark new ideas and result in changes that have a more immediate or tangible impact on community members. An important factor contributing to the choice of an approach, regardless of the agency's size and reach, is its experience and history addressing issues from a social determinants of health perspective. Also critical is the degree of political will—especially among the highest levels of leadership—for employing tactics that, while innovative, may also be disruptive. Finally, comprehensive and thoughtful training in LCT for all involved—staff, agency stakeholders, and community members—is essential to achieve cohesion around shared values and a paradigm shift for a new way of doing business.

To ensure the success of efforts that take a novel approach to entrenched public health problems, there must be consensus—both internally and among external partners—about the need to move away from approaches that focus on individual behavior change to those that recognize how social inequality results in neighborhood conditions that do not foster good health for its residents. Helping all parties involved to recognize the connection between place and health—and the role that racism and segregation play in the development of suboptimal neighborhood conditions—is the first step in developing interventions that take into account the roots of health inequities and aim to address them in a meaningful way. More on the importance of achieving a paradigm shift around the concept of health equity can be found in Chapter 2.

CASE STUDIES: PUTTING THE LIFE COURSE THEORY TO WORK

North Carolina's Perinatal Health Strategic Plan

Background

North Carolina ranks 42nd in the United States for high rates of infant death.[4] Even though North Carolina's infant mortality rate has declined over the past 20 years, the gap in infant death between Black and White infants has widened, with the result that Black infants are two and a half times more likely to die before their first birthday than White infants.[5,6] This disparity affects more than just one community: the infant mortality among American Indian infants is close to that of Black infants.[5]

In 2011, the University of North Carolina Center for Maternal and Infant Health received a small grant from the National Institute of Child Health and Human Development to bring academic and community partners together to develop strategies to close the gap in birth outcomes between African American and White mothers. Focus groups were conducted with 10 community-based infant mortality prevention coalitions, reaching 130 participants across North Carolina. Key informant interviews were conducted with consumers as well as leaders in public health, education, and community and economic development. An equity council was convened to review the data, discuss current research, and learn from experts in health equity and framing.

A year later, North Carolina joined the Collaborative Improvement and Innovation Networks (CoIINs) to reduce infant mortality. In keeping with CoIINs' focus on areas that lend themselves to rapid-cycle quality improvement, North Carolina chose to prioritize topics around which there was already significant momentum in their state. With this structure providing some direction, 11 lead agencies and more than 125 partners came together in 2014 to create North Carolina's Perinatal Health Strategic Plan. North Carolina's plan is constructed on the 12-point life course framework proposed by Lu et al., which covers three major domains: improving health care for women and men, strengthening families and communities, and addressing social and economic inequities.[2] Within these domains, the plan calls for actions in 12 specific areas (Box 10-1).

Members of the North Carolina partnership developed strategies and specific action steps for each of the three domains. For example, in the area of strengthening families and communities, priority action steps include partnering with men's organizations to support fathers, preventing violence, improving transportation systems, providing tobacco-free housing, and fully engaging women and communities in the design and delivery of services. The plan advocates significant policy changes such as paid parental and sick leave, a guaranteed living wage, and equity in compensation to address social and economic

Box 10-1. Life Course Approach for Reducing Infant Mortality

1. Provide interconception care to women with prior adverse pregnancy outcomes.
2. Increase access to preconception care.
3. Improve the quality of prenatal care.
4. Expand health care access over the life course.
5. Strengthen fathers' involvement in families.
6. Enhance coordination and integration of family support services.
7. Create reproductive social capital in communities.
8. Invest in community building.
9. Close the education gap.
10. Reduce poverty among families.
11. Support working mothers and families.
12. Undo racism.

Source: Lu et al.[2] Adapted with permission of ISHIB, publisher of *Ethnicity & Disease*.

inequities. The plan also highlights the necessity of increasing high-school and post–high-school graduation rates, promoting access to early childhood education and affordable quality childcare, and collaborating with agencies that focus on poverty reduction. The most critical and perhaps most challenging component of this section of the plan calls for promoting community and systems dialogue on racism, infusing equity into the provision of health care services, and promoting quality training about institutional and structural racism and its impact on poor communities and communities of color.

Securing Leadership Buy-in

As many of the proposed activities are far-reaching, with implications outside the health sector and across the life course that may make them challenging to implement, securing the approval from the highest level of health department leadership to include these components was a significant accomplishment, especially in a conservative state like North Carolina. Their inclusion in the plan was a result of persistent efforts on the part of the partners to educate decision-makers about the powerful influence of social conditions, including exposure to racism and discrimination, on the health of women, children, parents, and communities. And, although it was important to address the impact of racism on the health status of communities of color—as one of the initial reasons for bringing the partnership together was to address the startling Black–White gap in birth outcomes—it became evident to partnership members that the plan's underlying framework and strategies were appropriate for all populations, not just African American families.

Indeed, creating the political will that ultimately resulted in the approval and publication of the plan took some time. The plan was officially released and published on the North Carolina Division of Public Health website in 2016, more than two years after its initial development. The implementation of the plan is now being overseen by a multidisciplinary steering committee of more than 40 people who represent a range of affiliations, including local health departments, university researchers including Historically Black Colleges and Universities, state Medicaid and other insurers, and stewards of Mental Health and Substance Use Services funding. The Women's Health Branch Head at the Division of Public Health provides oversight for the group. The plan is considered a living document that will be reviewed and updated annually. A consumer and community version of the plan is being developed as the group continues to welcome input from consumers, community leaders, and other experts in the field. The full plan can be viewed at http://whb.ncpublichealth.com.[7]

Keys to Success

Through the development of a long-term, collaborative strategic plan for perinatal health, North Carolina has succeeded in building a strong foundation for health equity work in the state. Identifying connections between programs across the health department by topic or age group, taking the time to build relationships with staff in various programs across the health department, and inviting them to be part of the growing partnership allowed the connection of previously separate activities so that each section of the health department could see its role in achieving the health of individuals across the life span. Engaging established partners from outside the health department who already had a successful track record of collaboration, while at the same time building on the leadership base within the health department, helped to ensure the institutionalization of the plan. Securing the buy-in and respect of decision makers in the state also paved the way for gradual implementation of the plan's recommended activities and lent political and institutional power to the plan's critical assertion that racial and social equity must be realized for women, children, and their families to be healthy.

Next Steps

The Division of Public Health will use some of its Maternal and Child Health Block Grant funding for a staff person who can serve as the overall driver of the perinatal health strategic plan—spearheading new efforts while also integrating them into existing activities. A priority for this staff person will be to focus on areas in which there is already some momentum. For example, thanks to an existing learning collaborative on long-acting reversible contraception (LARC) organized by the Association of State and Territorial Health Officials, progress has been made in increasing Medicaid reimbursement rates for LARC, and there has been an improvement in immediate postpartum insertion of LARC, a strategy that is tied to steps one and two of the 12-step plan. There is also momentum around perinatal regionalization efforts, including a proposed study bill pertaining to high-quality, risk-appropriate maternal and neonatal care, which relates to step three in the plan—improve the quality of prenatal care.

North Carolina has also begun to tackle some of the activities that are more complex and do not sit squarely within the health arena. A Social Determinants of Health Workgroup has been convened within the Division of Public Health along with some of its partners. One of the group's initial activities was to attend the Racial Equity Institute Foundational Training to gain further knowledge on the historical nature of institutional racism.[8] The group is adapting the City of Seattle's Racial Equity Toolkit and piloting it with one of its state programs to help ensure that the program was designed in a manner to support health equity.[9] Developed as part of Seattle's Race and Social Justice Initiative—a citywide effort to end institutionalized racism and race-based disparities in city government—the toolkit describes a concrete methodology to guide the development, implementation, and evaluation of policies, initiatives, programs, and budgetary decisions that promote racial equity. North Carolina's integration of Seattle's Racial Equity Toolkit illustrates both the importance of sharing innovative practices to achieve health equity across the nation and the universality and relevance of many of these approaches, despite the cultural and demographic differences that exist between states.

Wisconsin's Life Course Initiative for Healthy Families

Background

Like their counterparts in North Carolina, public health leaders and advocates in Wisconsin are also grappling with persistent perinatal health disparities. Though Wisconsin's overall infant mortality rate is low compared with that in the rest of the United States, infants born to African American mothers in Wisconsin are nearly three times more likely to die before their first birthday than those born to White mothers—one of the worst disparities in the country.[10] These stark racial disparities persist beyond the child's first year of life; the Annie E. Casey Foundation's Race for Results Policy Report identified Wisconsin as the worst state to be a Black child.[11]

The Wisconsin Department of Health Services was quick to adopt life course principles to inform strategies to reduce maternal and child health disparities.[1] In 2003, the health department invited Dr. Michael Lu to introduce the life course perspective to state and local maternal and child health advocates at a Healthy Babies Summit. Leaders at the state and local levels embraced this approach, worked to educate a broad base of stakeholders, and began to implement LCT into programs and policies across the state.[1] The efforts of the Department of Health Services converged with local initiatives in Racine, Kenosha, Beloit, and Milwaukee to address the high African American infant mortality rate.[1,12,13]

The Wisconsin Partnership Program at the University of Wisconsin School of Medicine and Public Health, motivated by the values of the Wisconsin Idea—a general principle guiding university outreach efforts that education should influence people's lives beyond the boundaries of the classroom—sought to actively support the community in addressing this critical public health problem.[14] They commissioned a white paper titled "Elimination of racial and ethnic disparities in birth outcomes in Wisconsin" to outline recommendations for funding strategies to have an impact on this issue. The paper specifically included the recommendation that any initiative should honor, respect, and include communities in every phase; build on existing infrastructure; and take a multilevel, intergenerational approach.[13]

In 2008, following the publication of this white paper, the Wisconsin Partnership Program convened a conference to examine the paper's recommendations and potential avenues forward.[12] After the conference, the Wisconsin Partnership Program launched the Life Course Initiative for Healthy Families (LIHF) and made a $10 million commitment to improve community conditions that lead to healthier birth outcomes among African Americans in Wisconsin.

A Community–Academic Partnership

The development of LIHF was guided by a large, multisector steering committee including strong representation from each community. This community–academic partnership model is informed by the LCT, community coalition action theory,[15] and Dr. Michael Lu's proposed 12-point plan to close the Black–White gap in birth outcomes, the same framework that served as the foundation for North Carolina's perinatal health strategic plan. LIHF is grounded in the evidence that maternal, infant, and family well-being are influenced by factors that span the life course and that healthy birth outcomes result from more than just high-quality prenatal care and healthy individual behaviors.[12] The Centers for Disease Control and Prevention's (CDC's) Racial and Ethnic Approaches to Community Health (REACH) program also influenced the development of LIHF in design elements such as action planning, collaborative formation, capacity building, use of systems thinking, and facilitating change among change agents to realize widespread health improvements.[16,17]

LIHF's theory of change has its foundation in the premise that locally driven collaboratives can build awareness and capacity in the communities most heavily impacted by perinatal disparities. Increased awareness at the community level and multisector collaboration will lead to policy, systems, and environmental changes that improve health care and community conditions. With a Life Course Approach, ultimate outcomes include improved birth outcomes, as well as improved health and well-being for African American women, their children, and their families.[12]

Understanding the importance of centering the initiative around the priorities of the communities most affected by high African American infant mortality, LIHF initially launched in the four counties in Wisconsin where 85% of the live births and 89% of the infant deaths to African American women occur: Kenosha, Milwaukee, Racine, and Rock.[12] During the planning phase of the initiative, the LIHF counties engaged in a comprehensive, community-driven process to create community action plans. This process began by convening local collaboratives that included multisector partners (representing health care, nonprofit, public sector, business, and faith-based organizations) and emphasized involvement of African American organizations and multigenerational community members. Through convening, conversation, and extensive local data collection, the collaboratives assessed local needs within the framework of the 12-point plan. The life course perspective was dominant in public dialogue about infant mortality and expanded the scope of the conversations with support from local media.[12]

The resulting community action plans recommended approaches within each county for improving health care for African American women, strengthening African American families and communities, and addressing social and economic inequities. Today, each LIHF collaborative is housed at a convening agency that provides infrastructure, leadership, and unique, local expertise. The convening agencies and collaboratives are each supported by a five-year grant to engage their communities, build on the local vision for addressing infant mortality, and implement policy, systems, and environmental change strategies. Additional funding has supported project grants and program offices focused on technical assistance, epidemiological surveillance, evaluation, and research.

Community Collaborative Model

Using their community action plans as the local vision of how to address racial disparities, each collaborative identified priorities and strategies for implementation. These local action agendas varied. The Racine Collaborative identified the need to enhance coordination among home visiting programs, support breastfeeding, and improve preconception care starting with adolescent health. In Kenosha, fatherhood, housing, and mental health emerged as important concerns. The Rock Collaborative identified culturally competent health care as its major action area. In Milwaukee, one of the most segregated cities in the United States, preterm birth was identified as one of the principal drivers of infant mortality and their collaborative's action agenda was organized around reducing prematurity.

Some early wins resulting from work in these priority areas are already emerging. Racine is working to normalize breastfeeding and increase community support for the practice. Activities have included increasing the capacity of lactation consultants to serve African American women, having a breastfeeding promotion booth at the Juneteenth Celebration, and establishing and celebrating a Black Breastfeeding Week. Collaborative members in Kenosha have guided the development of a project to promote fatherhood engagement at local Special Supplemental Nutrition Program for Women, Infants, and Children (WIC) sites. Kenosha is also working to improve systems navigation around maternal mental health and has led efforts to ensure that those eligible for the Earned Income Tax Credit actually receive it. In Milwaukee, the role of pregnancy intention and birth spacing as contributors to preterm birth led the Milwaukee collaborative to implement a pilot of One Key Question[18] in four clinic sites to encourage medical providers to engage their patients in a clear conversation about reproductive health needs.

The recommendations in Dr. Michael Lu's 12-point plan that are most challenging to implement are those related to changing the social fabric of our nation, such as investing in urban renewal and undoing racism. The LIHF Collaboratives have devoted considerable time and energy from the outset to having meaningful and straightforward conversations about the impact of racism on maternal and infant health outcomes. Each has reviewed local data (such as Fetal Infant Mortality Review and Wisconsin Pregnancy Risk Assessment Monitoring System [PRAMS] data) illustrating the disproportionate share of adverse maternal and child health outcomes among African Americans. Using LCT to frame these differences as health inequities resulting from social inequality, the collaboratives have built compelling local cases about the role of racism in determining the health of women, children, and families. They have also facilitated collaborative members' participation in workshops focused on unlearning racism and have continued conversations about racism as a means to dismantle deeply entrenched beliefs and practices. Each collaborative educates the broader community through ongoing conversations about how broader socioeconomic factors contribute to preterm birth and other drivers of infant mortality.

Project Grants

While the LIHF Collaboratives were beginning their implementation phase, the Wisconsin Partnership Program also made funds available through a competitive Request for Partnerships that focused on interventions and promising practices to address the needs identified in the community action plans. These grants were intended to support and stimulate this work and build community capacity. The result was 22 LIHF Project Grants mapped to the three overarching strategies in Lu's 12-point plan (Table 10-1). These grants enabled community-based organizations to design, pilot, or implement a variety of life course strategies focused on one or more of these areas in a LIHF county. Each organization worked with an academic partner from across the University of Wisconsin System. Examples of grant-funded projects include expansion of a home visiting program in Milwaukee for families with mental health issues to include pregnant women and the development of a fatherhood involvement project in Kenosha that resulted in the implementation a statewide indicator of paternal engagement at WIC sites. The LIHF projects were conducted from 2014 to 2017 and many grantee organizations continue to be participants in the LIHF Collaborative in their community.

Table 10-1. Mapping the Life Course Initiative for Healthy Families Project Grant Strategies to the 12-Point Plan

Improving Health Care for African American Women		Strengthening African American Families and Communities		Addressing Social and Economic Inequities	
Provide interconception care to women with prior adverse pregnancy outcomes.	1	Strengthen father involvement in African American families.	12	Close the education gap.	0
Increase access to preconception care to African American women.	2	Enhance coordination and integration of family support services.	6	Reduce poverty among African American families.	4
Improve quality of prenatal care.	7	Create reproductive social capital in African American communities.	1	Support working mothers and families.	8
Expand health care access over the life course.	4	Invest in community building and urban renewal.	2	Undo racism.	1

Source: Lu et al.[2] Adapted with permission of ISHIB, publisher of *Ethnicity & Disease*.
Note: Projects may fall into more than one point of the plan.

Support for Implementation and Regional Impact

The LIHF Regional Program Office, based in Milwaukee, was developed to provide guidance and support for the work of the community collaboratives. The primary role of this office is to provide training and technical assistance to collaborative leadership and staff to successfully achieve their goals. Staff assist with priority-setting exercises, conduct trainings on topics such as critical race theory and policy/legislative processes, and facilitate cross-community exchange by creating a space for learning, sharing, and developing ideas.

Data Surveillance and Evaluation

The Program Office based at the University of Wisconsin School of Medicine and Public Health partners with the state health department to enhance maternal and infant health data surveillance. With additional funding from the Wisconsin Partnership Program, the Wisconsin Department of Health Services was able to significantly increase the number of African American women in the LIHF counties included in the Wisconsin PRAMS survey. PRAMS is an ongoing survey of new mothers conducted jointly by the CDC and state health departments. Collaborative members and leaders ensured inclusion of questions that reflected community priorities and aligned with a life course perspective. PRAMS now provides a rich data source for the initiative, and the state as a whole, about differences in maternal experiences before, during, and after pregnancy.

Evaluation of the initiative emphasizes short-term measures of collaborative functioning as well as intermediate changes in risk and protective factors related to birth outcomes. Long-term impact evaluation tracks the initiative's three overall goals of (1) improving African American infant survival, (2) improving African American women's health status, and (3) eliminating racial disparities in birth outcomes.

Successes and Ongoing Innovation

Many innovative outcomes and promising practices have emerged from this work. LIHF has seen unique partnerships forged and new groups work together because of the life course focus, including those focused on fatherhood, adolescent health, and preconception health strategies. Other strategies focused on social and economic drivers of infant mortality, such as increasing uptake of tax credits, are promising practices that can influence birth outcomes and overall community health. The communities have been successful in raising awareness about the social determinants of health and the life course perspective, and local media now speak about infant mortality by using these lenses. In addition, the PRAMS statewide data surveillance system has improved data collection for African American women, resulting in more robust analyses of maternal health disparities and the variety of factors contributing to them. In the years to come, LIHF plans to build on momentum to continue to achieve policy and systems change. It is clear that the life course perspective has provided a useful unifying construct for building a foundation to take on these strategies.

Building Health Equity in Alameda County, California

Laying the Foundation

Despite having health outcomes that are among the best in the country, Alameda County, California—located in the San Francisco Bay Area—faces disparities in health by income, race/ethnicity, and neighborhood.[19] The Alameda County Public Health Department (ACPHD) has a long history of working to address these disparities and advance health equity by partnering with local agencies, key stakeholders, and neighborhood residents to improve community conditions and support good health. ACPHD's nationally recognized work to promote health equity began more than 20 years ago under the leadership of then–Director Arnold Perkins, who re-envisioned the health department as an entity that could only realize community change by involving the community itself. During his tenure, deep and lasting partnerships were formed with local nonprofits and neighborhood leaders that continue to this day.

As a result of these community partnerships, the health department leadership became increasingly aware of the need to address neighborhood conditions to achieve good health. With this awareness came the unavoidable realization that adverse neighborhood conditions are driven by social inequalities stemming from discriminatory policies and practices, such as "red lining," which is the practice of denying services, either directly or through selectively raising prices, to residents of certain areas on the basis of the racial or ethnic composition of those areas.

To realize optimal health and well-being for all of the county's residents, the health department chose to place more emphasis on policy and systems change efforts and began to think of itself as a social justice organization. Subsequent health department directors continued to champion the health equity cause. In 2006, a Place Matters team was convened and housed at ACPHD. Place Matters is a local partner of the national initiative of the Joint Center for Political and Economic studies at the Health Policy Institute and is designed to improve the health of communities by addressing social conditions that lead to poor health.

In 2008, ACPHD published a landmark report—"Life and Death from Unnatural Causes: Health and Social Inequity in Alameda County"—which garnered much attention locally and was also nationally recognized.[19] This report set the stage for a new way of looking at health in the county. As a result of the report, many organizations outside the health sector, such as the Oakland Unified School District (OUSD), began to see their role in ensuring the health of families in the county and to speak of themselves as health-promoting organizations. OUSD staff had been involved with the Place Matters work and were therefore learning about the impact of social conditions on health. The publication of the report helped them to solidify and clearly articulate their commitment to this new perspective and way of working. Similarly, at a county Board of Supervisors meeting, one of the supervisors presented maps from the report that show the clustering of poor health outcomes in low-income, disinvested neighborhoods, repeating a phrase that one of the former ACPHD directors had coined: "Your zip code is more important than your genetic code." A paradigm shift had occurred.

Integrating Health Equity Efforts Into Maternal and Child Health

Shortly after the report was published, a group of ACPHD leaders and program managers working with families during the perinatal period formed a learning community to study the life course perspective, review local data, and redesign the department's approach to improving perinatal outcomes. Black infant mortality rates in Alameda County are still two to three times higher than those of Whites despite generally good access to early prenatal care.[20] The group soon realized that ensuring healthy community conditions would be necessary to address inequities in perinatal and child health and that this work could not be done by a health department alone but instead needed to be driven by a strong coalition of multisector partners.[21]

In September 2009, ACPHD hosted a symposium called Building Blocks for Healthy Babies, Healthy Families, Healthy Communities, which centered on the theme of building cross-sector partnerships. Invited speakers included national health equity and life course leaders. The symposium generated tremendous interest in collaboration to advance health equity through a life course perspective, leading ACPHD to launch the Building Blocks Collaborative (BBC), a countywide initiative to engage community partners in remedying inequitable conditions for children. BBC partners are from diverse arenas—local economic development agencies, food access projects, city and county government, community clinics, housing, and parks and recreation—and represent stakeholders committed to community transformation throughout Alameda County. With one in three Alameda County children born into poverty, the BBC united around a singular vision—that every child in Alameda County should have the best start in life. One of the first products BBC participants created was a Bill of Rights—a shared vision that reflects the contribution of multiple stakeholders (Box 10-2). This document acknowledges the various ways that partners' organizations intersect and their unique roles in contributing to positive health for children. As one partner described, "over the past year, East Bay Asian Local Development Corporation has begun the conversation about how our work would shift if we considered ourselves health providers and not just affordable housing developers and managers."[21]

In early 2010, ACPHD received a grant from the Kresge Foundation for a multisector demonstration project—Food to Families (F2F). F2F, centered in two neighborhoods

Box 10-2. Building Blocks Collaborative Bill of Rights

All children in Alameda county have a right to be born healthy and to

- Be believed in;
- Live, play, and grow in a clean, safe place;
- Receive a quality education;
- Be loved by a caring adult;
- Eat healthy food;
- Explore nature;
- Enjoy economic opportunity and financial security;
- Access health care that promotes well-being;
- Be free from discrimination and violence; and
- Be included and valued by a supportive community.

Source: Shrimali et al.[21] Reprinted with permission from Springer Nature.

with a disproportionate burden of poor outcomes, was conceived and designed by BBC members on the basis of input from residents in both communities about the need to have access to fresh produce in their neighborhoods, to increase youth employment opportunities, and to improve local economic development. The project provided fresh food "prescriptions" to pregnant women receiving health services at local health centers, which were then "filled" at local food businesses where community youth were employed. The project engaged Mandela MarketPlace (a community-owned food cooperative), the Deputy Sheriff's Activity League, and two community health centers—all BBC members who had been involved in securing input from neighborhood residents about what they felt were the pressing problems in their communities.

F2F was unique, not only in its efforts to address multiple community issues through cross-sector partnerships but also because it was collectively designed and implemented. Even the grant-writing process was collaborative, with BBC members taking responsibility for different sections. The idea for the project was initially conceived by the BBC steering committee who, on the basis of initial brainstorming by the whole BBC, developed a framework for the project. The framework was then brought back to the larger group for a vote. Anticipating concerns from BBC members whose agencies were not located in the chosen neighborhoods about being left out, the steering committee members opted to include mini grants as part of the project. The mini grants were made available to BBC members to fund small-scale projects that were in line with the overarching goals of the F2F project, such as backyard gardens or neighborhood cooking classes. This strategy, along with continuous updates about the progress and outcomes of F2F that were provided to the BBC throughout the course of the project, helped to build consensus and ensure ongoing support for the project from the collaborative. The work of the BBC paved the way for the development of the Building Blocks for Health Equity unit within ACPHD.

Home Visiting and Healthy Start

In 2012, Alameda County stakeholders came together to collaboratively define and develop a comprehensive, integrated local home visiting system of care to serve pregnant women and families with children up to the age of 3 years. One of the most innovative aspects of the Alameda County Early Childhood Home Visiting System of Care is its commitment to addressing the social determinants of health through the integration of community transformation efforts with direct services through the Healthy Start program and Project HERA—Health Equity and Resource Advocates—which develops client-focused solutions to social and environmental factors that adversely affect the health of the families served through home visiting.

Currently, Alameda County's Healthy Start Initiative (ACHSI) serves the population at highest risk for infant mortality: African Americans in select zip codes. The Best Babies Zone (BBZ) is located in a census tract in East Oakland that is contained within one of these zip codes. This co-location has provided an opportunity to combine the BBZ's efforts to transform the neighborhood through economic development and resident engagement activities with ACHSI's delivery of direct services—such as case management and group activities—thereby achieving maximum impact. After several years of working together, BBZ and ACHSI staff have achieved a high level of synergy between the direct services provided in the neighborhood—home visiting, Club Mom, Community Baby Showers, a neighborhood playdate run by residents, a swim club at the high school, and Boot Camps for New Dads—and the BBZ community transformation efforts, specifically the development of a resident-driven community market.

A Focus on Financial Security

Project HERA builds on the work of the Robert Wood Johnson Foundation–funded Prosperity Project, which operated in Alameda County from 2011 to 2013. The project sought to improve health and financial well-being by increasing availability of and access to fair financial services and products, especially in communities where predatory financial services are disproportionately located. With a grant from the California Wellness Foundation (TCWF), the project is piloting a new program, called Financial Tools and Solutions (FT$), which consists of financial coaching and asset-building grants that have been integrated into the home visiting system of care. The grant was secured as a result of the relationship with the asset-building community, linking with TCWF's interest in funding a project that blended financial security and wealth-building strategies with direct service programs reaching low-income pregnant women and young families.

In recognition of the impact that financial insecurity has on health and well-being, FT$ was designed to provide tools and resources to help low-income families achieve financial stability. Home visitors routinely encounter situations in which families are experiencing potentially life-changing financial crises—such as a car breakdown or funeral that forces the household to choose between paying for medicine or keeping the lights on—or who are unable to make a small business idea come to fruition because of a lack of resources, credit, or information. FT$ aims to help families weather financial storms—without making their situations worse through utility shut-offs, eviction, or the use of debt traps such as payday lenders—and to assist them in developing income-generating strategies and building financial assets through a strengths-based approach.

FT$ started with an all-day training for all home visiting staff on financial fitness as well as an introduction to the concept of financial coaching. As a result of the training, all home visiting staff are expected to have conversations with their clients about their finances and refer interested clients for further financial coaching. In-depth coaching is then provided to the family, both individually and through group workshops, by ACPHD staff, some of whom have been trained and certified as financial coaches.

Once clients successfully complete four coaching workshops, they are eligible to receive an asset-building grant in one of two categories: emergency funds (to cope with potentially life-altering financial crises) or developmental pathways (grants to help build financial self-sufficiency through supporting small business ideas, education, or family development needs such as childcare). Coaches provide ongoing support and skills building necessary to help both staff and clients link their financial choices to their personal aspirations and realities.

Home visitors and coaches can also link interested clients to other programs that aim to build wealth, lift clients out of poverty, and set them on a different life trajectory. One of these programs is an entrepreneurship training—birthed in the BBZ—that was made possible through a generous three-year grant from the San Francisco Foundation to support ongoing work in the neighborhood. The training was developed in response to feedback received from Castlemont community market vendors about the challenges to formalizing small local businesses and the lack of trainings that were culturally and practically responsive to their particular business needs. The seven-week training provides individuals who may not identify as entrepreneurs with foundational business planning skills in a culturally relevant context. One of the graduates of the inaugural training series was a home visiting client who used the skills she learned, coupled with an asset-building grant from the FT$ program, to realize her dream of having her own eco-friendly cleaning business.

The Building Blocks for Health Equity unit's success in obtaining funding from the San Francisco Foundation for innovative work integrating neighborhood-based wealth-building strategies into public health programming came about as a result of long-term relationship building with the local foundation community. Team members took advantage of every opportunity to network with foundations interested in funding projects addressing the social determinants of health through neighborhood-based strategies. Staff pitched ideas for projects to many foundations that declined to fund them but they were always encouraged to continue with the work and were often referred to contacts at other foundations. It took more than three years to secure the kind of substantial moderate-term funding that every project hopes for—$1.5 million over three years—and in the end it came about organically. The lesson here is to not be discouraged by foundation rejection but to continue to talk about these innovative proposals to anyone who will listen. Doing so will not only further the paradigm shift that the success of this work requires but may also result in an infusion of funds when it is least expected.

Finally, ACPHD has also been collaborating with the City of Oakland over the past two years to design and implement a newborn college savings account program—another financial product that is being offered to home visiting clients. Building on the research showing that children from low-income families who have a college savings account in their name make better progress in their early social–emotional development, the City of Oakland secured millions of dollars from local foundations to support the new Brilliant Baby program.[22] Through partnerships with the home visiting system of care and other programs that serve families with children aged younger than 1 year, the city will open a college savings account for participating babies, seeded with an initial $500 deposit. Parents who choose to participate in a coaching and savings training will also have an opportunity to open a matched savings account that will be incrementally seeded with funds up to an additional $500 that they can use to further their own personal goals. This two-generation savings account approach is intended to be a source of inspiration and hope for parents about their baby's future as well as a remedy for financial stress, helping parents to build confidence about the future and have more energy for parenting.

PRACTICE ESSENTIALS

There is much value in re-engineering the public health approach to improving maternal and child health issues to include a life course perspective. Although considerable work is involved in embracing a new perspective, once the beginning of a paradigm shift has occurred, the work can fall into place quite nicely. This final section describes some ideas for practice that may be useful, especially when challenges arise.

Building Trust Through Persistence and Ongoing Communication

North Carolina's Perinatal Health Strategic Plan was thoughtfully built through a collaboration among leaders and communities across the state. Although keeping stakeholders engaged over the five years required energy, the investment and longer-term relationship building has paid off in many ways. Because the plan explicitly calls out racism as a contributor to poor health outcomes and recommends policy changes that might seem radical, especially in a southern state, it took some time to reach consensus on how to craft the language in the plan from the stakeholders involved. In addition, getting the attention of the state's Department of Health and Human Services leaders was challenging because of competing priorities inherent in the public health administrative environment, although this did not stop practitioners from using the plan in its draft form. Persistence, patience, and continuous communication with stakeholders were essential to the eventual publication and evolving success of the plan.

This was also the case in Wisconsin and Alameda County, where the free flow of information between the regional/county organizing body and the neighborhood coalitions and leaders was critical. For example, a great deal of time was spent in the early meetings of the F2F project not only building relationships but also repairing them, as some of the partners who had worked together previously were not on the best of terms. It was also important to ensure bilateral communication between the funder and the community partners—so that partners were well aware of their obligations and the funder could also benefit and learn from the experience—and to be realistic and transparent about the county's occasional slow pace, especially when it came to cutting checks for grant payments to the partners.

Shifting the Paradigm Within: Fostering Awake and Aware Staff Is Critical

Even within health departments with a long-standing commitment to addressing health equity, this ethos may not permeate all levels of the organization, and staff may view upstream approaches as time-consuming, amorphous, and impractical. At the ACPHD, the health equity work was initially confined to a small unit housed within the Office of the Director. The staff in this unit were young, mostly White, and highly educated. Despite their express commitment to addressing the social inequalities that contribute to health inequities along race and class lines, their way of talking about the work often did not sit well with staff who were working directly with marginalized families in low-income communities of color and/or who came from those communities themselves. Direct service staff communicated that it was difficult to hear about how poorly their communities were doing from people who they perceived as privileged, even though they were framing health disparities as a social justice issue. Furthermore, these staff felt that the upstream solutions being proposed, although understandable, could never be implemented on a scale that would make a difference.

Forging Alliances and Building Teams

Although home visiting staff were confronted with the stark reality of the connection between social conditions and health on a daily basis, the negative associations with health equity work persisted. There were still vast differences in staff culture between the direct service staff and health equity staff, not only in terms of race and socioeconomic status but also in their work style and perspective: direct service activities are much more concrete, whereas upstream approaches such as economic development, community collaboratives, and policy change are less clearly defined and may be perceived as overly process-oriented with few tangible results.

Several strategies ultimately served to dissolve these internal barriers. Focusing on specific projects that were of obvious benefit to home visiting clients was a turning point in staff relationships, and the eventual resounding success of the FT$ program was achieved by soliciting ongoing input from home visiting staff and clients and tweaking the program to meet their expressed needs at every step of its development and implementation. Also contributing to its success was the fact that the FT$ program coordinator shared his personal experience of growing up in a family that experienced multiple financial challenges, which helped him to secure the confidence of the staff in a way that was genuine and meaningful.

Having the right person in the job, especially for work that can be deeply personal and even painful for some staff because of their own lived experience, is a key to success. In particular, taking the time to listen—with patience and with humility, both cultural and otherwise—is an important skill. The FT$ project was a success because the home visitors' commitment was solid, because they truly believed in the project, because they realized that it could address critical client needs that they often feel powerless to fix, and because they saw themselves as integral to the project's success. The home visitors supported this project because they wanted to, not because they were asked by their supervisors to do so. Without their buy-in, client recruitment would not have been as successful as clients largely chose to enroll in the program on the basis of their trusted home visitor's strong endorsement.

Success Takes Time

It can take years to get the recipe right. Success may take just the right combination of funding and staffing, as well as an intervention that is carefully and collaboratively designed, to shape a project that met client needs, energized staff, and excited funders. Taking the time up front to engage in frank explorations of how race, power, and privilege are operating within one's own organizations, rather than dealing with issues as they arise—which can be messy and time-consuming—is an important starting point. Hiring the right people to do the work—including recruiting neighborhood residents as staff and dedicating the time and effort to provide them with the training they need to be successful in a work environment that is not necessarily familiar to them—is also critical. Finally, the importance of ongoing dialogue and intensive team-building efforts cannot be underestimated.

Program Planning, Evaluation, and Sustainability

Getting Started

Because LCT suggests multiple avenues for intervention, there are many potential starting points for the work. One way to begin, especially if a successful multisector collaborative to undergird the work has been established, is to identify a specific issue of importance to the community in which there is already significant momentum. To build a solid infrastructure for institutionalizing the work, organizations may also consider assigning staff to various programs and aligning budgets accordingly or braiding funding to make it more difficult to eliminate programs when a time-limited funding source ends. Also not to be forgotten is the potential for innovation that is perhaps hiding under the surface of an organization's staid exterior. Using techniques such as Design Thinking to encourage staff to envision new solutions to persistent issues and problems or offering internships to students who can bring a fresh perspective to the work can result in unique approaches that might not otherwise have been uncovered.

Managing Effective Collaboratives

Collaboratives have been mentioned extensively in this chapter as they are essential to the design and implementation of efforts that aim to address social conditions. However, in multisector collaboratives, turf issues may arise, despite best efforts to define mutually beneficial common goals and activities, causing competition among members or concerns about who is getting credit for the work. The perception that some entities, such as universities or public health departments, may have more resources and should prioritize funding to community-based organizations can also cause tension. Strategies to address this tension include anticipating it up front, being clear about the possibility of it happening, and developing a process for how to manage it when it does occur. Encouraging collaborative members to remember why they came together in the first place and reminding everyone about the group's common goals and shared vision, perhaps by posting it on the wall at every meeting or making laminated cards with these principles on them for members to carry with them, are also possible strategies for dealing with conflict.

Designing Relevant Evaluations

Evaluation of life course initiatives is challenging and there are few road maps. It takes time for interventions that focus on community transformation efforts to have a measurable impact on population health, particularly in the area of health disparities. For this reason, it is important to focus on proximal and intermediate outcomes. In Wisconsin's LIHF, proximal outcomes included measures of collaborative functioning and capacity, whereas intermediate outcomes centered around levels of stress, feelings of connectedness to other neighbors, or increased receipt of the Earned Income Tax Credit by participants. Tension between maintaining the fidelity of evidence-based interventions and being responsive to community and stakeholder priorities may also complicate the design of evaluation plans that must be both methodologically sound and culturally relevant. Chapter 13 in this book on assessment and evaluation offers a variety of strategies and ideas for advancing this work.

Funding Strategies

Taking a gradual approach and adding new staff to an existing county budget one at a time over a period of years—perhaps by choosing not to fill some positions when employees retire and instead dedicating those funds to health equity staff—can help organizations to build their health equity teams. Adding specific LCT–inspired activities to maternal and child health scopes of work also allows health departments to potentially use Title V or even Title XIX funds to support a portion of a health equity staff person's time, if the activities can be framed as helping Medicaid-eligible clients to access services and supports. Finally, successful programs that clearly show the connection between addressing social conditions and the health and wellness of women and children in a visceral and emotionally resonant way can draw the attention of county leaders who make decisions about how general fund dollars are spent. Even better, they may catch the eye of local business leaders who are looking to put their mark on a project that is making a meaningful difference in the community.

Looking Out and Looking In

Changing the way maternal and child health programs are designed and implemented to address the social conditions that affect the families served is not easy. It requires the development of approaches that go beyond conventional maternal and child health strategies that focus on individuals—such as coordination of direct services or health education campaigns that target individual behavior change—to address the root causes of health inequities and the systems that perpetuate them. Such approaches require leaders to scrutinize not only the world around them—with its legacy of discriminatory policies and practices that have influenced the health of communities—but also their own institutions. It involves thinking and talking about difficult and sensitive issues, such as racism and classism, that may be beyond one's comfort level and that are not typically discussed in work settings. And, for this work to be successful, these conversations must be held at all levels of the organization, including among top-level leaders and decision makers.

The success of life course initiatives ultimately depends on whether organizations are willing to make lasting change within their institutions' walls. Committing to address issues of race, class, power, and privilege in work with communities and in professional relationships with coworkers also means ensuring that hiring practices and other human resources functions such as internal promotions are aligned with this philosophy and are clearly communicated, open, and transparent. Thinking about the budget from an organizational perspective, rather than a programmatic one, can help liberate resources for different purposes and encourage a funding framework that supports cross-program collaboration within organizations and facilitates staff understanding of the role they play in ensuring health for individuals across the life span. Making a concerted effort, perhaps at annual all-staff meetings, to engage in dialogue about more effective ways to collaborate internally and develop some small, yet concrete, ways to work on joint program activities, can help to further weave a life course approach into the fabric of the organization.

Future Directions

This chapter has demonstrated that there are many different ways to integrate a life course focus into work with children, families, and communities. What is important is not to get discouraged by committing to address the vast array of social issues that seemingly need to be solved before communities can achieve optimal health. Setting this high standard is unrealistic. Instead, starting in small ways that may result in modest yet notable important changes on their own and that may also build a foundation for more in-depth work is a more reasonable tactic.

It is also critical to consider that ongoing conversations with key partners and policy makers about the social determinants of health and related policies can result in the gradual diffusion of a new paradigm that can shift decisions about the strategies that both public health agencies and entities outside the health sector choose to embark upon. University of California San Francisco Benioff Children's Hospital Oakland recently launched an online data platform called FINDconnect, which was developed to give health care providers the knowledge, skill, and capacity to treat social determinants of health such as food insecurity and housing instability, issues not normally addressed within the traditional medical model. Similarly, the mayor of Oakland's high-profile investment in the Oakland Promise—a cradle-to-career initiative that aims to triple the number of college graduates from Oakland within the next decade—was likely influenced by the continuing dialogue in the county about the long-term impact of education on one's health and life trajectory. The initial success of these efforts, and the influence that community members had on their design, underscores the important role that residents can play in shaping policy and points to the untapped potential of populations served by public health departments, such as home visiting clients, to serve as neighborhood activists.

In proceeding to design and implement interventions influenced by LCT, practitioners would be wise to embrace innovation, try novel and untested strategies, and embrace failure, knowing that it may point them in new directions that will likely have more success. Fostering ongoing dialogue and being prepared for any challenges to the work that may arise from within their own organizations is critical. Rather than viewing disruption and doubt as barriers, they should be seen as a sign that people are engaged and, if invited and well managed, can lead to lasting change within an organization.

KEY POINTS

- There are many ways to put life course principles into practice. Rather than setting a high standard that seems unreachable, consider starting small. Join an online learning community or host a journal club focused on health equity in one's institution. Invite one new nonhealth organization a month to come to an existing collaborative meeting.
- Strategies can range from small changes, such as designing intake and screening forms that are strengths-based rather than deficit-based, to more comprehensive efforts such as establishing multisector collaboratives in geographic areas heavily impacted by maternal and child health disparities. The size and scale of the organization and the degree of political will to address the root causes of poor health outcomes will influence the strategies that public health practitioners may choose.
- Changing the way maternal and child health programs are designed and implemented to address the social conditions that affect the families served is not easy. The work is time-consuming, difficult to define, and may seem impractical, as it can take years to realize an impact on health outcomes. Fostering ongoing dialogue and being prepared for any challenges to the work that may arise, even from within one's own organization, is critical.

KEY ACTION STRATEGIES

- Diverse multisector collaboratives are often the backbone of successful initiatives that aim to put life course principles into practice.
- Statewide action plans to improve perinatal health that are based on life course principles can bring together stakeholders from multiple sectors and create momentum to address health disparities in innovative ways.
- Identifying geographic areas with a disproportionate burden of maternal and child health disparities and convening local collaboratives that can identify local needs and priorities, and design interventions accordingly is a strategy that has shown promise.
- Choosing one social determinant of health, such as financial insecurity, and developing concrete tools to address it that can be integrated into existing direct service programs is another approach that can yield tangible results.

REFERENCES

1. Lu MC, Halfon N. Racial and ethnic disparities in birth outcomes: a life-course perspective. *Matern Child Health J.* 2003;7(1):13–30.

2. Lu MC, Kotelchuck M, Hogan V, Jones L, Wright K, Halfon N. Closing the Black-White gap in birth outcomes: a life course approach. *Ethn Dis.* 2010;20(1 suppl 2):62–76.

3. Elder TE, Goddeeris JH, Haider SJ, Paneth N. The changing character of the Black–White infant mortality gap, 1983–2004. *Am J Public Health.* 2014;104(suppl 1):S105–S111.

4. United Health Foundation. Infant mortality rate in the United States as of 2015, by state. 2015. Available at: http://www.statista.com/statistics/252064/us-infant-mortality-rate-by-ethnicity-2011. Accessed July 11, 2016.

5. North Carolina State Center for Health Statistics. North Carolina Infant Mortality Report: infant death rates (per 1,000 live births) by race/ethnicity and year. Raleigh, NC: Department of Health and Human Services; 2016. Available at: http://www.schs.state.nc.us/data/vital/ims/2014/table3.html. Accessed July 11, 2016.

6. Mathews TJ, MacDorman MF, Thoma ME. Infant mortality statistics from the 2013 period linked birth/infant death data set. *Natl Vital Stat Rep.* 2015;64(9):1–30.

7. Pettiford B, Ahmad S, Aina A, et al.; Perinatal Health Strategic Planning Committee. North Carolina's Perinatal Health Strategic Plan, 2016–2020. North Carolina Department of Health and Human Services. 2016. Available at: http://whb.ncpublichealth.com. Accessed December 20, 2017.

8. The Racial Equity Institute. Services and workshops. Available at: https://www.racialequityinstitute.org. Accessed June 9, 2017.

9. City of Seattle Race and Social Justice Initiative. Racial Equity Toolkit. Available at: http://www.seattle.gov/Documents/Departments/RSJI/RacialEquityToolkit_FINAL_August2012.pdf. Accessed June 12, 2017.

10. Matthews TJ, MacDorman MF, Thoma ME. Infant mortality statistics from the 2013 period linked birth/infant death data set. *Natl Vital Stat Rep.* 2015;64(9):1–30.

11. Annie E. Casey Foundation. Kids Count Policy Report: Race for Results 2014. 2014. Available at: http://www.aecf.org/resources/race-for-results. Accessed June 9, 2017.

12. Frey CA, Farrell PM, Cotton QD, Lathen LS, Marks KM. Wisconsin's Lifecourse Initiative for Healthy Families: application of the maternal and child health life course perspective through a regional funding initiative. *Matern Child Health J.* 2014;18(2):413–422.

13. Arronson RA. Elimination of racial and ethnic disparities in birth outcomes in Wisconsin. University of Wisconsin–Madison, School of Medicine and Public Health. 2008. Available at: https://www.med.wisc.edu/media/medwiscedu/documents/service/wisconsin-partnership-program/annual-reports/wpp-2008-annual-report.pdf. Accessed June 8, 2017.

14. Board of Regents of the University of Wisconsin System. The Wisconsin Idea. Available at: http://www.wisc.edu/wisconsin-idea. Accessed June 8, 2017.

15. Butterfoss FD, Kegler MC. The community coalition action theory. In: DiClemente R, Crosby R, Kegler M, eds. *Emerging Theories in Health Promotion Practice and Research*. 2nd ed. San Francisco, CA: Jossey-Bass; 2009.

16. Giles WG, Tucker P, Brown L, et al. Racial and ethnic approaches to community health (REACH 2010): an overview. *Ethn Dis*. 2004;14(suppl 1):5–8.

17. Rohan AM, Onheiber PM, Hale LJ, et al. Turning the ship: making the shift to a life-course framework. *Matern Child Health J*. 2014;18(2):423–430.

18. Bellanca HK, Hunter MS. One Key Question: preventive reproductive health is part of high quality primary care. *Contraception*. 2013;88(1):3–6.

19. Alameda County Public Health Department. Life and death from unnatural causes: health and social inequity in Alameda County. 2008. Available at: http://www.acphd.org/media/53628/unnatcs2008.pdf. Accessed May 25, 2017.

20. Community Assessment, Planning and Education Unit, Alameda County Public Health Department. Data from Alameda County vital statistics files, birth, fetal death, and death files. Available at: http://www.acphd.org/data-reports.aspx. Accessed December 11, 2017.

21. Shrimali BP, Luginbuhl J, Malin C, Flournoy R, Siegel A. The Building Blocks Collaborative: advancing a life course approach to health equity through multi-sector collaboration. *Matern Child Health J*. 2013;17(5):767–776.

22. Huang J, Sherraden M, Youngmi K, Clancy M. Effects of child development accounts on early social–emotional development: an experimental test. *JAMA Pediatr*. 2014;168(3):265–271.

11

Policy

Julia Caplan, MPH, MPP, and Lauren Gase, PhD, MPH

The health of mothers, infants, children, adolescents, and families is shaped by a variety of social, environmental, and policy factors, including economic and housing policies; the criminal and juvenile justice systems; educational and economic opportunities; access to parks, clean air, and water; transportation options; and availability of affordable, healthy foods. Public health alone cannot address these complex issues; rather, solutions require collaboration across sectors to ensure that governments, as a whole, prioritize the well-being of people throughout the life course. This chapter will describe Health in All Policies (HiAP) and will discuss how maternal, child, and adolescent health practitioners can use this approach to improve health across the life course.

WHAT IS HEALTH IN ALL POLICIES AND WHY IS IT RELEVANT TO MATERNAL, CHILD, AND ADOLESCENT HEALTH?

HiAP is defined as "a collaborative approach to improving population health by incorporating health considerations into decision making across sectors and policy areas."[1] While many of the principles of HiAP can be used in private or nonprofit sectors, HiAP originated as a government strategy and today continues to largely be implemented within government. HiAP aims to break down government silos, increase government efficiency, and engage multiple sectors in promoting the social determinants of health and equity. This strategy can help governments use collective problem solving to tackle complex, multifactorial problems that require collaborative approaches and pooled resources. The HiAP approach seeks to improve existing systems as opposed to creating new ones. Such an approach may not add significant cost and may help nonhealth partner agencies achieve their own goals more effectively.

Public health and social work have a long history of pursuing health-promoting policies such as living wage ordinances, paid family leave, and restrictions on tobacco advertising and sales. For example, California's Contra Costa County Family, Maternal, and Child Health Program launched Building Economic Security Today (BEST), which works to improve financial security and stability for low-income families through financial education and assessments.[2] Programs like the Special Supplemental Nutrition

Program for Women, Infants, and Children (WIC) have long supported improvements in children's nutrition and economic security for families. HiAP builds on this history of collaborative public health work and seeks to embed health, equity, and environmental sustainability considerations into the early stages of policy development and implementation across government sectors.

In 2011, the Institute of Medicine recommended that "states and the federal government develop and employ a Health in All Policies (HiAP) approach to consider the health effects—both positive and negative—of major legislation, regulations and other policies that could potentially have a meaningful impact on the public's health."[3] HiAP work can be strengthened by considering health and equity across the life course, and maternal, child, and adolescent health practitioners can play an important role by sharing their expertise and community connections. For example, scholars have suggested that "policies related to land use, housing, parks and recreation" should be informed by a life course perspective, and that "activities related to 'systems of care' might place greater emphasis on multisector systems of care."[2]

HiAP is also being embraced globally as an approach to supporting health and equity across the life course. Physicians and elected officials in Scotland and Wales have recently called for a HiAP approach to address child poverty as a determinant of health.[4,5] In addition, in 2013, an international multigovernment team made an explicit case for a connection between early child development and HiAP:

> New social accountability initiatives should consider the burden of responsibility of policymakers promoting early child development and Health in All Policies (ECD-HiAP) in terms of the social costs of not intervening with active policies towards the promotion of equity from the cradle . . . There is a need to integrate time (life course), contexts (social determinants) and actors (across sectors) for effective policies towards equity from the cradle. This constitutes a new paradigm tackling the intergenerational cycle of poverty perpetuation . . . Governments can make major and sustained improvements in the quality of environments experienced by children in society by implementing policies that take note of this powerful body of research while, at the same time, fulfilling their obligations under the CRC [United Nations Committee on the Rights of the Child].[6]

The HiAP approach has seen significant uptake across the United States at the city, county, and state levels (Box 11-1). Governments have established HiAP ordinances and adopted structures to establish ongoing collaboration across sectors to advance health and equity. A 2017 report from the National Association of County and City Health Officials[8] describes the spread of HiAP across the United States and shares key findings, promising strategies, and recommendations for supporting HiAP in local jurisdictions. Several public health conferences have featured a HiAP theme, and both state and local health departments across the United States have provided HiAP trainings to staff department-wide.

Box 11-1. California's Health in All Policies (HiAP) Task Force

California's HiAP Task Force is an example of a formal HiAP structure. The HiAP Task Force brings together 22 state agencies and departments to promote a vision that "California government advances health, equity, and sustainability in all policies."[7] Much of this work is carried out by embedding equity and health metrics and guidelines into decision making by nonhealth agencies. The public health department plays an important role in providing subject matter expertise. The HiAP team is staffed jointly by the health department, the Public Health Institute, and a branch of the Governor's office, which ensures public health expertise, access to high-level leadership across government, and connections to a variety of partners inside and outside of government.[1]

WHAT IS POLICY?

Public policy is defined as "a system of laws, regulatory measures, courses of action, and funding priorities concerning a given topic promulgated by a governmental entity or its representatives."[9] In other words, the term "public policy" refers to a wide range of activities carried out by government. While legislation is one mechanism for promoting health throughout the life course, the range of government activities is much broader than legislative action and presents myriad opportunities to promote health and equity. This chapter focuses primarily on nonlegislative approaches to public policy.

In *A Practical Guide for Policy Analysis*, Bardach and Patashnik provide a nine-page list of "things governments do" to spark ideas about the wide range of policy mechanisms available to solve public problems.[10] Drawing on this list, the following are examples of "things governments do" that have an impact on health throughout the life course. Many of these can be decided by government employees who have discretion to determine how their work is implemented, without going to a formal vote:

- Recruitment, hiring, and retention: Government has significant influence over who it employs, how much they are paid, and whether they are given opportunities for advancement. For example, agencies can take action to conduct outreach to communities that are underrepresented and provide professional development opportunities to women and low-income staff.
- Personnel policies: Government can promote healthy parenting by implementing supportive policies, such as breastfeeding policies, flexible schedules, paid parental leave, and predictability of scheduling.
- Agency budgets: Government can direct program resources to identify and target resources to communities with the greatest needs.
- Community engagement: Government can conduct community engagement in ways that are more likely to solicit input from working parents and their families. Examples are scheduling input meetings during evenings and in convenient locations, providing

food and childcare, providing language translation, and structuring input meetings to be discussion-oriented, as opposed to formal hearings.

- Grants: When local agencies develop proposals to fund affordable housing, social services, parks development, tree planting, and other projects, they can focus resources in communities that face the highest need, including prioritizing projects that are most likely to benefit children and families. State agencies develop criteria for how they disseminate dollars to local communities and can require local communities to prioritize high-need populations in their proposed projects.

- Data collection and analysis: Agencies can partner to gather and share data. For example, a maternal, child, and adolescent health program may be able to add family status questions to a questionnaire being administered by a local parks department. In addition, agencies can stratify data by subpopulations, such as gender, race, ethnicity, age, geographic location, or other categories, to ensure that their services and programs are reaching communities that need them the most (Box 11-2).

THE FIVE KEY ELEMENTS OF HEALTH IN ALL POLICIES

In 2013, the American Public Health Association, the California Public Health Institute, and the California Department of Public Health developed and released *Health in All Policies: A Guide for State and Local Governments*. The Guide identifies five key elements of a HiAP approach (Box 11-3).[1] The following discussion will consider each of these in light of promotion of health across the life course:

1. Promote health, equity, and environmental sustainability.
2. Support intersectoral collaboration.
3. Benefit multiple partners.
4. Engage stakeholders.
5. Create structural or procedural change.

Box 11-2. Health in All Policies (HiAP) Blend Policy and Politics

While public health seeks solutions through evidence and best practices, implementation of public policy generally requires a political process to gain support, secure commitments, and make decisions to act. Politics are often ideological and based upon public and personal opinion rather than science. An Australian HiAP evaluation team found that the "convergence of problems, policy and politics, as well as the strategic action of those involved, have been integral to HiAP's success in remaining on the policy agenda."[11] HiAP work must be rooted in the science of health and policy studies, but HiAP leaders must also engage in political processes, keep an eye out for windows of opportunity, and be prepared to act when these opportunities arise.

Box 11-3. What is in a Name?

Communities can use the Health in All Policies (HiAP) approach without explicitly calling it HiAP. The name is not important—what is important is the key principles and how the work is done.

Key Element 1: Promote Health, Equity, and Environmental Sustainability

HiAP simultaneously emphasizes the need to understand the health impacts of a given policy area, issue, or project as well as differential impacts on populations and impacts on the sustainability of the natural environment.

Applying an Equity Lens: A Key Role for Health in All Policies

Equity has been defined as "just and fair inclusion into a society in which all can participate, prosper, and reach their full potential"[12] and health equity is the "attainment of the highest level of health for all people."[13] Promoting equity means valuing all people equally, creating conditions that allow all people the opportunity to attain their highest level of health, and addressing inequities—in other words, differences that are avoidable, unfair, and unjust.[14]

One of the key roles for HiAP practitioners is to apply an equity lens to government processes to help government entities direct resources toward the communities that need them the most and focus on activities that will help close gaps in health, educational, economic, and social outcomes. There is a need to consider how decisions might affect different groups and to use that information to ensure that government practices and policies are equitable and avoid unintended harm. Public health and social work organizations have a lot to offer others in this regard, through data, expertise in community engagement, and evidence regarding health and equity impacts of various policies.

Because the social determinants of health are so complex, solutions are rife with unintended consequences; well-intentioned decisions can inadvertently exacerbate inequities. For example, a city may decide to add resources for transit lines, bike lanes, and parks to a neighborhood that faces high rates of poverty. These can be important investments for ensuring that families have access to jobs, safe places to play, and social cohesion. However, they could ultimately cause rents and housing prices to increase, leading to the displacement of existing residents. An equity approach would raise these concerns early in the process and consider antidisplacement strategies such as rent control and affordability requirements for new developments that can be implemented alongside neighborhood improvements.

Climate Change Is a Public Health Issue

The American Academy of Pediatrics reports that climate change threatens children's health through "physical and psychological sequelae of weather disasters, increased heat stress, decreased air quality, altered disease patterns of some climate sensitive infections, and food, water, and nutrient insecurity."[15] Children's mental and physical health is already impacted and increasingly threatened by potential "far-reaching effects of unchecked climate change, including community and global instability, mass migrations, and increased conflict."[15] The American Public Health Association concurs with the severity of the threat of climate change:

> The science is clear: climate change is a **serious threat** to human health . . . Vulnerable populations such as communities of color, the elderly, young children, the poor and those with chronic illnesses bear the greatest burden of injury, disease and death related to climate change.[16]

Climate change mitigation (reducing emissions of the greenhouse gases that cause climate change) also presents new opportunities for HiAP. For example, one of the key climate change mitigation strategies is to reduce fossil fuel dependency by increasing use of transit, walking, and biking (active transportation). This strategy also improves physical activity, social cohesion, air quality, and financial impacts on users.[17] At the same time, it is important to apply an equity lens and ensure that these improvements are accompanied by appropriate safety measures, as children, older adults, communities of color, and low-income communities are disproportionally impacted by traffic-related injuries and deaths.[18] The 2015 *Lancet* Commission on Health and Climate emphasizes that "tackling climate change could be the greatest global health opportunity of the 21st century" because many actions to reduce and prepare for climate change can simultaneously improve health and equity.[19]

Climate change adaptation and resilience—the ability of communities to prepare for, survive, and even thrive despite impacts of climate change—will increasingly join other factors such as transportation, education, and access to jobs as determinants of healthy communities. HiAP initiatives can help ensure that nonhealth sectors include climate change adaptation strategies to promote health. For example, schools and housing developments may need to consider new cooling and air filtration systems to respond to rising temperatures and related changes in air quality. Transportation planners can join with foresters, youth, and communities to plant trees along walking and cycling routes. Trees cool the air, filter the air and water, and make the route more pleasant, thus incentivizing activity and improving mental and physical health in addition to absorbing greenhouse gases.

Because climate change exacerbates existing health inequities, the HiAP approach can help ensure that processes to address climate change deeply engage and share decision-making power with communities facing inequities, so that resultant climate change policies and programs increase equity by prioritizing resources such as facilities, services, job training, and employment for these communities. Maternal, child, and adolescent health practitioners know where families gather and can share expertise in how to effectively engage them in planning and decision making.

Key Elements 2 and 3: Support Intersectoral Collaboration and Benefit Multiple Partners

HiAP approaches build intersectoral collaboration to achieve changes that cannot be made by any single actors on their own, and they do this largely by pursuing actions that provide benefits to multiple partners, often called co-benefits. All government entities are bound by mission statements, organizational goals, and strategic plans. Engaging nonhealth partners in HiAP work requires ensuring that they receive some benefit from participation, particularly benefits that will help them achieve their own goals.

Public health entities must make collaboration appealing to the other sectors they work with, and one way to do this is to identify additional nonhealth benefits, or co-benefits, to nonhealth sectors. As relationships are built with new partner agencies, it is important to ask what their goals are, what their challenges are, and how public health can help meet their needs while also advancing health and equity. For example, increasing access to locally grown produce not only increases consumption of healthy foods but also benefits the local agricultural economy and supports the preservation of agricultural lands, which is a key strategy for mitigating climate change. Farmers and environmental protection leaders may both be interested in supporting such efforts. Projects that reduce air pollutants or increase access to asthma treatment may reduce school absences, which can increase academic performance, reduce losses of school per diem funding, and reduce the number of missed work days by parents who are caring for sick children. For these reasons, schools and employers may be interested.

It is important to note that not all health issues yield co-benefits for nonhealth partners. In some situations, health organizations will support policies that are not popular with colleagues from other government entities. The stakeholder engagement processes of a HiAP approach may bring these issues to the surface, but solutions may require the engagement and leadership of nongovernment entities, advocates, community groups, and legislative action. Even while those processes are underway, a HiAP group may be able to help by providing health evidence, identifying areas of common values, and facilitating information-sharing and learning among sectors.

Key Element 4: Engaging Stakeholders

Stakeholder engagement can help create better solutions, provide insights into partner agencies' roles, catalyze community action, garner support for the initiative, facilitate development of new partnerships, identify resources, and understand potential problems early in the process.[1] Stakeholders can include community residents and organizations,

Box 11-4. Recommendations for Equitable Community Engagement

The Bay Area Regional Health Inequities Initiative developed a Health Equity and Community Engagement Report[20] based on qualitative assessments in seven local health jurisdictions. Some of the recommendations they identified are to

- Build meaningful, ongoing relationships with community partners.
- Partner with communities to mobilize and create more cohesion.
- Engage community partners in all steps of program planning.
- Provide community-based, culturally appropriate services.
- Prioritize community capacity building and leadership development.
- Engage partners to include health considerations in all policies (i.e., land-use zoning, transportation, criminal justice).
- Institutionalize professional development for staff regarding social determinants of health and health equity.
- Provide flexibility in staff time and priorities to allow effective community and health equity work.

policy and issue experts, funders, other governmental jurisdictions, and private sector companies. Many processes can be used to engage stakeholders, and the specific tactics employed will depend on the context, such as the information being sought and individuals being engaged. Attention should be paid to the needs of community members to ensure that they can access input opportunities (Box 11-4).

Key Element 5: Create Structural or Procedural Change

Although it is beneficial to bring a health and equity lens into specific projects, HiAP is about fundamentally changing the culture and business of government so that health, equity, and environmental sustainability are viewed and considered as key components of any decision-making process. This represents a fundamental shift in how government operates, to create shared goals across sectors and to put human well-being at the center of all decision making.

Structural and procedural change can be supported by the following:

- A top-down directive or leadership promoting HiAP, such as from a city council, board of supervisors, mayor, or governor: This can come in the form of legislation, executive action, or other statements.
- Structures for cross-sectoral collaboration, such as a formal HiAP body or seats for health representatives on decision-making or advisory boards for nonhealth policy issues: For example, a transportation agency could create officer positions that are responsible for ensuring that health, equity, and environmental sustainability are pursued.
- Adoption of health, equity, and environmental sustainability goals, which can be either shared across all of government or embedded in individual nonhealth agencies: These can include goals that are health-promoting but focus on social

determinants such as high-school graduation rates, workforce development opportunities, and access to healthy food.

- Institutionalized processes for analyzing health, equity, and environmental sustainability impacts of policy options and shaping decisions: For example, the Washington State Board of Health conducts health impact reviews of legislation, at the request of the governor or state legislature.[21]
- Workforce development, including building HiAP capacity into ongoing training activities, incorporating health and equity into duty statements in nonhealth agencies, and making it easier to hire staff with cross-sectoral subject matter expertise.
- Backbone staffing: Implementing HiAP requires a core staff that can facilitate shared decision making, conduct research, engage stakeholders, and help partners maintain momentum.

BUILDING COLLABORATIVE RELATIONSHIPS

In practice, HiAP centers on relationships and depends upon building trust, developing a shared vision, and engendering a culture of generosity and reciprocity. High-level leaders such as mayors, county supervisors, or city council members can play an important role in building institutional bridges and championing this work, but staff at any level of an organization can take steps in this direction. One of the most important things a practitioner can do is to ask nonhealth partners or potential partners about their priorities, goals, and challenges. This builds trust and can help practitioners identify potential opportunities for collaboration. Successful HiAP practitioners tend to employ the following practices in building relationships:

1. Create opportunities for informal conversations across sectors, such as coffee dates, phone calls, or walks in the park (Box 11-5).
2. Share information and ideas freely: Tell colleagues in other departments about new data or publications that they might find useful, educational events, or ideas.
3. Take time to build expertise: Before offering opinions about somebody else's field, read articles, talk to subject matter experts, and ask others what they think.
4. Help others build networks: Help colleagues connect to stakeholders or make introductions between colleagues in different departments who are working on similar issues.
5. Keep an eye out for windows of opportunity: Planning processes, new programs, and even community crises can create openings for new partnerships and new ways of thinking.
6. Be clear about health, equity, and environmental sustainability values, but be flexible about how time is spent, to easily respond to changing political realities and capitalize on emerging opportunities.

7. Offer support to others to help their work go well: This includes understanding the goals of partner organizations and articulating how HiAP projects can help them.

8. Be willing to make mistakes, apologize, and try again: HiAP requires courage to try out new ideas and approaches. It is OK to make mistakes, and it may even be a necessary part of the process.

EIGHT HEALTH IN ALL POLICIES IMPLEMENTATION ACTIVITIES: A FRAMEWORK

HiAP can take many forms, and the scope, structures, and activities undertaken to work across sectors are likely to vary. Although the five key elements describe underlying principles of HiAP work, multiagency partnerships can take on a wide range of activities. To support HiAP practice, Gase et al. identified eight commonly used activities to facilitate implementation of a HiAP approach.[22,23] These activities were identified on the basis of a review of US-based HiAP work being implemented at the local, state, and national level, as well the authors' own experience as practitioners (Figure 11-1). The eight HiAP activities complement each other and are often implemented in combination—that is why they are shown as integrated pieces of a puzzle. Building support and awareness and developing and structuring cross-sector relationships are shown as the foundation, because these two activities are often essential to getting HiAP work off the ground.

It is important to note that a formal HiAP initiative, such as a governmental task force with an explicit mandate to implement a HiAP approach, is not necessary to carry out these activities. Rather, these activities can be pursued as part of a more informal HiAP structure, such as a group of partners working together or a maternal, child, and adolescent health program looking to do more cross-sectoral work. These activities provide a helpful starting place to understand the kinds of HiAP projects that could be pursued in different practice settings.

Activity 1: Building Support and Awareness

One of the core activities to implementing a HiAP approach is creating awareness about the multiple factors that have an impact on health and well-being and the role that non-health partners can play in improving health across the life course. Practitioners can use both numerical data and personal stories to convey the impacts of social and

---

Box 11-5. First Steps in Building Health in All Policies (HiAP) Relationships

One of the best things a budding HiAP practitioner can do is ask a colleague from another agency to meet for coffee. Ask them what they do, what their goals are, what their challenges are, and how you can help.

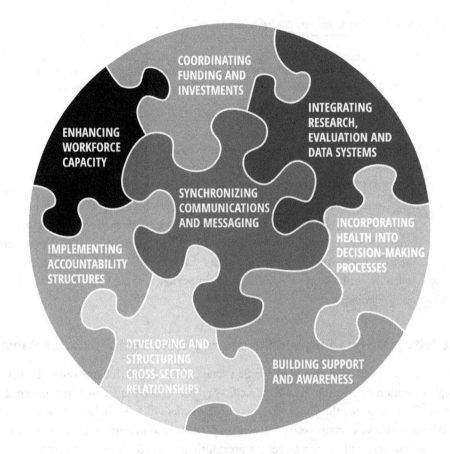

Source: Based on strategies for implementing Health in All Policies described in Gase et al.[22,23]

Figure 11-1. Activities for Implementing Health in All Policies

environmental factors on health and well-being and help partners find common ground. Helping others understand how health, equity, and environmental sustainability affect their goals can help with cultivating buy-in from champions in nonhealth fields, whose support is often foundational to being able to implement other activities. This can include policymakers, governmental leaders, business leaders, community-based organizations, academics, and the general public (Box 11-6).

Through its #SchoolsNotPrisons music and arts tour, The California Endowment helped reframe the public narrative around juvenile justice, supporting a new vision for community safety centered on education, health, healing, investing in youth, and civic engagement. The tour traveled to 11 California communities to highlight ways to invest in safe and healthy communities. The tour promoted the importance of voting, especially for young people, and supported local campaigns against the overuse of punishment and incarceration, including issues such as exclusionary school discipline, the lack of services

Box 11-6. New York City's Multisector Children's Board

Cultivating high-level, visible champions can help support health across the life course. New York City recently announced the members of the newly created Children's Cabinet Advisory Board. These high-profile leaders from academia, faith, media, business, technology, the nonprofit sector, and the judiciary will support the Cabinet's mission to protect and promote the well-being of children.[24]

for the formerly incarcerated, and the impact of incarceration on families.[25] Figure 11-2 provides an illustration of the messages used in this work.

Children's HealthWatch is a nonpartisan network of pediatricians, researchers, and children's health and policy experts that aims to improve children's health in America. They actively disseminate their research findings with academics, legislators, and the public to help them better understand the social and economic factors that have an impact on children's health. A recent news story titled "Food as Medicine: Rethinking Hunger Relief as Health Care" emphasized the importance of fresh, accessible food to treat and prevent disease.[26]

Activity 2: Developing and Structuring Cross-Sector Relationships

The Institute of Medicine recommends that state and local governments support HiAP implementation by creating "health councils of relevant government agencies convened under the auspices of the Chief Executive."[27] Regardless of how formal or informal a HiAP approach is, it is necessary to identify partners and determine how interaction between partners will be organized. As previously described, there are many ways to structure relationships, ranging from formal committees, councils or task forces, memoranda of understanding, and permanent structures for management, to informal mechanisms such as temporary workgroups or teams, voluntary networks, and consultation. Although high-level leadership is important for securing formal institutional partnership, staff at all levels can support collaboration and relationship building between organizations. The specific sectors and partners that need to be a part of a HiAP initiative will depend on its scope, political will, and staffing resources.

In 2009, the Kansas Health Institute launched the Children's Health in All Policies initiative, engaging more than 30 stakeholders from the Kansas Legislature, government agencies, and nongovernment organizations to examine ways to improve health by engaging sectors such as agriculture, education, and transportation. The initiative explores a range of children's health topics including poverty, infant mortality, obesity, children with special health care needs, oral health, access to health care, childhood injury, and adolescent risk behaviors.[28]

The Children's Environmental Health Network is a national multidisciplinary organization that aims to protect the developing child from environmental health hazards and promote a healthier environment. The network includes a number of structures,

Source: Fulton.[25] Reprinted with permission from The California Endowment.
Figure 11-2. The California Endowment's 2016 #SchoolsNotPrisons Tour

including a board of directors, an advisory council, five multiagency workgroups, and organizational staff.[29]

Activity 3: Incorporating Health Into Decision-Making Processes

Many HiAP initiatives integrate health considerations into decision-making processes, including policies, programs, projects, and plans. As previously described, policies can range from bills being considered by the legislature, to regulations written by governmental departments, to organizational funding decisions, protocols, and processes. Health criteria can be integrated at various time points and in various ways, such as during strategic planning, needs or community assessments, policy development, policy implementation, and policy enforcement. Tools can include health lens analyses, health impact assessments (HIAs), checklists, guidelines, and protocols.

In 2014–2015, the University of Nevada, Las Vegas, School of Community Health Sciences and partners conducted an HIA to assess the possible health impacts of changes to the availability of full-day kindergarten in Nevada. Results suggested that access to full-day kindergarten could improve short-term test scores, especially for at-risk students; access to school-based meals; and students' nutrition education and physical activity, especially when implemented through evidence-informed strategies. The HIA was useful in illustrating the connections between education and health issues in Nevada and provided information and recommendations that could inform development and implementation of existing and future policies. The HIA process helped strengthen partnerships and built interest in and capacity to conduct additional multidisciplinary assessment projects.[30]

The California Department of Housing and Community Development applied a health and equity lens to its planning process and data analysis when it was developing its statewide housing plan. Staff at the department developed a matrix to help them ensure that each section of the document used an equity framework that considered both people and place (i.e., geographic differences). The assessment included information about the possible negative health effects from exposure to poor air quality when housing is located in areas near heavy automobile traffic and identified options to address housing and access needs for vulnerable populations through greater interagency coordination, program design, and evaluation.[31]

Activity 4: Enhancing Workforce Capacity

To effectively work across sectors, staff from public health and nonhealth fields need to speak a common language, understand each other's priorities, and have the interpersonal and analytical skills to work together on environmental, policy, and systems change. This includes "soft skills," such as building trust and shared agendas, negotiation, and collaborative decision making. A range of tactics can be used to enhance workforce capacity, including formally training staff, creating opportunities for diverse staff to interact (e.g., though networking meetings or joint conferences), implementing hiring or reward practices that incentivize cross-sector collaboration (e.g., hiring "nontraditional" staff or providing incentives that reward cross-sector efforts), and implementing physical changes (e.g., co-locating staff or facilities).

Many health, public health, and social service staff work directly with residents, as community health workers, outreach workers, community health representatives, and *promotores de salud*. These staff are often trusted members of the community and serve as liaisons to increase access to health and social services, improve service quality, and improve client outcomes. These frontline workers can be trained to help address the multifaceted needs of children and families, such as securing employment, transportation, public benefits, and health care services.

The California HiAP team has provided trainings to several public health departments and at times has included nonhealth colleagues in the training groups. For example, in 2016, the Las Cruces, New Mexico, Wellness Committee organized a HiAP training that included representatives from the local health department, academic institutions, and health care, as well as local government partners from land use planning, schools, and parks. The training curriculum focuses on two primary areas: (1) the social determinants of health and equity, using a root cause mapping exercise to understand the upstream nonhealth causes of poor health outcomes, and (2) training on diplomacy and relationship building across sectors, including exercises to identify co-benefits and opportunities to achieve gains for multiple partners through HiAP activities.

Activity 5: Coordinating Funding and Investments

HiAP can support more efficient use of government dollars by ensuring that spending provides multiple benefits, including supporting healthy, equitable, and environmentally sustainable communities. Coordinating funding and investments can incentivize cross-sector work and can be achieved through a range of tactics, including jointly issuing funding announcements; building criteria into funding announcements, scoring criteria, or performance measures; and providing input on funding applications of partner agencies. Multiple partners can also coordinate investments in communities (e.g., through place-based approaches that aim to improve multiple outcomes, such as health, environmental, economic, and social). Building health, equity, and environmental sustainability goals into existing funding streams and program budgets can increase the value achieved without increasing overall spending.

Several of California's nonhealth agencies have incorporated health- and equity-promoting considerations into their grant programs. This includes grants that promote active transportation (Department of Transportation), urban greening (Natural Resources Agency), and affordable housing and land use planning (Governor's Strategic Growth Council). All of these programs require that the funds benefit disadvantaged communities. California's Affordable Housing and Sustainable Communities program encourages grant applicants to collaborate with local health departments as they develop their proposals and identify community needs and requires proposed affordable housing developments to be smoke-free, incorporate urban greening, and provide reduced-cost transit passes to residents.

New York City's Health Bucks are distributed as a Supplemental Nutrition Assistance Program (SNAP) benefit at more than 120 farmers' markets. For every $5 that SNAP recipients spend at the market using Electronic Benefits Transfer, they receive one $2 Health Buck coupon, which can be used to purchase fresh fruits and vegetables at all New York City farmers' markets. Such financial incentives are a promising strategy to increase awareness and use of farmers' markets, helping to improve health and boost the local economy.[32]

As part of the White House Neighborhood Revitalization Initiative, the Promise Neighborhoods program sought to align federal funding streams to help "transform neighborhoods of concentrated poverty into neighborhoods of opportunity." Communities use the funding to take a comprehensive approach to the health of youth and families, providing access to educational, health, and safety services to build a continuum of "cradle-to-career" solutions. The program had an explicit focus on integrating programs and breaking down agency silos.[33] Another program that uses a similar approach is the Best Babies Zone Initiative (BBZ), which brings together national and local funders to support a "multi-sector approach to reducing infant mortality and racial disparities in birth outcomes and improving birth and health outcomes by mobilizing communities to address the social determinants that affect health." Activities focus on economics, education, and community, as well as explicit health-related actions.[34]

Activity 6: Integrating Research, Evaluation, and Data Systems

Cross-sector research and evaluation can facilitate a more comprehensive look at the health and equity impacts of policies or programs that are traditionally considered to be outside the purview of the public health system, such as full-day kindergarten programs, tenant-based rental assistance programs, active transportation programs, and violence prevention strategies. Establishing systems to generate and share knowledge across agencies can support evidence-based practice and continuous quality improvement. This can include developing or supporting cross-sector research and evaluation projects, taking steps to integrate data from different agencies and organizations, and developing common measurement or tracking systems.

In Los Angeles County, California, agencies are forming a Probation Research and Evaluation Unit, with a multisector research agenda that highlights critical areas that must be measured and assessed to build effective juvenile justice practices and policies. The county's plans reflect the multiple dimensions of system functioning—for example, how young people "touch" and "flow" through governmental systems including law enforcement, probation, juvenile court, children and family services, public and social services, mental health, and health services. The unit plans to assess the impacts of services on a range of youth outcomes including recidivism, educational achievement, living stability, supportive relationships, mental health, and substance use. The county will use the results to hold systems accountable for their work, creating a critical feedback loop to improve practice.

The Children's Data Network links administrative data from public agencies that reflect youth and families' interactions with systems over the life course (e.g., birth records, screening records, emergency department records, educational records, home visiting records, homeless records). Linked data can be used to examine the health, educational, and social impacts of a wide variety of programs and policies, such as early home visiting services, early childhood education, nutrition strategies, and screening services. Data can also be used to better understand youth and family trajectories over time, thus supporting the Life Course Approach. The network is a partnership of public agencies, philanthropic funders, and community stakeholders that have worked together to help address the "ethical, political, operational, and scientific challenges" often present in building integrated data systems.[35]

Activity 7: Synchronizing Communications and Messaging

Communications and messaging are essential for conveying the importance and co-benefits of working across sectors and building a common vision and language for collaborative work. Tactics for synchronizing communication and messaging may include using language that shows the relationship between activities and multisector goals; developing intersectoral commitment statements, such as a vision or mission; developing common messages used by multiple sectors; and establishing shared platforms for cross-sector communication, such as a newsletter or website (Box 11-7).

The Whole School, Whole Child, Whole Community (WSCC) model is a tool for communicating the impact of education and health on the economy and society as a

Box 11-7. Partnership Example: Sex Education in Schools

A health agency may want to partner with schools to provide comprehensive sex education. Although achieving the goals of healthy sexual relationships, preventing teenage pregnancy, and avoiding sexually transmitted infections in and of themselves is important, the partnership will likely be more successful if the health agency can articulate the benefits of comprehensive sex education in helping to keep kids in school and increasing graduation rates. This helps schools make the case for directing scarce resources to support this program and shows them that the health agency also values—and is concerned about—having an impact on educational attainment as a shared objective.

whole, making the case that multiple sectors must work together and that "schools are a perfect setting for this collaboration." WSCC was developed jointly by the US Centers for Disease Control and Prevention (CDC) and the ASCD (formerly the Association for Supervision and Curriculum Development), a nonprofit organization that represents more than 125,000 educators. The WSCC model calls for greater alignment between education and health to improve each child's cognitive, physical, social, and emotional development.[36] The model recognizes that integrating health services and programs more deeply into the day-to-day lives of students will raise academic achievement and improve learning. WSCC has developed a variety of written and visual communications materials to convey the value and importance of its collaborative approach.[37]

Activity 8: Implementing Accountability Structures

Accountability structures are important for clarifying roles, creating a sense of shared responsibility, and providing direction and oversight for multistakeholder work. They also need to be flexible enough to allow changes on the basis of emerging opportunities, lessons learned, and the ever-changing priorities of political environments. Examples of accountability structures include oversight or management organizations, budget spending reviews, shared objectives or performance measures, cross-sector monitoring or enforcement of laws, and public reporting. Accountability structures can also support continuity over time, particularly when there is a high level of turnover among staff and leadership.

The National Prevention, Health Promotion, and Public Health Council (NPC) leverages the work of 20 federal departments and agencies, including Transportation, Housing, Labor, and Justice, to integrate health and prevention into their policies, practices, and programs. Each year, as required by statute, the NPC describes its progress in increasing the number of Americans who are healthy at every stage of life in its Annual Status Report, which is delivered to Congress. The reports include a list of NPC agency commitments and achievements, giving each agency a platform to describe what it has done to advance health.[38]

The California Home Visiting Program helps "vulnerable families independently raise their children." As a part of their performance monitoring system, state grantees (local health departments) measure and report on the percentage of women who after 12 months increased their (1) income and (2) educational attainment or employment status. To help achieve these objectives, grantees partner with local education and employment agencies to create referral networks, connect families to resources, and monitor outcomes. State objectives around family economic self-sufficiency help bring additional focus to and accountability for facilitating local partnerships.[39,40]

How Strategies Interact to Advance Health and Equity

Figure 11-3 shows how the eight HiAP activities can lead to improvements in policies, systems, health, and equity.[23] The activities being implemented as a part of a HiAP approach will depend on its context and goals and may change over time. Developing and implementing a HiAP approach is not linear; the processes used to build relationships, train staff, communicate with decision makers, frame problems, analyze data, and develop policy alternatives operate in a complex web. Feedback loops and interactions connect the activities, outputs, outcomes, and contextual factors depicted in the model. For example, early successes in one area may lead to changes in the level of stakeholder buy-in, which may facilitate implementation of additional activities. Over time, a HiAP approach can foster continuity and institutionalization of health and equity–focused practices and, in the long term, can lead to improved social and physical environments, more efficient and effective government, and improved population health and equity.

Evaluation is an important part of implementing a HiAP approach. Evaluation can be used to identify opportunities to improve ongoing work, foster shared learning among partners, and demonstrate impact, but it can be challenging. To date, there have been very few in-depth evaluations of HiAP initiatives. Evaluation can be difficult because of the nonlinear nature of this work, the multiple feedback loops, the complex web of social and environmental factors that shape health outcomes, and the distal impacts on population health of upstream prevention measures. It can be useful to identify short-term performance measures that are tied to long-term goals and to ground early evaluative inquiry in areas that can foster improvement, such as ways to improve partnership functioning.

Partners should work together to develop an evaluation plan and approach that matches their needs and goals. A helpful resource for thinking about evaluation can be found in the *Journal of Public Health Management and Practice's* article, "A Practice-Grounded Approach for Evaluating Health in All Policies Initiatives in the United States."[22] Practitioners and researchers can use the tools presented in the article to facilitate dialogue among stakeholders, clarify assumptions, identify how they will assess progress, and implement data-driven ways to improve their HiAP work. Researchers in South Australia have also conducted HiAP evaluation and published an article, "Evaluation of Health in All Policies: Concept, Theory and Application," which provides recommendations on the basis of their experiences.[11]

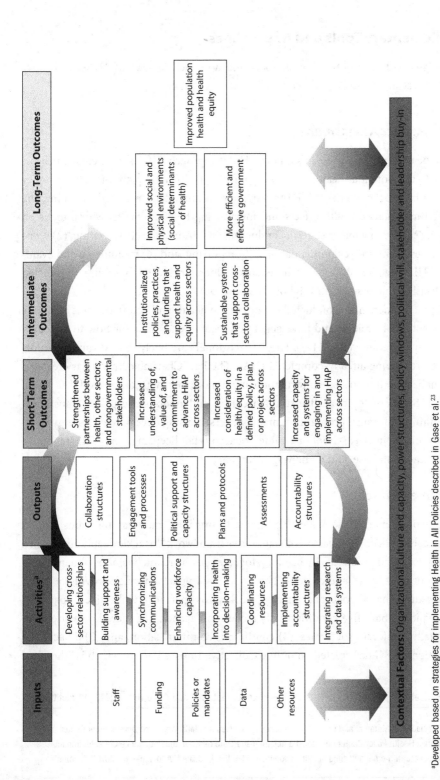

[a]Developed based on strategies for implementing Health in All Policies described in Gase et al.[23]

Source: Gase et al.[22] Reprinted with permission from Wolters Kluwer Health.

Figure 11-3. How Health in All Policies (HiAP) Can Lead to Improvements in Policies, Systems, Health, and Equity

Complementary Tools and Approaches

HiAP aligns with a variety of other tools and approaches, such as HIAs, Collective Impact, and strategies to advance equity.

Health Impact Assessment

HIA can be used on its own or to support a HiAP approach. HIA is a systematic process to evaluate the potential health and equity effects of a specific plan, project, or policy before it is built or implemented. HIAs provide recommendations aimed at minimizing or mitigating negative health effects and maximizing health benefits, with a focus on promoting equity. The major steps in conducting an HIA include (1) screening, (2) scoping, (3) assessment, (4) recommendations, (5) reporting, and (6) monitoring and evaluation.[41,42] HIA practice routinely includes stakeholders, including those directly affected by the decision under study, throughout the process.

HIA practitioners have conducted studies of the health and equity impacts of a wide range of potential projects and have generated recommendations for how to best promote health and equity (Box 11-8). HiAP practitioners are likely to find valuable information by reviewing already-completed HIAs. The Pew Charitable Trusts has created a data visualization tool to share information about more than 400 completed HIAs across the United States, on topics as diverse as agriculture and food systems policy, transportation planning and transit programs, rental vouchers, housing development, energy strategies, restorative justice, school discipline, tobacco retail licensing, nutrition standards, paid sick leave, land use, and living wage ordinances.[44]

Collective Impact

HiAP practitioners can use Collective Impact to organize multisectoral teams around specific goals. Collective Impact is a collaborative framework "to tackle deeply entrenched and complex social problems" by bringing together government, business, philanthropy, nonprofit organizations, and citizens. The Collective Impact approach provides a structure for setting shared goals and aligning work across partners. Collective Impact initiatives typically have five conditions: (1) a common agenda, (2) shared measurement, (3) mutually reinforcing activities, (4) continuous communication, and (5) a backbone organization.[45] FSG has created an online Collective Impact Forum, which is "the place

---

Box 11-8. Health Impact Assessment (HIA) Resource for Maternal and Child Health (MCH) Practitioners

The Association of Maternal and Child Health Programs, the National MCH Workforce Development Center, and the Georgia Health Policy Center developed a helpful resource to describe the importance of health impact assessment for maternal and child health, including a video titled, "Using HIA to Influence MCH Outcomes."[43]

for those practicing collective impact to find the tools, resources, and advice they need." The website includes unique resources and opportunities for funders, backbone staff, and partner organizations.[46]

Equity Tools and Resources

Equity is a growing field in its own right. Many tools exist that can help jurisdictions promote equity through HiAP work. Race Forward has developed a short, 2-page Racial Equity Impact Assessment Guide that provides messaging about why racial equity assessments are important and walks practitioners through questions to help them identify and engage stakeholders, identify and document racial inequities, examine the causes, and propose alternatives or improvements.[47] The City of Seattle has created a 7-page Racial Equity Toolkit to Assess Policies, Initiatives, Programs, and Budget Issues. The toolkit "lays out a process and a set of questions to guide the development, implementation and evaluation of policies, initiatives, programs, and budget issues to address the impacts on racial equity."[48] The Government Alliance for Race and Equity has created several resources for practitioners, including a 28-page Racial Equity Toolkit and a 30-page how-to manual for developing racial equity action plans.[49,50]

As interest in health equity has grown, several organizations have developed tools to assist governments with measurement, data, and modeling. The Public Health Alliance of Southern California has developed a composite index, called the Health Disadvantage Index (HDI) to identify cumulative health disadvantage in California in order to prioritize public and private investments, resources, and programs. HDI includes diverse nonmedical economic, social, political, and environmental factors that influence physical and cognitive function, behavior, and disease.[51] The University of California Davis Center for Regional Change Regional Opportunity Index (ROI) integrates "economic, infrastructure, environmental, and social indicators in to [sic] a comprehensive assessment of the factors driving opportunity." The goal of the ROI is "to help target resources and policies toward people and places with the greatest need, to foster thriving communities of opportunity for all Californians."[52] The SF Indicator Project is an online framework and data repository that examines how San Francisco neighborhoods perform across eight dimensions of a vision for a healthy, equitable community. The eight community well-being dimensions are environment, transportation, community cohesion, public realm, education, housing, economy, and health systems.[53]

AREAS FOR FURTHER WORK AND RESEARCH

HiAP is a relatively young field, particularly in the United States, and practitioners would benefit from advancement in several related areas of inquiry and development. First, to gain the support of legislators and finance and budget offices, HiAP practitioners often need to demonstrate that promoting social determinants of health translates this into population impacts and cost savings. HiAP practitioners may formally or informally change policies or organizational practices, but it can be difficult to subsequently track and report on impacts of this work, including population-level impacts. This requires a level of evidence and analysis that is beyond the capacity of most public health organizations. National foundations and research institutions may want to consider partnering to create tools or provide technical support to help practitioners make the case to nonhealth decision makers for the value of healthy and equitable public policy.

Second, to build the case for HiAP and related work, it is important to counter the dominant narrative in our society about individual responsibility for health. The United States has a predominant ethic of individualism, which often leads to blaming individuals for poor health as a result of their choices, as opposed to calling upon society and government to promote health through health-promoting environments. The fields of public health and social work, among others, need to do more to communicate the degree to which health is shaped by our environments and about the value of government collaboration and all-of-government focus on human well-being and health.

Finally, HiAP projects need to be studied and evaluated to identify effective practices and implementation models. These are questions to consider: What inputs are needed to develop a successful model? What activities are associated with intentional and unintentional success? What is the role of community-based partners in driving activities and outcomes? HiAP initiatives should build evaluation into their work and should actively share their experiences, success factors, lessons learned, and findings.

NEXT STEPS AND CONCLUSIONS

Every practitioner can begin to take steps to pursue a HiAP approach. In her 1944 essay titled "Give," Anne Frank wrote, "How wonderful it is that no one has to wait, but can start right now to gradually change the world!"[54] Regardless of positional authority, everyone can act to pursue a society in which our governments consider human well-being at the center of every major decision.

Some actions may take a lot of work and political support, such as launching a multiagency committee or embedding equity and health into a planning process, whereas other things can be done without any infrastructure or additional resources. For example, budding HiAP practitioners can begin by asking equity questions about current projects, arranging for a social determinants of health training, or attending a public input forum for a nonhealth issue such as housing, education, workforce development, or transportation. Anyone can connect with a colleague at another agency to learn about their work and opportunities for partnership.

Not only do practitioners need people in other fields to help address public health issues, but partner agencies that are working on issues such as climate change, transportation, or education also need public health. Even within public health, this approach can help break down silos. As the field of HiAP grows, there are great opportunities for maternal, child, and adolescent health practitioners to get involved, build partners across sectors, and make sure that the HiAP approach considers health and equity throughout the life course.

Policy is a key component of driving the changes that society needs to promote heath across the life course, and HiAP is a lever to do this. Governments act in a wide variety of ways, including disseminating resources, administering programs, collecting and analyzing data, investing in community programs and neighborhoods, setting policies, and acting as employers. Too often, these decisions are made in isolation, without consideration of the overall impacts on the communities that governments serve. Fortunately, governments are increasingly taking a holistic approach to policymaking. HiAP provides a way to bring a health, equity, and environmental sustainability lens into government operations and create opportunities for health for all people across the life course.

KEY POINTS

- HiAP is a collaborative governance approach that engages all sectors of government as partners in promoting healthy community conditions, with an intentional focus on populations already disproportionately affected by poor health outcomes.
- HIA is one of many tools that HiAP practitioners can employ to analyze health and equity impacts of potential policies and make recommendations for future action.
- Public health policy, including HiAP, requires unique skills, including strategic thinking, cross-sector relationship building, collaborative decision making, and the ability to articulate the mutual value proposition of investing in health across other sectors.
- HiAP can increase government efficiency by creating linkages between existing programs and practices.
- HiAP initiatives generally require backbone staff to support collaboration, gather input from subject matter experts, engage stakeholders, and facilitate shared goal setting and decision making.

ACKNOWLEDGMENTS

The authors would like to thank several colleagues for their assistance providing subject matter expertise, sharing examples, and reviewing this manuscript: Linda Helland, Meredith Lee, Connie Mitchell, Amelia Plant, and Wendy Hussey.

REFERENCES

1. Rudolph L, Caplan J, Ben-Moshe K, Dillon L. Health in all policies: a guide for state and local governments. Washington, DC: American Public Health Association; 2013.

2. Fine A, Kotelchuck M. Rethinking MCH: the life course model as an organizing framework. Rockville, MD: US Department of Health and Human Services, Health Resources and Services Administration, Maternal and Child Health Bureau; 2010.

3. Rudolph LB, Caplan J, Mitchell C, Ben-Moshe K, Dillon L. Health in All Policies: improving health through intersectoral collaboration. Institute of Medicine of the National Academies, 2013. Available at: https://nam.edu/wp-content/uploads/2015/06/BPH-HiAP.pdf. Accessed December 5, 2017.

4. Smith M. Doctors describe the devastating impact of poverty on children's health. Wales Online. 2017. Available at: http://www.walesonline.co.uk/news/health/doctors-describe-devastating-impact-poverty-13016534. Accessed June 5, 2017.

5. Behan P. Poverty and poor child health should be tackled, says councillor. *Dumbarton and Vale of Levin Reporter.* 2017. Available at: http://www.dumbartonreporter.co.uk/news/15060111. Poverty_and_poor_child_health_should_be_tackled__says_councillor. Accessed June 5, 2017.

6. Mercer R, Hertzman C, Molina H, Vaghri Z. Promoting equity from the start through early child development and health in all policies (ECD-HiAP). In: Leppo K, Ollila E, Peña S, Wismar M, Cook S, eds. *Health in all Policies: Seizing Opportunities, Implementing Policies.* Helsinki: Finland: Ministry of Social Affairs and Health; 2013:105–124.

7. California Strategic Growth Council. The California Health in All Policies Task Force. 2015. Available at: http://sgc.ca.gov/Initiatives/Health-In-All-Policies.html. Accessed June 7, 2017.

8. National Association of County and City Health Officials. Health in All Policies: experiences from local health departments. 2017. Available at https://www.naccho.org/uploads/downloadable-resources/HiAP-Report_Experiences-from-Local-Health-Departments-Feb-2017.pdf. Accessed December 5, 2017.

9. Kilpatrick DG. Definitions of public policy and the law. National Violence Against Women Prevention Research Center. 2000. Available at: https://mainweb-v.musc.edu/vawprevention/policy/definition.shtml. Accessed June 5, 2017.

10. Bardach E, Patashnik EM. *A Practical Guide for Policy Analysis: The Eightfold Path to More Effective Problem Solving.* Washington, DC: CQ Press; 2015.

11. Baum F, Lawless A, Delany T, et al. Evaluation of health in all policies: concept, theory and application. *Health Promot Int.* 2014;29(suppl 1):i130–i142.

12. PolicyLink. The equity manifesto. 2015. Available at: http://www.policylink.org/about/equity-manifesto. Accessed June 5, 2017.

13. Office of Disease Prevention and Health Promotion, Healthy People 2020. Disparities. Available at: https://www.healthypeople.gov/2020/about/foundation-health-measures/Disparities. Accessed June 5, 2017.

14. Health Equity Institute, San Francisco State. Defining health equity. Available at: https://healthequity.sfsu.edu/content/defining-health-equity. Accessed June 5, 2017.

15. Ahdoot S, Pacheco SE. Global climate change and children's health. *Pediatrics.* 2015;136(5): e1468–e1484.

16. American Public Health Association. Climate change. 2017. Available at: https://www.apha.org/topics-and-issues/climate-change. Accessed June 5, 2017.

17. Maizlish N, Woodcock J, Co S, Ostro B, Fanai A, Fairley D. Health cobenefits and transportation-related reductions in greenhouse gas emissions in the San Francisco Bay Area. *Am J Public Health.* 2013;103(4):703–709.

18. Frumkin H. Guest editorial: Health, equity, and the built environment. *Environ Health Perspect.* 2005;113(5):290.

19. Watts N, Adger WN, Agnolucci P, et al. Health and climate change: policy responses to protect public health. *Lancet.* 2015;386(10006):1861–1914.

20. Bay Area Regional Health Inequities Initiative Community Committee. Health equity and community engagement report: best practices, challenges and recommendations for local health departments. Bay Area regional summary. Oakland, CA: Bay Area Regional Health Inequities Initiative; 2013.

21. Washington State Board of Health. Health impact reviews. 2017. Available at: http://sboh.wa.gov/OurWork/HealthImpactReviews. Accessed June 5, 2017.

22. Gase LN, Schooley T, Lee M, Rotakhina S, Vick J, Caplan J. A practice-grounded approach for evaluating health in all policies initiatives in the United States. *J Public Health Manag Pract.* 2017;23(4):339–347.

23. Gase LN, Pennotti R, Smith KD. "Health in all policies": taking stock of emerging practices to incorporate health in decision making in the United States. *J Public Health Manag Pract.* 2013;19(6):529–540.

24. City of New York. Mayor Bill de Blasio announces NYC Children's Cabinet Advisory Board. 2016. Available at: http://www1.nyc.gov/office-of-the-mayor/news/109-16/mayor-bill-de-blasio-nyc-children-s-cabinet-advisory-board. Accessed June 6, 2017.

25. Fulton ML. Announcing the 2016 #SchoolsNotPrisons tour. The California Endowment. 2016. Available at: http://www.calendow.org/schoolsnotprisons-tour-launch. Accessed June 6, 2017.

26. Zimmerman R. Food as medicine: rethinking hunger relief as health care, March 23, 2017. *WBUR Radio, Boston.* Available at: http://www.wbur.org/bostonomix/2017/03/23/food-bank-evolution. Accessed December 5, 2017.

27. California Strategic Growth Council. Affordable housing and sustainable communities program: FY 2016–2017 program guidelines draft. Sacramento, CA: California Department of Housing and Community Development; 2017.

28. Lin T, Homan S. Children's health in all policies: policy options for addressing the health of Kansas children with special health care needs. Topeka, KS: Kansas Health Institute; 2010.

29. Children's Environmental Health Network. About CEHN. Available at: http://cehn.org/about/committees. Accessed June 6, 2017.

30. Pharr J, Gakh M, Coughenour C, Clark S. Health impact assessment as an instrument to examine the health implications of education policies. *Public Health*. 2017;145:83–92.

31. California Department of Housing and Community Development. California's housing future: challenges and opportunities. State of California. 2017. Available at: http://www.hcd. ca.gov/policy-research/plans-reports/docs/California's-Housing-Future-Full-Public-Draft. pdf. Accessed June 7, 2017.

32. New York City Health. Health Bucks. 2016. Available at: https://www1.nyc.gov/site/doh/health/health-topics/health-bucks.page. Accessed June 6, 2017.

33. US Department of Education. Programs: Promise Neighborhoods. 2016. Available at: https://ed.gov/programs/promiseneighborhoods/index.html. Accessed June 6, 2017.

34. Best Babies Zone. About us. 2017. Available at: http://www.bestbabieszone.org/About-Us. Accessed June 5, 2017.

35. Children's Data Network, University of Southern California. Generating new knowledge. 2017. Available at: http://www.datanetwork.org/research. Accessed June 5, 2017.

36. Lewallen TC, Hunt H, Potts-Datema W, Zaza S, Giles W. The whole school, whole community, whole child model: a new approach for improving educational attainment and healthy development for students. *J Sch Health*. 2015;85(11):729–739.

37. Association for Supervision and Curriculum Development. Whole school, whole community, whole child. 2017. Available at: http://www.ascd.org/programs/learning-and-health/wscc-model.aspx. Accessed June 5, 2017.

38. US Department of Health and Human Services. Prevention. Available at: https://www.surgeongeneral.gov/priorities/prevention/index.html. Accessed June 6, 2017.

39. Let's Get Healthy California. Reducing infant mortality. 2016. Available at: https://letsgethealthy. ca.gov/goals/healthy-beginnings/reducing-infant-mortality. Accessed June 5, 2017.

40. California Department of Public Health. California home visiting program. 2017. Available at: https://www.cdph.ca.gov/Programs/CFH/DMCAH/CHVP/Pages/default.aspx. Accessed December 6, 2017.

41. Centers for Disease Control and Prevention. Health impact assessment. 2016. Available at: https://www.cdc.gov/healthyplaces/hia.htm. Accessed June 6, 2017.

42. National Research Council. Improving health in the United States: the role of health impact assessment. Washington DC: National Academies Press; 2011.

43. MCH Navigator, National Center for Education in Maternal and Child Health, Georgetown University. Health impact assessment. Available at: https://www.mchnavigator.org/transformation/resources/health-impact-assessment.php. Accessed June 6, 2017.

44. The Pew Charitable Trusts. Data visualization: health impact assessments in the United States. 2015. Available at: http://www.pewtrusts.org/en/multimedia/data-visualizations/2015/hia-map. Accessed June 6, 2017.

45. Kania J, Kramer M. Collective impact. *Stanford Social Innovation Review*. 2011(Winter): 36–41.

46. Collective Impact Forum. About us. 2014. Available at: https://collectiveimpactforum.org. Accessed June 6, 2017.

47. Keleher T. Racial equity impact assessment. New York, NY: The Center for Racial Justice Innovation; 2009.

48. Racial equity toolkit to assess policies, initiatives, programs, and budget issues. Seattle, WA: Race and Social Justice Initiative, City of Seattle; 2012.

49. Nelson J, Brooks L. Racial equity toolkit: an opportunity to operationalize equity. Seattle, WA: Local and Regional Government Alliance on Race and Equity; 2016.

50. Curren R, Nelson J, Marsh DS, Noor S, Liu N. Racial equity action plans: a how-to manual. Berkeley, CA: Haas Institute for a Fair and Inclusive Society; 2016.

51. Public Health Alliance of Southern California. California health disadvantage index. 2015. Available at: http://phasocal.org/ca-hdi. Accessed June 6, 2017.

52. Regional Opportunity Index, University of California Davis Center for Regional Change. About. 2014. Available at: http://interact.regionalchange.ucdavis.edu/roi/about.html. Accessed June 6, 2017.

53. Program on Health, Equity and Sustainability, San Francisco Department of Public Health. The San Francisco Indicator Project. Available at: http://www.sfindicatorproject.org. Accessed December 6, 2017.

54. Frank A. Give! Anne Frank Fonds. 1944. Available at: http://www.annefrank.ch/annes-world-reader/items/give-march-26-1944.html. Accessed June 6, 2017.

12

Communication

Jennifer Farfalla, MPH, and Glynis Shea, BA

Communication matters when it comes to advancing the promise and potential of a Life Course Approach. Communication is also a challenge as Life Course Theory (LCT) can be hard to describe! For example, LCT includes complex concepts such as epigenetics and intergenerational factors. Implementation of LCT in public health and social service settings challenges typically categorical organizational structures, funding sources, policies, and even professions. Finally, LCT promotes an expansive view of health impacts, which in turn broadens the range of possible strategies for change.

With LCT as a backdrop, however, communication has the potential to illuminate critical and often underrecognized components of health over the life span including human development, the social determinants of health, and the impact of structural racism and oppression. Life course–focused messages align with public health framing recommendations, which include painting a complete picture of people in their environment and elevating the factors that help or hinder health. Life course messaging can engage nontraditional partners, community gatekeepers, policymakers, legislators, and professionals that interact with consumers (such as school nurses or home visitors) through presentations, reports, infographics, short videos, interactive digital tools, or simply talking. Successful communication of life course messages with these audiences could lead to increases in funding for programs, new partnerships, and innovative approaches. Alternately, talking about LCT has the potential to reinforce implicit bias and biological determinism and to place blame on individual behavior as the priority player in health outcomes.

In the face of these risks and rewards, communicating effectively about LCT demands a strategic approach. Although the practice of communication is one of the maternal and child health (MCH) leadership competencies and one of many responsibilities for epidemiologists, social workers, management, and program professionals,[1] expertise and resources are lacking. For example, access to graphic designers, social media experts, and professional writers is rare. Approval processes and restrictions can also make it challenging for professionals in government-funded agencies to be nimble on social media.

To address these communications challenges and build practitioner capacity, this chapter will demonstrate how to develop a basic life course–focused communications strategy, explore relevant framing research, provide concrete ways to effectively communicate LCT, examine common communication road blocks, and offer examples from states that embraced life course messaging. The chapter also includes "Action" recommendations to apply or practice the skills and ideas included to communicate LCT concepts effectively.

STRATEGIC COMMUNICATIONS

What am I trying to accomplish? Who am I talking to? What do I want them to do? These seemingly simple questions are the basic building blocks of a communications strategy. There is no single, uniform method to create a strategy; these questions were adapted from an advertising agency. Boxes 12-1 and 12-2 provide a series of important questions for consideration in strategy design. As demonstrated by the case studies at the end of this chapter, a basic communications strategy serves as a road map, logic model, and set of directions for the development of messages, media materials, fact sheets, data reports, presentations, and conversations. There are many considerations and decisions to be made when one is developing a communications project. The size and scope of the project may require a communications strategy that breaks down key goals, objectives, tactics, budget

Box 12-1. Communications Strategy Worksheet

Name What is the organization, group, topic?	
Big Goal/End Result/Problem What is your action/programmatic/intervention/policy goal? Is there a specific problem you are trying to address?	
Audience? Who is your most important audience? Provide description. Include key insights from brainstorm (refer to Box 12-2).	
Audience Adoption (Accepted Belief → Desired Result) On the basis of your audience analysis—where is your audience in terms of adopting your ultimate goal? Where do you want them to be as a result?	
Role of Communications What do you want to happen as a result of your communications that will ultimately support reaching your end result?	
Reason to Care/Values Why should they care about your topic? What values frame the issue?	**Single Message?** What is the one message the audience should hear?
Data What data prove, support, or illuminate your message? Provide three points.	
Call to Action What do you want them to do?	**Presentation, Tone, and Manner** Choose your form factor, length, visuals, style.

Source: Shea.[2] Adapted with permission from the Konopka Institute.

Box 12-2. Audience Brainstorm—What Makes Them Tick

Audience Defined

- Title/function
- Organization type
- Demographic generalizations

General

- What are their priorities?
- What are their top concerns?
- What is a day like? What are their daily challenges?
- Success is defined as . . .
- Who is their community? With whom do they most closely affiliate?

Subject Matter (may be multiple areas here!)

- What does your audience think about your focus, health topic, population, or issue?
- Why should they care? Where do your interests overlap?
- How much do they know about your specific health topic? (Sophisticated, novice, etc.)
- Do they have any professional, organizational, or cultural biases or preferences?
- Any hot (related) trends for them?
- What do they think about health in general?
- Where does your focus, health topic, population, or issue rank in their priorities? Do they see it as core to their success? Necessary but only tolerated?
- Is it their responsibility?

Your Organization/Staff

- What does the audience think of your type of organization?
- What do they think about your organization specifically?
  - Do they know you exist?
  - Are specific people in your organization particularly visible, respected, credible?
  - Are you known for/have a reputation for something specific? How does that intersect (or not) with what you are offering?

Source: Shea.[3] Adapted with permission from the Konopka Institute.

size, stakeholder/partner/team capacity, branding concerns, specific audience reach, media outlet priorities, digital and social protocols, event logistics, and evaluation measures. Public health, social work, and other professionals should partner with a communications specialist as the budget and scope increase. Regardless of the potential size of a project, this chapter emphasizes the core elements that all professionals will have to answer about their project: who is the audience, what are the goals, and what action should happen.

The "Larger" Goal Versus the Communications Goal

Communications efforts always serve a larger goal. Unlike the marketers of snack foods, sneakers, or cars—whose goal is to sell their product—public health goals largely look to change behaviors and improve conditions for health and well-being. To be successful, it is necessary to untangle the role communications can play to support the audience in moving from where they are to a different perspective or action.

This "untangling" is needed because communication is only one part of the overall marketing of an idea, behavior, or product. Standard marketing components are known as the "Four Ps"—product, price, promotion, and place. For example, sneaker marketers know that success depends on having a highly desirable product, a price that fits within their competitive niche and their audience's reach, sophisticated methods for promoting their product (advertising, events, placements, sponsorships, etc.), and an appealing, convenient place or way to buy their product. With this in mind, clearly a single poster, flyer, or advertising campaign is unlikely to accomplish ambitious public health goals. Impacting behavior or improving policy is a process; strategic communications can play a role in that process, but it cannot overcome an unwelcoming health clinic waiting room (product) or lack of access to family planning services (place).

The communications planning tool in Box 12-1 prompts practitioners to think about their "larger goal," which tends to be a health or behavior outcome or an improvement in systems, processes, or policies as compared with the "communications goal," which is the role communication will play in reaching the larger goal. For example, a behavior change goal of reducing sexually transmitted infection rates among young people may be led with a communication goal of connecting young people to sexual health services. A behavior change goal of reducing obesity rates in urban settings may be led with a communication goal of building systems support for place-based strategies to eliminate food deserts.

Who Is the Audience?

What marketers know, which health and social work professionals rarely have the time to consider, is that **what their audience thinks and believes is as important—if not more important—than what they think is great about their product.** Consumer research is a competitive advantage: marketers seek to identify the right audience, uncover an insight that links audience and product, then communicate that insight in a compelling and attention-getting way. It is not enough to describe the audience through demographics (adult men, aged 45+) or a job title (local public health staff); a deep understanding is essential.

In practice, the public health community has access to great deal of health outcome and behavior data but limited access to more qualitative "consumer research." Short of a substantial budget to conduct this research, there are two viable, accessible options: (1) a do-it-yourself (DIY) approach that captures insights of teams, partners, or impacted communities and (2) use of existing "framing" research to understand broad American perspectives on health topics. Framing research will be discussed later in this chapter in the specific context of LCT and health disparities.

The DIY approach to understanding an audience is exactly that—the process is simply to reflect on a series of questions about how and what the audience thinks and feels.

Box 12-2 includes a full "audience brainstorm" question list, with questions such as these: What are their priorities, top concerns, daily challenges? How much do they know? Is it their responsibility? Why should they care? What do they think about your type of organization?

Although this may seem simple, it can be complex because there are often many possible audiences. For example, the strategy of ensuring that all students receive evidence-based sexuality education involves multiple audiences: education professionals, parents, and policy-makers, as well as health professionals. Each has different priorities and relationships to the issue or topic. Even within a single audience—parents, for example—different attitudes are prevalent. All of this leads to a hard truth: trying to talk to everyone results in probably talking to no one. Because the logistics of creating multiple messages for multiple audiences is over-whelming, this process creates the opportunity to thoughtfully and strategically set priorities.

Understanding the audience's current thoughts and beliefs about the topic, issue, or program and the desired response as a result of the communication is critical. Insights from a brainstorm help to characterize the audience mindset and set a reasonable goal for an outcome. For example, a health department analyzing potential audiences to support schools' use of evidence-based sexuality education identifies the school principal as the primary decision maker. Their audience brainstorm reveals that educational outcomes remain the principal's top priority. As such, engaging the principal with information about the connection between health and educational outcomes is a strategic approach. Spending time reading blogs, following Twitter conversations, monitoring Instagram photos and videos, joining Facebook pages, and reading websites from people who are in your audience on related topics (influencers) can also build your understanding of images and language that resonate with them. Finally, using a process to understand the audience also informs the content, tone, and feel of the communication. If it is not possi-ble to include the audience in a DIY approach, proceed with caution as the analysis is based on assumptions and may not be suitable for use in all situations (Box 12-3).

Audience analysis and feedback does not end once a communication product is devel-oped. As the plan is rolled out, it is important to take insights learned from audiences and incorporate them back into the communication strategy. This point is illustrated well in the Louisiana case study at the end of this chapter, where they continuously revise their presentation and scripts.

Box 12-3. Life Course Communication Caution!

When you are forced into a "Do It Yourself" (DIY) approach that does not include the audience, be very aware that this process is based on assumptions and generalizations. It is far from ideal and should be considered an incremental step forward. Improve the process by sharing the results of the audience brainstorm with as many other people as possible. A DIY approach should never be used when members of marginalized communities are the most important audience.

Call to Action: What Should the Audience Do?

What should the audience do now? A call to action is an ask of the audience to *do something*. In advertising, the call to action is clear: "Buy now"; "Click here"; "Sign up today!" Including a call to action in a communication strategy avoids communicating for the sake of communicating. Practitioners should ask themselves what action makes sense on the basis of the following:

- The communications goal (e.g., Prove the link between health and educational outcomes);
- Audience insights (e.g., Principals want to hear from other principals); and
- What they believe is a viable, easy next step (e.g., Join a meeting with other principals).

The call to action should be a fairly easy and realistic step for the audience that works toward achieving the communicator's larger goals. The message gives the audience the information they need to take the step that is asked of them in the call to action. The call to action on web-based properties should be as direct as possible; one click should guide the audience to the exact page, information source, contact information, or other information needed for the consumer to take action. The case studies at the end of this chapter identify life course–specific calls to action:

- Reach out to nontraditional partners (with a list of nontraditional partners).
- Apply for funding to address social issues.
- Incorporate LCT into a university public health education program.

ACTION: Practice using the audience brainstorm tool in Box 12-2 to think about how a different division or discipline within your agency would respond to LCT.

INSIGHTS FROM FRAMING RESEARCH

Research from cognitive science shows all information humans process go through frames.[4] Frames are mental models that help people to understand what they see and hear and what they think about it.[4] A dominant health frame in the United States is to attribute health outcomes to individual choices.[5] Unless audiences are provided with a new frame when discussing key elements of the LCT, particularly social determinants of health, their brains will likely process this information through the existing, dominant frame of individualism.[4]

The public health, social work, and health community benefits greatly from framing research conducted by organizations such as the FrameWorks Institute and academic institutions such as the Berkeley Media Studies Group (BMSG). The FrameWorks Institute is a nonprofit organization committed to identifying, translating, and modeling relevant scholarly research to frame the public discourse on social problems.[6] BMSG is a nonprofit organization that serves to improve social and public health advocates' ability to strategically use media.[7] Although neither has specifically researched LCT, their investigations of public beliefs about health, disparities, racism, early child development, human services, obesity, soda taxes, aging, adolescents, and after-school programs offer many insights to guide effective communication.

ACTION: Visit the FrameWorks Institute website and explore their "Issues Research."[6] Visit BMSG's website and subscribe to their e-newsletter for weekly media advocacy updates.[7]

TALKING ABOUT SOCIAL DETERMINANTS OF HEALTH

LCT elevates attention to issues around housing, transportation, education, access to care, employment, and "-isms" (the social determinants of health) and specifically seeks to address persistent racial/ethnic health disparities.[8,9] These points situate LCT communication in a massive framing challenge.

In part, this is attributable to a long-standing American belief that health (or success, for that matter) depends primarily on individuals—their choices and actions.[10] This narrative dominates how Americans think about health, poverty, and achievement. This is not the only American value—Americans also prize their interconnections, but for most health topics, that frame remains a secondary consideration.[10] For this reason, data on health outcomes or behaviors are likely to be interpreted by public audiences as proof of a failure on the part of those most impacted unless communication is crafted to short-circuit those standard connections.

In recognition that this is the mental shortcut for most audiences, illuminating the health impacts of external, social, and community factors becomes job one. The Robert Wood Johnson Foundation (RWJF) released a resource titled "A New Way to Talk about the Social Determinants of Health" in 2010 to increase effective communication on this topic. RWJF's resource is explicit: people do NOT understand the phrase "social determinants of health."[5] Furthermore, although audiences may not be conscious of endorsing cultural stereotypes, the existence and their knowledge of these stereotypes influence how they process information.[4] The unintended bias that results from this influence is known as "implicit bias."[4] This concept is especially important in messages that deal with race or ethnicity because research shows conscious and unconscious attitudes about race often do not align.[5] Public health's ongoing efforts to focus attention on health disparities by promoting disproportionate impacts are likely to trigger attribution to individual causes and reinforce existing biases.

RWJF's work includes message testing to identify a way to talk about social determinants that was meaningful, easily understood, and not aligned with an existing political perspective or agenda.[3] Six phrases tested well in conveying the concept of social determinants:

1. Health starts—long before illness—in our homes, schools, and jobs.
2. All Americans should have the opportunity to make the choices that allow them to live a long, healthy life regardless of their income, education, or ethnic background.
3. Your neighborhood or job should not be hazardous to your health.
4. Your opportunity for health starts long before you need medical care.
5. Health begins where we live, learn, work, and play.
6. The opportunity for health begins in our families, neighborhoods, schools, and jobs.[5]

The public health community has largely embraced the phrase "Health starts where we live, learn, work, and play." This phrase also works for descriptions introducing LCT.

ACTION: Visit RWJF's *A New Way to Talk about Social Determinants* resource[5] and check out the seven lessons learned from their research to support better and persuasive messaging around social determinants.

VALUES

Public health professionals place a high priority on rational, data-driven messages. However, cognitive linguists and advertising agencies agree: engaging and appealing to an audience is best accomplished by talking about values, beliefs, and benefits. Patent and Lakoff[11] not only emphasize the importance of discussing values in communications but also instruct communicators that it should be the first item on the agenda. By leading with values, communication starts at a place of agreement and alignment. For example, this recommendation suggests that when the health department approaches the school principal to discuss teenage pregnancy prevention and sexuality education, the "opening line" addresses her values (educational success) and links to theirs (health). Clearly, this value must be one that is shared; fortunately, there are many shared American values that undergird this work including prosperity, freedom, and fairness.

Consumer marketers' more transactional approach places messaging priority on the "benefit" to the audience. Compelling messages focus on the benefits of a product or service, not simply its features. Stated more baldly, does the product address a need or solve a problem for the audience? Not just any value or benefit is sufficient—it needs to be believable, salient, and connected to the topic at hand. Although general American values exist, they are not always applied in the same way to every topic. For example, the American value of "fairness" proved to be compelling when applied to places: "It isn't fair that some places don't provide the same opportunities for people to get healthy."[12] The fairness frame was not effective when applied to people or populations.[12]

Box 12-4. Strategy Snapshot for Proposed Life Course Theory Communications Recommendations

---

Audience: You are talking to the public health community not currently engaged in Life Course Approaches (aware, but not well informed or actively implementing).

Larger goal: Improve practice/systems by incorporating a Life Course Approach.

Communications goal: Demonstrate benefit/value of the Life Course Approach; increase audience's ability to grasp key components of the theory.

Call to action: Forge nontraditional partnerships to implement a Life Course Approach to addressing health outcomes (e.g., public health and top employers in a county).

TALKING ABOUT LIFE COURSE THEORY

Despite the fact that LCT has been on the public health agenda for some time, there appears to be little change to systems, processes, programs, or data collection. For this approach to be salient in the public's eye, it must be embraced and modeled by practitioners first. The following recommendations were developed to support MCH programs at state health departments to communicate about LCT. This section addresses commonly expressed communications needs and includes simplified descriptions, word choices, a basic outline, examples of answers to strategy questions (Box 12-4), key talking points, and visual approaches.

Values, Benefits, Context

Although LCT is based on effective, science-based strategies, the context for applying it to existing public health and social challenges or systems is not well articulated. In the current context, barriers to the adoption of a Life Course Approach, such as silos created by funders, can seem to outweigh the benefits. As states in the case studies discovered, LCT is still not well understood. Thinking back to the communication strategy of starting from a place of shared values, two key characteristics of LCT align neatly with public health values: (1) Innovation that increases effectiveness is highly prized in the public health community, and (2) Health equity is a collective priority, despite its seemingly intractable status.

These shared values make a compelling case for why adopting a Life Course Approach is needed; it also instructs on how to improve practice and have an impact on population health. Leading with these values when one is talking about life course starts communication from a place of agreement and explains why the audience should care. Examples of messaging around these values include the following:

- Introductory messaging focused on health equity: Although we have reduced the rates of many diseases and conditions over the past hundred years, there has been a lack of progress on eliminating health disparities.

- Introductory messaging focused on innovative approaches: A narrow focus on treating disease and individual factors or behaviors limits solutions. Innovative approaches come from a broadened perspective on disease prevention and health promotion that addresses the impact of social, economic, and physical environments across the life span, guided by the idea that there are critical and sensitive time periods when we can have maximum impact.

This language frames addressing health disparities through the broader, innovative Life Course Approach in contrast to existing approaches and can also be presented in the context of health challenges and opportunities:

- Current systems place priority solely on biology and individual behaviors in determining health. Alternatively, the Life Course Approach includes emphasis on biological, social, and environmental factors in determining health outcomes.
- Whereas current systems are separated and built around life stages and diseases, life course incorporates integrated approaches focused "holistically."

Life Course Theory Components

LCT contains multiple components, which are complex in nature, creating a challenge to clear communication. In an effort to simplify and streamline, three basic groupings may be used: (1) timeline and timing, (2) the social–ecological model/social determinants, and (3) risk and protective factors (Box 12-5).[13] Within these primary groups, it is then possible to organize more detailed elements of LCT for messaging.

Organizing Structure: Story Outline

The proposed shared values and benefits (innovation and health equity) also establish an organizing structure for content and visuals that describe LCT components. Table 12-1 contains sample statements, organized by values that strategically answer the question "What is Life Course Theory and why should professional audiences care?"

Phrasing from any of the listed core LCT elements (timeline and timing, social–ecological model, risk and protective factors) can be used in the organizational structure from Table 12.1 to customize the outline for varying interests, priorities, and audiences. Table 12.2 contains suggested wording and talking points to create simple life course descriptions using innovation as a leading value.

ACTION: Use the outline in Table 12.1 and the phrases and wording in Table 12.2 to create a 5-minute elevator speech about LCT and why a professional audience you interact with should care about viewing their work from this lens.

Box 12-5. Talking Points for Life Course Theory

Talking points of varying levels of complexity for audiences at different levels of understanding are listed under each key LCT concept. These words and phrases can be mixed and matched to talk about what LCT is and why people should care.

Timeline/Timing

- Health across the life span, not individual stages or periods
- Interconnected, integrated whole
- Over the life span
- Developmentally critical points or periods
- Cumulative
- Intergenerational

Social-Ecological Model

- Defined as the complex interplay of biological, social, and environmental factors
- Goes beyond biology and individual decision making/behaviors to address broad social, economic, and environmental factors
- Sectors, spheres of influence, factors
- The broader community, outer rings of model, beyond the individual
- Social, economic, and neighborhood environments, conditions, factors
- Social determinants

Risk and Protective Factors

- Health improves or diminishes based in part on exposures to risk and protective factors across time and contexts
- Interventions that reduce risks and increase protective factors can change the health trajectory of individuals and populations

Source: Based on Fine and Kotelchuck,[13] Pies et al.,[14] and Rohan et al.[15]

Visual Approaches

Even after the model is simplified into two overarching goals and three descriptive areas, LCT remains complex and involves a great deal of jargon for lay audiences. Even professionals, without adequate time to study the larger context of LCT, may be lost in the details. Visual treatments such as infographics or simple visual representations of the concepts can be more appealing, compelling, and engaging.

Talking About Time: Show the Life Span

Drawing a timeline that represents the life span is a clear way to describe the time element of LCT. Use a basic design to illustrate critical developmental stages or life experiences with corresponding health behaviors and impacts. Low-cost design elements that represent time and interconnection are a staple of infographic programs. Programs such as easel.ly (https://www.easel.ly/create) or Canva (http://www.canva.com) online graphic design tools allow one to create infographics and a variety of

Table 12-1. Life Course Messaging: Sample Story Outline Structure and Statements

	Value: Innovation	Value: Health Equity
Overview statement Emphasizes the reason to care	Life course is an updated and broader way of looking at health.	Life course is a public health approach that illuminates the causes of disparities and informs strategies to achieve equity.
Proof Highlights the most compelling and well-aligned elements	Life course is an updated and broader way of looking at health because it includes social and environmental considerations as well as biological factors while looking at the entire life span, not just individual stages or specific health experiences.	Life course is a public health approach uniquely suited to health equity efforts because it addresses the underlying causes of health disparities: social, structural, and environmental factors.
Description Includes all basic components	Life Course Theory shows how health develops over a lifetime, with health improving or diminishing based in part on exposures to risk and protective factors that go beyond biology and individual behaviors to include social, economic, and environmental impacts.	By focusing on how social determinants and exposure to risk and protective factors impact health over a lifetime, Life Course Theory illuminates the causes of health disparities and informs strategies to achieve equity.

Source: Association of Maternal and Child Health Programs.[16] Adapted with permission.

customizable graphics with their templates.[17,18] Keeping the audience in mind, varying language and literacy levels, depth of content, culturally relevant factors, and other factors can be modified for multiple LCT graphic versions. Methods to dispersing this timeline graphic should be tailored by audience—whether shared online, mobile, or print.

Talking About the Social–Ecological Model: Pictures Over Words

Visually displaying the multiple factors that have an impact on health will help to challenge public perceptions that individual factors or behaviors are the most significant and impactful cause of negative health outcomes. A simplistic concentric circle, visually representing the various "spheres" of the social–ecological model, delivers this content. Figure 12-1 shows the social–ecological model illustrated by using SmartArt in Microsoft Word. It also creates opportunities to highlight risk and protective factors and strategies. Again, this visual is easily created with basic software or free online graphic tools (such as Canva.com[18]). An even simpler tactic is to create icon representations for the risk and protective factors and present their impact on the social–ecological spheres of influence in a graphic way. By simply presenting individual and societal-level factors in the same graphic, you are redirecting the default thinking about individual responsibility.

Table 12-2. Sample Life Course Descriptions and Phrasing: Innovation as a Leading Value

Key Characteristic	Suggested Phrasing
Value/benefit Innovation; transformation of historical, standard model	Life course is an updated and broader way of looking at health . . .
Phrasing emphasizes Timeline/timing	. . . because it considers health across the life span, not just individual stages or periods.
Phrasing emphasizes Ecological model and social determinants	. . . because it considers the complex interplay of biological, social, and environmental factors.
Phrasing emphasizes Risk and protective factors	. . . because it considers how risk and protective factors impact health over time and across contexts.

Source: Association of Maternal and Child Health Programs.[16] Adapted with permission.

Video and Storytelling

The camera is the new keyboard. New digital and social channels have rapidly evolved how consumers ingest and engage with content and how creatives share messages and materials. Audio and video clips can provide a shareworthy, more memorable message consumption—bringing a deeper understanding through thought-provoking imagery, statements, and music. Leveraging tools to easily create and edit videos, practitioners are able to share their messages in a compelling way. Consider the budget, message, and platform when deciding the quality and technical needs to video filming and editing. Where these videos will be shared? Social media typically does not require the same caliber of filming and editing as websites and media outlets. In fact, when it comes to social media and real-time video sharing, consumers expect it to feel authentic and less edited. Almost every social media channel has integrated video into its platform for audiences to watch, engage, learn from, and share. Social video "stories" and live options allow others to see different points of view and perspectives in real time. While social media clips and live videos can be shot and edited with mobile phones, there are online services, apps, and tools that can be used to create high-quality (and budget-friendly) videos.

With a public health focus toward behavior change, communicators can utilize storytelling as a method to make an audience care about and remember a message in a way simple data presentation cannot. Linking data and words with people and stories can create powerful, relatable content that will resonate if consumers can see themselves in the campaign or feel emotionally moved by the narrative. Several health campaigns use short videos to tell a story that gets a message across to the audience. In the resources section at the end of the chapter there are three examples of storytelling through video clips and a video on what makes an effective story from the *Atlantic*.

ACTION: Jefferson County Public Health in Colorado compiled health data and health information for a 2013 community health assessment.[20] The report is titled

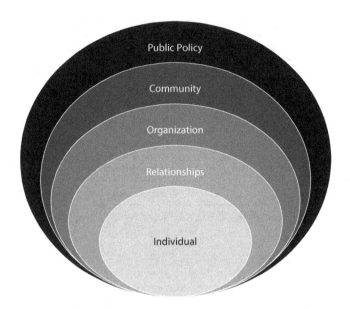

Source: Based on Centers for Disease Control and Prevention.[19]

Figure 12-1. The Social–Ecological Model

"Healthy People, Healthy Places" and contains a range of well-done visualizations on life stages, factors that influence health, and social determinants. Visit the 2013 Jefferson County "Healthy People, Healthy Places" community health assessment and examine the visuals used to explain factors that influence health in different life stages beyond health care.

Call to Action

Any discussion of LCT must also include a call to action. What should the audience do with the information? To address health according to a Life Course Approach, there is a need for different sectors (e.g., MCH, chronic disease, occupational health, social services, city planning, housing) to collaborate.[16] As such, a call to action may focus on asking for nontraditional collaboration to address the following:

- Rethinking and realigning the organization and delivery of health services[16];
- Linking health services with other services and supports (e.g., transportation, employment)[16];
- Transforming social, economic, and physical environments to promote health[16]; and
- Developing public policy in all sectors to include health considerations (e.g., working with the education sector to include nutritional standards for school lunches).

COMMUNICATION CHALLENGES

LCT uses life trajectories to illustrate how genetics, exposures, and life experiences interact to have an impact on health. While this opens up new opportunities for innovation, the complexity can also cause some significant challenges that can create harm and derail progress.

Life Course Is Deterministic

A main component of LCT is "sensitive periods."[8,9,21] Risk factors that occur during these periods may have a greater impact on health trajectories than if the same events occurred during other life stages.[9] Fetal development, infancy, and early childhood are all recognized as sensitive periods.[9] For example, studies found that family poverty before the age of 5 years has an impact on adult earnings and increases the likelihood of depressive symptoms later in life, but family poverty after age 5 did not show an effect on these outcomes.[22] Talking about early programming and sensitive periods opens the door for the criticism that it seems health is already determined before people are out of early childhood, maybe even before they are born. However, a child who experiences family poverty before the age of 5 is not determined to experience depressive symptoms later in life. There are multiple factors that can protect that child (e.g., strong, loving family structures) from the worst insults of poverty. How can communications make that point clear while also stressing the importance of sensitive periods? Messaging to avoid sounding too deterministic includes (1) stressing the importance of interventions in sensitive periods and (2) highlighting that even after exposure to risk factors during sensitive periods, protective factors over time can improve health trajectories.

Protective factors are as much a part of LCT as are risk factors. While risk factors over time drive health trajectories down, protective factors drive health trajectories in a positive direction.[21] Children who experience family poverty but also read with their parents, have a positive school environment, and have access to quality health care may match or surpass the health trajectory of children born into a family of higher socioeconomic status.[21] Messaging about "sensitive periods" should include a discussion not only on risk factors but also on the importance of interventions during early life stages to boost protective factors.

Clearly there will be cases in which an adolescent or adult has already experienced a number of risk factors throughout infancy and early childhood. If public health systems already missed the opportunity to intervene in these critical periods, how does the messaging change? While LCT recognizes the importance of early life stages in health development, it also states that health develops continuously over the life span.[8] A case study at the Iowa Department of Health illustrates how they identified 12 risk and protective factors for the adolescent health period that had the ability to affect health into adulthood. They targeted a life course–based intervention to the adolescent life stage because increasing protective factors and reducing risk factors in this stage will still improve the health and future well-being for these youth. The same is true over other transitional periods of time in life, including menopause and retirement. While we recognize the importance of infancy and early childhood in the life course, it is important to stress that steps can still be taken at any life stage to optimize short- and long-term health at that particular point in time.[13,21]

Avoiding the Blame Game

According to LCT, chronic disease in adulthood could be traced back to exposures in utero.[8,21] Dominant frames for pregnancy in the United States hold the pregnant woman responsible for influencing prenatal development in either positive or negative ways.[4] This means that when there is messaging about in utero exposures leading to chronic disease later in life, current "mental short-cuts" can easily lead to "mom-blaming" for the development of any future disease of her child.[4] The way Americans typically process information fails to account for the environmental conditions to which the pregnant woman is exposed and how society affects an unborn baby through affecting the mother.[4]

Winnet et al.[4] offer communication recommendations to avoid the unintended consequence of "mom-blaming" in the development of their offspring's disease. The first recommendation is to reframe the conversation with contextual information from the start. Maternal choices, such as what a mother eats, are influenced by societal factors including availability of healthy food in her community or the affordability of that food. This contextual information should be a part of the communication from the start.[4] Second, word choices matter and invoke previously discussed frames. Practitioners might feel it is innocuous to message "Help mothers make healthy choices," but this message still puts the responsibility of the choice directly and solely on the mother without context.[4] Instead, Winnet et al.[4] suggest words and phrasing that help give context and do not trigger unintended frames (e.g., "Helping society ensure that affordable and healthful foods are accessible to mothers and families").

These suggestions can also be deployed to avoid placing blame on individuals and communities. The "just world hypothesis" states that people want to believe that people get what they deserve.[5] This belief causes blame to be placed on victims, whether or not they had any choice in their experience.[5] When professionals communicate place-based data showing that census tracts with higher rates of poverty also have higher rates of preterm birth, without context, the audience may place blame on the people in those communities. The Robert Wood Johnson Foundation found that when people were first presented with messaging on social determinants, they were more likely to identify factors such as income, neighborhood, education, and pollution as influencers of health rather than just factors over which people have individual control.[5] Framing, word choices, and context can steer away from blaming individuals and communities and toward talking about improving systems and services.

CASE STUDIES IN COMMUNICATING LIFE COURSE

A Life Course Approach to Promoting Adolescent Health in Iowa

An adolescent health collaborative at the Iowa Department of Public Health (IDPH) wanted to elevate the importance of the adolescence years and the impact that risks and protections could have on their life (Box 12-6). Their first step involved creating an effective communication strategy, which included identifying a target audience and creating a clear communication goal. Although IDPH sought to have an impact on the health and health trajectory of adolescents, they did not target adolescents as their audience. The total population of adolescents in Iowa is a large, wide audience, which creates difficulty in developing targeted, audience-specific messaging. Instead, IDPH created a communication tool to bring awareness of the importance of the adolescent period within the life course to a narrower audience: adolescent health providers. Eventually, IDPH further narrowed its audience from adolescent health providers to school nurses because of the perceived readiness of school nurses to engage in change and their ability to interact with adolescents. The goal of the communication tool also narrowed after a target audience was identified. A goal of simple awareness of LCT is not conducive to creating a call to action for the audience. The communication piece was instead designed to give school nurses information and talking points to have conversations with adolescents about risk and protective factors that are crucial during the adolescent life stage and influence their health over time.

First, school nurses needed data. IDPH chose 12 adolescent health indicators that affect health trajectories: physical activity, smoking, oral health, obesity, illicit drug use, human papillomavirus immunization, early sexual intercourse, depression, childhood screening, bullying, alcohol use, and exposure to violence or abuse. The indicators

Box 12-6. Strategy "Snapshot" for Iowa Department of Public Health Life Course Communication

---

Audience (Who am I talking to?): You are talking to school nurses, who are likely not aware of a Life Course Approach to health.

Communication goals: Introduce school nurses to life course. Use life course as a framework to connect multiple risk and protective factors in the adolescent life stage. Increase conversations between adolescents and school nurses about these factors.

Larger goal (What am I trying to accomplish?): Improve 12 health indicators in Iowa from the adolescent health period that may have an impact on health trajectories of youth.

Call to action: The communication product asks school nurses to talk to adolescents about these risk and protective factors.

chosen were "upstream" and, if improved during adolescence, should have an impact on their health now and far into the future. An epidemiologist at IDPH calculated a state-level prevalence estimate for Iowa for each indicator, compared with the national average. IDPH visualized trend data for both state and national data to illustrate whether the indicator was improving, staying the same, or getting worse in Iowa among adolescents.

IDPH worked with an in-house graphic designer to create an interactive resource to present this information so school nurses could access it on tablets or laptops. The web-based resource starts at a home page visualizing the status of each indicator by using green, yellow, and red arrows. When school nurses hover their cursor over each indicator, they are taken to a page dedicated to that indicator, showing talking points to use with adolescents, supplemental information, and state and national data trends. The resource uses LCT as a framework to communicate why it is important for school nurses to discuss the selected risk and protective factors with adolescents and contains the information they need to have these conversations.

After receiving positive feedback and requests for additional information from school nurses, IDPH began a monthly webinar series on each of the indicators. The webinars discussed why each indicator was important within the life course and included additional resources. The webinars provided an opportunity to engage with new partners, including the Iowa Department of Education, the Center for Violence Prevention, the Mentors in Violence Prevention Leadership Institute, and the Iowa Poison Control Center, and to strengthen relationships between divisions within IDPH. Evaluation results indicated that the communication tool and webinar series made an impact with school nurses—97% found them useful. The frequency of school nurse conversations with youth increased as did the self-rated comfort level of school nurses with each of the 12 indicators. The work by IDPH illustrates success in using LCT as a framework to connect multiple health indicators from different sectors, justifying the importance of addressing risk and protective factors within the adolescent life stage through a life course framework, and getting an audience to answer a call to action through a well-developed communication strategy.

Communicating Concentrated Disadvantage in Louisiana

Louisiana's Title V program through the Office of Public Health, Bureau of Family Health (BFH) wanted to better communicate about Life Course Theory and concentrated poverty (Box 12-7). First, the BFH team created a communication strategy by answering questions such as these:

1. What is the point of the communication product?
2. Who is the intended audience for the communication product?
3. What action should the audience take after the communication?

Box 12-7. Strategy Snapshot for Louisiana's Bureau of Family Health Life Course Communication

Audience (Who am I talking to?): You are talking to colleagues in the Louisiana Department of Health.

Larger goal (What am I trying to accomplish?): Eliminate health disparities by adopting life course approaches.

Communications goals: Provide Louisiana Department of Health colleagues with tools to discuss life course concepts and concentrated disadvantage internally to prepare them for future external communication.

Call to action: Address concentrated disadvantage in funding and policy decisions, engage with nontraditional partners, and share information presented with partners.

BFH began by developing a presentation for their colleagues on LCT to ensure leadership was prepared to discuss life course and concentrated disadvantage among themselves and with outside audiences such as policymakers and funders. The presentation uses life course as a framework to discuss why place matters to health and to introduce the audience to concentrated disadvantage as a place-based health indicator. Concentrated disadvantage is a measure designed to capture the synergistic effects of economic and social factors that cluster geographically to create disadvantaged neighborhoods.[23] This measure is calculated from five census tract variables related to income, household structure, employment, poverty, and age to create a numerical index that represents the economic strength of a community. Neighborhoods with a high concentrated disadvantage index (low economic strength) experience an impact on the health trajectories of residents in ways that go beyond simple biology—to reduced access to services, employment opportunities, safe neighborhoods, and nutritious foods.[23]

To communicate their message that it is important to support and engage with residents living in communities of high concentrated disadvantage to improve MCH outcomes, BFH used a combination of storytelling and targeted audience messaging. Feedback from their audience was used to continuously revise and improve the presentation.

BFH was careful to avoid jargon and provided ample visualizations of complex points. They framed their data by telling the story of two infants born at the same hospital and living only a few blocks away from one another—one in an area of high concentrated disadvantage and the other with low disadvantage. The presentation includes quotes gathered during Louisiana's Title V needs assessment process from women living in areas of high concentrated disadvantage about their economic struggles and trying to take care of their family's health. The presentation's call to action includes addressing concentrated disadvantage in funding and policy decisions, engaging with nontraditional partners, and sharing the information presented with partners. BFH sought feedback from several groups in the course of developing the communications product, including the People's Institute for Survival and Beyond (PISAB). PISAB recommended including historical drivers of inequity in the presentation and including images depicting a diverse variety of individuals in the slides. Internal LDH test audiences found some wording was polarizing, such as "female-headed households," a variable in the concentrated disadvantage index. This feedback prompted edits to wording on slides to avoid potential negative reactions or placing blame on the people in these communities.

The presentation was given more than 20 times in 2016 to community groups, public health colleagues, BFH contractors, city council members, and students at Tulane University. The slides and script are regularly reviewed to ensure that the content remains current based on continuous feedback from audiences. In 2016, BFH used the presentation to secure a grant from the Robert Wood Johnson Foundation to work on packaging social determinants of health and concentrated disadvantage data in communication materials for conversations about community, economics, and health with large employers in Louisiana. This work is currently ongoing and is an example of the call to action at the end of the presentation coming to fruition.

CONCLUSIONS

Successful LCT communications plans incorporate basic communications strategies (think: communication goals, priority audience, simple call to action) with specific audience understanding, content curation, and delivery. By taking the time to listen to and understand the audience and develop a targeted communication strategy, messages will not only be received but also will resonate. Ongoing feedback and analysis are needed to ensure that the tone, content, and delivery reach the audiences where they are, in a timely manner, with information framed in an accurate, appropriate way.

Communicating about LCT requires creativity, flexibility, and innovative messaging—which *can* be done, even among departments with strict public communications policies. Use the tools and resources in this chapter to develop targeted, strategic communication around LCT and use your own creativity to test new communication channels and develop innovative messages to address long-standing health issues through a Life Course Approach. Connect with nonprofits and business groups who may be able to help amplify your message in unexpected ways. After all, the most innovative approaches, best services, and most interesting coalition gatherings will not create change if no one knows about them!

KEY POINTS

- Start with a communication strategy that includes a description of the audience, clear goals, and a call to action.
- Simplified language and visuals are key tools to introducing a Life Course Approach to audiences. Compelling graphics and videos that are easy to digest provide valuable, sharable, relatable "at-your-fingertips" information.

- Lead all communications with shared values and illuminate the social determinants of health. Innovation and achieving health equity are compelling values.
- Use context and frames to overcome key challenges such as the deterministic nature of LCT and blaming individuals for negative health outcomes.

RESOURCES

- The Association of Maternal and Child Health Programs' (AMCHP's) Talking about Life Course Tip Sheet: http://www.amchp.org/programsandtopics/data-assessment/Documents/Talking%20about%20LC%20Tip%20Sheet_Final.pdf.
- The *Atlantic*'s video: *What Makes a Story Great*: https://www.theatlantic.com/video/index/374941/what-makes-a-story-great.
- Examples of storytelling videos.
    o David Cornfield Memorial Fund's *Dear 16 Year Old Me*: http://dcmf.ca/tag/dear-16-year-old-me.
    o The Centers for Disease Control and Prevention's *Personal Stories: Why Flu Vaccination Matters*: https://www.cdc.gov/cdctv/diseaseandconditions/influenza/why-flu-vaccinations-matter.html.
    o Pew Charitable Trust's *Absolute vs Relative Economic Mobility* created by Duke and the Duck: http://www.dukeduck.com/portfolio/economicmobility.
- Louisiana's life course presentation, Iowa's interactive life course resource, and other communication products developed by state-level MCH programs are available on AMCHP's website: http://www.amchp.org/programsandtopics/data-assessment/Pages/LifeCourseMetricsProject.aspx.
- FrameWorks Institute website: http://frameworksinstitute.org.
- Berkeley Media Studies Group website: http://www.bmsg.org.
- The Robert Wood Johnson Foundation's A New Way to Talk about the Social Determinants of Health: http://www.rwjf.org/content/dam/farm/reports/reports/2010/rwjf63023.

ACKNOWLEDGMENTS

We thank Rebecca L. Majdoch, Addie Rasmusson, and Mary Greene for their contributions to the case studies in this chapter, and Suzanne K. Woodward for her contribution to the social media and marketing content in this work.

REFERENCES

1. Maternal and Child Health Leadership Competencies Version 3.0. MCH Leadership Competencies Workgroup. 2009. Available at: http://devleadership.mchtraining.net/mchlc_docs/mch_leadership_comp_3-0.pdf. Accessed May 27, 2017.

2. Shea G. Communication strategy worksheet. Minneapolis, MN: Konopka Institute for Best Practices in Adolescent Health, Healthy Youth Development, Prevention Research Center.

3. Shea G. Audience brainstorm. Minneapolis, MN: Konopka Institute for Best Practices in Adolescent Health, Healthy Youth Development, Prevention Research Center.

4. Winett LB, Wulf AB, Wallack L. Framing strategies to avoid mother-blame in communicating the origins of chronic disease. *Am J Public Health*. 2016;106(8):1369–1373.

5. A New Way to Talk about Social Determinants of Health. Robert Wood Johnson Foundation. 2010. Available at: http://www.rwjf.org/content/dam/farm/reports/reports/2010/rwjf63023. Accessed May 27, 2017.

6. FrameWorks Institute. FrameWorks Institute mission. Available at: http://frameworksinstitute. org/mission.html. Accessed June 23, 2017.

7. Berkeley Media Studies Group. About Berkeley Media Studies Group. Available at: http:// www.bmsg.org. Accessed June 23, 2017.

8. Lu MC, Kotelchuck M, Hogan V, Jones L, Wright K, Halfon N. Closing the Black–White gap in birth outcomes: a life-course approach. *Ethn Dis*. 2010;20(1 suppl 2):62–76.

9. Gee GC, Walsemann KM, Brondolo E. A life course perspective on how racism may be related to health inequities. *Am J Public Health*. 2012;102(5):967–974.

10. Lawrence R. Issue 12: American values and the news about children's health. Berkeley Media Studies Group. 2002. Available at: http://www.bmsg.org/resources/publications/issue-12-american-values-and-the-news-about-childrens-health. Accessed June 22, 2017.

11. Patent J, Lakoff G. Conceptual levels: bringing it home to values. March 2006. Available at: https://neighborhoodpartnerships.org/wp-content/uploads/2011/10/Rockridge-on-the-Levels-and-Values.pdf. Accessed December 1, 2017.

12. Manuel T, Gilliam FD. Framing healthy communities: strategic communications and the social determinants of health. FrameWorks Institute. 2008. Available at: https://www. frameworksinstitute.org/assets/files/food_and_fitness/social_determinants_of_health.pdf. Accessed June 22, 2017.

13. Fine A, Kotelchuck M. Rethinking MCH: The life course model as an organizing framework. US Department of Health and Human Services, Health Resources and Services Administration, Maternal and Child Health Bureau. 2010. Available at: https://www.hrsa.gov/ourstories/ mchb75th/images/rethinkingmch.pdf. Accessed May 15, 2017.

14. Pies C, Parthasarathy P, Kotelchuck M, Lu M. Making a paradigm shift in maternal and child health: a report on the National MCH Life Course Meeting. Family, Maternal, and Child Health Programs, Contra Costa Health Services. 2009. Available at: http://cchealth.org/ lifecourse/pdf/2009_10_meeting_report_final.pdf. Accessed June 15, 2017.

15. Rohan AM, Onheiber PM, Hale LJ, et al. Turning the ship: making the shift to a life-course framework. *Matern Child Health J.* 2013;18(2):423–430.

16. Association of Maternal and Child Health Programs. Life course indicators tip sheet: talking about life course. 2015. Available at: http://www.amchp.org/programsandtopics/data-assessment/Documents/Talking%20about%20LC%20Tip%20Sheet_Final.pdf. Accessed June 15, 2017.

17. Easel.ly. Available at: https://www.easel.ly/create. Accessed December 4, 2017.

18. Canva. Available at: https://www.canva.com. Accessed December 4, 2017.

19. Centers for Disease Control and Prevention. The social–ecological model: a framework for prevention. 2015. Available at: https://www.cdc.gov/violenceprevention/overview/social-ecologicalmodel.html. Accessed December 4, 2017.

20. Jefferson County Public Health. Jefferson County Community Health Assessment: Healthy People, Healthy Places. 2014. Available at: http://jeffco.us/public-health/certificates-and-health-data/community-health-assessment. Accessed June 22, 2017.

21. Halfon N, Hochstein M. Life course health development: an integrated framework for developing health, policy, and research. *Milbank Q.* 2002;80(3):433–479.

22. Najman JM, Hayatbakhsh MR, Clavarino A, Bor W, O'Callaghan MJ, Williams GM. Family poverty over the early life course and recurrent adolescent and young adult anxiety and depression: a longitudinal study. *Am J Public Health.* 2010;100(9):1718–1723.

23. Life course indicator: concentrated disadvantage. The Association of Maternal and Child Health Programs. 2013. Available at: http://www.amchp.org/programsandtopics/data-assessment/LifeCourseIndicatorDocuments/LC-06_ConcentratedDisad_Final-4-24-2014.pdf. Accessed May 27, 2017.

13

Assessment and Evaluation

Caroline Stampfel, MPH, and Lauren J. Shiman, MPH

As a field, maternal and child health (MCH) is shifting from thinking about life course as a theory to implementing the life course in practice. Some state and federal agencies have realigned programs according to the core life course principles, and in some cases funding has begun to follow these realignments. Initiatives at the local, state, and national levels have embedded life course in their work, and the connections of social and biological contributions to intergenerational health are better understood and more explicitly documented than they were 15 years ago when Lu and Halfon published their seminal paper on this topic.[1] Alongside progress in action comes a need to better understand the impact of the work. Amidst building urgency to take novel approaches to infant mortality prevention, leaders need to quantify and articulate the outcomes and benefits of life course–based programs. To demonstrate return on investment, programs modeled on Life Course Approaches must first be shown to influence change. Without rigorous evaluation, articulation of the full value of the Life Course Theory (LCT) will remain elusive.

This chapter will explore key evaluation approaches and methods that can be employed to measure the effectiveness of a Life Course Approach. Evaluation methods to assess outcomes from life course–based programs are in the development and testing phase. The techniques discussed are offered as suggestions for starting points and strategies to try, rather than a definitive guide to what works. Evaluation of life course programs is nascent, though there is much to be learned from the work being done today. The truth is, evaluating the type of work required to operationalize this theoretical construct of life course is hard. Compared with more traditional strategies, life course programs may be broad in scope, longitudinal in design, and extremely complex. Fortunately, although the characteristics of life course work present barriers, basic principles of evaluation and options for evaluation design still apply. This chapter acknowledges challenges associated with life course evaluation and makes recommendations about frameworks, tools, and methods that help navigate these potential road blocks. Promising practices will be discussed in this chapter along with a menu of options to consider in designing life course evaluations.

One word of caution is required upon exploration of life course evaluation challenges and potential solutions. Professionals seeking to evaluate life course efforts should adopt the suggestions of this chapter as part of discussions with colleagues and thoughtful consideration of the goals of their evaluation. Rigorous evaluation requires responsiveness to the unique complexities of each situation.[2] This chapter explores promising practices and emerging trends in the field but does not assert that the discussed approaches are appropriate or effective in every setting. It is important to note that contextual factors of an intervention play a significant role in designing an appropriate evaluation. This chapter presents challenges and offers corresponding mitigating approaches to consider. An evaluation tailored to the specific context of an intervention will be the most successful in measuring and documenting change.

USING GUIDING FRAMEWORKS, A THEORY OF CHANGE, AND KEY INDICATORS TO MEASURE WHAT MATTERS

When LCT started to gain traction in state MCH programs, it seemed that movement toward life course was the next "big thing." As more people in the field became familiar with the core components of the theory and interest in using the theory in programmatic work grew, a fundamental question emerged: how does one move LCT to practice? MCH programs have operationalized LCT in a number of ways. For example, the state of Rhode Island reorganized the structure of its Department of Health, which included the creation of the Division of Community, Family Health, and Equity, which capitalizes on the potential for internal collaboration by exploring the common, unifying themes across chronic disease, environmental health, and MCH. Several states created staff positions in MCH that had "life course" in the title to bring this lens intentionally into existing and new work.

As LCT is broad and encompassing, it inherently raises questions about what to measure. The Maternal and Child Health Bureau (MCHB) of the Health Resources and Services Administration has provided strong leadership in advancing life course measurement. The Bureau invested Special Projects of Regional and National Significance resources to set measurement parameters on the implementation of LCT through state and national funding opportunities. MCHB State Systems Development Initiative grantees collaborated to create a set of life course metrics. Furthermore, MCHB funded a Life Course Research Network (Box 13-1) to continue to fuel public health practice with connections to high-quality research. These investments have set the stage for the evaluation of life course programs.

Box 13-1. Life Course Research Network

The Maternal and Child Health Life Course Research Network (LCRN) is a virtual collaborative network of researchers, service providers, and thought leaders committed to improving health and reducing disease by advancing life course health development research. LCRN brings together diverse expertise and perspectives to examine the origins and development of health, and to inform meaningful and evidence-based changes in practice, systems, and policies affecting children and families. To learn more, visit http://www.lcrn.net.[3]

USING FRAMEWORKS TO DETERMINE WHAT TO MEASURE

LCT and the socioecological model (SEM) are frameworks that consider the complex interrelationships and diverse factors contributing to health. LCT stresses processes that occur over time (e.g., by explaining weathering[4] and allostatic load[5]) and the significance of the timing of exposures and experiences (e.g., critical or sensitive periods). SEM elevates interactions among subsystems (individual, interpersonal, organizational, community, policy).[6,7] The complementary nature of the SEM and LCT offers a new perspective about what to measure in life course evaluation by considering a wide variety of factors, allowing the evaluator to determine which are most likely to be influenced by the targeted intervention. Some key LCT and SEM components, pregnancy and the social determinants of health, are discussed in the next paragraphs.

Pregnancy is the focus of a breadth of research on life course because the experience of stressors during pregnancy affects not only a woman's health and her birth outcomes but also health outcomes across generations. For example, studies focused primarily on birth weight have demonstrated that a mother who was born low birth weight is more likely to have a child born low birth weight, that the fetal environment (including exposure to maternal stress) is associated with higher coronary artery disease and hypertension risk in adulthood, and that the weight of her offspring is independent of factors such as receipt of adequate prenatal care.[8-11] This longitudinal nature of life course indicates that ideal measures must be longitudinal, perhaps measured over decades and generations. However, most policymakers and funders are looking for results demonstrated over a much shorter time frame. In many cases, a 5-year grant cycle is the longest offered to programs to demonstrate significant outcomes. Frameworks that use environmental and longitudinal outcomes modeling may better meet shorter-term evaluation constraints.

Social determinants of health are the stressors, exposures, and context within which a person lives, works, learns, and plays and are critical in the life course equation.[12] The protective or risk factors of these determinants are particularly important during sensitive periods of development and provide important measurement opportunities for exposures and outcomes. Collecting data about social determinants of health during developmentally critical periods is essential to understanding the exposures and outcomes and their impact on life course trajectories. As disparities in critical MCH indicators such as birth outcomes are in part attributable to social determinants of health, such as racism experienced by African Americans over generations,[1] it is essential to monitor these experiences of discrimination immediately before and during pregnancy, as well as the experiences of discrimination experienced by children, youth, and adults over time. The particular social determinants of health (e.g., housing, employment, access to health care) selected as evaluation measures for life course programs may depend in part on the partners engaged in the effort and whether the modification of those determinants is within their locus of control.

Title V Performance Measures

The transformation of the Title V MCH Services Block Grant, a key funding support for state and local level MCH efforts, considered new national performance and outcome measures in the context of LCT. In the current Title V language, cross-cutting and life course is one of the six performance measure domains, along with the traditional population groups: women's and maternal health, infant health, child health, adolescent health, and children and youth with special health care needs.[13] The transformation has enabled states to create critical connections between health issues that affect people's lives across the life course (e.g., access to health care, oral health care, tobacco use) and key MCH outcomes (e.g., low birth weight and preterm birth), thus raising the bar for state health departments across the country and drawing attention to the need for life course–based evaluation strategies.

Leveraging Theories of Change

With myriad guiding frameworks, from academic theory to concrete public health practice, there is still a critical question to be answered: what should be measured when one is evaluating a program that uses a Life Course Approach? A cornerstone of evaluation planning is developing a theory of change and visual logic model to depict the pathways through which intervention activities may effect change. As life course interventions are often complex and longitudinal in nature, developing an appropriate theory of change and logic model can be challenging. Articulating the theorized mechanisms through which an intervention may have an impact on specific aspects of health and well-being can help determine the answer to the question of what to measure.

Understand the Pathway

It is nearly impossible to plan an effective evaluation without first understanding and being able to communicate how the intervention is intended to work. Developing a theory of change and accompanying logic model can help a practitioner to explain the idea behind a complex intervention to funders, evaluators, partners, and other stakeholders. Articulating this pathway also helps to identify measures that would indicate success. Ideally, these measures can be tracked before the long-term outcome, as explained in the next paragraphs.

Consider Short-, Mid-, and Long-Term Outcomes

Developing a theory of change can provide insight about what to measure and responds to the longitudinal nature of the intervention and outcome. It can take many years before the ultimate target of a life course intervention has changed (e.g., decreased preterm birth for African American infants). However, there may be upstream indications of change that can be measured in the more immediate future to demonstrate progress to the practitioner, participants, funders, and others. This also offers opportunities to course-correct if the intervention is not proving effective or successful.

For example, a theory of change documents a life course intervention that aims to reduce preterm birth (long-term outcome) by increasing employment rates in the target population (mid-term outcome) through an intervention that seeks to help community members develop new job skills (short-term outcome). In this case, it would be possible to measure particular skills of program participants by using a pre–post test to document short-term outcomes. Using this as a guide to evaluation, one could identify if program participants are gaining the intended skills by participating in the program, and if gaining these skills is associated with an increase in the percentage of the population who are employed within a few years. Tracking these short- and mid-term outcomes allows an opportunity to alter program design or implementation if needed. If the evaluation results demonstrate that participants have increased skills and are more likely to be employed within a few years but long-term preterm birth rates in the population do not change, then the practitioner cannot show that the intervention had an impact on preterm birth even if it had other positive benefits for participants. Without measuring these interim outcomes, it would be impossible to know at which point in the pathway the program was not having an impact on the participant as hypothesized.

Be Mindful of Locus of Control

Before identifying a set of key indicators to measure as part of a large-scale evaluation, one should consider where the locus of control for each measure actually lies. One of the biggest pitfalls for many programs is attempting to measure a life course outcome that the program has very little ability to influence. For example, it might be tempting to choose poverty reduction as a measure for a life course intervention. However, who has the ultimate responsibility for reducing neighborhood poverty? If an MCH program at the local, state, or national level chooses poverty as its life course outcome and fails to demonstrate a reduction in poverty for its participants, is that a failure of the life course intervention? Programs are cautioned against choosing outcomes whose locus of control lies beyond their ability to have a measurable impact. Articulating a theory of change and demonstrating pathways through a logic model before selecting the indicators to measure in an evaluation can help to avoid this pitfall. A clear mechanism through which the inputs and intervention activities will influence an outcome should be established up front.

Determining Key Indicators for Life Course Programs

When articulating the theory of change for a program employing a life course approach, one may struggle with how to apply the guiding frameworks to identify reasonable short-, mid-, and long-term outcomes. In response to a call from the field to identify a set of key indicators that should be measured when one is examining life course approaches to MCH, the Association of Maternal and Child Health Programs (AMCHP) underwent a process to identify a set of life course indicators.[14] A National Expert Panel guided the framework for the project, and the selection of the final set of indicators took place over a 12-month collaborative process with seven state teams in Florida, Iowa, Louisiana, Massachusetts, Michigan, Nebraska, and North Carolina. The teams assessed proposed indicators using three data and five life course criteria. The project ultimately identified 59 life course indicators, with a set of 13 on the "short list" for examining life course approaches at the state level (Boxes 13-2 and 13-3). The indicators, drawn primarily from

Box 13-2. Association of Maternal and Child Health Programs (AMCHP) Life Course Indicators

1. Adverse childhood experiences among adults
2. Adverse childhood experiences among children[a]
3. Substantiated child maltreatment
4. Breastfeeding support—Baby-Friendly Hospitals
5. Fluoridation
6. Concentrated disadvantage[a]
7. Homelessness
8. Homicide rate
9. Household food insecurity[a]
10. Poverty
11. Small for gestational age
12. Bullying
13. Experiences of race-based discrimination or racism among women[a]
14. Perceived experiences of discrimination among children[a]
15. Perceived experiences of racial discrimination in health care among adults
16. Racial residential segregation, by community
17. Early intervention
18. WIC nutrition services
19. Early childhood health screening—EPSDT
20. High-school graduation rate
21. Mother's education level at birth
22. Unemployment
23. Adolescent smoking
24. Adolescent use of alcohol
25. Children with special health care needs
26. Diabetes
27. Exclusive breastfeeding at 3 months
28. Exposure to secondhand smoke in the home[a]
29. Hypertension
30. Illicit drug use
31. Intimate partner violence, injury, physical or sexual abuse
32. Obesity[a]
33. Physical activity among high-school students
34. Cervical cancer screening
35. Children receiving age-appropriate immunizations

(Continued)

Box 13-2. (Continued)

36. Human papillomavirus immunization
37. Medical home for children[a]
38. Asthma emergency department utilization
39. Inability or delay in obtaining necessary medical care, dental care, or prescription medicines
40. Medical insurance for adults
41. Oral health preventive visit for children
42. Depression among youth[a]
43. Mental health among adults
44. Postpartum depression
45. Suicide
46. Capacity to assess lead exposure
47. Data capacity to support integrated childhood research
48. States with P-20 longitudinal data sets
49. Diabetes during pregnancy
50. Early sexual intercourse
51. HIV prevalence
52. Postpartum contraception
53. Repeat teen birth
54. Teen births
55. Preterm birth[a]
56. Stressors during pregnancy[a]
57. Fourth graders scoring proficient or above on math and reading[a]
58. Incarceration rate[a]
59. Voter registration

Source: AMCHP.[15] Adapted with permission.
Note: EPSDT = early and periodic screening, diagnosis, and treatment; WIC = Special Supplemental Nutrition Program for Women, Infants, and Children.
[a]Items on the short list.

commonly calculated MCH measures, have become a set of tools for needs assessment, program and policy planning, monitoring and evaluation of MCH outcomes, and engaging and educating partners within and beyond the MCH field.

Although the indicators themselves may be a useful starting point in selecting evaluation measures, the life course criteria (intergenerational impact, ability to leverage and realign resources, implications for equity, public health impact, and consistency with life course science) used to determine whether an MCH indicator was truly a life course indicator are perhaps more instructive and more broadly applicable to life course evaluation. These criteria provide a roadmap for how a life course–oriented theory of change can influence selection of short-, mid-, and long-term outcomes.

For example, a key consideration in selecting life course indicators was whether the indicator, if improved, would improve the health and wellness of an individual and/or their children, or more succinctly, whether there was a link to intergenerational health. Often these indicators are focused on reproductive potential as one of the major ways

Box 13-3. Mortality and Life Course

When selecting a set of life course indicators, state teams chose to include preventable measures that contributed to mortality rather than mortality indicators. Mortality is relatively rare and thus mortality rates are small. This leads to statistical fluctuation, which in turn makes trends difficult to interpret. States made exceptions for indicators that they felt were indicative of overall community issues (e.g., homicide rate and suicide rate) or highlighted a significant mental health issue (e.g., suicide rate).

The discussion on including infant mortality centered on whether the indicator added something to the final set that was not already captured. Although state team members thought it was a broader marker for community well-being and equity, there was not strong support that it added more than preterm birth and small for gestational age, which had already been included in the set. Similarly, the argument for the inclusion of maternal mortality centered around the impact on the family left behind; maternal mortality was ultimately not included in the final set in favor of upstream factors such as diabetes during pregnancy, stressors during pregnancy, mental health among adults, postpartum depression, obesity, hypertension, illicit drug use, and intimate partner violence.

that exposures are "transmitted" across generations. Reproductive potential is the internal pathway for stressors that affect the biology of the body in a way that can be transmitted to children and possibly grandchildren. Several sentinel MCH indicators, such as infant mortality, do not fully meet this definition because they lack implications for intergenerational health via this internal pathway.

The potential for indicator data to spur action among nontraditional partners such as urban planners, justice system stakeholders, representatives of transportation, and housing as well as private business partners is another key consideration. Data that are reflective of programs, services, and policies that expand beyond the traditional MCH focus are needed to make change happen.

Intentionally incorporating ways to measure equity has important implications for what is uncovered in an evaluation. The equity impact criterion explores how well the selected indicators reflect social, psychosocial, and environmental conditions. This work considers whether there were measurable disparities in the indicator and includes dimensions of disparity beyond race, including educational attainment, income, age, gender, and sex. These disparities result from an external pathway of transmission of stressors, primarily through policies and laws that perpetuate inequitable institutional decision making and/or distribution of resources. Racism, for example, travels multiple pathways to affect health, and restoring equity may be achieved through a Life Course Approach whose theory of change addresses each of the different levels of racism (institutionalized, personally mediated, and internalized).[16]

The public health impact screening criteria assess the impact of a positive change in the indicator attributable to program or policy interventions or the potential for population-level impact. An indicator that meets other life course criteria but whose potential for population-level impact is low might not be worthy of selecting for evaluation purposes because it might be extremely difficult to detect change in the target population.

An example of this situation is phenylketonuria, a rare genetic condition that prevents the body from processing the amino acid phenylalanine, which can cause a toxic build-up with lifelong health implications.[17] The condition is inherited and there is an effective public health intervention—newborn bloodspot screening can identify the condition at birth and a diet free of phenylalanine prevents health problems. For the individual, the disease is severe and the potential for impact is high, but phenylketonuria is a very rare condition. At most, only 0.019% of infants will have this condition. By comparison, preterm birth affects 9.6% of infants in the United States, with three states experiencing rates of 11% or higher in 2016.[18]

These criteria provide guidance about how to select indicators to measure when evaluating Life Course Approaches by providing some structure for discerning what distinguishes life course measures from those that are simply MCH measures. There are limitations in using cross-sectional data when one is considering longitudinal concepts; considering whether the indicator has connections to intergenerational health, equity, public health impact, and engagement of diverse partners addresses some of those limitations. The list of 59 life course indicators is included here to provide some guidance and to spur ideas. Data availability and the practicality of actually measuring each indicator are also important considerations in selecting indicators; these ideas are discussed later in this chapter.

Measuring What Matters

In the evaluation field, it is widely acknowledged that what is measured matters a great deal in what will be valued about the work. Although life course inherently presents challenges with regard to what to measure, the departure from traditional public health programs also presents unique opportunities to measure what is truly valuable. The next section will review some measurement possibilities that take advantage of these opportunities, including measuring partnerships, disparities, and spatial comparisons.

Measuring Partnerships

Inherent in the complex problems Life Course Approaches attempt to address is complexity in solutions—and these solutions are rarely able to be implemented by just one organization or entity without strong partnerships. Furthermore, because many life course exposures and outcomes belong across different sectors, multisector partnerships are often essential to implementation. For these reasons, it is likely that a program or policy that implements a Life Course Approach will have as part of its theory of change a set of key and strategic partnerships. Particularly in the case in which strong partnerships with key stakeholders do not already exist, evaluation might measure newly created partnerships as one of the outcomes of the program. If they already exist, one might consider some measure of maximizing partnership. Qualitatively and quantitatively tracking changes in partnership can help to measure a valuable component of the program or policy; for example, one might measure changes in level of trust among partners, changes in collaboration or referrals, or data and information sharing among organizations.

In the case in which an intervention includes developing or strengthening a network of partners, Social Network Analysis (SNA) is a tool that can measure the presence and strength of connections between partners in the network.[19] SNA is typically conducted by asking each partner or individual in a network to identify their relationship with all of the other partners in the same network, either by using a scale ranking level of collaboration or by simply indicating if they are connected or not connected with the other agencies. One appeal of SNA as a tool is that the data lend to mapping partners in an easily accessible visual. A single SNA map may contain information about all existing relationships in the network while simultaneously presenting other helpful information to inform future use of partnerships, including which partners are critical bridges to certain sectors or specific clusters of individuals or organizations, which partners are most connected within the network, or which partners are most effectively situated to disseminate messages throughout the network. If repeated at appropriate time intervals, metrics collected through SNA can also demonstrate changes in a network of partnerships over time. SNA can be a useful tool for multiple contexts, including summative and formative evaluations.[20] One note: if a project is subject to institutional review board oversight, partners' identities may need to be kept confidential, thus limiting the depth of knowledge that can be shared in SNA maps or tables.

Measuring Disparities

Life course experts have emphasized the importance of looking not just at the overall health potential over the life course but also at the striking differences in that potential by race and ethnicity.[21] There is evidence that minority racial and ethnic group members experience more stressors than non-Hispanic White or majority group members; these differences in exposure contribute to well-documented differences in health outcomes.

As such, evaluation should examine disparities in exposures and outcomes. There is evidence that highly effective interventions can exacerbate racial and ethnic disparities if access to the interventions or response to the interventions is different.[22] Wise presents the example of exposure X, which has a varying impact on mortality among three groups. It may appear that there is something different about the underlying risk status among three groups or that there is an existing effective intervention, but access to the intervention is differential across the groups, causing mortality rates to be 5 and 18 times higher in some groups compared with others. The fictional exposure X was the sinking of the Titanic, and the highly effective intervention was life boats. Only 3% of female passengers in first class did not survive, but for female passengers in second and third class, whose access was limited, mortality rates were very high. There are public health corollaries to this story—for example, surfactant and other clinical interventions are highly effective at reducing infant death, but access to these may be limited by the ability to get to a regional level III/IV hospital for perinatal care.

When one is evaluating life course interventions, it is essential to measure baseline and ongoing disparities by monitoring exposures and relevant outcomes by individual characteristics such as race, ethnicity, educational attainment, and income. Anand et al. outline seven dimensions of health status that may exhibit difference: risk; perception; care-seeking behavior; diagnosis; treatment; incidence of disease, disability, and death; and socioeconomic consequences.[23] Measurement across each of these dimensions allows the program to determine not only whether the intervention is effective but also whether there are differential experiences of the intervention that lead to the stagnation or widening of gaps in outcomes. If the intervention is targeting a reduction in disparities as the primary outcome, measurement of the disparities at multiple time points can determine if the gap is closing for the right reason (narrowing the gap by improving the rates of the group experiencing the worst outcomes) rather than the group who experiences the best outcomes getting worse.[24]

Furthermore, in assessing disparities in important risk and protective exposures, it is important to distinguish between disparities in determinants of health (i.e., differing exposure to safe and affordable housing among subpopulations) and determinants of health equity, the systems and structures that drive disparities in determinants of health (i.e., history of "red lining" policies that contribute to specific populations having more limited access to safe housing). Measuring differences in exposure or outcome across a population may expose disparities in determinants of health or disparities in health outcomes. To truly move the needle on disparities, interventions need to look upstream to the historical and institutional practices that have designed a system in which health potential is based on neighborhood, skin color, gender, and other factors. Interventions designed to mitigate disparities need to focus, too, on historical or systematic processes that drive these differences in exposure and/or outcome, including structural racism or policies and processes that distribute resources inequitably. Understanding and measuring changes in determinants of health equity includes explicitly measuring metrics such as experienced racism, criteria for allocation of resources, and the extent to which vulnerable populations are explicitly considered in policy and program development. Such measurements require an equity lens in evaluation design[25] and a willingness to consider qualitative and quantitative data as complementary and equally credible.

Measuring Spatial Comparisons

Because many life course influencers are tied to the places where people live, learn, work, and play, examining spatial distributions and making spatial comparisons of the factors may be another way to measure, and thus value, what matters in a life course intervention. Spatial comparisons, typically visualized with maps, help tell a story of the spatial distribution of risk and protective factors as well as outcomes. Maps can also be very compelling for lay audiences because they are easily consumable comparisons. Spatial comparisons may provide insight into the ability of a program to penetrate a geographic area, such as neighborhood, community, county, or state. There are several spatial comparisons that may be appropriate to consider, including looking across generations at the same geographic area, comparing adjacent geographic areas, and comparing similarly composed populations that are not adjacent.

When one is performing spatial comparisons, it is important to remember that people living in a community, neighborhood, county, or state are influenced by the policies and programs acting in that geographical area. When one is attempting to address social determinants of health by using a Life Course Approach, the context of a place is extraordinarily important; policies and programs that have existed over time influence the outcomes for the population. Concentrated poverty, "red lining" and home ownership, creation of housing projects, and siting of hazardous waste facilities are all examples of how policies and procedures that may remain in place for generations influence the health and well-being of populations without the members of that population explicitly participating in those policies and procedures.

Concentrated disadvantage, defined by the AMCHP life course indicator project as a measure combining poverty, use of public assistance, female-headed households, unemployment, and density of children, constitutes a proxy measure for community economic disadvantage.[26-28] Communities with concentrated disadvantage may have less collective efficacy or social capital.[29] As collective efficacy is a critical way that neighborhoods inhibit the perpetuation of violence, people who live and grow in disadvantaged neighborhoods are more likely to experience violence because of where they live.[30] Concentrated disadvantage, when calculated for use at the state level, provides a yardstick for geographic comparisons built from census tract information, allowing the user to identify tracts of high and low concentrated disadvantage that can be overlaid on other factors related to program implementation and impact.

It is important in spatial comparisons that the metrics used are comparable from one selected area to another. For example, areas of "high concentrated disadvantage" are defined as those census tracts whose averaged z scores (defined as percentage of individuals below the poverty line, on public assistance, in female-headed households, unemployed, and aged younger than 18 years) fall within the 75th percentile of values. When calculated within a certain geography, such as a state, the values for concentrated disadvantage are only valid for that geography because the percentiles are developed according to an internal standard. Therefore, although MCH programs in New Mexico, Louisiana, Nebraska, and Wyoming have each calculated and mapped concentrated disadvantage to explore areas of high and low disadvantage, these maps are only meaningful within their states and cannot be directly compared. To truly compare concentrated disadvantage across states, percentiles need to be established by using the entire nation's data. In 2016, the America's Health Rankings Health of Women and Children Report presented concentrated disadvantage calculated on a national level for the first time, allowing direct comparison of high disadvantage across the United States.[30] Provided that the scores and values used to calculate each of the components are held constant over time, the report and associated map can be used to examine how concentrated disadvantage changes (or does not change) over time.

Now that some strategies for determining what to measure have been explored, the next step is to determine if what is measured is actually related to the intervention being evaluated. In the next section, the challenge of attribution versus contribution toward demonstrated impacts is explored, including a discussion of comparison groups and baseline measures.

MITIGATING THE CHALLENGES OF ATTRIBUTION PART 1: UNDERSTANDING THE COUNTERFACTUAL AND SELECTING COMPARISON GROUPS

The gold standard of research and evaluation is considered to be a randomized control trial (RCT). This methodology offers an opportunity to consider the counterfactual[31]—what outcomes would have been realized if the intervention had not occurred. Examining a counterfactual allows one to determine if detected outcomes are, in fact, attributable to the intervention. Attribution is a defining factor in knowing "what works," but demonstrating attribution is challenging across public health evaluations. It is rarely ethical to randomly assign comparably vulnerable communities to receive a life course intervention or not to receive the same intervention. It is rare that equipoise, or genuine uncertainty about the benefits of an intervention, exists for public health interventions the way it might exist for pharmaceutical interventions. More often, in nonclinical interventions, there is already good reason to believe that participation in the intervention would be more likely to benefit a person in the target population than nonparticipation would, whether or not there is evidence to support the specific impact under study. In addition to ethical constraints, the long period of time over which the impacts of life course interventions are expected to be realized often makes RCT an impossibly expensive design.

So, if the gold standard cannot be used, what evaluation design can be used? Often, quasi-experimental designs offer the next best thing—they allow evaluators and researchers to measure the intervention group against a comparison group that seeks to emulate the intervention group had the intervention never occurred. If quasi-experimental design is also not feasible, understanding the unknowable counterfactual and striving to determine attribution to the extent possible can help guide decisions about selecting evaluation methods. The sections that follow explore methodological options that life course evaluators should consider to maximize efficiency, effectiveness, and rigor.

Including Comparison Groups

Employing methods to understand the counterfactual should be considered in life course evaluation design. If it is financially and logistically feasible to include a comparison group in the evaluation, an evaluator may choose to use a quasi-experimental design. The inclusion of a comparison group can serve as a stand-in for a true nonintervention arm. Comparing the intervention group to a separate but similar nonintervention population is a helpful, if imperfect, way to attribute outcomes to the intervention rather than to external factors or random chance.

To do this, one must confront a time-honored question in epidemiology: who makes up the comparison group? The population of the intervention group should be clear. The nonintervention group, or comparison group, should be as similar as possible in terms of any factors that may influence the outcomes you seek to measure. This may include eligibility for the program, demographic characteristics, and place-based factors. While the goal is to get as close as possible to the characteristics of the intervention group, there will always be some measurable and unknown or unmeasurable differences.

The premise for using a comparison group is to get as close as possible to understanding what the counterfactual case would look like by choosing similar populations and statistically adjusting for measured differences in confounding variables. Collecting baseline data for the intervention and comparison group allows measurement of these key factors and performing these adjustments. Administrative data sources that are readily available for both the intervention group and the comparison group may prove useful when a comparison group cannot be directly assessed. The more granular the administrative data, the easier it is to select a similar comparison group and measure differences in potential confounders. Although the general benefits and challenges of comparison groups apply to other public health evaluations, life course interventions face specific added concerns in selecting appropriate comparison groups. The long period of time over which one expects impacts from the program to occur increases the likelihood that other interventions or changes may occur in the comparison group, but not the intervention group, that have a positive or negative impact on outcomes of interest. The extent to which these changes can be captured and measured may help to mitigate, but not fully resolve, this challenge.

If it is not possible to construct a nonintervention comparison population, there are other options to draw comparisons between the intervention population and some other standard. One source of comparison data may be the rate of the primary outcome for a geographic area, such as a census tract, a county, or the whole state. Depending on the availability of selected metrics, another possibility is to choose a theoretical standard rather than a real community as a point of comparison—for example, a Healthy People 2020 goal. Typically, this theoretical standard is used as a point of relative comparison but does not help with attributing change in the intervention population to the intervention itself. For interventions with multiple participating sites, another option would be to stagger the implementation of the program in each site to create comparison groups by using a step-wedge design. Most commonly, communities or populations serve as their own comparison group by measuring indicators before and after the intervention took place, although at the preintervention (comparison) time point it is likely that the community or population was different in several important ways that are external to the impact of the intervention. More about the collection of baseline data, which is useful whether or not it may serve as a comparison "group," is presented in the next section.

Statistically accounting for the limitations of any selected comparison group is critically important to appropriately applying any of the outlined suggestions. This may include adjusting for measured confounding variables, applying difference-in-differences techniques to intervention and nonintervention groups that are measured at multiple points over time, or using other standard methods to account for imperfections in the comparison as a counterfactual. These statistical methods are not specific to life course evaluation and are discussed in depth in many epidemiological and statistical resources.[32]

Collecting Baseline Measures

Whether or not it is feasible to use a quasi-experimental design by considering a veritable comparison group, collecting baseline data on the key risk indicators and health outcomes for the target population and for the comparison group, if applicable, is an important first step in measuring future change. Detailed baseline data can inform the program approach, set the stage for rapid-cycle process improvement during the implementation phase of the program, and provide the "pre" measurements for pre–post designs. Collecting baseline data from the target population for the program will likely be easier than collecting data from a comparison group, especially if the comparison group is made up of a population with which the program will not have regular, direct contact.

National, state, and sometimes county-level information on key indicators for life course can usually be obtained from publicly available data sources, allowing one to assemble a cadre of data points that tell a story about the state of the population before the intervention took place. Comparison and reference points are helpful to place data points in context, particularly for indicators that a program has never considered part of its work before. How many MCH programs have considered measures of civic engagement, such as voter registration, as elements of a public health effort to address a MCH outcome? If a program has never examined voter registration, it can be challenging to identify whether the target population for the intervention experiences high, low, or typical civic engagement. Similarly, measures of adult and youth incarceration may be completely foreign to a program that attempts to decrease preterm birth; national indicator comparisons and time trends establish reasonable baselines for life course concepts that are not part of the everyday MCH conversation. Collaborating with partners from different fields who understand these data well is beneficial.

MITIGATING THE CHALLENGES OF ATTRIBUTION PART 2: MIXED METHODS AND THE ART OF WORKING WITH WHAT IS AVAILABLE

Because of the inherent complexity of life course interventions, it can be difficult to differentiate between findings that can be attributed to the intervention versus to the activities and actions of other important change agents. This question of attribution cannot be solved by a comparison group alone, particularly if the intervention is taking place in the context of a network of related programmatic work, policy and social changes relevant to outcomes of interest, or restructured systems that may include new partnerships or improved coordination and collaboration. Life course efforts often involve multiple partners, program or policy components, and points of intervention. For this reason, relying on singular outcomes to measure change will not produce a full picture of what works and what does not. Piecing together a package of evaluation activities with both qualitative and quantitative components allows an evaluator to demonstrate a more complete understanding of the effectiveness of the program or policy.

Mixed-Methods Evaluation

Mixed-methods evaluations offer an opportunity to explore not only "Does it work?" but also "How does it work?" By collecting both qualitative and quantitative data, the evaluator has an opportunity to contextualize and triangulate findings. For example, the Best Babies Zone Initiative (BBZ) seeks to measure changes in financial literacy and economic independence among residents living and working in the BBZ Castlemont zone in Oakland, California. To measure change over time, BBZ considers publicly available indicators such as median household income to demonstrate population-level trends over time at the census tract level. The initiative also makes use of publicly available comparison data including the surrounding city of Oakland. However, national and local external factors make it impossible to attribute change in median income in the census tract to the work of BBZ alone. The difference between median income in Castlemont and the median income in the city of Oakland may change over time because of national and local economic trends, policies, or external programs unrelated to BBZ work. Given the small sample size in a census tract, variations may also simply reflect fluctuations in the data attributable to random change.

To understand trends in economic indicators and provide additional information about outcomes not measured by the American Community Survey or other secondary sources, the evaluation team has also conducted focus groups with program participants in the community. Qualitative data collected during focus groups demonstrated progress toward other economic outcomes, including that participants have experienced increased job training, increased financial literacy, and increased microfinance opportunities. Participants identified specific pathways through which BBZ programming influenced positive trends in these indicators, providing evidence not only that participation in the program had an impact on financial health but also how this impact occurred for focus group respondents. In this way, mixed-methods evaluation allowed for a more nuanced and deeper interpretation of information. Furthermore, this additional information allowed demonstrated progress that can be attributed to BBZ programming and partnerships.

Including qualitative methods in an evaluation design also invites the opportunity to consider hard-to-measure metrics like the experience of racism or discrimination, referenced previously in this chapter. Too often, evaluators and practitioners are either not able to understand or try to address complex drivers of health disparities because of limitations in what can be measured or what data are available in a particular region. Considering documented stories and experiences as equally credible data as statistically significant risk ratios broadens what *can* be measured and, thus, what we can attempt to address.

With a clearer understanding of what to measure and what evaluation methods to use to increase one's ability to determine attribution, there is one final obstacle: the inherent complexity of life course work, which can make designing the right program and the right evaluation on the first try nearly impossible.

NAVIGATING COMPLEXITY

Interventions intended to benefit not only the participant but also future offspring of that participant are complex in design. Complex interventions require real-time learning to make adjustments as the intervention unfolds. As such, practitioners implementing life course interventions recognize a unique need for feedback loops between evaluation and program implementation to facilitate critical course-corrections. There is a practical element to this; if life course interventions may take many years or even a generation to influence intended outcomes, it is economical to make adjustments to the intervention design or implementation in response to short- or mid-term outcomes rather than to wait 10 or 30 years to determine that the intervention did not work as intended. Real-time learning, when shared with appropriate stakeholders, can also support the generation of new funding and the development of new or deeper partnerships.

Participatory Evaluation

Life course work itself often focuses on empowering participants to change the structures and systems of oppression that contribute to multigenerational disparities in health outcomes. In programs of this nature, including participants in the evaluation planning, data collection, and analysis can be an important part of shifting the power dynamics that contribute to inequities. Participatory evaluation is a way to increase capacity of the program participants or broader target community while simultaneously working to strengthen the program plan and implementation through evaluation learnings.[33] Participatory methods may mitigate issues of complexity, as participants navigate multiple systems of service, implications of policy and systematic pressures, siloed sectors, and other challenges in their daily lives.

As experts in their own communities, program participants and community residents in turn offer an expertise that practitioners and researchers cannot contribute to the work. Participatory evaluation affirms the expertise and experience of community members and participants and can provide valuable insights that are otherwise unknowable to outside researchers and even to practitioners. Furthermore, participatory evaluation methods are one way to ensure that the practitioners and evaluators do not reinforce historical power dynamics by controlling the evaluation and the results. Participatory methods include a broad range of activities and vary in level of community engagement. This approach can be in coordination with mixed-methods designs, as participatory research often introduces a strong qualitative component.

Developmental Evaluation

In many approaches to summative evaluation, in which the focus is on the outcome(s) of the program, an intervention must be applied in precisely the same way over time to make an overall judgment of the extent to which the work has moved the needle on outcomes of interest.[34] For obvious reasons, life course practitioners balk at the idea of adhering to this principle. Alternatively, if learning in real time would benefit the life course intervention, practitioners should consider adopting elements of a developmental evaluation approach in their evaluation design. As founder of this method, Michael Quinn Patten points out in his illustrative book about this approach that systems-change work is often best measured with developmental evaluation because the structures of traditional evaluation approaches are poorly suited for "turbulence."[34]

One way that developmental evaluation differs from more traditional approaches is by including the evaluator(s) more intentionally as members of the initiative team. In this approach, evaluators focus on asking key questions and communicating findings back to the initiative team in real time rather than packaging all findings to report out at the end of the project. This information can be used to make adjustments to the program model or implementation, to include community members in participatory research practices, and to move the field forward with lessons learned and emerging successes.

Details about how to apply developmental evaluation concepts are readily available in the references cited at the end of this chapter, as well as in many other papers and presentations; this chapter does not intend to instruct about how to do a developmental evaluation. Rather, the intention is to raise the practice as a possible solution to the inhibitions of traditional evaluation. When some aspects of traditional evaluation are required to demonstrate outcomes, it is still possible to integrate aspects of the developmental evaluation approach to respond to the complexity of the work. In particular, life course evaluations may benefit from building in interim points to share findings and allowing results-driven adjustments to be made to the intervention on the basis of short- and mid-term findings.

FUNDERS CAN HELP MITIGATE THESE CHALLENGES

Making smart, cost-efficient investments is important. The field needs to know what works and what does not to think about how to improve it, scale it up, expand it, or just keep it going with sustainable resources. Funders play an important role in addressing some of these challenges. Innovation in translating LCT to practice is fundamental to the growth of this area of work. Valuing innovation is one way that funders can encourage complex solutions for complex problems rather than more straightforward solutions that have already been demonstrated to be insufficient. Similarly, valuing qualitative data, strong partnerships and collaboration, and other nontraditional outcomes are ways that way funders can support life course practitioners in measuring what matters. Generation-long investments could mitigate the challenges of evaluating work that inherently relies on longevity and complexity.

Finally, funders play a key role in exacerbating or mitigating challenges related to attribution. It is important to design an evaluation that will help both funders and practitioners to understand the ways in which the program is or is not working as hypothesized. However, it is equally important to acknowledge that all complex interventions occur in the context of a broader network of multisector efforts to enact change and that there is an extent to which attribution cannot and should not be valued over contribution. If a life course initiative is contributing to positive change, it could be that all change is attributed to this intervention only if it occurred in a vacuum. Luckily, multiple efforts to improve the lives of children and their families are often underway simultaneously in the most vulnerable communities. While a perfect research setting would allow only one intervention at a time, the problems to be addressed by life course efforts are urgent and complex; it is not actually desirable to have only one intervention taking place at a time. Collaboration and coordination with other efforts simultaneously underway supersedes the importance of attributing success when players are all working toward related goals.

IT IS CHALLENGING, BUT IT IS WORTH DOING

Life course interventions pose numerous challenges when it comes to evaluation. This chapter provides some foundational knowledge, a review of the key challenges, and some viable options to address these challenges to achieve a reasonable evaluation design.

There is no perfect evaluation method for life course interventions, but there are many good reasons why it makes sense to apply imperfect methods to these complex programs. Without solid evaluation efforts, practitioners in the field will never be able to demonstrate impact, make critical decisions about what works, and funnel practice information back to the evidence base. Innovation in practice demands innovation in evaluation, and the field continues to build on lessons learned and successes of early efforts. Life Course Approaches have tremendous potential to improve the health outcomes for generations of women, children, and families; evaluation as a learning tool is the key pathway to ensure that programs and policies realize that potential.

ACKNOWLEDGMENTS

The authors would like to acknowledge Tegan Callahan for her contributions to the analysis of life course and the socioecological model.

REFERENCES

1. Lu MC, Halfon N. Racial and ethnic disparities in birth outcomes: a life-course perspective. *Matern Child Health J.* 2003;7(1):13–30.

2. Patton MQ, McKegg K, Wehipeihana N. The developmental evaluation mindset: eight guiding principles. In: Patton MQ, McKegg K, Wehipeihana N, eds. *Developmental Evaluation Exemplars: Principles in Practice.* New York, NY: The Guilford Press; 2016:289–312.

3. Maternal and Child Health Life Course Research Network. Available at: http://www.lcrn.net. Accessed November 26, 2017.

4. Geronimus AT. The weathering hypothesis and the health of African-American women and infants: evidence and speculations. *Ethn Dis.* 1992;2(3):207–221.

5. McEwen BS, Stellar E. Stress and the individual. Mechanisms leading to disease. *Arch Int Med.* 1993;153(18):2093–2101.

6. Bronfenbrenner U. Ecological systems theory. In: Vasta A, ed. *Six Theories of Child Development: Revised Formulations and Current Issues.* Vol 6. Greenwich, CT: JAI Press; 1989.

7. Braveman P, Egerter S, Williams DR. The social determinants of health: coming of age. *Ann Rev Public Health.* 2011;32:381–398.

8. Emanuel I. Maternal health during childhood and later reproductive performance. *Ann N Y Acad Sci.* 1986;477:27–39.

9. Barker DJ, Gluckman PD, Godfrey KM, Harding JE, Owens JA, Robinson JS. Fetal nutrition and cardiovascular disease in adult life. *Lancet.* 1993;341(8850):938–941.

10. Coutinho R, David RJ, Collins JW. Relation of parental birth weights to infant birth weight among African Americans and Whites in Illinois: a transgenerational study. *Am J Epidemiol.* 1997;146(10):804–809.

11. Collins JW, David RJ, Prachand NG, Pierce ML. Low birth weight across generations. *Matern Child Health J.* 2003;7(4):229–237.

12. Robert Wood Johnson Foundation. A new way to talk about the social determinants of health. 2010. Available at: http://www.rwjf.org/en/library/research/2010/01/a-new-way-to-talk-about-the-social-determinants-of-health.html. Accessed August 16, 2017.

13. Kogan MD, Dykton C, Hirai AH. A new performance measurement system for maternal and child health in the United States. *Matern Child Health J.* 2015;19(5):945–957.

14. Callahan T, Stampfel C, Cornell A. From theory to measurement: recommended state MCH life course indicators. *Matern Child Health J.* 2015;19(11):2336–2347.

15. Association of Maternal and Child Health Programs. Life course indicators online tool. 2014. Available at: http://www.amchp.org/programsandtopics/data-assessment/Pages/LifeCourseIndicators.aspx. Accessed February 2, 2018.

16. Jones CP. Levels of racism: a theoretic framework and a gardener's tale. *Am J Public Health.* 2000;90(8):1212–1215.

17. Williams RA, Mamotte CD, Burnett JR. Phenylketonuria: an inborn error of phenylalanine metabolism. *Clin Biochem Rev.* 2008;29(1):31–41.

18. March of Dimes. 2016 Premature Birth Report Card. Available at: http://www.marchofdimes.org/materials/premature-birth-report-card-united-states.pdf. Accessed August 16, 2017.

19. Scott J. *Social Network Analysis.* 4th ed. Los Angeles, CA: Sage; 2017.

20. Fredericks K. Using Social Network Analysis in evaluation: a report to the Robert Wood Johnson Foundation. 2013. Available at: http://www.rwjf.org/en/library/research/2013/12/using-social-network-analysis-in-evaluation.html. Accessed August 16, 2017.

21. Fine A, Kotelchuck M. Rethinking MCH: the life course model as an organizing framework. Rockville, MD: US Department of Health and Human Services, Health Resources and Services Administration, Maternal and Child Health Bureau; 2010.

22. Wise PH. The anatomy of a disparity in infant mortality. *Ann Rev Public Health.* 2003;24: 341–362.

23. Anand S, Diderichsen F, Evans T, Shkolnikov VM, Wirth M. Measuring disparities in health: methods and indicators. In: Evans T, Whitehead M, Diderichsen F, Bhuiya A, Wirth M, eds. *Challenging Inequities in Health: From Ethics to Action.* New York, NY: Oxford University Press; 2001.

24. Pearcy JN, Keppel KG. A summary measure of health disparity. *Public Health Rep.* 2002; 117(3):273–280.

25. Equitable Evaluation. The project. Available at: https://www.equitableeval.org/project. Accessed August 16, 2017.

26. Sampson RJ, Morenoff JD, Earls F. Beyond social capital: spatial dynamics of collective efficacy for children. *Am Sociol Rev.* 1999;64(5):633–660.

27. Sampson RJ, Morenoff JD, Gannon-Rowley T. Assessing "neighborhood effects": social processes and new directions in research. *Ann Rev Sociol.* 2002;28(1):443–478.

28. Sampson RJ, Sharkey P, Raudenbush SW. Durable effects of concentrated disadvantage on verbal ability among African-American children. *Proc Natl Acad Sci U S A.* 2007;105(3): 845–852.

29. Sampson RJ. Neighborhoods and violent crime: a multilevel study of collective efficacy. *Science.* 1997;277(5328):918–924.

30. United Health Foundation. America's health rankings health of women and children report. 2016. Available at: http://assets.americashealthrankings.org/app/uploads/hwc-fullreport_ v2.pdf. Accessed August 16, 2017.

31. Rothman KJ, Greenland S, Lash TL. *Modern Epidemiology.* 3rd ed. Philadelphia, PA: Lippincott Williams and Wilkins; 2008.

32. Jewell NP. *Statistics for Epidemiology.* Boca Raton, FL: Chapman and Hall/CRC Press; 2003.

33. Minkler M, Wallerstein N. *Community-Based Participatory Research for Health: From Process to Outcomes.* 2nd ed. San Francisco, CA: Jossey-Bass; 2008.

34. Patton MQ. *Developmental Evaluation: Applying Complexity Concepts to Enhance Innovation and Use.* New York, NY: The Guilford Press; 2011.

14

Resource Development and Funding

Sara S. Bachman, PhD

Advances in the science of human development, coupled with knowledge generated by recent biopsychosocial and epigenetic studies, have led to the acceptance of the idea that social, psychological, environmental, and other influences have an impact on a person's health over her or his life span, perhaps to a greater degree than illness or injury.[1] The Life Course Theory (LCT) integrates mounting evidence that health status is influenced by social determinants of health and that chronic diseases in adulthood have their origins in early childhood.[2] Effective application of the LCT requires changes in the way health and social support services are financed, including integration of funding from multiple sources and greater emphasis on a systems outlook over the life span. This chapter briefly describes the historical trends that have led to current funding streams for maternal and child health (MCH) services. Strengths and barriers to innovation in resource development and allocation are discussed, and ideas for new ways to advance and sustain adequate resources and funding for MCH, grounded in a life course perspective, are presented.

A BRIEF HISTORY OF MATERNAL AND CHILD HEALTH CARE FINANCING

In the late 1800s and early 1900s, as child labor practices and care for orphans revealed child maltreatment, concerned citizens advocated increasing attention to the welfare of American children, and the federal Children's Bureau was established in 1912.[3] The Bureau focused its initial activities on child labor laws as well as a study of infant mortality, identifying socioeconomic factors as important determinants of unequal infant mortality rates. The work of the Bureau, combined with other events, such as World War I and the Great Depression, led to the signing of the Social Security Act in 1935; Title V of the Act gave the Children's Bureau responsibility for MCH services, care for "crippled children," and child welfare services.[3] Title IV of the Social Security Act authorized the Aid to Dependent Children's program, which provided grants from the federal government to the states for financial aid to mothers. Thus, the earliest national American social welfare programs established financing of health and social care specifically for children.

In 1965, the Medicaid program was established through Title XIX of the Social Security Act, further focusing national programming on children. Medicaid is jointly sponsored by the federal and state governments, with federal funding matching that of the states through the Federal Financial Participation formula.[4] Children receiving Aid to Families of Dependent Children (AFDC, formerly Aid to Dependent Children) were automatically eligible to receive health care coverage through the Medicaid program along with their mothers. Adults with disabilities were also determined eligible.[2] Simultaneously, older adults were eligible to receive health care benefits through the Medicare program. With the establishment of Medicaid and Medicare, and building on the already established Titles IV and V of the Social Security Act, the connection between age and eligibility for specific health care coverage programs was established and the development of siloed financing became entrenched.

Other, often disconnected sources of health and social care financing and coverage for children evolved, including employer-sponsored health care coverage, offered to individuals and families while they are employed by a selected employer; services for people with mental health, substance abuse, and developmental disability conditions; the Special Supplemental Nutrition Program for Women, Infants, and Children (WIC); and the Supplemental Nutrition Assistance Program (SNAP) for low-income individuals and families. Still more resources and supports evolved through other agencies and departments such as special education supported through the Individuals with Disabilities Education Act (IDEA), public housing, child welfare services for children placed in foster care, and cash supports through Temporary Assistance to Needy Families (TANF, formerly AFDC) among others.

Although current iterations of these programs provide essential services; meet the needs of specific populations, including children and their families; and sometimes serve the same individuals, integration among them is variable. Eligibility criteria do not necessarily overlap and funding is not often coordinated. Many programs are means tested and thus are not available to some children and families that have employer-sponsored health care coverage. Family financial hardship can negatively affect families that are underinsured, particularly when they have limited employer-sponsored private health care coverage, especially high-deductible health plans.[5] This fragmented and often inadequate system of coverage and financing options has its roots in the historical trends that spawned each program. The cumulative potential impact of the universe of available programs is not leveraged, and the gains that might be afforded from a life course perspective have not been realized.

TRENDS IN THE CURRENT MATERNAL AND CHILD HEALTH FINANCING LANDSCAPE

The Patient Protection and Affordable Care Act (ACA; Pub L 111-148) was passed in 2010 amid hope and expectations that this fragmented system of funding and resources would be improved. Initial ACA impacts included reduction in the number of uninsured Americans, expansion of eligibility for Medicaid, and development of essential health benefits as standards for basic health care coverage. However, without Medicaid expansion implementation in all states, the ACA may not provide the sustainable framework needed to move toward comprehensive and lifelong coverage for health and social support services. There are several trends ushered in through the ACA that, when considered along with the progress in financing MCH services that was ongoing before the ACA, may promote development of a life course perspective for MCH health funding and resources. These trends include an emphasis on value, integration of payment systems, and a focus on person-centered care; each of these topics is discussed in the following paragraphs.

Value-Based Purchasing

There is increasing interest in developing new health care financing and reimbursement strategies that mitigate the consequences of the historical use of fee-for-service reimbursement, in which providers are paid a fee for each service delivered. Fee-for-service reimbursement promotes fragmented systems of care and little accountability. Value-based purchasing (VBP), in contrast, aims to maximize value in health care purchasing by promoting delivery and payment strategies that emphasize cost-effectiveness and achieving the best health outcomes possible given available resources. One example of VBP includes the financing and reimbursement mechanisms used by pharmacy benefit management companies.[6]

Payment reform provisions in the ACA promote VBP strategies to advance the triple aim of lower cost, increased efficiency, and improved population health. However, VBP is a concept that has been used by private employers or health insurance plans for many years. Although these VBP program sponsors may have accrued a record of the outcomes associated with these strategies, this information is proprietary to the employers and health plans and so is not generally available to makers of public policy for use in designing and implementing VBP programs. As a result, evidence-based strategies for VBP are not emerging. Moreover, there is not one definition of VBP; instead, there is a growing landscape of purchasing and insurance design strategies that are generally considered VBP and include a broad range of innovative financing approaches such as bundled payments, accountable care organizations, and integrated care systems that link primary care and behavioral health services, among others. A key limitation of expanding VBP is identifying outcomes that can be achieved through specific, improved financing or purchasing strategies.

To promote use of VBP, payers need information about measuring value and health outcomes for the people they insure. The Children's Health Insurance Program Reauthorization Act of 2009 mandated the Pediatric Quality Measurement Program. Through this initiative, various measures of quality have been identified such as the

Consumer Assessment of Healthcare Providers and Systems and the National Research Corporation Picker Pediatric Inpatient Survey.[6] However, these measures are not consistently used by all MCH providers, thus making it difficult to design a VBP program based on them. More work is needed on the validity and reliability of existing measures as well as the implementation of expanded measures, such as characteristics of the medical home or the development and use of an integrated comprehensive care plan. Better measures of care integration, care coordination, and integration of mental, developmental, and physical health into a comprehensive care system within the medical home are high-priority topics for measure development.[6]

Developing strategies to gather and analyze the measures is also a significant barrier. Information about health outcomes is contained in health records, but if the records are electronic, there are likely to be compatibility issues among the different health information systems. And the specific data elements needed to determine "value" may not be easily retrieved from electronic medical records. Resolving this barrier will require a significant investment on the part of payers, providers, information systems, and other stakeholders to create and implement standard strategies for health information.[7] These issues become even more complicated when applied to Medicaid claims data, which vary by state and are also subject to significant delays in processing.[8] Without consistent and agreed-upon quality and outcome measures, providers will not be able to meet benchmarks and performance incentives as required by VBP to manage patient care and financial risk.[9]

Bundled Payment Systems

Aggregating the expenditures associated with a set of services into so-called bundled payments has become a key strategy for achieving value in health care purchasing. For many years, Medicare has promoted bundled payments to control program spending through a reduction in the number of hospitalizations and more judicious use of health care resources and to reduce postdischarge costs, including unnecessary post–acute care services and avoidable readmissions. Medicaid programs have also long advanced agendas that include use of capitated purchasing of health care services for eligible populations. However, the impact of these payment systems on vulnerable populations has not been well documented, and the incentives to withhold care under capitation are powerful, with potentially devastating consequences. High-risk or high need patients are particularly vulnerable to underservice if provider payment systems are not linked to meaningful quality and outcome measures. Providers may opt not to serve Medicaid beneficiaries at all. Or inadequate payment rates that do not cover the costs of serving high-risk or high-need patients may cause providers to skimp on necessary services or avoid serving vulnerable patients entirely, thus exacerbating existing inequities according to income, severity of illness, race, ethnicity, or other characteristics. For example, in the case of postpartum care, when the prenatal services bundle includes postpartum health but is paid upon delivery, there is little financial incentive for providers to ensure that quality, comprehensive postpartum care occurs.

One solution to this issue is the development of risk adjustment mechanisms to "level the playing field" among capitated plans. Through risk adjustment, health plans receive a greater capitation amount for individual patients with greater health care needs. Bundled payment rates are often risk-adjusted in an effort to account for differences in patient-level characteristics or severity of illness. However, the accuracy of risk-adjustment methodologies remains uncertain, especially for high-cost populations such as children with special health care needs. The development of accurate risk adjustment strategies has not kept pace with the trend toward moving to bundled payments.[6] As a result, some very high-risk (and, thus, high-cost) populations may be excluded from bundled payment arrangements or at risk for inadequate care.

Patient-Centered Care and the Medical Home

The Patient-Centered Medical Home (PCMH) is a model of primary care that is conceptualized as being delivered through strategies that make it accessible, continuous, comprehensive, family-centered, coordinated, compassionate, and culturally effective. Its goals include improving the quality of care through team-based care coordination, increasing access to health care services and supports, and improving patient engagement and partnership. These goals align with those of the LCT.

While over time individual therapies and health care interventions have become more effective and thus, more value driven, the extensive array of continuing health care needs facing many patients are difficult for families, physicians, and other health care providers to manage and coordinate without additional supports. Children and families often interact with a variety of different systems; these systems, as described previously, are not designed to communicate easily or effectively with one another. Financing mechanisms, lack of integrated or compatible electronic records to speed communication, and provider competition about roles and practice domains are examples of system design flaws that all have an impact on quality of care and outcomes.

Although care coordination has been proposed as a solution to these issues and is thus seen as an essential service, sustainable funding for care coordination continues to be a primary challenge. A currently underfunded system of care coordination, when it does exist, presumes there is care to coordinate, which is not always the case, especially for families in rural communities, those in plans with inadequate provider networks, and those who require services that are impacted by long-standing workforce shortages, such as home nursing and personal care attendant services. Delivery reform, such as the PCMH and its essential reliance on care coordination, must be linked more directly with VBP payment reforms, such as risk-adjusted bundled or global payments, to more effectively leverage the benefits of both.[5]

CURRENT FUNDING MECHANISMS: IMPLICATIONS FOR TRANSLATING LIFE COURSE THEORY INTO PRACTICE

Multiple sources of funding for the health and social support services needed by MCH populations have evolved over the past century. Specific characteristics of this system of care offer both strengths and barriers to developing and sustaining the LCT as the conceptual underpinning of an improved system of care. This section briefly discusses these characteristics and their impact on promoting use of the Life Course Approach.

Categorical Eligibility

To receive many MCH benefits, individuals or families must meet certain eligibility criteria under specific categories of aid. The categories of aid are typified by demographic and income characteristics, such as gender, family composition, or family income in relation to federally determined poverty levels, among others. The WIC program, for example, is available only to selected categories of women, infants, and children, including women who are pregnant, postpartum, or breastfeeding. Once determined to be eligible for a selected categorical program, the individual or family may also be eligible for other benefits. For example, if a mother and her children are determined to be eligible for cash benefits under the TANF program, the family may also be automatically eligible for other benefits such as child care or job training programs.

Age is a common categorical eligibility criterion and categorical eligibility based on age is particularly relevant for MCH populations. For example, IDEA provides for a free appropriate public education for all students including children with disabilities. However, children are eligible for IDEA only until they turn 22, at the latest. At that time, regardless of whether the child would still benefit from a free, appropriate public education, the child is no longer eligible for these services and must transition to the adult system of care.

Categorical eligibility generally serves as an impediment to the LCT, as children and families predictably flow among the different criteria that are used to determine eligibility in this way. Children inevitably age, for example, and thus lose eligibility for services and supports that are available only for individuals who are aged younger than 22 years, a typical age eligibility criterion. Effective use of the LCT will not be possible if funding is based on categorical eligibility.

Siloed Programs

Many health and social need programs are not connected at all through eligibility, benefits, or program administration, even though individuals or families may simultaneously receive services or benefits from these disconnected programs. For example, families that are receiving cash benefits under the TANF program may or may not be receiving housing or rental assistance through public housing programs. Furthermore, the gap between selected programs may be mandated through law or regulation: although health and housing are intricately connected, Medicaid programs are not authorized to pay for housing services. Public health funding sources, such as federal grants from individual agencies, tend to focus on one specific disease or issue. The targeted audience for these key resources impedes effort at the state or local level to integrate funds to achieve broader goals.

Separate, independent programs inevitably exacerbate underfunding of needed services and lead to gaps in coverage and a fragmented system of services and supports. To translate LCT into practice, there must be more integration among the various programs, services, and supports developed for children and families. The bundled payment systems described previously have evolved in part to mitigate this problem, but the complexities of these strategies have made solutions difficult to realize.

Limited Sustainability

Although programs such as Title V have been in operation since the Social Security Act was passed, children and families do not typically experience stability and sustainability in the benefits they receive over time. Medicaid eligibility levels, for example, are variable among states; they rise and fall within a particular state as budget priorities and political leadership inevitably change. Individual income levels may also fluctuate and thus Medicaid eligibility for children and families may fluctuate or "churn" as family income increases and decreases in relation to Medicaid income eligibility criteria. Family eligibility for employer-sponsored health insurance can also fluctuate as employers select new health care coverage plans or adult family members move among employment opportunities. Thus, coverage for health and support services is not typically sustained over the life course. For example, if a head of household for a Medicaid-eligible family works additional hours for a short period of time, the supplemental income temporarily earned may put the family's income above Medicaid eligibility levels. Until the family income declines to below eligibility levels, the family will not receive Medicaid benefits. This "churning" within health and social support programs is an important barrier to sustainability of beneficial services and an important threat to translating the LCT into action.

Adequacy of Coverage and Financial Hardship

As a result of characteristics such as categorical eligibility, siloed programs, and limited sustainability, the public and private programs that provide funding and resources for MCH and social supports offer variable and limited amounts of coverage for these services. When health plans and benefit programs have limits on the quantity, duration, or cost of coverage, expenses are shifted to the consumer, especially in the context of the high-deductible health plans that have become more common among employer-sponsored health care coverage options. When this happens, family financial hardship results.[5]

Family financial hardship can accumulate over time, especially for families that have children with medical complexity or special health care needs. As children receive more and more needed services over the course of their development, families cannot afford to pay the out-of-pocket costs, such as co-pays and deductibles, that are an essential element of employer-sponsored health care coverage plans. Obviously, as children age, these costs accumulate and can burden a family with overwhelming debt. This clearly affects not only the health and opportunities of the affected child but also that of the entire family. Families that accumulate substantial medical debt as a result of limits on their employer-sponsored or private health care plan may become impoverished and thus eligible for Medicaid. Translating LCT into action must include provisions for adequate funding to cover the actual costs of care, thus making coverage affordable for all families, helping them to retain employment and their employer-sponsored health care coverage.

Health Inequities Over the Life Course

As has been documented in many ways, there are significant inequities in health care access and outcomes among subpopulations of women and children. These inequities exist among subgroups according to race, ethnicity, class, disability, gender, age, and a range of social determinants of health. Over the life course, inequities mount and become compounded. Characteristics of funding strategies and recent trends in health care coverage do little to mitigate these effects. The financial incentives that have become integral to health care coverage encourage biased selection of less complex cases and, without adequate risk-adjustment protections, certainly do not encourage providers to address the social determinants of health that drive some health inequities.

A critical mass of evidence indicates that health inequities compound over the life course, and adult health status is shaped by events and social determinants in childhood. Systems of financing do little to alleviate these trends, including the barriers described here. The United States spends far more on the health care of older adults, working to mitigate the compounded ill effects of fragmented service delivery, poor housing, or inadequate nutrition that began in childhood, the symptoms of which have been manifested as expensive chronic conditions in adulthood. To translate the life course perspective into practice, this trend must be reversed, with a focus on equitable access to quality services beginning with maternal health and continuing throughout childhood. Funding the life course perspective will require resources to pay for comprehensive services and supports that address the broad range of social determinants of health, including housing and education as well as services that are more traditionally identified as in the realm of health care. For historically marginalized groups, additional efforts will be needed to address their even worse health status, resulting from compounded years of poor access to quality health care.

Performance Measures and Outcomes

The problem of identifying appropriate performance measures, described in the section about VBP, is made even more difficult when considered in the context of the LCT. The causal pathways between events of childhood and outcomes in adulthood are complex and multilayered; it is difficult to consistently ensure the use of a parsimonious set of outcomes measures that give the best indication that programs are working, especially in the context of many potentially impactful social determinants of health. One strength in this area is the steady advancement of sophisticated information technology systems and electronic medical records that make it possible for health information to be accumulated over an individual's lifetime, to connect childhood and adult health and other data. These comprehensive data sets could support the development and application of performance and outcome measures to document impact over a lifetime. For example, monitoring measures of the social determinants of health in childhood, such as safe housing and adequate nutrition, could result in improved health status in adulthood. However, these types of performance measures are not in use, thus limiting their integration into a Life Course Approach to program development and financing.

Demonstrating Return on Investment

There are research and practice outcomes that demonstrate the value of investing in MCH programs; see, for example, resources from the Association of Maternal and Child Health Programs.[10] Although these resources offer suggestions for demonstrating return on investment, they do not typically rely on data gathered over a longer period of time to document economic benefits of MCH care over the life course. An extension of the barriers related to developing performance measures, as described previously, is the limited information about the quantity and variety of investments in child health and well-being that will lead to the greatest improvements in health status over the life course. A small body of research is accumulating that demonstrates the return on investment of access to child health care that is provided through the Medicaid program.[11]

Longitudinal data analysis suggests that Medicaid provides long-term benefits with respect to health; the effect of Medicaid on other social determinants of health such as income or medical debt is less clear. Another body of research has focused on evaluating the long-term impact of school-based early childhood education programs. These data suggest that there is a return on investment for preschool education, including reduction in felony arrests and improvements in socioeconomic status.[12] Confounding variables and potential bias are weaknesses in the methods that limit the evidence base about the return on investment of early childhood programs. Resources are available to support return on investments in MCH programs such as asthma prevention or newborn screening. Visit the Association of Maternal and Child Health Programs website for more information.[10] Practitioners can extend these activities to include a life course perspective by tracking health and well-being outcomes over a longer period of time.

Translating the LCT into practice will be accomplished with greater efficacy with a deeper understanding of the impact of health, education, and social service investments in childhood. Given the number and variety of programs that might improve individual and family health status and well-being over the life course, it is essential that policymakers and funders have information about program impacts not only during childhood but also during working age and older adulthood. Public and private resources, including out-of-pocket spending by individuals and families, are all limited and, thus, precious. Understanding how to maximize the impact of each dollar spent for child and family well-being is an essential element of transitioning to an effective system developed by using LCT.

Grounded in the historical roots of their development, current funding and resources that support health and social services for children and families offer important benefits that promote well-being. However, characteristics associated with the mechanisms by which these programs have been implemented also present important barriers to their efficacy. Translating LCT into practice will necessitate intentional efforts to mitigate these barriers and create financing methods that can support sustained program impact over the life course.

RECOMMENDATIONS FOR INNOVATION AND EXTENSION

Since the initial funding of health and social support programs for children and families more than a century ago, policymakers, advocates, payers, and consumers have all recognized the weaknesses associated with each program. At some point following each program's implementation, stakeholders have taken steps to make improvements. Thus, there is an accumulating body of knowledge about the intended and unintended consequences of program design elements. For example, we know that fee-for-service reimbursement, in which providers are reimbursed for each service they deliver, creates incentives to provide more services, sometimes when the services are not needed. Other program characteristics discussed previously, such as categorical eligibility, have attendant weaknesses that serve as barriers to quality and efficiency of service delivery.

Developing a system of funding and resources that will support the translation of LCT into practice demands another cycle of financing reform with attention to the weaknesses that have plagued implementation of more sensible financing strategies to date. Given that health care financing reform generally occurs incrementally in the

United States, it seems safe to assume that incremental reform will be needed to achieve comprehensive funding of life course health and social service delivery models. Stakeholders are thus charged with identifying and implementing strategies that can serve as fundamental building blocks that will initiate the process of creating a new funding system with the understanding that the system will need to be extended to maximize impact of the life course perspective. The next sections identify and briefly discuss some of these innovative strategies that might serve as springboards for the comprehensive reform that is required.

Integrated Funding With Incentives for Systems Development

LCT is characterized by the conceptual underpinning that stages of human development flow with little demarcation among them. Thus, it follows that the funding for services provided under the LCT would similarly flow smoothly without consideration of age, categorical eligibility, or time period. For many years, policymakers have been attempting to develop a financing system that is grounded in integrating multiple funding streams to promote this fluid funding ideal. Although these efforts have not been framed as supporting the LCT, funding integration could be considered one of the building blocks on which model development could occur.

For example, a provision in the Medicare Modernization Act of 2003 authorized the development of Special Needs Plans (SNPs), a type of Medicare managed care plan reimbursed using bundled payments.[13] SNPs are authorized to enroll people who are dually eligible for both Medicare and Medicaid. A person who is dually eligible may be an older adult who is poor and thus eligible for Medicaid benefits as well as Medicare or an adult with disabilities who has had Medicaid coverage and aged into Medicare eligibility. As is typical of many health coverage programs, there is not usually coordination between Medicaid and Medicare for individuals eligible for both programs. Under the SNP provision, states can elect to develop a managed care option through their Medicaid program that would serve as a companion to an existing Medicare managed care plan. As might have been anticipated, given the variability in state Medicaid programs previously described, SNPs targeting dual eligibles are not uniformly available across all the states, and the majority of dually eligible SNP enrollees are found in a minority of states. However, in the states that have elected to implement SNPs, individuals who are dually eligible for Medicaid and Medicare report that they receive services that are better integrated.[12] Thus, SNPs are an example of an integrated funding mechanism that could be leveraged to make more systemic improvements in funding integration. Other examples of integrated funding projects include those developed by Medicaid by using an 1115 waiver such as a recent Massachusetts program to integrate primary and behavioral health care, building on the state's rich experience with 1115 waivers.

There are many ways that funding integration could be pursued. For example, state or local MCH and social service programs could look at their overall agency budget more holistically and co-mingle funds and staff across programs. The potential to show return on investment over the life course (discussed previously) would create incentives for agency leaders to think creatively about this integration. Care coordination is an effective tool for implementing integrated care models over the life course.[14] Care coordination can be provided by professionals or family members and is best financed through integrated payments models. Integration can extend beyond siloed public agencies; employers are also invested in healthy children and families and have made the business case for access to MCH programming.[15]

Continue to Improve Value-Based Purchasing Strategies

The application of LCT to practice must build on current efforts to improve health outcomes by purchasing services only from providers that demonstrate cost and outcome effectiveness. The barriers suggest that issues such as siloed programs and impediments to sustainability perpetuate inefficiencies and less robust outcomes than might be achieved if these problems could be resolved. Thus, greater attention to increasing value in purchase of health and support services appears to be a worthy goal, especially in the context of increasingly constrained resources.

With that said, VBP appears to be a conceptual model in need of practice translation in the same way that LCT needs mechanisms for implementation. The two models share a dependence on outcome measures to demonstrate impact. However, as discussed previously, work is needed on the identification of performance measures for LCT, as well as indicators of return on investment. Outcome measures might encompass domains such as cost-effectiveness measured by reduced health care use or activities of daily living measured by school attendance. Once these measures are identified, they can be used to improve purchasing strategies through an increased emphasis on identifying and using only providers that can demonstrate value over the life course. Without a consensus-driven process to identify the outcomes that providers, payers, policymakers, and consumers aim to achieve, however, it will be difficult to implement financing and reimbursement strategies that promote the desired outcomes.

Social Entrepreneurship

Partially in response to the weaknesses and gaps in current health and social service systems as described previously, there has been increased attention on organizations that create social as well as economic value through social entrepreneurship models.[16] Through these models, a social problem is identified, and capital and economic assets are harnessed to develop solutions to the problem. Economic investors forgo some monetary return in favor of the social benefits that result from the entrepreneurial model. Existing public and private programs are often bypassed in these solutions, and the focus is on entrepreneurial innovation and creativity in addressing health, social service, educational, environmental, or other needs.[17]

Much of the research on social entrepreneurship has focused on individuals or organizations that serve as the impetus for developing and implementing a creative social innovations model.[16] Much less work has been done about how this strategy can be used to support a system of care or a broader approach such as the LCT.[16] Interestingly, there is some research that suggests that a social entrepreneurial model can be both a resource mechanism and an intervention.[18] For example, a social entrepreneurial model has been used as the underpinning of a youth development model, in which entrepreneurial activities form the basis of an intervention to improve economic and health outcomes among youth who are homeless or unstably housed.[18] Thus, the benefits of using a social entrepreneurial model may extend beyond funding and resources to improved health and well-being outcomes. Especially as improved outcomes may be associated with employment, there is also potential for the social entrepreneurial model to serve as a foundation for the life course and it may be an effective way to translate LCT into practice.

A significant amount of advance work would be required to make these adaptations, such as research to learn more about how social entrepreneurs develop and implement innovative models and how these efforts would be more specifically linked to MCH.[16,17] Regardless, social entrepreneurship holds promise as a model that might usher in the significant reforms that would be needed to transform the centuries-old structure of financing and delivering MCH services into a seamless life course system of services and supports.

Philanthropy

Recent literature suggests that philanthropic organizations are playing an increasing role in translating theory into transformative action for practice. For example, the Robert Wood Johnson Foundation has developed a major initiative to spark and support a social movement called The Culture of Health.[19] The Foundation's initiative is holistic, addressing multiple aspects of health including social determinants of health, as well as a long-term view, with a 20-year time frame.[19] These perspectives certainly align with the life course theoretical perspective and suggest that philanthropy can play a major role in translating the theory into practice. Other roles for philanthropy have also been identified. For example, Fukuzawa and Karnas[20] suggest that philanthropic organizations can reconnect health and housing, in support of the social determinants of health framework. Certainly, improved housing quality for children would serve as a platform for improved health over the life course.

Conversion foundations, often established when nonprofit health care institutions are acquired by for-profit organizations, have been created for many years. Maurana et al.[21] describe the transformative potential of a conversion foundation in Wisconsin, suggesting that this type of philanthropic effort can promote community and public health outcomes that would be consistent with life course perspectives. Philanthropic organizations can have a significant impact on health equity, particularly with respect to engaging other sectors, including public health and sectors related to the social determinants of health.[22] Thus, philanthropy represents an opportunity to engage resources and financing that can help transform the current system of care and support to one that is grounded in the life course perspective. Little work has been done to develop the evidence base about this strategy, however, thus offering an opportunity for new research and analysis.

CONCLUSIONS

Since the initial funding of health and social support programs for children and families more than a century ago, policymakers, advocates, payers, and consumers have struggled to create sustainable sources of financing and resources that will promote health and well-being for all mothers and children. The effective application of the life course perspective of human development will require significant overhaul in the way the current health and social support services are financed, including integration of funding from multiple sources and greater emphasis on a systems outlook over the life span. As demonstrated in this chapter, there is an accumulating body of knowledge about financing methods developed to promote efficacy and value. Advancing a system of funding and resources that will support the translation of LCT into practice demands another cycle of financing reform, with attention to the weaknesses that have plagued implementation of more sensible financing strategies to date. Given that health care financing reform generally occurs incrementally in the United States, it seems safe to assume that incremental reform will be needed to achieve comprehensive funding of life course health and social service delivery models.

Health status accumulates over a lifetime and is directly determined by MCH, in the context of social determinants of health. Cross-sectoral strategies implemented through integrated mechanisms can ensure not only that mothers and children receive high-quality, cost-effective care but also that children and families live in environments that promote health. The strategies discussed here can serve as fundamental building blocks to create a new, comprehensive funding system that will support the health, social care, and overall well-being that we know mothers and children need for a lifetime of health. MCH practitioners, policymakers, and advocates must take action to implement the strategies discussed in this chapter to develop adequate and sustainable resources and financing that advance the LCT.

KEY POINTS

- Funding for MCH populations has evolved over time, but funding impact continues to be limited by factors such as siloed programming, categorical eligibility, and fee-for-service reimbursement.
- The effective application of the LCT requires further improvements in the way health and social support services are financed, including integration of funding from multiple sources and greater emphasis on a systems outlook over the life span.
- New performance measures are needed to demonstrate impact and outcomes over the life course.
- Exploration of philanthropy, social entrepreneurship, and other innovative models is important for advancing this work.

RESOURCES

- The Catalyst Center—the national center for health insurance and financing health care for children and youth with special health care needs—has a great variety of resources on financing: http://cahpp.org/project/the-catalyst-center.
- The Association of Maternal and Child Health Programs is a national resource, partner, and advocate for state public health leaders and others working to improve the health of women, children, youth, and families, including those with special health care needs: http://www.amchp.org/AboutAMCHP/Pages/default.aspx.

REFERENCES

1. Halfon N, Larson K, Lu M, Tullis E, Russ S. Lifecourse health development: past, present and future. *Matern Child Health J.* 2014;18(2):344–365.

2. Russ S, Garro N, Halfon N. Meeting children's basic health needs: from patchwork to tapestry. *Child Youth Serv Rev.* 2010;32:1149–1164.

3. US Department of Health and Human Services. Children's Bureau timeline. Administration for Children and Families. Available at: https://cb100.acf.hhs.gov/childrens-bureau-timeline. Accessed December 28, 2016.

4. Bachman S, Comeau M, Tobias C, et al. State health care financing strategies for children with intellectual and developmental disabilities. *Intellect Dev Disabil.* 2012;50(3):181–189.

5. Bachman SS, Comeau M, Dworetzky B, Hamershock R, Hirschi M. The Louisiana Family Opportunity Act Medicaid Buy-in Program. *Matern Child Health J.* 2015;19(12):2568–2577.

6. Bachman S, Comeau M, Long T. Statement of the problem: health reform, value-based purchasing, alternative payment strategies, and children and youth with special health care needs. *Pediatrics.* 2017;139(suppl 2):S89–S98.

7. Bailey LC, Mistry KB, Tinoco A, et al. Addressing electronic clinical information in the construction of quality measures. *Acad Pediatr.* 2014;14(suppl 5):S82–S87.

8. Gidengil C, Mangione-Smith R, Bailey C, et al. Using Medicaid and CHIP claims data to support pediatric quality measurement: lessons from the 3 centers of excellence in measure development. *Acad Pediatr.* 2014;14(suppl 5):S76–S81.

9. Delbanco SF, Andersen KM, Major CE, Kiser MB, Toner BW, Hamilton BA. *Promising Payment Reform: Risk-Sharing With Accountable Care Organizations.* New York, NY: The Commonwealth Fund; 2011.

10. Association of Maternal and Child Health Programs. Available at: http://www.amchp.org/AboutAMCHP/Pages/default.aspx. Accessed November 22, 2017.

11. Boudreaux MH, Golberstein E, McAlpine D. The long term impacts of Medicaid exposure in early childhood: evidence from the program's origin. *J Health Econ.* 2016;45:161–175.

12. Reynolds AJ, Temple JA, Ou S-R, Arteaga IA, White BA. School-based early childhood education and age-28 well-being: effects by timing, dosage and subgroups. *Science.* 2011; 333(6040):360–364.

13. Bachman SS, Gonyea J. Improving health care delivery to aging adults with disabilities: social work with dual eligibles in a climate of health care reform. *J Gerontol Soc Work.* 2012; 55(2):191–207.

14. Bachman SS, Comeau M, Jankovsky KM. *The Care Coordination Conundrum and Children and Youth With Special Health Care Needs. What Is Care Coordination? Who Should Receive It? Who Should Provide It? How Should It Be Financed?* Boston, MA: Lucile Packard Foundation for Children's Health; 2015.

15. Campbell KP, ed. *Investing in Maternal and Child Health.* Center for Prevention and Health Services, National Business Group on Health. 2007. Available at: https://www.businessgrouphealth.org/pub/?id=f3004374-2354-d714-5186-b5bc1885758a. Accessed May 11, 2017.

16. Heinze KL, Banaszak-Holl J, Babiak K. Social entrepreneurship in communities: examining the collaborative processes of health conversion foundations. *Nonprofit Manag Leadersh.* 2016;26:313–330.

17. Hernandez D, Carrion D, Perotte A, Fullilove R. Public health entrepreneurs: training the next generation of public health innovators. *Public Health Rep.* 2014;129(6):477–481.

18. Jennings L, Shore D, Strohminger N, Allison B. Entrepreneurial development for US minority and unstably housed youth: a qualitative inquiry on value, barriers and impact on health. *Child Youth Serv Rev.* 2015;49:39–47.

19. Trujillo MD, Plough A. Building a culture of health: a new framework and measures for health and health care in America. *Soc Sci Med.* 2016;165:206–213.

20. Fukuzawa DD, Karnas F. Reconnecting health and housing: philanthropy's new opportunity. *Environ Justice.* 2015;8:86–94.

21. Maurana CA, Lucey PA, Ahmed SM, Kerschner JE, Bolton GA, Raymond JR. The Advancing a Healthier Wisconsin Endowment: how a health care conversion foundation is transforming a medical school. *Acad Med.* 2016;91(1):42–47.

22. Doykos P, Gray-Akpa K, Mitchell F. New directions for foundations in health equity. *Health Aff (Millwood).* 2016;35(8):1536–1540.

15

Leading for Change

Sarah Verbiest, DrPH, MSW, MPH

Applying the Life Course Approach to practice offers the chance to turn current thinking and strategies upside down. Restructuring programs to align with an intergenerational perspective, seeing the individual as part of an interwoven web of relationships within the context of community, and focusing on improving health and wellness equitably is exciting work indeed! At its heart, Life Course Theory (LCT) lifts up the dynamic nature of people within communities influenced by shared history and policy at all levels. While this may overwhelm some practitioners, readers who have made it to this last chapter are clearly invested in ensuring that women and men, children and adolescents, and families can attain their fullest potential.

It is true, however, that practitioners in the field of maternal and child health (MCH) can have a solid grounding in LCT yet find it challenging to advance these novel and innovative approaches to solving long-standing problems. As discussed throughout this book, applying the LCT to practice is founded on the intention of addressing inequities head-on. This requires disrupting systems that contribute to oppression—from criminal justice to immigration, health care to social services, and more. LCT requires that practitioners are mindful about their communication—framing issues to shift people out of old patterns of thought and speaking in a way that reaches each audience in a manner unique to their specific needs. Furthermore, LCT compels practitioners to reconsider how they evaluate outcomes and results, share resources, and connect with new and unusual partners. And, as this last chapter describes, this approach requires a new look at leadership.

This final chapter weaves together several strategies for moving words and ideas into action and change. Given the considerable body of literature on leadership, this chapter is not intended to be an exhaustive summary of that work. Rather, the ideas included are offered to spark new possibilities about ways organizations and teams can work, as well as to reaffirm time-proven techniques, such as quality communication, self-awareness, and adaptability. Leadership at all levels is important, from program managers to agency executives, from community residents to local champions, and from students who are learning the craft to faculty who are connecting the dots in new ways. As such, this chapter is not just for those with formal leadership positions; rather, it is also for anyone who wishes to approach their work in a more complete, life course–aligned manner.

RELATIONSHIPS MATTER

Quality relationships with one's team, organization, clients, partners, and the broader community are foundational. Several chapters in this book provide information about technical skills such as evaluation and planning. Although these skills are the ones that make it to the resume, it is the soft skills that matter in many ways. Cultivating emotional intelligence along with flexibility, adaptability, active listening, active learning, critical thinking, communication, and interpersonal skills is essential for taking on the tasks required by the Life Course Approach. While organizational skills are useful in coordinating a meeting, the ability to sense the mood of a room, read unspoken cues between people, and consider who is and is not speaking is what will lead to tangible outcomes from that event. The emotional work of leadership is absolutely essential.

When working with individuals, teams, or groups, practitioners should take the time to create a shared language and learn about where each person comes from—what are their frames? What experiences do they bring to the table? Creating a contract as to how individuals within a group are to be with each other may take time, but it can offer parameters and "bumper pads" that may foster deeper, more courageous conversations. The Guidelines for Dialogue from the William C. Friday Fellowship for Human Relations in Box 15-1 are an example of strategies to support productive conversations.[1] Whatever guidelines are developed, make sure they remain visible to the group and are reviewed regularly. Furthermore, leaders ignore the visible and invisible power balances at their peril. When convening groups, listening for what is not said and considering who is not at the table is imperative. Exploring ways to create teams, committees, and spaces where all voices are valued is important. It is not uncommon for people from historically excluded groups to be invited to the table but never truly heard or seen. Not only does this delete their contributions but it also wastes their time and increases their stress. Inclusion of leaders (formal or informal) from the place an agency is working (e.g., a community) or population to be served (e.g., foster youth) should happen at the beginning of the group or coalition formation—not at the end as an afterthought nod to diversity. Finally, relationship building takes time—both in the immediate connection and over months and even years as people have shared experiences and a trust that comes from getting to know each other.

Relationships within teams and organizations and between organizations are important. But connection with the people who are receiving services (clients, consumers, customers, families) and who live in communities with many needs is equally essential yet often undervalued. Throughout history, people in the "helping professions" like public health, social work, and nursing have developed and sometimes tested programs to meet a wide range of identified needs without ever consulting the people whom they have designated as needing these services. Unlike the for-profit sales industry, which collects detailed information about their target audience's preferences, interests, and patterns, public health and social work often offer services, assuming that the customers will adapt

Box 15-1. Guidelines for Dialogue

Speak from the "I."

Speak your truth, expressing your thoughts, feelings, and experiences by making "I" statements rather than "you," "we," or "one." In our culture, it is very common to use "you" instead of "I." As you pay attention you will see how much more powerful using "I" statements will be—speaking only for yourself, not for a community as a whole, not for the person sitting next to you.

Disagree but do not shame, blame, or attack.

Disagree with each other; it is absolutely OK to. One of the necessary ingredients for differences to be expressed and valued is that people let go of the need to be, think, or act the same. Asking someone to feel shame for what they believe to be true, blaming someone for his/her experiences, or for thinking or feeling the way he or she does, attacking each other, because of anger or feeling offended because of another's perspective, all undermine continued effective dialogue. Please be open to disagreements on perspectives and do so respectfully.

Accept messiness and practice nonclosure.

Be messy and realize that complex issues will not be resolved in one dialogue. You don't have to have your statements worked out before you start talking or have any answers—your perspectives and thoughts are enough. A common fear is that you will offend someone—but we are here to learn from one another and get as much as we can into the dialogue. Please accept both yourself and others being disorganized in their thoughts and share as openly as possible. And, know that learning comes from the process of delving into complex perspectives, issues, and identities, a process that is never ending.

Embrace paradox and use both/and thinking.

Look for ways in which ideas fit together and avoid setting up an either/or process or a competition between ideas. One does not have to be false to make the other true. It is quite possible that both are true. Being able to accept that two seemingly contradictory views of the world could both be true is challenging and important, as we know people experience realities differently for quite authentic reasons.

Lean into discomfort and each other.

By design, authentic dialogue challenges participants. Discomfort signals that you are being challenged and perhaps even growing from the experience. Support each other to reflect on discomfort with a spirit of inquiry and wonder to reach new awareness and meaning individually as well as collectively. The process can be useful and meaningful only with everyone's full participation. Support each other to participate fully.

Maintain confidentiality.

In agreeing to maintain confidentiality it will be much safer to share your thoughts, perspectives, and ideas. We must agree that nothing that is said here is shared elsewhere and that nothing that is shared is used against each other either, in any way. In addition, it will be important when you see each other outside of this context to respect that people may or may not want to discuss issues raised here after they leave.

Source: William C. Friday Fellowship.[1] Adapted with permission.

to how the program is delivered as they often have no choice. This happens for many reasons: willful ignorance, trying to work quickly to meet a grant deadline, or lack of funds and "know how" to do the work.

This is a very skewed power balance that has perhaps kept many programs from being successful and perpetuates systematic oppression among people who have been historically oppressed by the collective system. Practitioners must acknowledge that they are a part of "the" system, both influenced by and acting as agents of that system and others. Being in relationship with the people to be served means taking the time to get to know them, shop (spend money) in their neighborhoods, attend local events, prove that one's words can be trusted, hold meetings at times and places when they can come—see the people behind the "consumer" and listen to their suggestions about what works for them. Many communities that have been historically excluded have a deep distrust of institutions for good reason. LCT and community engagement may spark new ideas about how, when, and by whom services are administered—ideas that are critical if the profession is to make real progress on closing gaps in life course trajectories. Chapter 9 by Berkowitz et al. offers one strategy—Human-Centered Design—for approaching projects, actions, and resource allocation in a way that is more likely to result in sustainable change.

Given the propensity for people to socialize, strategize, and communicate with people who hold similar beliefs, life course practitioners are compelled to seek out different perspectives. In this American season, dichotomies such as red versus blue, rural versus urban, millennials versus baby boomers, pro-life versus reproductive justice, conservative versus progressive, and so forth are creating deep divides across the country. People who can bridge differences and offer a way to leverage myriad perspectives into workable strategies for change are needed. Respecting and understanding difference does not require agreement, but it does model the intention to really see people, learn about their perspective, and find common experiences and values. Developing emotional intelligence, being self-aware, and having an open heart and mind are crucial leadership skills. Again, investing in relationships takes time, but the reward is invaluable.

EMBRACE COMPLEXITY

LCT offers an opportunity for practitioners to challenge themselves to look at interlocking systems and circumstances influenced by human behavior and needs as they identify policies and strategies for change. Stampfel and Shiman underscore the complexity introduced by LCT in Chapter 13 on evaluation when they highlight the variety of factors that might be attributed to an improvement in a single outcome. Leaders need to be able to see the whole of a problem or situation, understand interrelationships, and envision patterns of change. Fortunately, there are tools such as system dynamics modeling, concept mapping, social network analysis, and the field of implementation science that can assist practitioners in this work. Taking advantage of training opportunities, such as conference workshops or technical assistance resources to learn more about these methods is highly recommended for today's life course practitioner.

One easy way to start is to try the "Why times 5" method.[2] Developed by Sakichi Toyoda and used within the Toyota Motor Corporation, this is an iterative technique that explores causes and effects in greater detail. When someone mentions a problem that they think should be addressed, ask them a simple "why" question. For example, a clinic may have low rates of postpartum utilization among low-income patients. A first "why" question might elicit a response that new mothers may not care about coming in for the visit. A second "why" might draw out that new mothers do not find the effort to attend the visit equal to the value they perceive they will get from this care. A third "why" might elicit the fact that the visit is only scheduled for 15 minutes. A fourth "why" could find that the clinic is paid in a bundle for their services and, as such, the implicit "reward" system in a clinic favors keeping slots in a busy clinic open for prenatal visits as there is not an economic incentive for providing postpartum care. Finally, a fifth "why" might reveal that this lack of focus on postpartum care on the part of clinic management has trickled down to clinic staff, who themselves may start to see the postpartum visit as low value and provide services as such. There may be multiple responses to each level of "why," but digging deeper will identify the right place to begin to address change. In this case, one would not start with a new program to try to get women in for care; rather, engage in a review of the value of postpartum care within the culture of the clinic itself and a need for a policy change in reimbursement to support higher-quality services.

Remembering that everyone works in and is surrounded by interconnecting systems is essential. A life course–aligned leader will make the time to learn how these systems may intentionally or unintentionally advantage some groups of people over others, thereby shining a light on the work that needs to happen to reduce chronic stress, augment protective factors, and build equity. This underscores the work of Abresch and Wyche-Etheridge in Chapter 2. As their work on equity suggests, when analyzing the way a system functions, practitioners must also be keenly aware of the vantage point they have in seeing a particular system and recognize that there are many other positions and ways of seeing within that system that must be respected if they are to understand the whole. As described in Chapter 1, individuals are nested within families who live in communities that are influenced by organizations and set on a foundation of policy. Simple approaches to complex problems (e.g., handing out educational resources) will reap limited success. Programs and practitioners who accept the complexity of the lives of young adults and families are more likely to develop multifaceted, even intergenerational, strategies that can actively address the "why" of the problem and lead to sustained change.

BE ADAPTIVE

Fostering change in the face of complexity requires the ability to diagnose problems within a program or organization and leans into the discomfort that arises as systems and people within them are pressed to change. In truth, any social system (family, team, agency) is the way it is because the people in the system (with the most leverage) want it to be that way. As such, the work of shaking up the system to get different results is not easy. The art of adaptive leadership—the practice of mobilizing people to tackle tough challenges and thrive—is a perfect approach for the life course leader. Successful adaptation builds on the past, occurs through experimentation, relies on diversity, significantly reregulates/rearranges the old way of being, and takes time.[3]

Heifetz et al. posit that the most undervalued leadership capacity is the ability to diagnose the root cause of problems.[3] Leaders need to focus both on the organization/system and themselves as part of that system. In the midst of multiple pressures and immersion in the daily life of an organization, it is challenging for a leader to step back and really see problems. Furthermore, taking the time to identify an issue that will require some upheaval and discomfort to address is not something that most people want to add to a busy calendar. To do this effectively, Heifetz et al. (and others) suggest that leaders need to take a step back and observe their organization from a higher vantage point to truly see what might really be happening in an agency or system.[3] The capacity to understand a system and oneself within that system takes time to cultivate, but the ability to hold both perspectives is important for advancing real change.

Adaptive leadership also requires the ability to distinguish between technical fixes (problems that have known solutions that can be solved by the organization's current ways of doing things) and adaptive challenges (problems that require a change in people's priorities, beliefs, and habits).[3] Both actions are important, but most organizations stop with the easier "win." For example, an agency claims that it is committed to supporting a diverse workforce yet finds that the majority of its employees have similar backgrounds and skill sets. The executive director might reallocate resources in the budget to advertise positions to reach different audiences, revise job descriptions, and conduct interviews in a different manner. However, the real problem might be that the agency itself is not really interested in bringing in different perspectives and opinions as that will challenge the status quo and introduce discomfort. The approach to addressing organizational culture and norms is the adaptive and more difficult work that must be done.

Honestly, it is easy to write and read about the necessity of disrupting systems that are not getting results. Actually doing something is entirely different. It is risky to lead adaptive change. Heifetz et al. offer strategies for staying in "the productive zone of disequilibrium," where there is pressure to make change, but the work is measured so as to create conditions for change—not blow up the organization and lose one's job![3] Ultimately, the space of creative tension—the point where the old way no longer makes sense—can provide the energy to stand forward and take risks. That sense of energy is necessary to move people out of their comfort zones into a new space that opens up to a different approach to work and new ideas. To use an apt metaphor for an MCH audience, the process of giving birth is painful and very challenging, but the result is life changing across generations. It is impossible to learn how to be an adaptive leader in a few paragraphs. The book *The Practice of Adaptive Leadership, Tools and Tactics for Changing Your Organization and the World* by Heifetz et al. (Harvard Business Review

Press) is an excellent resource for practitioners at all levels who wish to advance a life course perspective.[3]

DIVERSITY IS MORE THAN A CHECKBOX

Dismantling long-standing systems of discrimination and oppression is not a simple process. Addressing these challenges requires time and energy focused on an understanding of power and privilege at the personal, interpersonal, and organizational levels. Simply ensuring that people who may represent different types of communities and cultures are around the table is not enough to include and integrate their different talents, perspectives, and energy into the work at hand. In truth, this work is about organizational culture—and culture change.

The impact of systems built around White culture and power is evident in seen and unseen ways. For example, people from historically oppressed groups may feel pressured to continuously prove their competency. This pressure can make their leadership and management style look different and, over time, create stress that can have an impact on their life course trajectory. What appears to be a lack of interest in taking on new roles may instead be a lack of confidence. The inability or reticence to self-promote during interviews and performance reviews can easily create barriers to being hired and promoted. Women may be more likely to assume they are unqualified to step in to a role or position, even though their experience and skills may be very well aligned for that work. Achieving a goal of having a more diverse workforce will not be reached in a workplace that is not genuinely ready to embrace difference of experience, approach, and culture.

For readers who are White and readers who have had access to resources, such as higher education, it can be particularly difficult to see the systems in which one is immersed. Leaders who want to lead differently need to begin by reassessing their perceptions of the world around them. Attending trainings such as those by the Racial Equity Institute and participating in discussion groups about books, journal articles, blogs, and documentaries that share a different view on life are good places to start. Being willing to hear the voices of others who are different is essential. As Mellody Hobson noted,

> It's time for us to be comfortable with the uncomfortable conversation about race. If we truly believe in equal rights and equal opportunity in America, we need to have real conversations about this issue. We can't be color blind, we have to be color brave.[4]

Diversifying one's personal networks and experiences can also be helpful. Taking on power structures and applying new ways of tackling long-standing challenges demands work on the part of practitioners for whom those systems have worked.

Practitioners need to know and own their privilege and use it accordingly. The reality is that people with privilege have less to lose in questioning the system than those who are disadvantaged within that system. Courage in the face of a press for change will look different based on privilege—do not judge another's bravery without understanding that individual's level of risk. The emerging understanding of prophetic leadership is an important example of how advocacy can look different for some groups. People who are managing pervasive exclusion tend to focus their leadership efforts toward a future time, especially when they cannot see the possibility of change happening in the present. It is important to recognize this slow and steady, often behind the scenes, progress and success. There are valuable strategies employed by people who have been able to effectuate major change while underresourced and without a voice at the highest levels of power. After all, a people who could not vote or drink out of certain water fountains managed to change the US Constitution. There is much to be learned from these leaders and their legacies and applied to current times.

LIFE COURSE AT WORK

A diverse, healthy, and engaged workforce is a critical component of success for any agency, business, or program. There are many opportunities for leaders and managers to apply a Life Course Approach to the development of policies, procedures, benefits, and organizational culture. An organization that is outwardly focused on providing services and resources to vulnerable populations may likewise ignore the way its own payment and reward structures advantage some groups of employees over others. Recruiting a truly diverse workforce requires attention to the unique needs of these employees, as well as being aware of the way the social determinants of health (e.g., transportation, education, housing) can act as barriers for the very people they may wish to hire. Bringing diverse perspectives to one's team also requires consideration of where one posts job announcements, how the announcements are written, the preparation of the search committee, and a review of the process once a decision has been made. Retaining and supporting diverse staff and team members once hired is of equal importance for a thriving, multifaceted team that is capable of solving life course–focused problems.

Human resource policies offer great potential for supporting health and wellness across the life course for everyone. Vacation and paid sick time provide an opportunity for stress reduction and can prevent the spread of illness at the workplace. Paid family leave, onsite childcare, retirement benefits, and comprehensive health care plans serve as protective factors that can improve wellness trajectories at many stages of the life course. Opportunities such as flexible work schedules, access to standing desks, modified breaks or duties to accommodate for pregnancy or temporary health issues, facilities that have comfortable rooms for expressing breast milk or resting during the day, onsite health care or wellness programs, or the option to work remotely even occasionally to accommodate a home repair service or a child or grandchild's school event can support workers in reducing stress, being healthy, and meeting the needs of the other people in their lives. MCH care managers and employees alike should be observant of human resource policies and advocate improvements that can better align with the needs of workers over time. Incremental change is possible, and aligning with advocacy groups such as Moms Rising can be helpful in gathering the evidence as to how changes can improve productivity and health simultaneously. Taking on these issues within one's own agency and with workers in other industries (e.g., large retail stores, processing plants, and fast-food restaurants) has the potential to reshape the meaning of work–life harmony. Practitioners can also foster a sensitivity and sense of community among their teams that leads employees to show compassion to each other across the many different stages of life that are being experienced.

Mentoring and being mentored is an excellent way for practitioners to build their skill across the ages and stages of their lives and careers. Good mentors can foster self-awareness and reflection, support critical decision making, assist with systems thinking, support goal setting, and provide coaching during leadership challenges. Traditional mentors are seen as people who are at higher levels of prestige, knowledge, or position who can bring others forward in their career. However, a new mom who has just returned to work or a person who has to sort out elder care for a parent may find mentors to help them navigate these unique and sensitive periods of their life. Likewise, mentors may be people who have expertise in a particular field, community, or skill. For example, less savvy, often slightly older leaders can benefit from working closely with younger mentor who under-stands social media in different way. Observing seasoned mentors navigate challenges around career advancement and eventual retirement offers value as does seeing emerg-ing professionals find their passion and build their skills. At its heart, mentoring is an investment in relationship. Set guidelines for communication and commit to spending time together. Seek out a variety of mentors for a diversity of opinion. Be intentional in finding mentors and offering mentorship—this is a time-tested method for supporting each other across the professional life course.

Challenging the way in which organizations do business is important. In the late 1880s, Mary Parker Follett, a social worker, offered a unique perspective on management and organizational behavior science. Follett suggested that the actions of managers or organizations affect employees (and clients) and employee (and client) behavior in turn influences managers. She proposed a management structure focused on power "with," a jointly developed co-active power, as opposed to power "over." Her vision saw organiza-tions as relational as compared with structural, and she felt that fair decisions are those that involve all individuals who have a stake in the decision and its outcomes. Follett was being mindfully critical of power structures and pointing out their inappropriateness as a way to manage human beings.[5] Current hierarchical structures have been re-enforced over time as cultural justifications for power "over" relationships have shifted from birth-right in feudal times, to colonialism, and then to industrialism. Follett used science as a way to challenge the re-enactment of the politics of exclusion and domination. Unfortunately, as a woman challenging entrenched power imbalances during that time, her voice was not taken seriously. Similarly, other cultures and communities—those indigenous to North America and globally—have unique approaches to organizational design that have likewise been ignored. Follett is starting to make a comeback in the field of social work, and efforts are underway to lift up other equally compelling approaches to leadership.

SERIOUSLY, JUST DO IT

Practitioners at all levels must examine and engage with leadership opportunities. Managers spend much of their time thinking about running programs, coordinating people, and delivering products on time. They often must respond to administration and shifting expectations and demands. Within this work there *is* space and opportunity for leadership. Practitioners at all levels can create positive subcultures on their teams, examine their assumptions, engage clients and community members in a meaningful way, encourage their staff, push upward to administration on critical issues, and insist on innovation and partnerships that can begin to consider new intergenerational approaches. Furthermore, leadership is not left at the office at 5 PM each evening. Extend the Life Course Approach to other spheres of one's life—through service on coalitions or boards, clubs or sororities/fraternities, in one's faith community, community groups such as the parent–teacher association and Scouts—the opportunities are boundless for thinking differently and shifting perspectives.

There are many approaches to leadership: positive leadership, authentic leadership, appreciative inquiry, servant leadership, transformational leadership, autocratic leadership, democratic leadership, and laissez-faire leadership, to name a few! There is not a single gold-standard methodology—the type of leadership needed by an organization can vary and the personality of the person "in charge" will shape the approach. Furthermore, a single person may employ traits and strategies from multiple frameworks. The heart of leadership focuses on the internal alignment of people with their own values and those that they aspire to achieve on behalf of their organization. The William C. Friday Fellowship for Human Relations in North Carolina has developed a set of leadership practices and competencies that aligns well with the work of advancing LCT. The practices include the following:

- Integrity: Acting in alignment with one's well-discerned and publicly stated values.
- Intention: Acting with purpose in accordance with one's passions and abilities.
- Inclusion: Engaging authentically across deep differences in identity, experience, and perspective.[6]

What would MCH look like if everyone were to engage with each other and their work in accordance with these values? Kouzes and Posner suggest that leaders need focus, passion, courage, wisdom, and integrity. They define passion as a deep emotional investment that is rooted in love—for the work, the people who do it, and the people who benefit.[7] Bolman and Gallo believe that leaders bring a deep sense of commitment and contribution to their work when they embark on a developmental journey, recognize that inner growth matters, embrace a sense of calling, accept that the journey is the challenge, lead with their soul, and demonstrate the courage to learn.[8]

Chances are that people who have made it this far in the book have a spirit of curiosity and personal growth. This is fortunate, as much of the work called for by LCT application begins with a genuine desire and humility to see the world and oneself differently. As Kotelchuck highlighted in Chapter 3, this time in history, this MCH era, is being defined now. Leading into the paradigm shift that the life course perspective offers might move practitioners of today to embrace activist Angela Davis's perspective that it is no longer right to just accept the status quo; rather we are called to create change.[9]

There are moments all around for applying LCT to push for action. Whether by learning more about specific systems, stepping into policy work (at the capital P or small p level), approaching strategic planning with a multilayered lens, or using Human-Centered Design thinking to address a community need, there are many opportunities to try on the ideas shared in this book. Hopefully this work has sparked an interest in embarking on a journey of experimentation and creativity in leadership and management practice. Ultimately, we have what we need to advance policies, programs, and systems that build equity and support conditions where all people can live to their full potential.

KEY POINTS

- LCT can feel overwhelming. Sometimes the best place to start is with one's own team. Work within your sphere of influence first.
- There are numerous opportunities for leaders to apply a Life Course Approach not only to those they serve programmatically (the outside) but also within their own organization through the development of policies, procedures, benefits, and organizational culture. Creating a diverse and strong workforce within MCH programs is important.
- Emotional intelligence, strong interpersonal skills, awareness of power and privilege, and self-knowledge are critical, especially for practitioners who wish to fully engage with the communities they serve.
- There are many approaches to leadership and there is not a single mold of a leader. True leadership focuses on the internal values of that individual and those values of the organization that they are working on behalf to achieve. Building leadership skills is a life-long pursuit.

RESOURCES

- Block P. *Community: The Structure of Belonging.* 1st ed. San Francisco, CA: Berrett-Koehler Publishers; 2009.
- Gregory T. Beyond winners and losers: diversity as a learning phenomenon. In: Senge P, Kleiner A, Roberts C, Ross R, Roth G, Smith B, eds. *The Dance of Change: The Challenges to Sustaining Momentum in Learning Organizations.* New York, NY: Doubleday Currency Books; 1999:274–279.
- Heffernan M. *Beyond Measure, the Big Impact of Small Changes.* New York, NY: TED Books Simon and Schuster; 2015.
- Heifetz RA, Linsky M, Grashow A. *The Practice of Adaptive Leadership: Tools and Tactics for Changing Your Organization and the World.* Boston, MA: Harvard Business School Publishing; 2009.
- Kimmerer RW. *Braiding Sweetgrass: Indigenous Wisdom, Scientific Knowledge and the Teachings of Plants.* 1st ed. Minneapolis, MN: Milkweed Editions; 2015.
- Starr J. *The Mentoring Manual: Your Step by Step Guide to Being a Better Mentor.* Upper Saddle River, NJ: FT Press; 2014.

ACKNOWLEDGMENTS

This chapter was informed by the work of Kathleen Crabbs Clark, Gita Gulati-Parti, Sterling Freeman, Sayra Pinto, Minda Brooks, and the William C. Friday Fellowship on Human Relations.

REFERENCES

1. William C. Friday Fellowship for Human Relations. Guidelines for dialogue. Available at: http://c.ymcdn.com/sites/www.fridayfellowship.org/resource/resmgr/Guidelines_for_Dialogue. pdf?hhSearchTerms=%22guidelines%22. Accessed December 18, 2017.

2. Mindtools. 5 whys. Getting to the root of a problem quickly. Available at: https://www.mindtools.com/pages/article/newTMC_5W.htm. Accessed December 2, 2017.

3. Heifetz RA, Linsky M, Grashow A. *The Practice of Adaptive Leadership: Tools and Tactics for Changing Your Organization and the World.* Boston, MA: Harvard Business School Publishing; 2009.

4. Hobson M. Color blind or color brave? TED2014. Available at: https://www.ted.com/talks/mellody_hobson_color_blind_or_color_brave. Accessed December 2, 2017.

5. Feldheim MA. Mary Parker Follett lost and found—again, and again, and again. *Int J Organ Theor Behav.* 2004;7(3):341–362.

6. NC Leaders for Courageous Action. The William C. Friday Fellowship for Human Relations. Available at: http://www.fridayfellowship.org/?page=fellowshipoverview2&hhSearchTerms=%22integrity+and+intention%22. Accessed September 26, 2017.

7. Kouzes JM, Posner BZ. *The Leadership Challenge*. 4th ed. San Francisco, CA: Jossey-Bass; 2007.

8. Bolman LG, Gallo JV. *Reframing Academic Leadership. Feeding the Soul*. San Francisco, CA: John Wiley and Sons; 2010.

9. Davis AY. *Freedom is a Constant Struggle: Ferguson, Palestine, and the Foundations of a Movement*. Chicago, IL: Haymarket Books; 2016.

Contributors

Chad Abresch, MEd
CityMatCH
University of Nebraska Medical Center
Omaha, Nebraska

Deborah Allen, ScD
Los Angeles County Department
of Public Health
Los Angeles, California

Thea Anderson, MPH, MSW
San Francisco, California

Helen Arega, MA
California Preterm Birth Initiative
School of Nursing
University of California, San Francisco

Sara S. Bachman, PhD
Center for Innovation in Social Work
and Health
Boston University School of Social Work
Boston, Massachusetts

Rebecca Bakal, MPH
Norton & Elaine Sarnoff Center
for Jewish Genetics
Chicago, Illinois

Rachel L. Berkowitz, MPH
University of California, Berkeley

Carol Brady, MA
Florida Maternal Infant & Early
Childhood Home Visiting Initiative
Florida Association of Healthy Start
Coalitions
Tallahassee, Florida

Monica Y. B. Braughton, MPH
Harder + Company Community
Research
Sacramento, California

Megan K. Calpin, MPH, MCP
San Francisco, California

Julia Caplan, MPH, MPP
Public Health Institute
Oakland, California

Dorothy Cilenti, DrPH, MPH, MSW
UNC Gillings School of Global Public
Health
The University of North Carolina at
Chapel Hill

Quinton Cotton, MSW
UW Institute for Clinical and
Translational Research
University of Wisconsin-Madison

Tyan Parker Dominguez, PhD, MPH, MSW
Department of Children, Youth and Families
USC Suzanne Dworak-Peck School of
Social Work
University of Southern California
Los Angeles, California

Deborah B. Ehrenthal, MD, MPH
School of Medicine and Public Health
University of Wisconsin-Madison

Jennifer Farfalla, MPH
Association of Maternal and Child Health
Programs
Washington, District of Columbia

Lauren Gase, PhD, MPH
Spark Policy Institute
Denver, Colorado

Gibbie Harris, MSPH, BSN
Mecklenburg County Public Health
Charlotte, North Carolina

Amy Locklear Hertel, PhD, JD, MSW
The University of North Carolina
at Chapel Hill

Faye Johnson, BS
Northeast Florida Healthy Start Coalition
Jacksonville, Florida

Milton Kotelchuck, PhD, MPH
Center for Child & Adolescent Health
Research and Policy
Division of General Academic Pediatrics
MassGeneral Hospital *for* Children/Harvard
Medical School
Boston, Massachusetts

Paul Lanier, PhD
School of Social Work
The University of North Carolina
at Chapel Hill

Michael C. Lu, MD, MPH
Prevention and Community Health
Department
Milken Institute School of Public
Health
The George Washington University
Washington, District of Columbia

Christina (Kiko) Malin, MPH, MSW
Alameda County Public Health
Department
Oakland, California

Erin K. McClain, MA, MPH
Center for Maternal and Infant Health
The University of North Carolina
at Chapel Hill

Monica R. McLemore, PhD, MPH, RN
University of California, San Francisco

Denise Pecha, LCSW
CityMatCH
University of Nebraska Medical Center
Omaha, Nebraska

Belinda Pettiford, MPH
Women's Health Branch
NC Division of Public Health
Raleigh, North Carolina

Cheri A. Pies, DrPH, MSW
School of Public Health
University of California at Berkeley

Glynis Shea, BA
Konopka Institute
University of Minnesota
Minneapolis, Minnesota

Lauren J. Shiman, MPH
New York, New York

Bina Patel Shrimali, DrPH
San Francisco, California

Elizabeth A. Smulian, MPH, CHES
School of Medicine and Public Health
University of Wisconsin-Madison

Caroline Stampfel, MPH
Association of Maternal & Child Health
Programs
Washington, District of Columbia

Jessica Vechakul, PhD, MPH, MS
Berkeley, California

Sarah Verbiest, DrPH, MSW, MPH
Center for Maternal and Infant Health
The Jordan Institute for Families
The University of North Carolina
at Chapel Hill

Jessica Wolin, MPH, MCRP
Health Equity Institute
San Francisco State University
San Francisco, California

Kimberlee Wyche-Etheridge, MD, MPH
Meharry Medical College
Nashville, Tennessee

Index

definition, 183–184f
diversity of team, 185, 201, 204
exemplars, 132, 133
funding, 205, 229
home visiting
  family engagement, 124–126, 127, 128, 132, 133
  implementation prototyping, 191
  project brief, example of, 187
  understanding phase, 187, 188
mindsets, 185–187, 186t, 201, 203
practice of, 191–192, 203–206
  recommendations, 201–202b
process, 184f–185, 203–206
  experimentation and Implementation, 184f, 189, 191, 205
  ideation, 184f, 188–189, 190f, 204–205
  understanding, 184f, 187–188, 204
training in, 205–206
hypothalamic–pituitary–adrenal (HPA) axis, 4

I

implicit bias, 269
Improved Pregnancy Outcome program, 64
incarceration
  environmental asset removal, 46–47
  health disparities and, 42, 82–83, 90
    children of incarcerated parents, 87–88
    women incarcerated, 86–87, 89
  intergenerational effects, 87–88
    health disparities, 42
    parental custody, 79–80, 89
  mass incarceration, 80–83
    definition, 81
    restorative justice approaches, 89–90
    women incarcerated, 83–87
  prison industry, 81–82
  prison vs. jail, 80–81
  rates of incarceration, 80, 83, 84, 85
  release, 88–89
    challenges of poverty, 80
    mothers released, 85, 89
    recidivism, 88–89
  restorative justice approaches, 89–90
  strategies to reduce, 88–90
  War on Drugs, 64, 82
  women incarcerated, 83–87
    health care, 86–87
    history of, 83–84
    motherhood and incarceration, 84–85, 89, 90
    release of, 85, 89
    victims of violence, 85
Indians. See American Indian populations
Infant Care (Children's Bureau), 59
Infant Mortality Collaborative Improvement and Innovation Network (IM CoIIN), 70–71
infants
  breastfeeding, 5 (see also breastfeeding)
  father–child relationship, 33–34 (see also fatherhood)
  infant mortality (see also birth outcomes)
    CelebrateOne initiative, 104
    as evaluation parameter, 294b

father involvement and, 35
  Healthy Start as exemplar, 120, 132
  history of campaigns against, 58–67, 68–69
  Life Course Theory and, 69–73
  North Carolina perinatal strategy, 212–216, 213b
  rates, 9–10, 41, 42t, 62
  societal well-being gauge, 9, 65–66
race and
  Alameda County (California) case study, 221–226, 223b
  Black–White gap closure, 13–14b
  CityMatCH Institute for Equity in Birth Outcomes (Equity Institute), 104–105, 111
  history of campaigns against, 60, 64
  infant mortality rates, 9–10, 41, 42t, 62
  Louisiana case study, 101–103, 107–108
  North Carolina case study, 212–216, 213b
  Wisconsin case study, 216–221, 219t
infographic software, 273–274
Institute of Medicine Health in All Policies recommendation, 236
institutionalized racism, 48
  breastfeeding barriers, 49
  Racial Equity Institute Foundational Training, 215, 333
insurance. See health insurance
integrated funding mechanisms, 319–320
interconception health, 8f, 46, 130
intergenerational health
  home visiting impacting, 117, 129–130
  incarceration and, 87–88
    parental custody, 79–80, 89
    social effects, 42
  Life Course Theory, 2, 11, 289
  pregnancy longitudinal effects, 289
  research as Life Course Approach, 14
  savings account, two-generation, 226
  tobacco use, 22–23
  whole-family clinical services, 151–152
internalized racism, 49
interventions
  American Indian populations, 30–31
  asset-based approaches, 50
  cautions in applying, 45
  ecological theory, 2, 3f
  evaluation, 290–291 (see also evaluation)
    demonstrating return on investment, 317–318, 320
    performance measures, 290, 311–312, 317, 320
  father involvement, 35–36, 218
  federal health disparity interventions, 41 (see also policy)
  Health in All Policies, 235–236 (see also Health in All Policies)
  history of, 59 (see also history)
  housing programs, 150–153
    supportive housing, 151, 162
    transitional housing, 162
  human-centered design, 191–192 (see also human-centered design)
  incarceration reduction, 88–90
  Life Course Theory, 6, 12–14b, 71
    research, 15

Sojourner Syndrome

environmental "risk scape"
  adverse health effects @
  lower doses
AL during key developmental
  periods